MW00781294

Secrets and Lies in Psychotherapy

Secrets and Lies in Psychotherapy

Barry A. Farber
Matt Blanchard
Melanie Love

American Psychological Association
Washington, DC

Published by
American Psychological Association
750 First Street, NE
Washington, DC 20002
www.apa.org

APA Order Department
P.O. Box 92984
Washington, DC 20090-2984
Phone: (800) 374-2721; Direct: (202) 336-5510
Fax: (202) 336-5502; TDD/TTY: (202) 336-6123
Online: http://www.apa.org/pubs/books
E-mail: order@apa.org

In the U.K., Europe, Africa, and the Middle East, copies may be ordered from
Eurospan Group
c/o Turpin Distribution
Pegasus Drive
Stratton Business Park
Biggleswade, Bedfordshire
SG18 8TQ United Kingdom
Phone: +44 (0) 1767 604972
Fax: +44 (0) 1767 601640
Online: https://www.eurospanbookstore.com/apa
E-mail: eurospan@turpin-distribution.com

Typeset in Goudy by Circle Graphics, Inc., Reisterstown, MD

Printer: Sheridan Books, Chelsea, MI
Cover Designer: Beth Schlenoff, Bethesda, MD

Cover Art: Summer J. Hart, b: 1975, detail: Further Evidence of Invasion, 2018, site specific installation, 15′ h x 10′ d x 13′ w, hand-cut Tyvek, fishing line, neon gouache.

Library of Congress Cataloging-in-Publication Data
Names: Farber, Barry A. (Barry Alan), 1947- author. | Blanchard, Matt, author. | Love, Melanie, author.
Title: Secrets and lies in psychotherapy / by Barry A. Farber, Matt Blanchard , and Melanie Love.
Description: Washington, DC : American Psychological Association, [2019] | Includes bibliographical references and index.
Identifiers: LCCN 2018044190 (print) | LCCN 2018057520 (ebook) | ISBN 9781433829482 (eBook) | ISBN 1433829487 (eBook) | ISBN 9781433830525 (hardcover) | ISBN 1433830523 (hardcover)
Subjects: LCSH: Deception. | Psychotherapist and patient.
Classification: LCC RC569.5.D44 (ebook) | LCC RC569.5.D44 F37 2019 (print) | DDC 616.89/14--dc23
LC record available at https://lccn.loc.gov/2018044190

British Library Cataloguing-in-Publication Data
A CIP record is available from the British Library.

Printed in the United States of America

http://dx.doi.org/10.1037/0000128-000

10 9 8 7 6 5 4 3 2 1

To my family: then, now, and always.
—Barry A. Farber

To M, C, and H, my constant companions.
—Matt Blanchard

To the lifelong friends I found at Teachers College who have turned into family; to Matt, my coauthor and the other half of my brain; and to Grandmere and Grandpere.
—Melanie Love

CONTENTS

ACKNOWLEDGMENTS

We are indebted to the many graduate students at Teachers College, Columbia University, who helped us over the years, designing surveys, coding data, transcribing interviews, performing literature reviews, constructing tables, tracking down references, and coming to endless lab meetings to discuss this project. They did so creatively, thoughtfully, enthusiastically, and conscientiously. Many have, deservedly, gone on to doctoral programs in the mental health field. Many thanks then to (in alphabetical order) Rachel Altman, Veronika Bailey, Bianca Cerosimo, Laura Curren, Matt DeMasi, Brianne Dickey, Lauren Grabowski, Alana Jorgenson, Mona Khaled, Lama Khouri, Adam Mitchell, Mandy Newman, Veronica Ozog, Ida Taghavi, Kaila Tang, Catherine Thompson, Katrina Wehmeyer, Jeffrey Wong, and Katelyn Zmigrodski. For particular help with our chapter on therapist dishonesty, we are grateful for the efforts of Devlin Jackson, a current doctoral student who runs a research lab investigating this issue, and several master's degree students, including Catherine Crumb, Whitney Hedgepeth, Parul Kaushik, Nadine Peppe-Bonavita, and Daniel Samost.

We are also very thankful for the insightful suggestions of some very smart colleagues, including Drs. Phil Blumberg, Jesse Geller, and George Goldstein. We appreciate as well the very helpful comments of three excellent reviewers of preliminary versions of this book, as well as the support provided to us by the editorial staff at APA Books, including Susan Reynolds, Tyler Aune, and Erin O'Brien. We extend our sincere thanks and appreciation to our friends, family, and significant others who listened to our ideas and supported our writing, even as they wished we were more available for playing. And last, we are indebted to those very many psychotherapy clients who shared their stories and struggles with us and who endeavored to honestly answer questions about their dishonesty.

Secrets and Lies in Psychotherapy

INTRODUCTION

From its inception, psychotherapy has always been considered a place where hard truths can and should be disclosed. Clients are exhorted to tell the truth, therapists are trained to deal with inevitable resistances to client truth-telling, and the outcome of the work is often thought to be dependent on the joint efforts of both to make better sense of previously withheld or distorted information. Although over the years clinical and empirical investigations have indicated that psychotherapy clients keep secrets, conceal information, and lie to their therapists, these studies, although heuristically valuable, tended to be small-scale, qualitative efforts. We were interested in designing a large-scale, multimethod research project that would enable us to understand more fully the nature of the secrets and lies of psychotherapy clients. We wanted to know what kinds of information clients tended to conceal or lie about, why they resorted to dishonesty, and what they saw as

http://dx.doi.org/10.1037/0000128-001
Secrets and Lies in Psychotherapy, by B. A. Farber, M. Blanchard, and M. Love

the consequences of their various attempts at keeping information away from the prying eyes and ears of their therapist.

We were interested in these phenomena as part of a long-standing focus of the senior author (BAF) on issues relating to disclosure in the psychotherapeutic process. Beginning in 1992 with a presentation by the senior author and a doctoral student (Desnee Hall) at a conference of the Society of Psychotherapy Research in Berkeley, California, entitled "Disclosure to Therapists: What Is and Is Not Discussed in Therapy," research teams based in the clinical psychology program at Teachers College, Columbia University, have pursued a series of related questions: In this most confidential therapeutic space, what's left out of the dialogue, and why? How can we best understand the nature of the dialectic between wanting to be known by one's therapist and wanting to be seen by oneself and one's therapist in a favorable light? What factors contribute to how this dialectic is played out? What does the therapist allow the client to know about him- or herself? And how does the tension between honesty and impression management manifest among other psychotherapeutic dyads, including the supervisor and supervisee? The answers, or at least preliminary answers, to these questions have been reported in books and articles and at professional presentations by the senior author and members of his research team over the past 25 years. But until work on this current project began, we had not yet tackled head-on the phenomena of client lies and secrets. We had not, for example, asked clients to report on the specific reasons they concealed or lied about specific topics.

A few other researchers, notably David Rennie, Clara Hill, Bill Stiles, and Anita Kelly, had made some inroads on understanding client concealment and secret-keeping before we undertook our studies. Rennie attributed client withholding to their attitude of "deference" to their therapists. Hill, who has studied multiple aspects of the therapeutic process, published a series of valuable studies with her students and colleagues (most notably, Sarah Knox) investigating such phenomena as client "hidden reactions," "things left unsaid," and secrets, finding these related processes to be more common and harder to detect than previously imagined. Stiles delineated the complications in attempting to determine the relationship between client disclosure and treatment outcome. Kelly suggested that withholding certain shameful information from one's therapist could prove beneficial, serving to maintain the therapist's positive feelings toward the client. In addition, a group of researchers, including John Archer, Jeffrey Kahn, Erica Shambaugh, and Robert Hessling, have done important work on measuring psychotherapy clients' tendency to disclose distressing information. Still, for the most part, clients' lies and secrets have been a neglected aspect of psychotherapy research—a peculiar omission and one perhaps motivated in part by the field's not wanting to believe that clients lie and keep secrets and that, therefore, therapists are quite imperfect in their ability to overcome resistance and invoke truth.

It was time, we felt, for a comprehensive examination of this phenomenon, one that would use both quantitative (survey research) and qualitative (in-depth interview) data. And so a research lab overseen by two doctoral students in the clinical psychology program, now the second and third authors of this book (MB and ML), began thinking about ways of collecting data. Several years later and after analyzing the responses of over 1,300 individuals who participated in our studies, we decided to write this book, reporting what we and others have discovered about the nature and importance of psychotherapy clients' secrets and lies. The narratives contained in this volume are taken directly from the written statements and interviews of research participants and, in a few cases, from clinical case material we have encountered as therapists. Quotations are generally verbatim with only minor alterations for the sake of grammatical correctness, with the exception of several passages of dialogue between client and therapist that have been recreated to the best of our ability. Names and other bits of identifying information are fictionalized to protect the anonymity of our respondents and clients.

We regard this book as a logical sequel to the senior author's (2006) book, *Self-Disclosure in Psychotherapy*, which drew on both clinical and research perspectives, focusing on the topics that patients tended to discuss in therapy and those they tended to avoid; it also considered the factors, including demographic and cultural variables, that facilitated or impeded disclosure. Furthermore, it addressed disclosure and nondisclosure among other participants in the therapeutic process, including therapists, supervisors, and supervisees. That book did not, however, delve deeply into the related phenomena of secrets and lies. Although instances of nondisclosure, or more commonly, minimal disclosure, are attributable to many of the same factors and result in similar consequences as client lies and secrets, these latter phenomena are also in many important ways distinct in their presentation and clinical implications.

Although our topic is relatively narrow—truth and untruth in the special context of psychotherapy—the scope of this book is quite broad. We begin in Chapter 1 with an overview of this general issue—the ways in which clients are typically deceptive in therapy, the difficulties therapists have in detecting secrets and lies, and the reasons why patient deception matters. The second chapter takes us outside the consulting room and into everyday life, exploring the various attempts made from multiple social science and philosophical traditions to define and categorize the lies, secrets, and deceptions used by the human animal in the eternal struggle for love, status, safety, and self-esteem. The third chapter returns to the world of psychotherapy, reviewing the clinical and empirical literature that tries to answer questions such as,

Why do clients lie? What are the ways in which client deception can be categorized? What topics tend to be concealed, minimized, or lied about? The fourth chapter focuses on factors that affect clients' tendency to disclose versus keep secrets or lie in therapy, including their perceptions of the benefits and costs of disclosure. This chapter also addresses three other aspects of the disclosure–deceit relationship: What is the process by which clients decide to disclose honestly rather than deceive? What is the relationship between disclosure and various forms of deception? And what are the consequences of keeping secrets and/or telling lies in therapy? Chapter 5 shifts the focus from client to therapist, reviewing the literature on therapist secrets and lies, a fascinating topic in its own right, and one with implications for clients' tendencies to conceal and deceive.

Chapters 6 through 11 focus extensively on the results of our ongoing studies of client secrets and lies. The first of these chapters reviews our basic findings: the most common lies told, personal and clinical factors affecting their occurrence, and the perceived reasons for and consequences of these lies. The next six of these chapters contain multiple clinical examples and delve into the nature of specific, common client lies and secrets: self-harm and suicidal thoughts, sexual issues, substance abuse, trauma, and clinical progress and feelings about one's therapist. The concluding chapter of this book deals with the training, research, and clinical implications of client lies and secrets, focused primarily on the question "What's a therapist to do?"

The primary audience for this book includes practitioners, academics, and students in the mental health fields. We imagine too that many psychotherapy clients, including those who have already terminated therapy and those for whom this extraordinary activity is still ongoing, will find much to identify with in these pages. For these readers, we offer a view of therapy at precisely those critical points where it may be going awry. We sift through client stories seeking the cracks and seams, tensions, and pressures that might bring a treatment down or significantly limit its effectiveness. The simple question "What can't you tell your therapist?" is our way of examining the core supports of psychotherapy: disclosure, trust, and the therapeutic alliance. We also hope this book will attract curious lay readers, perhaps those considering therapy and/or those who know something about (and are intrigued by) the therapies of friends and family members. But even those with no personal experience with or vicarious knowledge of therapy are likely to have felt some of the pulls toward not-quite-honesty that we discuss in the chapters ahead. For all these potential readers, we offer a judgment-free zone and the shared experiences of others who have struggled to disclose in therapy. Importantly, we believe all patients have a right to their secrets and elisions. We seek only to help with that subset of secrets that patients wish—or mostly wish—they did not have to keep.

Although this book was not influenced by contemporary media scrutiny of truth-telling among politicians and other famous people, its focus nevertheless is remarkably consistent with this cultural moment. Our emphasis on the many ways that truth can be defined and distorted, and the ways that individuals can and do rationalize their decision to avoid honest engagement with others, is certainly consonant with current reports on the statements and actions of prominent figures in our midst. There is, we think, an intriguing aspect to the tendency of many people to lie and conceal information in situations where we do not expect them to do so—including, as this book reveals, the psychotherapeutic setting. Perhaps in contrast to many political figures, what we found was that most psychotherapy clients want to be honest, though they struggle to do so consistently. The details of both sides of this issue are contained in the pages of this book.

1

TELLING LIES AND KEEPING SECRETS IN PSYCHOTHERAPY

> If you look for truthfulness, you might just as well be blind.
>
> —Billy Joel, "Honesty"

There is abundant evidence that in every context of their lives, people lie and keep secrets. They do so from childhood on, beginning with parents and teachers; they do so throughout their lives, with friends, dating partners, spouses, children, potential employers, coworkers, supervisors, and of course, various government agencies, especially the Internal Revenue Service. They sometimes lie when publishing research studies (Markowitz & Hancock, 2014) and writing purportedly nonfiction articles or books (e.g., James Frey, 2003, *A Million Little Pieces*). They certainly do so when it comes to politics. As *The New York Times* noted, the truth seemed to be "deeply out of fashion" in the 2016 presidential campaign (Barbaro, 2015, p. 1). "Fake news," both during and after the election, was prominent enough to warrant a *New York Times* story with the headline "As Fake News Spreads Lies, More Readers Shrug at Truth" (Tavernise, 2016, p. 1). Who could have predicted that, in the spring of 2017, the cover of *Time* magazine would read "Is Truth Dead?" These are strange days indeed for public discourse.

---

http://dx.doi.org/10.1037/0000128-002
Secrets and Lies in Psychotherapy, by B. A. Farber, M. Blanchard, and M. Love

In their private discourse, as per Billy Joel (in the epigraph), many individuals find it easier to be consistently kind than consistently truthful. Still, it feels somewhat surprising, even disconcerting, to accept that this occurs in psychotherapy—that even in that sacred space of near-absolute confidentiality, clients lie and keep secrets. Intuitively, or perhaps out of naive hope or expectation, we want this space to be different. We want our clients to trust us enough to tell us their truths, to believe we are trustworthy and safe, and to trust that their most profound, intimate, and shameful disclosures will be honored and respected. And to a great extent, many clients do trust us and disclose a great deal to us, including parts of their lives that are typically viewed as intimate (e.g., sex), private (e.g., money matters), immoral (e.g., cheating on a significant other), illegal (e.g., selling drugs), or especially difficult to acknowledge and talk about (e.g., the experience of being abused).

Nevertheless, in the psychotherapist's office, as in every other interpersonal situation, the pull for full and honest disclosure is often at odds with the powerful human needs to avoid or minimize shame and to affirm or aggrandize our sense of self. These motives and a host of others, including the wish to avoid hurting others' feelings, make it nearly inevitable that there will be some degree of secret keeping and lying by most clients in every therapist's practice. In fact, the emerging data indicate that lies are far more prevalent in the therapeutic process than most therapists realize. Although differing research methodologies and discrepant definitions of terms make it difficult to derive a single, accepted figure for rates of client lying or secret keeping, a definition that included the large and small ways we minimize, exaggerate, omit, deny, twist the facts, or pretend to agree with our therapists would probably state that "client dishonesty is almost universal" (Blanchard & Farber, 2016, p. 2).

In a recent study we conducted—and about which we will have far more to say later in this book—93% of a sample of over 500 clients in therapy acknowledged having lied to their therapist. Moreover, the mean number of topics they reported lying about was 8.4, with minimal differences as a function of client or therapist demographics. Although these numbers are likely inflated given the methodology of this study—people who had lied more to their therapist may have been more motivated to complete a survey on "lying in therapy"—a subsequent study we conducted in which there was no mention of "lying" found that 84% of nearly 800 respondents indicated there was a topic they had either deliberately avoided talking about or been substantially dishonest about in their therapy. That is, even in this second, more neutrally presented study, most clients implicitly acknowledged some form of concealment or deception.

These findings confirm a basic truth noted in other empirical and clinical studies: Although clients often tell the truth, dishonesty also seems to occur frequently and across multiple topics, clinical settings (private practice, clinics, hospitals), and therapeutic orientations. Given the confidentiality accorded to the therapeutic situation, these statistics might appear surprising, but the extremely intimate nature of the therapeutic relationship, including a near-constant focus on the self in the context of face-to-face interaction, may actually increase the frequency of lies and secrets. The therapist's scrutiny, even gentle and caring scrutiny, can be too much to bear. Much as we all sometimes feel the need to avert the intensity of a seemingly too-prolonged or too-intimate gaze, even from a loved one, our clients cannot always bear our need to know, understand, or care. The vulnerability can feel overwhelming—or, in the words of a song by Dan Hill, "Sometimes when we touch, the honesty's too much." As well, the wish to look good, to be seen as competent and reasonably well-adjusted, and to be admired by one's therapist often makes secret keeping and lying seem like viable options.

The findings of research studies (e.g., Baumann & Hill, 2016; Farber & Hall, 2002; Kelly, 1998; Pope & Tabachnick, 1994; Regan & Hill, 1992) suggest that some, perhaps many, clients adopt a strategy that can be summarized as "I can tell my therapist hard things about a few topics, but I need to maintain a basic level of self-esteem such that I need to minimize, conceal, or distort the truth on other matters. I cannot let my therapist come to think of me as deficient or incompetent in too many areas of life." These studies point to another common position, one that takes the form "I can reveal a good deal about a hard topic, but there are limits to how far I can go—some real bottom lines as to how vulnerable and shameful I'm willing to feel—and when I get to that point, some aspects of the entire truth about that topic are going to be compromised."

Thus, therapists often do not get the truth, the whole truth, and nothing but the truth (though hardly anyone does). Sometimes they get no version of it at all, no discussion of a topic of personal importance to the client. And sometimes they get a version of the truth that is sanitized or otherwise truncated in some significant way or perhaps even quite distorted—a truly fictionalized version of the truth. Sometimes they eventually get the whole story, the telling of a previously held secret or the recanting of a previously made-up tale. But sometimes clients leave therapy even after long-term treatment with significant parts of themselves unrevealed to their therapist. Our sense of self—including the way we view our thoughts, feelings, actions, wishes, fantasies, and fears—is often a fragile thing that needs protection from critical self-scrutiny and even seemingly trusted and relied-on others.

CLIENT SECRETS AND LIES: THREE VIGNETTES

Kevin

Kevin, a 28-year-old, White, married (for 2 years), heterosexual man working as a sales clerk, entered therapy for the first time complaining of anxiety related to his marriage and his job. Per the information offered at intake, Kevin had graduated on time from high school and had taken several courses during 1 year attending a junior college. He indicated that he had no history of trauma or drug or alcohol abuse.

Four months into treatment Kevin called to make an "emergency appointment" with his therapist. He had failed a random drug test at work and had been fired from his job. In discussing what occurred, Kevin acknowledged that he had not told the truth about his extensive drug habit (from marijuana to cocaine to assorted pills), fearing that the therapist would view him negatively and attribute all his problems to his drug use. Kevin further acknowledged that his wife had only a "slight" awareness of this problem and that no one else, except the friends with whom he got high, were aware of how much money he spent and how often he got high. During this discussion, the therapist was open to understanding Kevin's concerns regarding disclosure and accepting of his seemingly genuine apology. She also expressed concern about his ongoing drug use and wondered about his resolve to deal with this issue. During the last part of that session, she and Kevin discussed whether and how they could regain the trust necessary to continue their work together. Kevin did not show up for his next scheduled appointment, did not return repeated phone calls from the therapist, and never returned to therapy.

Catherine

Catherine, a 50-year-old, twice-divorced, currently unmarried White woman with three children in their 20s, who was employed as supply manager in a plumbing company, reentered therapy for the fourth time after a 3-year break from treatment. She first began therapy at the age of 14 at the request of her parents, who were concerned about her poor schoolwork, lack of motivation, and drug and sexual experimentation. She had been in therapy for a total of 16 years—her longest treatment with one therapist was 8 years—with complaints of depression, "not fitting in," anger and impulsive behavior, and poor relationships with family members, including her mother, her siblings, and her three children. On the basis of her complaints and symptom picture, her new therapist theorized she had been abused as a child, and Catherine acknowledged that this was so—and acknowledged too that although she had admitted to being physically abused to previous therapists, she had never spoken before about the sexual abuse perpetrated by her father. She had been explicitly asked about this possibility by previous therapists but had consistently denied any such abuse.

Therapist: Can you tell me what you were thinking or afraid of when those therapists asked you about that?

Catherine: I had told them so much about the physical abuse that had happened to me, gone into great detail, answered all their questions. . . . I felt so low, beaten, awful, terribly guilty, I just couldn't admit to anything more.

Therapist: And when they asked about whether your father had done anything else to you, whether he'd abused you in any other way, you (pause).

Catherine: They were okay—they seemed to care—but at those moments I just wanted to retreat and get out of there. I couldn't stand any more questions, especially about that [the sexual abuse]. So I just said no. Actually, now that I think about it, I said something to one of them—Jennifer, the therapist I worked with the longest—I told her that dad got all the kicks he needed out of beating me.

Therapist: I appreciate the fact that you're letting me know this now, but I also wonder why. Why now tell a therapist about this after all these years of it being a secret?

Catherine: I don't know. It's just time to let someone know. It's been on my mind. I was actually going to let my last therapist know, but then she pissed me off about something. I think I was a few minutes late to a session, and she wouldn't let go of that, and I just said screw it.

Therapist: I'm hoping that you can trust me enough to let me know some of the details of what happened, and we can go as slowly as you need to, but for now I'm wondering this: Do you think that keeping this secret got in the way of therapy in some way?

Catherine: I don't know. Maybe. It was a secret, maybe a lie, but I just didn't feel like I wanted to talk about it. It was too deep, worse even than the physical abuse, though sometimes they happened together, and I just couldn't imagine dealing with more guilt and shame. It was like the one piece of myself that I didn't want to share. I guess I felt defiant about it. You can get everything else from me, but I'm not going to talk about that. And I was scared too that talking about that was going to set me off, make me either want to kill someone else or myself. He [her dad] died when I was 24, but I still feel I could kill someone when I think of what he did to me . . . but you know what too? Those therapists, particularly Jennifer, helped me anyway. I was really out of control for a lot of years, and I'm better now. Not where I want to be yet, but not quite as out of control.

Therapist: Mm-hmm, I can understand, or at least try to understand why you wouldn't or couldn't talk about the sexual abuse, so why now? Why are you willing to do it now?

Catherine: I'm 50 years old. Maybe it's time to deal with this finally. And maybe if I deal with this, it'll get those last pieces of anger in me under control. Little things still piss me off, and I still lose it too easily with people . . . and my eldest [daughter] is getting married, and I'd really like that to go well. We've already started to argue, and I'm just tired of being angry and arguing with everyone all the time. It still doesn't take much to set me off.

Therapist: So there's a sense that talking about the sexual abuse might help with your anger, might help with getting along with people.

Catherine: Look, I know that talking about it is not going to be a miracle thing and make me a patient saint overnight, but I'm tired of it weighing on me. And I know this is crazy, but believe it or not, I actually feel guilty about it, as if some of this was my fault. And I hate thinking that.

Therapist: Does anyone else know about what happened to you? Your mother?

Catherine: Yeah, of course she knew, but she never wanted to talk about it, and when I was a kid and started to ask her about and ask her why she never did anything about it, she said she didn't want to talk about it, that was the past, and that she had tried to do something like ask him to stop, but then he'd beat her and threaten her. I mostly stopped asking her about it, though sometimes during some of our worse arguments I'd tell her that she was worse than he was, that she was mostly sane and didn't even protect her own kid.

Therapist: I'm sorry—sounds terrible. I am hoping we can work with this somehow to make it feel less toxic, less your fault, but am wondering too—are there other secrets you've kept from your therapists, including me, that may be useful to talk about at some point?

Catherine:	Yeah, maybe some things I've done in my marriage, but I don't want to talk about that now.
Therapist:	OK, that's understandable. I appreciate that you've shared what you have. How are you feeling now with this?
Catherine:	Shaky. We'll see what I feel later today or tonight. I'll let you know next week.

Catherine did return to therapy the following week, and she reported that she had experienced a difficult week with more frequent and vivid memories of her physical and sexual abuse. But she continued to discuss these experiences quite openly and with a great deal of crying and intense anger over the next few months of therapy. Going over what happened to her, including the subsequent effects on her life and her attempts to keep these experiences, especially the sexual abuse, out of consciousness and out of the awareness of others, became for a while the dominant focus of therapy. Catherine stayed in therapy for 3 more years after she first acknowledged the facts of her sexual abuse to her therapist. Both she and her therapist reported significant improvement in multiple areas of her life, especially in her relationships with her children and a new romantic partner.

Stephanie

Stephanie, a White, 45-year-old mother of two teenage girls, married for 18 years, working as a part-time paralegal, came into therapy complaining about her marriage and considering divorce. She had been in therapy briefly as a teen when her parents went through their divorce. She remembered vividly her struggles to come to terms with that—feeling angry, alone, and "abandoned" and "hating the shared custody arrangements." She did not at present fear being single or alone, but she did have great concerns about how her girls would react to the same situation she had faced as a child.

She and her husband had met in their early 20s and fallen "passionately in love." They were engaged within a few months of meeting and were married within the year. She described many common interests, including music and traveling, and she considered their first few years together "quite good." They had several good friends with whom they frequently got together; although they did not have a great deal of money, they had enough to go out to eat occasionally and go on modest vacations. Things changed, Stephanie noted, when they had their first child. Her husband was "all in favor" of having children but "struggled with parenting." He reacted poorly to the normal frustrations and stresses inherent in parenting a young child, leaving virtually all the parenting—feeding, bathing, preparing for sleep, and so forth—to Stephanie and occasional help from her mother. According to her, he became a "somewhat better" parent when the girls became older and more independent.

She acknowledged that his work as a middle-school teacher had become far more stressful for him with a transfer several years earlier to a more difficult school, but she nevertheless felt increasingly resentful of the burdens placed on her "with little help from him." They had frequent verbal spats, although there was no physical violence. He acknowledged his initial difficulties with being a father but felt he had gotten better over the years and was still "trying"; moreover, he accused her of not acknowledging his financial contributions to the household. According to Stephanie, their sex life, once active and mutually enjoyable, had become sporadic and far less enjoyable over the past several years. She acknowledged being "less interested" and attributed this to her fatigue over parenting and her resentment toward her husband.

What she had not told her therapist about—and what she did not think her husband knew about—was the affair she had started a few years after the birth of their second child, an affair that had been ongoing, if intermittent, for the past 10 years. This came to light when the therapist encouraged Stephanie's husband to attend a joint therapy session. The session started out amicably but devolved quickly into mutual criticism and was punctuated dramatically with her husband's accusations and apparent knowledge for at least a year of the affair. Stephanie's initial denials felt unconvincing to both her husband and therapist, and she moved quickly to an angry position of "Yes, but I deserved some happiness and loving and you weren't giving it to me."

The therapist referred them to couples counseling, but that ended when they agreed after 2 months to proceed to separation and divorce. The therapist continued to see Stephanie in individual therapy where they worked on three major issues: life for her and her children during this period of separation and expected divorce, the role she played in the dissolution of her marriage (i.e., how she dealt with frustration and disappointment), and questions of trust between the two of them (i.e., Stephanie and her therapist). Regarding this last point, Stephanie initially suggested that she did not share the fact of her affair with the therapist because it was not "relevant" to what they were discussing. She claimed that her resentment toward her husband and their waning emotional and physical intimacy were "real by themselves" and not affected by her affair. Moreover, she felt this to be a "really a private matter" and something she did not want to discuss in therapy. Following the acknowledgment of her affair, Stephanie wavered in her commitment to therapy, missing several sessions. But she did return each time and was able to acknowledge that she was "angry" at her therapist for pushing her to talk about something she did not want to talk about. They worked on this a good deal, with the therapist acknowledging her frustration with Stephanie concealing an important facet of her life and also apologizing for being "clumsy" in pursuing this issue. Stephanie reluctantly agreed that she had concealed something really important from her therapist and began talking about her difficulty in trusting others to believe her side of any story without distorting or concealing important details.

UNDERSTANDING THESE LIES AND SECRETS

Kevin lied to his therapist about his drug problem, a common topic of client avoidance and deception. He felt that his therapist, who was about 30 years older than he, would take a dim view of his alcohol and drug use and attribute all his problems at work and with his marriage to this one part of his life. Moreover, Kevin believed that he had this part of his life more or less "under control" and did not need help with it. The therapist, for her part, did not investigate fully Kevin's brief comments about "an occasional drink or two" nor about "occasional marijuana use in high school." She did not want to appear suspicious or otherwise too parental, fearing that doing so could damage the formation or maintenance of an effective working alliance. Of note, too, she had struggled with confronting her children when they were teenagers about their experimentation with drugs and alcohol. To a certain extent, then, the therapist's issues made it easier for Kevin to avoid telling the truth about his drug use. One could say she colluded with his deceit; from a psychoanalytic perspective, this therapist's countertransference made it all too easy for Kevin to lie. More generally, this situation reflects the principle that it takes two for a lie to succeed: the liar and the person (sometimes deemed "the dupe") who tacitly agrees to be lied to.

Although they had a good, open discussion of what happened at work and in the therapy itself, with a seemingly genuine apology on Kevin's part for not telling the truth, that discussion did not include the therapist's acknowledgment of her possible mistakes or even collusion in missing now-obvious clues or failing to ask the right questions. Nor did it include another aspect of therapy that Kevin was not open about: his lingering doubts about his therapist's ability to help him. Partly because he was still too ashamed of his deceit and fearful that his therapist would still be angry at him, partly because he experienced his therapist as not strong enough for him and not able to confront him on issues he preferred to avoid, and partly because he was still ambivalent about wanting or needing to give up these substance-abusing parts of his life, he terminated treatment.

Catherine's story of concealing sexual abuse had many of the same elements. Like Kevin, she feared acknowledging to her therapist a part of her life story that she felt made her seem too damaged. Like Kevin, she kept this secret from virtually everyone in her life. And like Kevin, her deception was a combination of secret keeping and lying—in previous therapies, she had explicitly denied any history of being sexually abused. But her most recent therapist was more persistently inquisitive than Kevin's, and Catherine, having been in therapy multiple times before this experience, may have realized on some level that her lack of candor in regard to her sexual abuse was frustrating her efforts to feel understood and to gain greater relief from her nearly constant states of distress and bouts of self-recrimination. She was ready to acknowledge what had happened to her with her father, though was not yet ready to speak about other parts of her life—things she had done in her marriage (an affair?)—that she had apparently kept secret or lied about. Catherine's story seems primed for a better ending. She seems committed to continuing her therapy, and we get a sense that she is resolved to be more honest with her therapist about multiple aspects of her life. Furthermore, her new therapist seems to be well-attuned to her style and needs, and they seem to be developing a strong working alliance. Nevertheless, the end of this story has not been written. Catherine's past behavior, including her impulsivity, anger, and struggles with interpersonal relationships, suggests that despite her current resolve there are likely to be future therapeutic conflicts, resulting in further instances of some form of resistance to treatment, including concealment of salient information.

Stephanie, like Kevin, attempted to compartmentalize her work in therapy—allowing her therapist to know a good deal about the history and current state of her marriage but leaving out a significant part of the story. Whether out of shame (for how she felt about herself for what she was doing) or guilt (for the affair itself), Stephanie did not allow her therapist to know about this part of her life. She convinced herself that she could be helped in her marriage without revealing this, contending that her affair was essentially a meaningless part of the larger story. But to her credit, and to the credit of her therapist as well, she began to work on her problems with trusting others. She was able to see how her patterns of avoidance and lies, both minor and major, were getting in the way of all her significant relationships. What helped too was her therapist's ability to acknowledge her role in making this topic difficult to address. According to Stephanie,

> A turning point was her saying to me something like, "my frustration at you for not telling me the truth wasn't meant to be a criticism of you, it was about my own frustration about not being to help, about something getting in the way between us."

Stephanie went on to say,

> I knew it was really my problem—I had lied my whole life about lots of things—but she made it easier for me to talk about something that was just so awful and embarrassing. It's so much easier to blame other people.

LIES AND SECRETS IN PSYCHOTHERAPY ARE HARD TO DEFINE

These examples—all drawn from interviews with current and former patients with all identifying information altered—are the "easy" illustrations of lying. That is, they depict clear instances of a client either omitting a significant detail of his or her life or, in response to therapist questioning, denying a historical fact or current instance or pattern of behavior. Furthermore, in each case, the client eventually acknowledged his or her lie; in two of these three examples, the client continued to work with treatment. Lying in therapy, however, is typically both harder to define and harder to detect.

It is difficult to define because there are so many varieties of lies, and finding common elements, other than that of general deceit, is surprisingly elusive. As CNN legal analyst Danny Cevallos noted in response to the threat of a prominent public figure to sue one of his many detractors for purportedly lying about an incident of sexual harassment,

> And that's the problem with the term "liar": what does it actually mean? Courts recognize that "lying" applies to a broad spectrum of untruths: white lies, partial truths, misinterpretation, deception and just general dishonesty. We all "lie" to some degree at some point—even presidents—maybe even under oath! (Cevallos, 2016, para. 12)

In this regard, too, we are taken with a 2018 *New Yorker* cartoon by David Sipress in which a person being sworn in for court testimony is asked the following: "Do you swear to tell the truth, the whole truth, and nothing but the truth, even though nobody has any idea what that is anymore?"

On a basic level, one can differentiate between lies of omission (secrets) and commission (lies per se), but in fact, there are multiple means of categorizing lies (see Chapter 2), none of which is entirely satisfactory and none of which reflects the complexity of most interpersonal dynamics, especially that of the therapist–patient situation. Secrets and lies are complicated and sometimes overlapping matters—lies, misdirected emphases, or half-truths can, for example, provide cover for secrets.

Furthermore, some lies of omission appear more in the form of secrets and nondisclosure of relatively minor events (e.g., a traffic violation) and some about secrets and nondisclosure of significant facts (e.g., suicidal thoughts or behaviors, feelings about one's therapist or the progress of therapy). And there are lies of commission that are manifest as exaggeration of details or feelings or behavior (e.g., effusive praise in the absence of genuinely positive feelings, lies that under- or overemphasize one's role in the success or failure of an event) and lies that take the form of explicit distortion of details (e.g., substituting accounts of verbal abuse for the reality of physical abuse, fabricating personal accomplishments).

Deceit can serve many different personal and social purposes and reflect both benign and malevolent motives. Different kinds of lies—"white lies," narcissistically induced exaggerations, distortion of significant historical material, and nondisclosure of current feelings between two individuals, among others—have significantly different "feels" to them and are barely containable within a common conceptual framework. White lies, for example, tend not to evoke the interpersonal anger or resentment as these others; by contrast, the awareness that someone close to us is withholding "obvious" negatively tinged feelings (e.g., anger) or being vague or otherwise disingenuous in reporting the details of an event may lead to apprehension and/or considerable annoyance.

More generally, lies are hard to precisely define and identify because, with rare exception (i.e., blatant distortions of agreed-on facts), they exist on a continuum with truth telling. Details are inevitably left out of narratives, memories are faulty, tact and so-called white lies are embedded in the fabric of most cultures and considered necessary and appropriate, and truth is always filtered through personal histories, needs, and cognitive biases. Several individuals, including the late French novelist Andre Gide, have been credited with the astute observation that "the color of truth is gray" ("Gray Is the Color of Truth," 2017). And, in a similar vein, though over 200 years ago, Jane Austen (1816) wrote in her classic book *Emma*, "Seldom, very seldom, does complete truth belong to any human disclosure; seldom can it happen that something is not a little disguised or a little mistaken" (p. 392).

Truth, though, is not only best seen as existing on a continuum but also as existing "in the eye of the beholder." Without verifiable information, where can the truth be located but in the differing perceptions of different actors in typically complicated situations? *Rashomon* (Jingo & Kurosawa, 1950), the classic Kurosawa movie, is often used as an example of how idiosyncratically the truth is constituted. The plot involves several characters—a bandit, a wife, a samurai, a woodcutter—presenting their conflicting versions of an incident, the death of a samurai that each professed to witness. As the film critic Roger Ebert noted in his 2002 review,

> Because we see the events in flashbacks, we assume they reflect truth. But all they reflect is a point of view, sometimes lied about. . . . The genius of "Rashomon" is that all the flashbacks are both true and false. True, in the sense that they present an accurate portrait of what each witness thinks happened. False, because as Kurosawa [the director] observes in his autobiography, "Human beings are unable to be honest with themselves about themselves. They cannot talk about themselves without embellishing." (Ebert, 2002, para. 6)

Like Kurosawa's witnesses, psychotherapy clients struggle to see things objectively. In therapy, the client is not only one of the witnesses but is also in fact all of the witnesses—the bandit, the wife, the woodcutter are all parts of self—turning to the therapist for help constructing one workable truth out of his or her fractured perceptions, competing desires, and internal conflicts. But therapists too are bound by their subjectivity and necessarily biased perceptions regardless of whether they have been in their own therapy. Personal therapy may illuminate and lessen the hold of a therapist's blind spots but cannot eradicate their influence entirely. Empathic lapses in therapy may represent the clinician's inability to go beyond his or her sense of the truth to sufficiently accept, believe, or synthesize the presented truth(s) of his or her client.

Truth has also become more difficult to define as Western culture has taken on a more postmodern bent. Within this emerging discourse, truth is said to be obscured or confounded by the limitations of language, be "constructed" or "coconstructed" by participants in the dialogue, and shift with context and/or observers (as in *Rashomon* or, more recently, the movies *The Usual Suspects* [McDonnell & Singer, 1995] and *Gone Girl* [Chaffin, Donen, Milchan, Witherspoon, & Fincher, 2014] or books that use the device of an "unreliable narrator," such as Yann Martel's [2001] *Life of Pi* or Julian Barnes's [2011] *The Sense of an Ending*). Furthermore, narrative truth may be considered as valid as previously held ideas about objective or documented truth. Thus, memories have been thought of as "true but inaccurate"—true to the belief of the narrator but false in regard to objective or verifiable facts (Barclay, 1986). From this perspective, unless the therapist concludes that the client is intentionally attempting to deceive, the therapist makes use of what the client is saying through the lens of "this is what it felt like to my client" or "this is the truth of his or her experience." In short, the failures of language and the ever-present effects of power and context add another layer of warping to any effort to locate the truth.

The nature of truth and honest disclosure in contemporary Western culture may be further entangled by the apparent lure and demands of social media. Not only do many people maintain an online presence that may or may not be entirely congruent with their offline presence, but also their online persona may vary across different forms of social media (e.g., Facebook, Instagram, Snapchat). The rise of the selfie, doctored with photo editing apps and filters has allowed individuals to continually shape their identities, to form "curated selves." This is reminiscent of Winnicott's (1960) ideas about the *false self*—the extent to which we conform to the expectations of others in our social environment. We can all choose to show the world certain aspects of ourselves while omitting others; we can even invent or greatly exaggerate aspects of ourselves. These days, it is far more than public relations people who routinely "spin" facts to create impressions. As the English writer, Jeanette Winterson (2016) observed, "The airborne contagion of advertising and spin, political lying and celebrity froth, makes authentic discourse difficult" (p. 21).

Of course, to a great extent, this has always been the case. As Goffman (1959) so brilliantly documented, we are all constantly preening and presenting ourselves in certain ways to meet social demands and personal needs for affirmation. But technology greatly facilitates this tendency to present a less-than-fully-honest version of ourselves to the world, one that tends to emphasize our uniqueness, importance, and worthiness to be seen, heard, and responded to. It is no wonder that many have suggested that social media serve to promote individuals' intense pursuit of self-esteem, allowing users to create exaggerated, unreal images of themselves for others to consume. It would hardly be surprising, then, if some of this carried over to the therapist's office, such that the painful, longstanding, detailed truth of personal experience may be elided, at least in the initial stages of therapy, in favor of other, more superficial truths favored by social media, truths steeped in recent accomplishments and pithy observations.

In considering the nature of truth, it is also important to consider that over time narratives and memories are often altered. Decades of research by psychologist Elizabeth Loftus and colleagues has suggested that eyewitness memories can be distorted simply by asking misleading questions (Loftus & Palmer, 1974)—that, in essence, memory is highly malleable. In a related vein, research into the neural basis of memory has illuminated the process of *memory reconsolidation* by which memories are vulnerable to distortion and reediting each time they are accessed in the brain (Schiller, Monfils, Raio, Johnson, LeDoux, & Phelps, 2010). Such findings seem to square with everyday life. Chatting with old friends, we find ourselves at odds over the details of time, place, and the people who were there. Images and memories may be lost, regained, or even revitalized under the impetus of "anniversary events" (e.g., the birthday or day of death of a loved one) or even viewing old pictures. As Gregory Cowles (2015), a book reviewer for *The New York Times* noted, "Even the most honest memoirs are necessarily conditional and incomplete, compromised as soon as they're pinned wriggling on the page" (p. 21). All this, of course, is not the stuff of lies but rather the changing panorama of truth.

The same can be said for narratives recounted in a therapist's office. Initial client accounts of important events or people may be fragmented, the details obscured by time or the need to forget that which is too painful to remember. These memories often fill out and become more differentiated over the course of treatment, details slowly restored. Client recollections of early abuse often reflect these influences. Under such circumstances, it often becomes the therapist's task to help assemble fragmented bits of experience into a more coherent truth. It is also true that these accounts may be distorted, influenced by client wishes, unconscious or otherwise, to make their lives or those of others grander or starker or more contemptible than they really were. But again, sketchy or inconsistent accounts of lives recounted early in therapy are not necessarily the stuff of secrets and lies; they are often preliminary, best attempts at the truth, though confounded by the usual influences of self-protection.

Furthermore, distinguishing an off-handed, not-meant-to-be-literal comment ("What happened at that party last night was the worst thing that ever happened to me") from a more significant distortion of the truth may demand a fair amount of clinical acumen. Among other possibilities, an off-handed comment may be a form of small talk, an attempt at humor, or an avoidance of a larger issue or reflect a habitual pattern of exaggerated reporting. Although each of these possibilities suggests an interpersonal strategy that might well be worthy of therapeutic comment, each has its own dynamic, and each suggests a distinct intervention. All attempts at impressing or even distracting one's therapist do not fall into the category of lies.

And still more nuances surround the nature of truth and lies in psychotherapy, here posed as questions: Does leaving out details of significant events with the vague assumption or expectation that they will be discussed with the therapist at some future point constitute secret keeping or lying? Under what conditions can omitting details be considered a function of the time limitations of a therapeutic hour or treatment rather than an instance of secret keeping? Are clients who prefer to talk about seemingly insignificant aspects of their lives—"people talking but not speaking," in the smart words of the songwriter Paul Simon—lying or keeping secrets or are they just "testing the waters" or going at their own pace? There are many gradations between deceit and truth and many obstacles in one person's communicating a thought or feeling accurately to another.

In some cases, particularly with secrets, the client's personal history and presenting problems are critical determinants of the distinction between nondisclosure and deceit. There is, after all, a true difference between nondisclosure of insignificant events and secret keeping in regard to quite significant events. Note, for example, the difference between a client without an eating disorder omitting any discussion of her meals and the secret keeping of a client with a history of an eating disorder failing to tell her therapist of her apparent relapse into eating-disordered behaviors over the past several weeks. In general, though, apart from egregious and seemingly conscious distortions of material or the withholding of significant information, discriminating between a client lie or secret and a yet-to-be-fully-and-honestly-discussed issue in psychotherapy can be a difficult proposition. Clients sometimes say or otherwise adopt the position of, "I'm getting there, it's just taking me a while to talk about something this hard." Or, "It's still fuzzy; I'm still filling in the blanks." Or, "I just don't want to talk about that now." Or even, "I'm not sure anymore of what did or didn't happen."

In short, within the context of a situation such as psychotherapy—one in which there are so many competing forces, especially that between the wish to be known fully and the wish to be judged favorably by oneself and others—it may be difficult, if not impossible, for a therapist to differentiate between narrative and objective truth or even to determine which aspects of the client's narrative reflect the best of his or her current abilities and which reflect some attempt to conceal or distort even known aspects of the truth in the service of avoiding shame or guilt. Although there is a psychoanalytic tradition dating back to Freud that encourages the therapist to assume the position of final arbiter of truth, few today would take this stance, accepting instead the notion that truth is elusive, iterative, and often coconstructed.

CLIENT SECRETS AND LIES ARE HARD TO DETECT

Client secrets and lies are not only difficult to define, they are also difficult for therapists to detect. In the clinical vignettes presented earlier, the lies eventually came out; that is, the client ultimately acknowledged a difficult truth. In fact, though, research (e.g., Hill, Thompson, Cogar, & Denman, 1993) has shown that most therapists cannot tell when clients are lying or leaving feelings or thoughts unexpressed. Clients, and nonclients too for that matter, are good at being deceitful. Freud (1905/1953) contended that "he that has eyes to see and ears to hear may convince himself that no mortal can keep a secret. If his lips are silent, he chatters with his fingertips; betrayal oozes out of him at every pore" (pp. 77–78). But contrary to Freud's assertion, many clients are quite capable of lying and keeping secrets forever—till death—without being found out. (There is an interesting literature on "deathbed confessions"; among the most intriguing of the stories is that of the man who confessed that he had faked the famous Loch Ness Monster.) As the novelist, Javier Marias, noted so wisely in his (2013) book *The Infatuations*,

> Yes, it's ridiculous, isn't it, that after all these centuries of practice, after so many incredible advances and inventions, we still have no way of knowing when someone is lying; naturally, this both benefits and prejudices all of us equally, and be our one remaining redoubt of freedom. (p. 246)

Apart from client persistence in keeping up a lie or holding onto a long-held secret, lies may stay intact because most therapists are inclined to believe their clients. Even when their issues do not overlap with their clients' issues—as in the case of Kevin (discussed earlier)—therapists often engage in "truth bias." They want to trust and believe their clients because doing so tends to promote a healthy therapeutic relationship and because most therapists (à la Carl Rogers) want to see the "good" in their clients. And it is not hard to see the good in most clients. Most are courageous in presenting themselves for therapy, are sincere in wanting to be helped, have qualities and competencies we admire, and will make us feel good about our abilities. Thus, as per the lyrics to a popular 1980s song "Eye in the Sky" by The Alan Parsons Project: "The sun in your eyes made some of the lies worth believing."

Given these considerations, questioning the consistency of a client's narrative, wondering whether there's "more" to the story, or gently challenging the credibility of a client's report ("Really?") can be courageous actions. When approached with great tact, these interventions can greatly deepen and improve the work. As per the advice to therapists proffered by our colleagues George Goldstein and Jessi Suzuki (2015), "If you see something, say something." But doing so can also pose dangers. The therapist can be wrong—even if one is sure, one can be wrong—and even if the therapist is right, the timing of this intervention and the exact choice of words and tone had better be near perfect. All individuals need some defenses against the wounds of the world. It is too easy for clients to become even further entrenched or defensive if they feel threatened or insufficiently held.

Therapists who suspect they are encountering clinically significant client concealment or deceit must deal with a host of issues. Some may start with a personal indictment of sorts, wondering why they did not pick up on this behavior earlier in the treatment: "I should have known better," "I knew something was wrong and didn't follow up on it." Some will surely, if unfortunately, silently condemn the client for his or her character flaws while using these instances of lying or concealment as confirmatory evidence of the client's personality disorder. But all thoughtful therapists will have to consider and discuss the reasons for a client's secrets or lies. Although many occurrences of omission and distortion can be attributed to the aforementioned needs to avoid shame or project an ideal self, other instances have more to do with legal issues (e.g., admission of a crime), fear of hospitalization (e.g., admitting to suicidal thoughts), a perceived need to not hurt the therapist's feelings, or culturally mediated mandates about protecting the reputation of family members. And sometimes, though not always, client secrets and lies are a form of "acting out" behavior, a way for the client to express some dissatisfaction with the therapist or therapeutic progress. Understanding the motive for a client's avoidance of an important truth is almost always a first step in considering therapeutic options, including the option of doing nothing at all, at least at the moment.

THE CLINICAL IMPORTANCE OF CLIENT LIES AND SECRETS

Client honesty has been central to psychotherapy since Freud (1913/1958) set out his "fundamental rule"—that the client should reveal everything that came to mind, as it came to mind, as honestly as possible. Rieff (1959), in his interpretation of Freud's contributions, contended that it was this "ethic of honesty" and "special capacity for candor" (p. 315) that distinguished psychoanalysis as a healing force. But this demand for total honesty, to say everything that came to mind without censorship, proved impossible for virtually all clients. Why did people struggle so much to speak honestly, especially about those very topics that were most impacting their lives? What was getting in the way of their forthright presentation of thoughts, feelings, fantasies, dreams, and behaviors? Sometimes, Freud understood, it was simply a learned habit. "It is hard," he wrote, "for the ego to direct its attention to perceptions and ideas which it has up till now made a rule of avoiding" (Freud, 1926, p. 159).

Freud and his followers began to advocate for the proposition that dealing with resistance to the work of psychoanalysis was a prerequisite to actually doing the work. Or rather, dealing with resistance was doing the work. Much later, research confirmed the idea that resistance to treatment—now more broadly defined to include oppositional, angry, avoidant, and devious client behaviors—is inimical to treatment effectiveness (e.g., Beutler, Moleiro, & Talebi, 2002). Fundamentally, though, the inability or refusal of clients to do the work of therapy, including speaking openly about their concerns, history, or current feelings toward significant figures in their lives (including the therapist), compromises the potential of psychotherapy to accomplish established goals.

Simply put, clients' disclosure of thoughts and feelings constitute the primary source material with which therapists work (Stiles, 1995). Although therapists are also cognizant of nonverbal behavior, much of our attention is directed toward what clients do and do not say. Therapists can and do question, clarify, interpret, and challenge clients' words—their skill is often reflected in the ways in which clients' words become more understandable and usable to both parties. But this becomes remarkably more difficult when clients either keep significant secrets or provide material that is substantially untrue. Whereas therapists are unlikely to assume full client disclosure, our sense is that they do assume client honesty. And although there is a fair amount of research on client disclosure—on what is and is not disclosed to therapists and the factors affecting this—there is a surprising paucity of studies on client secret keeping and lies. The study of client dishonesty can highlight problem areas in psychotherapeutic treatment, alerting therapists to topics about which they may not have sufficient accurate information to know how to proceed clinically.

One could argue that client lies and secret keeping should be considered normative and expected aspects of all psychotherapies and be dealt with like all other clinical material. That is, lies and secrets and other forms of concealment of the truth could be considered no more or less than other notable aspects of a client's defensive repertoire. From this perspective, therapists would deal with gaps in client narratives, perceived secrets, and other instances of distortions or deceit in ways commensurate with their perceived salience. If this pattern of behavior occurred habitually outside of therapy and interfered significantly with the client's life, including other, nontherapy relationships, it would have to be discussed. If the material left out or distorted was deemed important, if the client's distortion of events consistently interfered with his or her (or the therapist's) understanding of patterns of thoughts or behavior, or if what was missing or distorted seemed to reflect some rupture in the therapeutic relationship, the therapist would have to address these events in an attempt to overcome the resistance and prevent the therapy from growing stale or fading out entirely.

In fact, we believe these scenarios tend to play out as described—that therapists do tailor their interventions to the perceived extent and consequences of their clients' tendencies toward lies and secrets. The problem, as noted earlier, is that recent research indicates that client lies are far more prevalent than most therapists realize. These data, in conjunction with studies indicating that therapists tend to be unaware of the phenomena of client lies and secret keeping, suggest that therapists are in most instances oblivious to the fact that their clients are deceiving them. They may well detect the egregious lies, but many other lies and secrets go undetected—to the likely detriment of therapeutic progress.

We suspect too that a good percentage of premature termination from therapy—a significant problem in the field—is attributable to the fact that what clients need and on some level want to talk about does not fully or honestly get talked about. It is simple to say that it is the client who has the responsibility and agency to talk about whatever he or she wants at whatever level of depth or honesty; typically, in fact, the nondisclosing or explicitly deceitful client blames him- or herself for perceived failures in these realms. But a more complex equation includes the therapist's ability to establish and maintain a sufficiently effective therapeutic relationship for helpful levels of honest client disclosure to occur and for the therapist to have the requisite skills, including awareness of his or her "hot button" issues, to enable the patient to speak about sensitive, shameful, feared topics. If the therapist is perceived to have failed at making it possible for the client to speak honestly—and at least some clients prefer to shift the attribution of their reluctance to speak the truth to the therapist's failings or the inadequacies of therapy itself—the risk of early termination of treatment is likely to increase substantially. The client's belief in the usefulness of therapy may become fatally undermined. Paraphrasing a Billy Joel song ("She's Always a Woman"), she can ruin her faith with her casual lies.

A final reason the study of client lies and secrets is important has to do with evaluating the outcome of psychotherapy. Although we are strong proponents of psychotherapy and one of us (BAF) has spent many years teaching and serving multiple administrative positions in a doctoral program in clinical psychology, we wonder whether process and outcome data based on client evaluations of the treatment are entirely accurate. Client evaluations of treatment outcome correlate only minimally with evaluations provided by therapists and raters (Hill & Lambert, 2004), suggesting that perspective has a great deal to do with determinations of therapeutic effectiveness. Furthermore, our ongoing studies indicate that client lies about their feelings for their therapist and therapy are among the most common forms of deceit in therapy (Blanchard & Farber, 2016), a finding that leads to questions about the validity of previous client self-reports regarding their therapeutic experiences. Whether provided on a one-to-one basis to a specific therapist or on a survey administered anonymously by a team of researchers, evaluations of the effectiveness of psychotherapy may be affected by client tendencies to avoid certain hard truths. Hard truths about the effectiveness of psychotherapy may be especially prone to distortion given clients' deep investment (both emotionally and financially) in the process.

WHAT ABOUT THERAPIST LIES AND SECRETS?

To this point, we have discussed the phenomena of lies and secrets in psychotherapy as if these are solely in the realm of client behavior. This cannot be the case, and though research is even sparser on the issue of therapist lies and behaviors than it is on the corresponding deceit of clients, the existing literature (as well as common sense) suggests that therapists too are sometimes less than fully truthful. But sorting out what this means reveals complications. Therapists do not inhabit the same roles as clients; that is, therapists are not expected to reveal deeply personal information to their clients (though clients may sometimes push for this kind of material). The roles of therapists and clients are complementary, not reciprocal.

Most basically, though, there are different principles involved in identifying client secrets than in identifying therapist secrets. Therapists do not, generally speaking, have to reveal personal information to their clients. They are typically strongly advised by supervisors and teachers and ethics boards not to do so. But of course, this raises other questions, mostly focused on the need or advisability to withhold clinical information (e.g., feedback, including personal reactions) from clients: Where does the need for tact fit into therapists' decisions to reveal their feelings about clients or their own struggles with similar problems? Where do therapists' wishes or needs for authenticity of genuineness fit?

Despite the conceptual murkiness inherent in the concept of therapist deception, Internet blogs of therapists and clients, as well as some emerging research (Jackson & Farber, 2018), seem to suggest that at least some, and perhaps many, therapists lie to their clients at least some of the time. According to these reports, therapists lie about several issues, including what they have remembered about previous sessions, how tired or sleepy or preoccupied they are feeling at the moment (in response to client questioning or commenting on this), their lack of anger or disappointment in regard to a client's behavior (including lateness and payments for sessions), and perhaps most commonly, their romantic and/or sexual feelings toward their clients (a topic about which most therapists feel inadequately trained to deal with effectively). Although most of the following chapters deal with various types of client lies and secrets, the clinical importance of therapist lies led us to include material on this therapeutic situation as well.

CONCLUDING COMMENTS

Evaluations of the effectiveness of therapy aside, the primary reasons to focus on the related issues of client lies and secrets are that (a) they affect the process of psychotherapy; (b) therapists tend not to detect them as they occur; and (c) given their relative neglect in the literature on psychotherapy, therapists are not well trained to respond when they suspect clients are concealing or distorting significant clinical material. Therapists have to know more on those topics about which clients conceal information, the demographic and treatment variables that contribute to this behavior, and the motivations and clinical consequences of this behavior. Therapists should also, of course, be aware of the tools they might use to attenuate the tendency of clients to engage in these behaviors and deal with the consequences when these behaviors occur. Furthermore, therapists have to be aware of their own tendencies to either bend the truth or collude with client avoidance of the truth. Though sometimes such behavior is clinically justifiable, at other times such behavior is more obvious to clients than therapists believe and can lead to significant alliance ruptures and/or termination from treatment.

2

THE NATURE, PREVALENCE, AND FUNCTIONS OF LYING AND SECRET KEEPING: WHY DO WE DO THESE THINGS?

> From time immemorial we have been accustomed to lie. Or to put it more virtuously and hypocritically, in short, more pleasantly: we are much more the artist than we realize.
>
> —Friedrich Nietzsche, *Beyond Good and Evil*

Denise is cheating on her husband. Even though this infidelity is the most important problem in her life right now, she does not want to reveal it to her therapist. She explains, "I don't want her to think of me as a terrible person."

David came to therapy for help getting his career on track, but he lied to his therapist, claiming he had graduated from college when he has not. "I have a need for people to view me as smart and driven," he explains, "as opposed to a slacker."

Lynn is troubled by urges to physically hurt her mother, a woman who beat her as a child: "I see her physically and emotionally abusing my father and me, and I just really want to—I want to retaliate." Yet when her therapist asks her about her mother, Lynn conceals her feelings to avoid seeming out of control or possibly being reported. She believes there is no one she can tell about these feelings.

http://dx.doi.org/10.1037/0000128-003
Secrets and Lies in Psychotherapy, by B. A. Farber, M. Blanchard, and M. Love

Each of these clients is lying in therapy, which on the face of it can seem surprising. As noted in Chapter 1, psychotherapy in virtually all its forms has traditionally been a space of confidentiality and nonjudgment. It is designed to be outside the rules and norms of society. In this setting, clients can say whatever comes to mind without the consequences they would face in other contexts, often with the goal of discovering the emotional truth of their lives. Clients pay substantial hourly fees for this opportunity—even those who do not typically devote many hours of precious time to be in their therapist's office. Yet, as noted previously, our research has suggested that about 93% of therapy clients can recall specific instances of lying to their therapist in the past about such matters as their relationships, suicidal thoughts, how they feel about therapy, and the depth of their suffering (Blanchard & Farber, 2016). At any given time, 84% of clients surveyed report they are either being dishonest or deliberately avoiding some topic in their therapy. Why would the great majority of clients choose to be deceptive while they are investing so much in psychotherapy to help them find the truth?

The answer will be different for every client and different for every topic. Yet in great measure, each of these clients is also doing what people do in all types of social situations. Denise wants to avoid being judged for her affair. David wants to enhance his image in the eyes of his therapist and to enhance his self-image, too. Lynn wants to avoid the shame that comes with embarrassing questions ("Would you really beat up your mother?"). At work, at home, with friends, and in other arenas of everyday life, we often accomplish these communicative goals through the careful shaping of what we say, how much we say, and how we say it.

Indeed, lies in one context can highlight the unspoken truths of another. Noted psychotherapist Irvin Yalom (2002) wrote about paying special attention when his clients described some act of deception in their everyday lives, perhaps lying to their family members or coworkers. He seized the opportunity to make the link to possible deceptions perpetrated inside therapy:

> I find such an admission an excellent opportunity to inquire about what lies they have told me during the course of therapy. There is always some concealment, some information withheld because of shame, because of some particular way they wish me to regard them. A discussion of such concealments almost invariably provokes a fruitful discussion in therapy—often a review of the history of the therapy relationship and an opportunity to rework and fine-tune not only the relationship but other important themes that have previously emerged in therapy. (p. 74)

In this chapter, we follow Yalom's lead and look to the extensive research on lying outside of therapy to better understand lying that happens inside the clinical encounter. Clients like Denise, David, and Lynn present clear-cut cases in which the lies they tell in therapy provide a direct route to their most important issues. Conversely, even when our clients are completely honest with us—or at least trying to be honest with us—the lies they are telling everyone else may serve as important clinical material. As confidential listeners, we are privy to the lies and deceptions of everyday life, information that provides insight into our clients' character and that may determine the course of treatment. Understanding distortions, secret keeping, and lying is central to the work of psychotherapists across all theoretical orientations.

Scholars working on the study of deception and dishonesty come from a wide range of disciplines, including psychology, sociology, communications, history, political science, zoology, anthropology, philosophy, management, and neurosciences. They are part of a tradition of inquiry stretching back to ancient Athens that remains vibrant today. In just the last few years, scholars have reopened basic questions of the field: Who lies? What is a lie? And why do we do it? In the process, many commonly held beliefs about lying have been called into question.

For example, despite the widespread belief that liars fidget or avoid making eye contact—a belief we noted earlier was held by Freud, among others—research has suggested that although this sometimes happens, there are no physical "tells" that can reliably distinguish someone who is lying from someone who is not (e.g., Bond, Levine, & Hartwig, 2015). In fact, lies are most commonly detected by getting information from a third party or discovering incriminating evidence (Park, Levine, McCornack, Morrison, & Ferrara, 2002). This makes therapists as a profession fairly easy to fool. We meet our clients alone, keep their remarks confidential, and cannot very well phone or email their friends for corroborating evidence. Thus, the version of reality provided by our clients is often all therapists have to work with.

WHO LIES?

The degree to which people are dishonest in everyday life has been a topic of intense interest since ancient times. Legend tells of the Greek philosopher Diogenes searching Athens with his lantern held aloft, looking for a single "honest man" and coming up empty-handed. Diogenes's unstated argument—that all men are liars—was not addressed with the tools of empirical science until the late 20th century when scientists finally attempted to establish exactly who is lying and how much. The results are both intriguing and clinically useful.

Initial research supported Diogenes's intuition. In an oft-cited study, DePaulo, Kashy, Kirkendol, Wyer, and Epstein (1996) asked samples of college students and community residents to keep a diary for 1 week, recording every social interaction they had and every time they lied. The headline results, cited in more than a thousand subsequent academic papers, were that people told an average of between one or two lies per day and were lying in 20% to 30% of all social interactions. Individuals in this study lied about their feelings mostly but also their actions, future plans, and whereabouts, as well as facts about themselves, their achievements, and their possessions. Most of their lies were self-serving, mainly to protect themselves from embarrassment or to make themselves look good, but one of every four lies was chiefly altruistic, told to help or protect others from distress (e.g., "You look great in those pants!").

Although the DePaulo et al. (1996) sample was not statistically representative of the national population, the idea that Americans tell one or two lies per day has entered the popular media, where one can find claims about the prevalence of dishonesty that are even higher and somewhat alarming when generalized to situations outside the research context. For example, when pollsters asked the general public whether they are dishonest in everyday life, about 90% to 96% could recall specific instances of lying in the past (Kalish, 2004; J. Patterson & Kim, 1991). In her book, *Liespotting*, Pamela Meyer (2010) contended that we are lied to between 10 and 200 times in a typical day. Whether this statistic has any meaning must surely depend on where and with whom one spends one's days.

These questions have been reopened in just the last few years: Does everybody lie? And do they lie quite that much? The emerging answers add much-needed nuance to the picture. Seeking a nationally representative sample, Serota, Levine, and Boster (2010) asked 1,000 American adults to report the number of lies told in the prior 24 hours. Just as in previous studies, they found that on average Americans did indeed report telling somewhere between one and two lies per day (an average of 1.65 lies, to be precise). Yet statistical averages are only meaningful when we assume a normal, or nearly normal, distribution of data. That is, the bell curve allows us to assume that the vast majority of people fall somewhere near the average score.

Lying, it turns out, does not follow the bell curve. Serota et al. (2010) found that on a given day, only about 20% of Americans fell into the one-or-two-lies category (the statistical average), whereas a full 60% of American adults reported telling absolutely no lies at all. That suggests the average or most common experience (the mode) is actually telling zero lies in a given 24-hour period—a very different headline message about honesty in American life. Meanwhile, roughly half of all recorded lies were being told by a tiny minority, so-called prolific liars, who make up 5.3% of the population and who were telling as many as 38 lies per day. The curve of lying looks more like a ski jump than a bell, with a huge pile of honest people in the zero-lie category and a long, thin tail containing small numbers of hugely prolific liars. This deeply skewed distribution of lying has been replicated in studies of high school students (Levine, Serota, Carey, & Messer, 2013) and a large representative sample of adults from the United Kingdom (Serota, Levine, & Burns, 2012). The same deeply skewed distribution turned up in a reanalysis of the original data from DePaulo et al. (1996) and two other studies (Feldman, Forrest, & Happ, 2002; George & Robb, 2008).

For therapists, these findings raise questions about psychopathology: Could the 5.3% of prolific liars qualify for certain diagnoses? The picture is not yet clear. Truly compulsive, pathological lying is thought to appear in no more than 0.1% of the population. That makes it much too rare to explain the prolific lying group found by Serota et al. (2010). More common are the four Cluster B personality disorders (antisocial, borderline, histrionic, narcissistic) defined by the *Diagnostic and Statistical Manual of Mental Disorders* (fifth ed., American Psychiatric Association, 2013), which are indeed associated with prolific lying. It was said, for example, of the brilliant but notoriously narcissistic (and perhaps bipolar) writer, Ernest Hemingway, that "by the 1940s, [he] included an exaggeration or lie in nearly every sentence he uttered" (Dearborn, cited in Showalter, 2017, p. 16). Similarly, Harper Lee, the author of *To Kill a Mockingbird*, had this to say about her lifelong friend, Truman Capote, also long thought of as narcissistic: "I don't know if you understood this about him . . . but his compulsive lying was like this: If you said, 'Did you know JFK was shot?', he'd easily answer, 'Yes, I was driving the car he was riding in'" (J. C. Howard, 2017, C1).

But these Cluster B personality disorders only occur at a general prevalence of about 1.5% (Lenzenweger, Lane, Loranger, & Kessler, 2007). Substance use disorders are also thought to co-occur with a good deal of lying to conceal one's addiction, and these affect between 8% and 10% of the U.S. population (Center for Behavioral Health Statistics and Quality, 2015; Grant et al., 2004). Thus, it is probably the case that prolific liars are a heterogeneous group determined not merely by any single psychiatric diagnosis but also by changing life circumstances (e.g., someone having an extramarital affair) or even choice of profession (e.g., politicians). We have more to say about prolific liars—how they are made and their styles of deception—later in this chapter.

WHAT IS LYING?

Lying seems simple enough. As implied in the famous quote from U.S. Supreme Court Justice Potter Stewart about defining pornography, "You know it when you see it," we all have an instinctual sense of what it means to lie. But as we began to lay out in Chapter 1, things get a little tricky when we try to distinguish it from other types of human communication. We could think of a lie as simply the opposite of the truth, yet the objective truth is famously hard to know and is always up for debate—especially, as we have noted, in a postmodern age given to seeking out divergent perspectives on reality. Mankind is "condemned to tell lies," wrote the philosopher Maria Golaszewska (2010), "because he never knows what the truth is. . . . The same set of events can reveal different aspects and can suggest different appreciations depending on the nature and mood of the witness" (p. 137). Here, we are back in the territory of the film *Rashomon* (Jingo & Kurosawa, 1950), a place where truth is determined by the position of different actors viewing the same narrative. Dishonesty, then, cannot be defined in opposition to absolute truth but rather as a misrepresentation of what the liar believes to be true. Such a standard is central in American perjury law and everyday social life.

Scholars of lying must be more exacting. They usually consider four different criteria when defining a lie: (a) Lies are communications that the speaker knows to be false, (b) are intended to mislead others, (c) are used for some identifiable purpose, and (d) occur without notification or warning. Let us look at each in turn.

In their diary study, DePaulo and colleagues (1996) drew heavily on intentionality. They explained to subjects that "a lie occurs any time you *intentionally try to mislead someone*" (p. 981, italics in original). The intention to mislead serves to distinguish lying from situations in which the speaker was simply wrong. Young children will often categorize any counterfactual statement as a "lie" because they have not yet developed the cognitive capacity to fully imagine the mental experience of others. But to be deceptive, it is not enough to merely speak inaccurately. As philosopher Sissela Bok (1999) observed, "The moral question of whether you are lying or not is not *settled* by establishing the truth or falsity of what you say. In order to settle this question, we must know whether you *intend your statement to mislead*" (p. 6, italics in original). Intentionality also helps distinguish lies from more bizarre behaviors—for example, the delusional claims of those who believe they are God or the devil while experiencing psychosis. Although manifestly untrue, the emphatic claims of a delusional person are not intended to mislead the listener. Quite the contrary, such patients are often quite driven to reveal their version of the truth.

Purpose is a third important aspect of deception. The requirement that there be some purpose behind a lie serves to distinguish deliberate lying from pathological lying, which is defined by its lack of any discernable goal or practical reason why the liar would lie. Indeed, as we saw in the 2001 case of a disgraced California judge who could not stop making false claims about his education and military service—even with his job and reputation at stake—pathological liars may be highly functional people who face great costs for their compulsive deceptions. Similarly, types of confabulation brought on by brain injuries and psychiatric conditions are not deceptive or dishonest because the client has no intent to deceive, no awareness of lying, and no purpose to the deception. Such patients are struggling to make sense of reality.

An often-overlooked fourth element of lying is the lack of notification, which we could think of as the failure to be honest about the fact that one is lying. Ekman (2001) defined a *lie* as "a deliberate choice to mislead a target without giving any notification of the intent to do" (p. 41). In other words, *lying* is making a false claim in situations when the truth is expected. This insight helps us separate lying from a diverse set of communications in which listeners are alerted that the speaker is not being truthful. These include sarcastic remarks, which are meant to convey the opposite of their literal content (e.g., "I'm just loving this painful skin rash. It's a real treat"). This also includes theatrical performances, when everyone who enters the theater knows the actors onstage are likely to be saying things which are, strictly speaking, not true. When an actress playing Shakespeare's Juliet announces, "O happy dagger! This is thy sheath; there rust, and let me die" (*Romeo and Juliet*, 5.3.8) and makes to plunge the knife into her chest, few in the audience will believe the actress is committing suicide. Perhaps the best example of the notification issue is offered by our current president, Donald J. Trump. In an oft-quoted passage from his 1987 book, *The Art of the Deal*, Trump wrote,

> The final key to the way I promote is bravado. I play to people's fantasies. People may not always think big themselves, but they can still get very excited by those who do. That's why a little hyperbole never hurts. People want to believe that something is the biggest and the greatest and the most spectacular. I call it truthful hyperbole. (p. 58)

Trump's essential point is that because showmanship is a recognized part of sales, his exaggerations are merely giving the audience what they want and expect. He is, therefore, "innocent" and not really lying. In Ekman's (2001) terms, Trump believes his audience has been notified by the context of real estate sales, just as theatergoers are warned when they take their seats in a playhouse.

What we call lying, then, is not a unitary phenomenon, but rather comprises a host of behaviors in which some advantage can be gained, or loss prevented—materially, socially, or psychologically—by not telling the truth. The lie can benefit the liar in a self-serving fashion, or it can serve to help someone about whom the liar cares. The liar has access to a variety of tools and techniques, each useful for a range of tasks. For example, exaggeration is handy for selling real estate and also for securing friendships, lovers, jobs, and self-esteem. Omission and secret keeping are useful for escaping criminal prosecution, mollifying your worried mother, or saving your marriage. If you have an aggressive goal such as smearing the reputation of an enemy, your weapon of choice may be fabrication, the whole-cloth invention of a false version of events. Lies are in turn a subset of the larger category of deception, which can involve everything from military counterintelligence maneuvers to the false eyespots on the wings of moths. Throughout this book, however, we follow common speech and use the terms *lying*, *deception*, and *dishonesty* more or less interchangeably to capture intentionally deceptive communications conveyed by any means.

Scholars agree that lying does not require speech and that one does not have to actually tell a lie to be lying. Indeed, the most common forms of deceptive communication involve the omission of relevant information, rather than the utterance of untrue statements. Our research has suggested that omission is the most common form of dishonesty reported by therapy clients (Blanchard & Farber, 2016); that is, the nature of reported dishonesty is heavily weighted toward passive dishonesty (e.g., *omission*) and away from active dishonesty (e.g., fabrication, also known as *commission*). Whereas 42% omitted important information while speaking to their therapist, only 12% made up facts.

Nonverbal communication also offers a wide field of play for deceptions (DePaulo et al., 1996; Ekman & Friesen, 1969; Ford, 1996; Saarni, 1982). The many muscles of the face allow us to simulate emotions we are not feeling. We fake smiles so often it probably escapes our awareness until our faces start to hurt from the effort. We pretend to nod in agreement with those with whom we disagree or disrespect, and we raise our eyebrows in artificial delight when tasting a friend's inedible baked goods. Ford (1996) outlined four common strategies of nonverbal deceit. The first two parallel verbal forms of deceit: We use *minimization* when we dampen the expression of strong emotions, as when a surgeon whose patient is deteriorating simulates a calm demeanor to conceal his panic. *Exaggeration* is the false heightening of one's emotional expression, as when children simulate sorrowful crying to pressure their parents in a toy store. *Neutralization* is the adoption of a poker face, which Ford pointed out, is an especially important skill for psychotherapists as we listen to our clients' stories without conveying even the slightest hint of judgment. Finally, *substitution* involves the replacement of one emotional expression (e.g., indifference, disgust) with a more acceptable one (e.g., affection, delight). This is handy when friends invite you to adore their pets.

The moral stain of being a "liar" arises directly from our evolutionary history as a cooperative species. Unlike fireflies or foxes, most of humanity's evolutionary achievements—our cities and supermarkets and international commodity futures trading—all depend on what biologists have called *reciprocal altruism* (Leaky & Lewin, 1978; Trivers, 2011). As the name implies, this is a process of long-term cooperation by which individuals make real sacrifices to help others based on the expectation that the others will return the favor at a later time. Even when we have reason to be suspicious, we generally act as if we expect honest dealing from people we meet. Bok (1999) called this the *principle of veracity*, the idea that we all carry a foundational assumption that people will communicate honestly to the best of their conscious knowledge. Bok argued that social life as we know it would be impossible without this assumption, yet at the same time, such a trust-based system is easily exploited by cheaters. This may be why our species (like some others) has evolved attitudes that harshly punish certain forms of deception, such as outright lying, which seem to threaten the social order. Indeed, one ingenious study found that 35% of participants declined to tell a lie even when it would result in a $10 benefit to both the liar and the target, an example of pure "lie aversion" that may be bred into the genome of our species (Erat & Gneezy, 2012).

By contrast, most of us tacitly endorse other forms of deception, such as white lies, which serve as a social lubricant and thus support the social order. Children are taught from a young age to conceal their opinions when they might be offensive: "If you can't say anything nice, don't say anything at all." We know that adults are routinely expected to tell outright lies in service of politeness; recent research has even found that the degree of compassion we feel toward others increases the intensity of prosocial lying (Lupoli, Jampol, & Oveis, 2017). Indeed, to eschew white lies in favor of the dishing out the unvarnished truth inevitably provokes the shock and outrage of coworkers, family, and friends. This was put to the test by A. J. Jacobs, who for his (2009) book, *The Guinea Pig Diaries*, tried for a month to speak only the truth to everyone in his life. He concluded that it was "probably the worst month of my life," and in the end, he could not pull it off. As he put it, to continue being absolutely honest put him at clear risk of being "beat up, fired and divorced" (Jacobs, cited in Guthrie & Kunkel, 2013, p. 628). Actor, writer, and director Ricky Gervais mined similar territory in his movie *The Invention of Lying* (Gervais, Lin, Obst, Obst, & Robinson, 2009).

Thus, it seems behavior at the extremes of honesty and dishonesty can both leave one at risk of adverse consequences. Perhaps for this reason, the flow of natural discourse features little total honesty or total dishonesty, containing few of what deception theorist Steven McCornack called *bald-faced lies* or *bald-faced truths* (McCornack, Morrison, Paik, Wisner, & Zhu, 2014). To reiterate an earlier point, most deceptive messages—and arguably almost all messages—are mixtures of true and false information that must be judiciously blended to meet the goals of the communicator. Social communication requires a constant awareness of our audience as well as high-speed calculations about how others will respond to our remarks. These calculations allow us to deploy small instances of deceit—a cautious change of wording or a raised eyebrow to feign interest—which are so ubiquitous they often escape our conscious awareness.

Life in the borderland between honesty and deception was perhaps most famously explored by sociologist Erving Goffman, whose work we noted briefly in the previous chapter. In his landmark book, *The Presentation of Self in Everyday Life*, Goffman (1959) pointed out that people do not present anything we could call their real selves in society. Instead, they attempt to enact social roles appropriate to the occasion, engaging in constant modulations of their appearance and behavior intended to manage the impressions they are making on their audience. Goffman's theory of "self-presentation" posited a world of desperate little dramas in which people perform edited versions of themselves to appear coherent, believable, and worthy of respect. As with actors in the theater, these performances change strikingly, depending on whether they happen in *front stage* public spaces (e.g., office, street, or dining room during a dinner party) or *backstage* private spaces (e.g., bedroom, kitchen, bathroom) where the social actor can be more genuine, though almost never entirely genuine. Blunders in self-presentation result in the painful loss of face. Indeed, even when alone we may experience a *generalized other*, a sort of internalized social eye rendering judgments on our performance for whom we may endeavor to stage appropriate performances, acting as "normal" as possible even when we are entirely alone.

Goffman's (1959) ideas can also tell us something about psychotherapy. In his terms, therapy is a social practice designed to create a deep backstage, a space apart from normal social pressures, in which the self can experiment with new performances supported by the presence of a safe, structuring audience in the person of the therapist. Ideally, this support can give clients the courage to face the internalized judging eye and soften the stance they take when observing their performance of self. Though this process may evolve over the course of treatment, it may never be fully completed. Self-presentational concerns never entirely fade, either in "real life" or in therapy. The evidence indicates that the majority of lies told in therapy have their roots in self-presentational concerns, as clients seek to avoid shame before the audience of the therapist. Thus, for those many clients who at least occasionally lie in treatment but who also honestly disclose a great deal of the time, psychotherapy may be experienced as a confusing mix of backstage and front stage experiences—a setting in which they reveal many intimate details they would not discuss elsewhere but a setting too in which presenting one's best self is still a powerful motive. A case in point: the public (on-air) revelation of radio personality, Howard Stern, who on his show (7/18/17) acknowledged that although he reveals many intimate details of his life to his therapist, he has never discussed his preoccupation with "babysitter and step sister porn." His rationale: His therapist is "really smart, an MD, and I want him to think I'm an intellectual."

THE FOUR FEATURES OF ANY FALSEHOOD

Angela is a 30-year-old client in psychotherapy who presents a complex clinical picture of anorexia, social phobia, and symptoms of posttraumatic stress disorder. She is also concealing an unusual secret: She has been seeing three different therapists at the same time and telling none of them about the others. She explained:

> I have a really hard time ending therapy. So, I've ended up seeing three therapists at the same time. I lie because I don't want my therapists to be mad or hurt, and I feel like I'm being mean. I'm really not good at standing up for myself. Sometimes I feel like I'm balancing two divorced parents—trying to keep everybody happy.

Scholars have produced many—perhaps too many—different ways to classify Angela's deception. We might say it is a self-oriented lie as opposed to an other-oriented lie (DePaulo et al., 1996), a concealment versus a fabrication (Ekman, 2001), a defensive lie rather than an aggressive lie (Ford, 1996), a white lie rather than a black lie (Bok, 1999), a somewhat selfish lie rather than an altruistic lie (Erat & Gneezy, 2012), and a low-stakes lie rather than a high-stakes lie (Porter & ten Brinke, 2010). Such is the complexity of deceptive communication that no one system is likely to capture all the important qualities of Angela's lie.

We argue that the nature and significance of any given lie, including those manifest in therapy, can be understood by examining four features: (a) the *technique* or means of deception used by the liar; (b) the *moral status* or harm potential of the lie, for self and others; (c) the *external goal* that the lie is designed to achieve; and (d) the *internal function* that the lie may serve for the liar's psyche.

In Angela's case, we can see her technique is predominantly concealment; she seeks to hide her relationships with other therapists as part of a strategy to avoid imagined conflicts and complications. The moral status of her lie appears to be neutral; Angela is neither helping herself nor hurting others, and this fact makes her behavior all the more mysterious. Why exactly is she carrying on this complex deception? She explains that her external goal in lying is to avoid making her therapists "mad" or hurting their feelings; perhaps she uses such secrets to maintain a kind of covert control over significant people in her life. Finally, the internal function of Angela's lie is not clearly stated, but we can speculate that she finds the loss of relationships highly distressing. She offers a potentially significant hint when she reports feeling like she is "balancing two divorced parents" and "trying to keep everyone happy." The lie may allow her to feel taken care of by multiple others, perhaps a long-standing wish or fantasy. Relatedly, the lie may function to recapitulate a childhood dilemma she is compelled to revisit and resolve, events that may also relate to her trauma history and eating disorder.

Considering all four factors does not provide total certainty about client lies. Rather, it provides a scaffold on which to build useful hypotheses. Each part of the scaffold has a long history in the study of deception, and we address each in turn.

Technique refers to the verbal and nonverbal tactics used by the liar. Commonly understood notions of technique include exaggeration, minimization, omission, evasion, fabrication, telling half-truths, and innuendo, among many others. Ekman (2001) argued that all technique boils down to either concealment (hiding something true) or falsification (communicating something false), or as the writer Adrienne Rich (1979) suggested, lying is done with words as well as with silence.

A substantial body of research, including our own, has suggested that liars greatly prefer passive over active lying techniques. Not only is it easier but it is also seen as less of a transgression (Ritov & Baron, 1990; Spranca, Minsk, & Baron, 1991; Van Swol, Braun, & Malhotra, 2012). When caught in a passive lie, people anticipate less severe punishments than if the lie had been active (DeScioli, Christner, & Kurzban, 2011). In a similar vein, liars find it much easier to justify omissions ("I'm sorry, I meant to tell you") than to justify fabrications (Tenbrunsel & Messick, 2004).

What can the technique of a lie tell us about the liar? Nothing definitive, but considering the widespread preference for passive lying, clients who describe substantial incidents of active lying should be recognized as quite out of the ordinary. Active lying may be indicative of a certain recklessness, a desire to be caught, poor reality testing, or a tip-off to the presence of a personality disorder or addictive behavior.

The *moral status* of a lie is often not the first concern of psychotherapists, who tend to avoid moralizing in favor of a nonjudgmental stance. Yet consideration of the ethical status of a client's dishonesty is often warranted. Even if clients are outwardly dismissive of harm they may be doing to others or themselves through dishonesty, self-justifications ("My affair was helpful to our marriage," "Those insurance companies make so much money anyway") are rarely airtight. Guilt, shame, and/or regret typically percolate just beneath the surface.

Historically, most thinking about dishonesty has been focused on the moral question. Because lying is, paradoxically, both morally repugnant and absolutely necessary, thinkers since ancient Greece have struggled with rules to govern the use of dishonesty. Socrates condemned all lying, Aristotle thought self-deprecating lies were perhaps okay, and Plato explicitly endorsed lying by political leaders for the good of the polis. Augustine implicitly permitted certain lies by explaining that some lies were considerably less sinful than others. He provided eight categories by which followers could identify which of their lies might get more of a pass in the eyes of heaven.

How do people these days judge the moral status of their lies? Lies that benefit others are seen as most acceptable, followed by lies that benefit both the liar and the target, with lies that harm others being least acceptable. Lies with severe consequences are not okay, whereas low-stakes lies are often fine. And in most cases, lying to strangers is far more acceptable than lying to a spouse or someone in another close relationship. The moral logic that unifies these findings appears consistent with evolutionary logic—specifically, with humans' evolutionary reliance on reciprocal altruism for the species' survival (Sakamoto & Gupta, 2014). The basic rule seems to be lie to strangers if you have to, lie about trivial matters if you must, but never lie to close allies about important things.

Morally speaking, lies are generally grouped into three basic types. *White lies* are defined by their harmless, social nature (e.g., "I'm 5 minutes away," "I'm busy that day," "I gotta go"). *Altruistic lies* benefit other parties but do not benefit the teller. Such lies might even put the teller at risk, as in the classic case of Dutch families lying to the Nazis to save the lives of Jewish families during World War II. *Malicious* (or "black") *lies* are meant to harm others, as in the spreading of defamatory rumors around a workplace or the telephone or Internet manipulations of con men who pose as charity workers to swindle "donations" out of elderly persons. Clients who are suspected of malicious lying should be handled with great care because the clinician can quickly move from confidant to victim. Kottler and Carlson's (2011) essay collection, *Duped*, contains stories of clients whose duplicity involved stealing their therapist's identity or, in Carlson's own case, a client who initially lied to control her daughter but ended up taking vengeance against Carlson himself with a letter to the state ethics board accusing him of seductive behavior. As in the fable of the scorpion and the frog, clients who routinely use malicious lies to control others may sting even those who are trying to help them.

External goals are the core feature of most lying. Indeed, it has been experimentally demonstrated that people generally need an external reason to lie (Levine, Kim, & Hamel, 2010) and tend to avoid dishonesty if their external goals are attainable by honest means. There are multiple external goals or motives for lying, including the need to bolster the esteem of loved ones or, conversely, to hurt enemies and the need to achieve simple material gain, as when high school or college students feign attention-deficit/hyperactivity disorder symptoms to get psychotropic medications (e.g., Ritalin) to use as study drugs.

Some clients arrive in psychotherapy seeking to gain monetary rewards (e.g., disability benefits), obtain prescriptions, or escape responsibilities by securing a certain diagnosis (Newman & Strauss, 2003). Suicidal individuals may lie to try to avoid hospitalization, separated or divorced parents may lie in an attempt to secure better custody arrangements, and inpatients may deny psychotic symptoms to speed their release. But more commonly, clients lie because they are ashamed or afraid of the emotional consequences of telling the truth. These are internal reasons for lying, and it is to these that we now turn.

Internal functions of lies serve to regulate or gratify some aspect of the speaker's internal experience. Take, for example, a client who tells many lies to accommodate her demanding and uncompromising mother, misrepresenting her own feelings and friendships, perhaps even her attitude toward religion or her sexual orientation. The client says she lies to keep Mom happy, avoid conflict, and "keep the peace." Yet the dissembling also serves to prevent the expression of her own buried aggressive feelings toward her mother. Her lies, like those of many others, are in the service of emotional regulation. If she were to respond honestly to her mom, buried conflicts would quickly surface and who knows what would happen. In a sense, she lies to assist the repression of her emotions, as well as to meet external demands. Any lie, as we have noted previously, can serve multiple purposes.

There are several kinds of internal motives for lying. *Lies to aid emotional repression* are in the service of avoiding unwanted emotional states, as in the example of the people-pleasing daughter mentioned earlier. Another example is the frustrated client who remarks, "I'm fine" or "Nothing's wrong" when questioned by her therapist. Even if she is conscious of being upset, she lies about having those feelings because she has not developed a constructive way to express anger inside the relationship. As Freud (1933) noted, repression often takes precedence over expression.

Lies to preserve self-esteem are efforts to regulate self-worth. This can be done by concealing one's shameful or embarrassing behaviors, one's status as a loser in a competition, or experiences as a victim of abuse. As Goffman (1959) pointed out, the nature of social life makes shame an ever-present threat and dissembling an ever-present possibility. Avoiding shame is behind about half of all secret keeping in psychotherapy (Hill, Thompson, Cogar, & Denman, 1993) and a large proportion of lies (Blanchard & Farber, 2016). One may also lie to preserve or enhance self-esteem by inflating one's accomplishments to meet the demands of what Heinz Kohut (1966) called the "grandiose" or "narcissistic self." Ford (1996) provided the example of young men who exaggerate the number of their sexual partners, and old men who fabricate glorious sports achievements from their high school days. Under the sway of the grandiose self, many amateur athletes insist that the best shot they have ever made in their lives is the one they regularly continue to make. In the most extreme cases, such liars may approach the status of the "impostor," a character type explored by Helene Deutsch in a fascinating 1955 case study, in Woody Allen's *Zelig* (Greenhut & Allen, 1983), and in the characterization of the protagonist (played by Leonardo DiCaprio) in the movie *Catch Me if You Can* (Parks & Spielberg, 2002).

Another internal motive for lies is *to achieve psychological distance* from others. Thus, individuals sometimes manipulate information to keep others away, establishing or preserving their sense of autonomy by deceiving others about their feelings, plans, or whereabouts. Among children and adolescents, such lying is part of the normal developmental process of individuation. In adulthood, lies to achieve psychological distance can range from very modest to quite extreme. On the modest end of the spectrum, the era of text messaging has led to a form of dishonesty called the *butler lie* (Reynolds, Smith, Birnholtz, & Hancock, 2013). This species of deception has evolved to let people manage access to themselves in a digitally connected world, in the same way a butler might deceive unwanted visitors at the front door. Examples include texting "Sorry, just got your message" when you knowingly ignored some time-sensitive text and also "Headed into a meeting" or "Going to bed now" when you want to end an unwanted text exchange. A client who arrives late to a session because of ambivalent feelings about therapy can claim that traffic is responsible for the lateness, the excuse an attempt to preempt the clinician's inquiry into resistance.

Lies to vent sadism and aggression have the external goal of hurting others to satisfy an internal need to take revenge and/or banish feelings of weakness or victimhood. Those who lie in this manner work to position others as the "dupe" to revel in a sense of triumph. Lemma (2005) described the case of a client who invented false reasons for missing sessions. When asked about one of his inventions, the client replied with an expression of triumph: "You bought that shit? What I told you is a pack of lies. [Laughs.] I don't know, don't they teach you anything?" (p. 741). Lemma said she felt the violence of his aggressive act but doggedly worked her way toward an interpretation: "You seem to live in a world where it's safer to lie than to allow yourself to believe another person and to then risk being exposed as the duped one who believes the pack of lies." To which the patient tersely replied, "Lies keep me warm" (p. 741).

This is but a short list of internal functions that lies may serve. By considering all four dimensions of lying—the technique used, the moral status of the lie, the external goals of the lie, and the internal functions of the lie—psychologists hearing "suspicious" or seemingly deceptive material in therapy (or who later discover they have been lied to) can arrive at useful ideas about how to understand and respond to client dishonesty. We have more to say about such clinical strategies in later chapters. For now, we turn to another dimension of dishonesty: secrets.

SECRETS AND SELF-CONCEALMENT

What about keeping secrets? Gail Saltz (2006), in her popular book, *Anatomy of a Secret Life*, suggested that secrets are human "essentials," ranking only somewhat below food, water, and shelter. They are thrilling and dangerous. And they are important intrapsychically, allowing individuals to explore the depths of their selves, as well as interpersonally, providing the material for intimate exchanges of information. According to Saltz, there is an important distinction to be made between secrets that are manageable (and even at times life enhancing) and a secretive life that can control, overwhelm, and disrupt our existence. In the latter case, she strongly suggested psychotherapeutic treatment to help uncover the source and need to live a secretive life.

Perhaps the most popular current source of material on secrets—in fact, a worldwide phenomenon—is "PostSecret," which refers to both a website (http://www.postsecret.com) and a series of books by the website's creator, Frank Warren. Starting in 2005, Warren asked the public to mail him postcards containing one secret they needed to get off their chest, with a simple instruction: "Your secret can be a regret, fear, betrayal, desire, confession, or childhood humiliation. Reveal *anything*—as long as it is true and you have never shared it with anyone before." At the time of this writing, Warren had received over 1 million such postcards, the site had received more than 770 million visits, and the secrets keep pouring in. They include regrets ("My porn addiction made me unable to feel real love"), revelations ("I'd be happier if I quit law school"), and life-defining moments ("25 years ago I stopped my sister's abusive boyfriend at the door with a shotgun"). The wave of public interest generated a PostSecret TED Talk, a PostSecret traveling art exhibit, and for a time, a PostSecret app, as well as a partnership with a suicide-prevention hotline. The extraordinarily popularity of this enterprise seems to affirm theory, research, and popular wisdom that people seek to unburden themselves of secrets. It may be all the more appealing that they get to remain anonymous, and—in an era hungry for Internet fame—that there is a real chance that millions will read it.

What happens when we do not reveal our secrets? Arguably the most controversial aspect of secret keeping is its supposed adverse consequences. Secret keeping about traumatic experiences has been linked to stress, anxiety, and depression, as well as bodily symptoms and depressed immune functioning (e.g., Pennebaker, Kiecolt-Glaser, & Glaser, 1988). One fascinating set of studies found that people who were suppressing or preoccupied with an important secret tended to overestimate the difficulty of physical burdens, such as lifting weights or climbing hills, and were less likely to help others with physical tasks (Slepian, Masicampo, Toosi, & Ambady, 2012). But secret keeping has also been viewed as a typically benign activity with only rare negative effects (e.g., Vrij, Nunkoosing, Paterson, Oosterwegel, & Soukara, 2002). Advancing this latter argument, Kelly (2002) contended that although divulging secrets—for example, by writing about them, as in Pennebaker's studies—may improve health, concealing them has never been proven harmful. Her point is that although the person keeping a secret might miss out on certain health benefits, that possibility is not equivalent to positing that a person will become sick if he or she keeps a secret. Researchers and lay people get it wrong, she suggested (Kelly & Yip, 2006), when they fail to account for the fact that secretive people tend to be generally less emotionally and physically healthy than others.

Although secret keeping can be viewed as an activity or behavior, self-concealment—the tendency to actively conceal from others personal information that one perceives as distressing or negative—is best viewed as a trait-like individual difference that tends to stay stable across time and situations (Kelly & Yip, 2006; Larson, Chastain, Hoyt, & Ayzenberg, 2015). Self-concealment has been found to be conceptually distinct from low self-disclosure, highlighting a difference between the predilection to actively hide information that is distressing and not volunteering it because one simply does not wish to (Larson et al., 2015).

Another important concept comes from Kahn and Hessling (2001), who made a distinction between general self-disclosure and *distress disclosure*—an individual's willingness to disclose distressing personal information to others. In their conceptualization, distress disclosure is distinct from both self-concealment and self-disclosure, such that an individual who is a high self-discloser is not necessarily a distress discloser. A high self-discloser may discuss a large quantity of information, but all or much of this could be lacking in negative or personal valence. Kahn and Hessling theorized that distress disclosure represents a bipolar and unidimensional trait-like quality, with distress concealment (i.e., rare disclosure) at one end and distress disclosure (i.e., rare concealment) on the opposite end.

The trait of self-concealment, as opposed to secret keeping per se, has been found to consistently relate to negative outcomes regarding both psychological and physical health. Chronic concealment has been found to be significantly associated with outcomes such as depression, suicidality, disordered eating, and the early onset of smoking. It is inversely linked with social support and the willingness to use psychological services (Larson et al., 2015). What are the mechanisms through which self-concealment exerts such widespread negative effects? Pennebaker (1985) implicated behavioral inhibition, arguing that the deleterious effects of inhibition occur specifically when the individual desires to talk to someone but implements a measure of self-control not to do so. Consistent with Pennebaker's ideas, Larson et al. (2015)

asserted that the problematic effects of self-concealment occur when individuals desire to make their distress known to others and to receive support but encounter conflicts with their equally strong need to avoid shame. Their comprehensive review of this subject indicates that chronic suppression, avoidance, and inhibition serve to both compound distress and prevent its resolution through diminished social support and ambivalence toward accessing services.

Although many, even most, secrets are likely benign, some secrets do exert a powerful influence over lives. Here is an example from *45 Years* (Goligher & Haigh, 2015), the movie that brought Charlotte Rampling an Oscar nomination for best actress for her portrayal of a wife in a long marriage. The movie takes its time heating up, but ultimately, we are witness to the anguished and perhaps permanent impact of the revelation by her husband of a long-held secret. Circumstances force him to slowly reveal details about a premarital loving relationship about which his wife previously knew little. He wants to reveal little; from what he does reveal she surmises that there is a great deal more that he has been keeping from her for the entirety of their marriage. Details about the intimacy of that first love of his begin to emerge, including the possibility that had she not died in an accident he would have married her; shockingly, too, his wife finds out that at the time of this first love's (presumably) accidental death, she was pregnant. Even as the wife is preparing for their 45th wedding anniversary, she begins to doubt everything about their marriage, wondering, and in fact convincing herself, that most everything about their marriage has been affected by his secret. She confronts him with her belief that every significant decision they have made in their lives together has been tinged with his memories and longing for his first love and that their current house has been permanently filled with her perfume. We are left to believe that their decision not to have children was greatly influenced by his unshared memories of his first love and their unborn child. And we are left at the end of the movie to watch the married couple play out diametrically opposed versions of their postrevelation lives: he desperately wanting to refocus on the happiness they shared (i.e., to quickly get beyond the feelings and hurt of the newly revealed story) and she unable to do so, terribly hurt and wounded by the revealed secret that has now scarred her life and made her rethink every reality they shared.

INDIVIDUAL DIFFERENCES IN DISHONESTY

Earlier in this chapter we cited research (Serota et al., 2010) indicating that a minority of about 5% of individuals (at least among American and British populations) are responsible for about half of all lies being reported in a given period. And as we noted earlier, some, though not all, of these prolific liars represent individuals who have personality disorders. But what about the others? Might they just be fairly regular people who happen to lead especially complicated lives? Could they even represent, paradoxically, those people who are honest enough to tell researchers about the full extent of their lying? Although the overall picture is not yet clear, the substantial history of research on individual differences in lying provides some clues to a profile of prolific liars.

One line of research began in the 1970s with the development of a standardized measure of *Machiavellianism*, a personality construct defined as the tendency to be an amoral, manipulative, scheming deceiver—behavioral elements drawn from the philosophy of Niccolo Machiavelli's 16th century treatise on power, *The Prince* (Christie & Geis, 1970). The measure asks for agreement or disagreement with statements such as "Never tell anyone the real reason you did something unless it is useful to do so." Those found to be high in Machiavellianism are not necessarily more intelligent than others, but they are much more skillful liars, experiencing less guilt and anxiety while lying, and thus they manipulate more often and with greater success. More recent years have seen the focus shift to a trio of undesirable personality traits called the *dark triad* (Paulhus & Williams, 2002), which includes Machiavellianism, subclinical narcissism (featuring grandiosity, entitlement, and dominance), and subclinical psychopathy (featuring high impulsivity, low empathy, thrill seeking, and anxiety). The dark triad traits are overlapping but distinct traits said to produce "toxic employees," mean-spirited sexual libertines, and other troublesome people whose behavior is consistently focused on manipulating and controlling others.

Interestingly, Machiavelli's name has also been borrowed by evolutionary biologists to explain not only our deceptions but also the size and sophistication of our brains. Among several theories is the *Machiavellian intelligence hypothesis*, which holds that our brains evolved to deal with ever-larger social groups and the ever-more complicated social relations produced by such groups (Whiten & Byrne, 1988, 1997). Living in a big social group means great potential gains for individuals with the ability to manipulate those around them and great penalties for those who cannot play the game well. Thus, there may have been substantial evolutionary pressure selecting for those with the brainpower to keep track of social networks containing dozens, hundreds, and even thousands of different relationships. In fact, comparative studies of brain size in primates show a correlation between the relative size of a species' neocortex (sometimes known as the *social brain*) and the frequency with which tactical deception is practiced in social groups. As evolutionary biologist Robert Trivers (2011) explained, "Among apes and monkeys, the smarter the species, the more deception occurs" (p. 37). This may even extend to white lies told for the sake of social harmony; apes have been observed hiding inappropriate facial expressions with their hands and engaging in "face-saving" techniques (e.g., de Waal, 1986).

Although Machiavellianism captures the personality profile of prolific liars, it does not explain how liars get made. What developmental factors push someone in this direction? Interesting findings have suggested that lying and deception are more likely to take root among children who are raised in harsh, punitive environments (M. Lewis, 1993; Stouthamer-Loeber, 1986; Talwar & Lee, 2011). Lying emerges as the essential strategy for self-protection in environments where punishments are harsh.

The trait of self-consciousness is also thought to foster frequent lying, perhaps of a more low-stakes, social nature. Children with a heightened awareness of their own thoughts and internal states, as well as how they appear to others, may learn how to mask negative emotions earlier than other children (Talwar & Crossman, 2011). Although other children remain blissfully unaware of their embarrassing feelings and responses, self-conscious children are only too aware and may develop a deceptive facade to conceal their feelings from peers. Kashy and DePaulo (1996) found that, among adults, frequent liars are "most concerned about the impressions they convey to other people" (p. 1048). They score more highly on measures of self-consciousness and *social adroitness*, a construct that involves the ability to pretend to enjoy things you dislike, modify your behavior to satisfy others, and hold your feelings in check.

It is also worth noting that recent research has indicated the brain adapts to dishonesty—the extent to which individuals engage in dishonesty increases with repetition. As Garrett, Lazzaro, Ariely, and Sharot (2016) noted, "The extent of reduced amygdala sensitivity to dishonesty on a present decision relative to the previous one predicts the magnitude of escalation of self-serving dishonesty on the next decision" (p. 1727). Lying in multiple contexts, including psychotherapy, may take the form of a "slippery slope," such that lies become more common over time.

Lying appears to decrease across the life span, with several studies showing older age to be a significant predictor of fewer lies in everyday life (DePaulo et al., 1996; Serota et al., 2010). This is also true in psychotherapy; our two studies of lying by adult clients suggested that the strongest demographic predictor of a client's level of dishonesty is their age, with older clients being considerably more honest than the young (Blanchard & Farber, 2016). Lying may decline with age because it is no longer needed as much, having been generally replaced by mature coping skills.

What of the association of gender to lying? Research on this issue is inconclusive. Studies can be found in which men lie more than women, and vice versa (DePaulo et al., 1996; Levine, McCornack, & Avery, 1992). It is likely that men and women tell lies at nearly the same rate but lie for different reasons. On average, men tell more self-oriented lies to puff themselves up and protect their interests, whereas women tell more other-oriented, altruistic lies to prevent social discomfort and embarrassment (DePaulo & Bell, 1996; DePaulo et al., 1996; Feldman et al., 2002). These are, of course, broad generalizations and do not say much about what clinicians might encounter in an individual case.

There is also a fair amount of research indicating that the tendency to lie is influenced by the nature of our relationship to the person to whom we lie. A seeming paradox is that the bulk of our lies are told to people to whom we are not close. As a leading dishonesty researcher, Bella DePaulo (2004), put it: "We are more likely [with strangers and acquaintances] to tell puffed up tales of our own accomplishments, or devious untruths designed to dodge obligations and unpleasantries" (p. 10). But we can also be shockingly honest with strangers, as when we might spill our entire life story to the unknown person sitting next to us on the plane. The reason for both behaviors is the same: Strangers and nonclose others just do not know much about our lives. Thus, we are more likely to tell them whatever suits our purpose and worry little about being caught (DePaulo et al., 1996).

Close relationships are a different animal. They feature a lower rate of self-serving lies, perhaps because we feel more comfortable being our authentic selves and perhaps too because we know we are more likely to get caught. At the same time, close relationships feature a substantial number of altruistic lies (DePaulo & Kashy, 1998) as we seek to achieve a degree of unity in opinions and emotions with our loved ones and to support their self-esteem. "It is to our close relationship partners," DePaulo (2004) explained, "that we are more likely to claim, falsely but reassuringly, that they did the right thing and we know just how they feel" (p. 10).

A notable exception to this pattern is one's mother. Perhaps because several of the landmark studies on lying involved adolescents and college students, mothers appear to be the great dupes of the research literature; in one study, moms were lied to in one out of every two interactions (DePaulo et al., 1996). This may be because mothers are the closest relational bond most individuals have and thus are the object of the most aggressive efforts, including deception, that further an individual's ongoing attempts at individuation. Stated in somewhat less tactful terms: Mothers have a reputation for worrying and asking prying questions. Although these behaviors may well reflect evolutionarily driven needs for mothers to protect their children, they are also behaviors that elicit considerable lying and concealment from their children. In another study, 82% of adolescents reported lying to their parents on at least one of six hot-button issues: money, alcohol/drugs, friends, dating, parties, and sex (Jensen, Arnett, Feldman, & Cauffman, 2004). This is a finding that will surprise only those who have never been a teenager.

Lovers, too, are prey to a distinct pattern of deception. Often-cited research has suggested that 92% of college students have lied to a romantic partner (D. Knox, Schacht, Holt, & Turner, 1993). Much of this lying occurs in the early stages of a romantic relationship when people worry that their "true self" is not quite loveable enough to attract and keep partners (DePaulo & Kashy, 1998). Thus, men and women present themselves as smarter, sexier, and more confident than they really are, and these goals are served by billion-dollar industries in clothing and cosmetics. On dating sites, they present themselves as more desirable in terms of weight, height, and age; one study found that 81% of participants lied about one of these attributes on their profiles (Hancock, Toma, & Ellison, 2007). But again, if lovers stick around long enough to become spouses, the rate of lying will decline to be among the lowest of all relationship types (DePaulo & Kashy, 1998; Knapp, 1984; McCornack & Levine, 1990; G. R. Miller, Mongeau, & Sleight, 1986).

Other demographic, personality, and diagnostic factors that may affect the tendency to keep secrets or lie in psychotherapy per se are discussed in the next two chapters.

SELF-DECEPTION

This is a book about conscious, deliberate deception in psychotherapy. Yet self-deception is so central to the work of psychotherapy that the concept cannot be ignored. We are reminded of a 2018 *New Yorker* cartoon by Paul Toth in which the Easter Bunny is lying on a psychologist's couch. The therapist: "I'm more interested in hearing about the eggs you're hiding from yourself."

To deceive oneself is at first a paradox: How can one not know that which one knows (Ford, 1996)? Yet patients do convince themselves—or at least try to—that the person they are dating is wonderful, even when they know (sort of) that it is just not true. The paradox resolves when we accept that the human mind consists of overlapping brain systems that are only partially integrated. At various times these systems may operate independently, cooperatively, or in conflict and so may seem to "deceive" each other, as one part of the mind denies the reality of knowledge held by other parts. Often our favorite target for deception is the same hapless person who turns up each morning in the bathroom mirror. In this regard, Daniel Gilbert (2006), professor of psychology at Harvard University, wisely noted the following:

> How do we manage to think of ourselves as great drivers, talented lovers and brilliant chefs when the facts of our lives include a pathetic parade of dented cars, disappointed partners and deflated soufflés? The answer is simple: We cook the facts. (p. 179)

Self-deception is a staple of literature from Oedipus to Charles Dickens to Kurt Vonnegut, yet Sigmund Freud can rightly claim credit for systematizing the notion for modern times. As early as 1894, Freud was paying special attention to unconscious defensive behaviors, noting that painful or overwhelming emotions could be "dislocated or transposed" from certain ideas and then "reattached" to other ideas, with the apparent goal of protecting the ego from unacceptable impulses (1894/1953). First in 1905 and later in 1926, he identified several mechanisms of ego defense (e.g., humor, distortion, isolation of affect) by which the self deceives and distracts itself. A version of this hierarchy, further developed by Anna Freud and others, remains in use today (Cramer, 2006). Contemporary psychoanalytic case studies involving lies still invoke the language of an ego defending itself against awareness of some unbearable truth (e.g., sexual or possessive feelings toward a parent).

Evolutionary biologists explain self-deception in a very different way. In the early 1970s, Rutgers University professor Robert Trivers began arguing that self-deception exists because it confers a clear evolutionary advantage. In his view, the so-called defense mechanisms are, in fact, offensive mechanisms, keeping our conscious minds unaware of contradictions so that we can be even more effective at lying to others (Trivers, 2011). Because some particularly dangerous or unflattering truth is kept out of our awareness, we do not end up sending the clues (e.g., fear, nervousness, guilt) that might reveal our deception to the listener. Thus, our conscious minds can much more easily control our communications, and we are that much more likely to escape detection. Put simply, the most believable liar is the one who is not aware that he or she is lying. Much of this unawareness is achieved through biasing the way we process information, either by selectively avoiding unwelcome information, selectively discounting unwelcome information as unimportant, or selectively forgetting that we ever encountered the unwelcome information in the first place (von Hippel & Trivers, 2011).

Multiple studies have established certain patterns in human self-deception, revealing what might be called the "hidden agenda" of the unconscious mind (Smith, Trivers, & von Hippel, 2017). The goals of this agenda include believing the best about oneself and one's tribe or ingroup while derogating those who belong to outgroups, forgiving and/or forgetting our transgressions while carefully cataloging the faults and offenses of others, and imagining that we have control over our fate. In pursuit of this agenda, Trivers (2011) contended that the unconscious mind preferentially excludes or distorts information even before the conscious mind has time to process it: "If the mind acts quickly enough, no version of the truth need be stored" (p. 9).

Perhaps the most striking illustration of Trivers's (2011) theory involves Trivers himself, who reported a lifelong habit of unconscious thievery, always committed in the presence of his victims. Pens, pencils, lighters, and matches were the most common items to "appear" in his pockets, but in one incident he stole an entire set of keys from the desk of a high school principal whose office he was visiting—without any conscious knowledge of the theft. He wrote,

> There appears to be a little unconscious module in me devoted to petty thievery, sufficiently isolated to avoid interfering with ongoing activity, such as talking. . . . This organism will study the behavior of my victim but it will also devote time to my own behavior, in order to best integrate the thievery while not giving off any clues. (Trivers, 2011, p. 26)

Although a skeptic might regard this as improbable, an attempt by the author to justify criminal activity along the lines of "the devil [or my unconscious] made me do it," many serious scholars have endorsed the basics of Trivers's overall theory, seeing it as consistent with basic tenets of evolutionary psychology.

There is, in fact, little contradiction between the Freudian idea of a child repressing dangerous oedipal feelings about his parents (to express them could threaten his only source of food and safety) and the mind of Robert Trivers planning petty thefts outside of conscious awareness (to be aware could get him caught). Freudians, cognitive psychologists, and evolutionary biologists all describe a mind that actively distorts reality for its own purposes—whether that purpose is survival, ego protection, self-inflation, or stealing pens—and then works to keep those distortions out of consciousness. It is a mind composed of competing parts that mislead each other, and it is a mind for which the objective truth is not high on the agenda.

The diverse acts of deception covered in this chapter can be understood along the key dimensions we have proposed: their techniques, their many shades of morality, and their external and internal functions. Research on deception in everyday life has established that it is both ubiquitous and deeply ingrained in human communication—indeed that having secrets and telling lies are part of what makes us human. Secrets and lies as clinical material are something like dreams: mysterious yet richly informative. Or like a prism, perhaps—these forms of deceit can split the concentrated beam of a client's narrative into its constituent colors, revealing the many parts of a divided self. In the next chapter, we move from secret keeping and lying in everyday life to the nature of deception that occurs within the confines of the consulting room.

3

CLINICAL AND EMPIRICAL PERSPECTIVES ON SECRETS AND LIES IN PSYCHOTHERAPY

If you do nothing else in therapy, learn to tell the truth.
—John M. Grohol, cited by Tara Parker-Pope, "Do You Lie to Your Therapist?"

The very structure of psychotherapy is meant to encourage disclosure of one's most shameful and distressing thoughts: It is confidential and private, characterized by a relationship with a caring, interested other. This relationship is nevertheless still a human one and, like any other human interaction, subject to moments in which the client (and sometimes the therapist) minimizes, conceals, or distorts the truth. Previous clinical and research studies have sought to investigate this phenomenon more fully by seeking answers to a series of interrelated questions: How can dishonesty be defined and studied in the therapy setting? How frequently does it occur? Are there certain topics about which clients are especially likely to be dishonest? What are their motives for lying about or concealing information from their therapist? What do they perceive as the consequences of being more fully open versus being deceitful with their therapist? Finally, what are the factors associated with disclosure and nondisclosure in therapy?

http://dx.doi.org/10.1037/0000128-004
Secrets and Lies in Psychotherapy, by B. A. Farber, M. Blanchard, and M. Love

This chapter thus provides an overview of the clinical and empirical literature that has attempted to understand clients' experiences when they have made an active choice not to tell the truth about what matters to them in therapy. We begin by briefly noting the ways in which client disclosure has been addressed by some of the notable figures in the history of our field, including Freud, D. W. Winnicott, Carl Rogers, and Irvin Yalom.

CLIENT DISCLOSURE IN PSYCHOTHERAPY

Open disclosure has been conceived of as being at the heart of psychotherapy since Freud's (1913/1958) injunction that patients should "be absolutely honest and never leave anything out because for some reason or other it is unpleasant to tell it" (p. 135). He had patients pledge to *free-associate*—to attempt to say whatever was on their mind without censorship—believing that it was the suppression of secrets that generated conflict and suffering. As such, revealing deeply hidden material was considered to be the pathway to healing, defusing the secrets of their power. Beyond providing a valuable means of unburdening oneself, honesty was framed by Freud as a moral imperative (Rieff, 1959; M. G. Thompson, 2001), a call to arms for patients to create and foster a standard of truthfulness in their lives through confrontation with the unspoken and the seemingly unmentionable.

Yet often what is unspoken can become so unbearable that the patient turns away from reality—not in the sense of becoming psychotic but rather in withdrawing from full contact with others. Winnicott (1956) described children who grow up in a hostile or otherwise nonresponsive environment who develop a *false self* to protect themselves from feelings of worthlessness and neglect. Meanwhile, the true self becomes barricaded behind a façade to protect from any further encroachment from the environment. But the true self is never wholly lost. Winnicott wrote,

> The false self is no doubt an aspect of the true self. It hides and protects it. . . . In this way, the true self is not involved in the reacting, and so preserves a continuity of being. The hidden true self suffers an impoverishment, however, that results from lack of experience. (p. 386)

Although the divide between true and false self is more strikingly apparent in those individuals who have grown up in hostile environments, it is important to note that the tendency to shield some aspects of one's inner experience from others is universal. It is impossible to be wholly genuine all the time, in all situations, with all people. Thus, all individuals possess a false self, a presentational style that becomes activated as a protective mechanism against feelings of shame or judgment.

This deceptive presentational style is self-preserving but, nevertheless, ultimately stifling to one's ability to feel real and authentic. As such, the therapist's task is to provide a "good enough" setting in which clients feel safe enough to reveal themselves more honestly. As per Nancy McWilliams (2004), a leading figure in contemporary psychoanalytic circles, "The primary aim of the psychoanalytic therapist is to encourage free expression [such] that we give patients the experience of having a relationship in which honesty is possible" (p. 135). But because the false self is so deeply ingrained and because shame is present in all of us, the process of fostering the emergence of the true self is ongoing and challenging. Winnicott (1956) noted that this revelatory process is all the more intense because the client is aware, as the infant was not, of the risks involved in dismantling the protective false self and allowing his or her inner truth to be shown. Ultimately, it is through a healthy and trusting therapeutic relationship that clients become able to take the risk of being seen by another for who they truly are—an experience that may well be "emotionally corrective."

For his part, Carl Rogers believed that a consistently open and genuine attitude on the part of the clinician provides the fertile ground for the client to be genuine as well. Rogers (1957) asserted that individuals need to experience the sense that they are prized, cared for, and valued for who they are, not what they do. This promotes the development of *congruence*, or the alignment between clients' behavior (and resulting self-image) and their sense of an ideal self. By contrast, when clients are exposed to *conditions of worth*—when they sense that their actions, words, or thoughts are being judged—they experience a sense of incongruence. Too wide a split between one's self-image and one's ideal self leads to feelings of shame, in turn leading to denial, repression, and dissembling: The truth under these circumstances cannot be discussed in full because it becomes too painful to do so. Thus, it is through the therapist's modeling of genuineness and his or her provision of empathy and acceptance (positive regard) that clients can encounter and express their truths more fully.

In ways somewhat similar to Freud, Winnicott, and Rogers, Irvin Yalom, an existential therapist, reminded us that shame and the deep sense of not being good enough are essentially universal problems and inevitably manifest in the psychotherapeutic situation: "Many patients enter therapy with the foreboding thought that they are unique in their wretchedness, that they alone have certain frightening or unacceptable problems, thoughts, impulses, and fantasies" (1970, p. 10).

In his 2015 book, *Creatures of a Day*, Yalom recounted a case that exemplified his belief that "everyone has secrets" (p. 22) and that a key element of a client's growth lies in the therapist's ability to understand the role of secrets in the client's distress. The case was of a successful physician seeking treatment following the death of his estranged brother. Client and therapist began to discuss death, isolation, interpersonal connections, and intimacy—many of the most profound existential concerns. They began to focus more intensely on the client's issues with intimacy, including his connection to his therapist (Yalom). "I guess," the client stated, "I'm just at the 'private' end of the continuum. I like being alone" (p. 71). Yalom pushed a bit: "Yet just a few minutes ago you talked about how comforting it was for you to speak intimately to me and to experience my interest in you." The client responded, "That's true, but I don't need it all the time." (p. 72). Yalom began to wonder more generally about the client's social withdrawal: "I'd seen many isolated, withdrawn individuals before, but rarely anyone with such competent social skills and capacity for intimacy . . . there was something odd going on" (p. 72). In this statement, Yalom foreshadowed the denouement, the revelation of the client's secret that tied all these strands together. He encouraged his client to let Yalom visit his house, persisting in this request despite the client's clear attempts to dissuade him from doing so. The client ultimately relented, Yalom visited, and we as readers were exposed to the details of the client's extreme hoarding behavior—a secret far too shameful to share. The story ended as Yalom's housekeeper came to serve in the same roles for this client, leading to the tidying up of the house and ultimately the client's ability to marry and have children. One clinical lesson we are left with is that of the power of secrets to derail lives, including the progress of psychotherapy. Another is Yalom's belief—one shared by most contemporary clinicians—that the central task of therapy is to facilitate clients' ability to disclose and ultimately accept previously hidden and shameful parts of themselves. The syllogism is deceptively simple: Clients hide what they cannot accept; with the therapist's help, they disclose that which they have previously found unacceptable; their disclosure leads to acceptance; and their acceptance leads to change.

And what is the engine that drives this process? At the heart of most systems' efforts to either help clients uncover previously undisclosed material or to construct more accurate (or at least adaptive) narratives is the facilitative role of the therapeutic relationship. This relationship has variously been regarded as intrinsically healing as in person-centered therapy, as the means by which central historical truths can be discussed as in psychodynamically oriented therapy, or as the basis on which interventions are successfully implemented as in cognitive behavioral therapy. Whether disclosure in therapy affects the strength of the relationship or is a product of it—it is most likely an interaction of the two—it is has been shown that disclosure of important thoughts, events, and feelings is related to more favorable ratings of the therapeutic relationship (e.g., Farber & Sohn, 2007; Pattee & Farber, 2008).

And yet, clients are often unable to tell the truth about some of the topics, feelings, and behaviors that matter most to them. They omit crucial information, avoid certain subject matter entirely, minimize the extent to which they are suffering, fudge details, and sometimes explicitly lie. They are often unreliable narrators. Even clients who report that it is "always better to disclose" still admit having some secrets (Baumann & Hill, 2016; Farber, Berano, & Capobianco, 2004). Particularly in the early stages of therapy, critical omissions are common (Gediman & Lieberman, 1996) as clients test the waters of what seems acceptable to share and acclimate to how the therapist will react to and perceive them. Often clients' initial priority in psychotherapy is to gain the therapist's approval, presenting themselves in a way that minimizes flaws and vulnerabilities; thus, deception serves as a means of managing one's image, especially in front of a therapist who may be perceived as an authority figure with great potential to bestow positive or negative judgments (Kottler & Carlson, 2011).

Therapists too contribute to an atmosphere in which deception is nearly inevitable. Although most people tend to have a bias toward believing that others' communications are truthful, therapists are perhaps even more trusting than most (Langer, 2010), preferring to give clients the benefit of the doubt and devoting attention to their strengths. We suspect many therapists, especially early in their careers, have not followed through on their suspicions that the whole story is not being told. Or perhaps they have reflexively brushed aside or minimized some patient concern or behavior, with a statement such as, "Sounds like you did your best" or "Doesn't seem like that was really your fault." Or maybe they have colluded with the patient's focus on the many flaws of everyone else in his or her interpersonal world. This general, overbelieving therapeutic stance can unwittingly foster an atmosphere in which the client feels compelled (or relieved) to conform to a certain narrative, withholding from the therapist information that is incongruous with this rosier view of themselves. Of the expectations analysts have about client communications, Weinshel (1979) wrote,

> I assume that most analysts accept as inevitable the fact that patients, as a product of defense and resistance, will distort various elements of truth and reality; and further, I assume that most analysts are less prepared for conscious deception. (p. 505)

Though written about psychoanalysts per se, this statement seems to apply to therapists of all persuasions.

In short, because psychotherapy is at its core a human endeavor, it is subject to all the fears and evaluative concerns that emerge when one is asked to be fully transparent with another person. And like any other human interaction, dishonesty in this setting is cocreated by both members of the therapeutic relationship; each brings into the room his or her own attitude about how fully the truth can be addressed and explored.

DEFINING AND CATEGORIZING CLIENT DISHONESTY

Consistent with the general literature on lying and secrets, there is still no consensus on the definition of dishonesty in psychotherapy. As such, it has been difficult to capture a clear and reliable sense of the phenomenon that clinical intuition and empirical research tells us is widely prevalent. Differences in classifying the phenomenon of interest—from secrets, to lies, to things left unsaid, to personally significant topics rarely discussed—lead to broad differences in research design, ultimately resulting in a heuristically valuable but somewhat confusing picture of client dishonesty. As detailed in the previous chapters, the act of being dishonest spans a wide spectrum of presentations and related motives.

Our sense, one consistent with the focus of this chapter and the balance of this book, is that client deceit is best understood and limited to instances of *conscious dishonesty*: occasions when clients are aware of their choice to conceal from or mislead the therapist about something relevant. As such, this definition excludes all forms of unconscious dishonesty, including repression, self-deception, and delusions. That said, a persistent problem in measuring and categorizing deceitful behavior is that of distinguishing between lies and secrets. Does lying require an explicit deceitful communication, or can the act of willfully withholding information be classified as lying? Some therapists, including Akhtar and Parens (2009), have suggested that both phenomena can be folded into the wider category of deception—in both circumstances, they suggested, one person will not possess significant knowledge of the reality of another's situation. Others, including Gediman and Lieberman (1996), have contended that lying is a distinct act of commission that creates a new form of false reality, whereas omissions simply alter reality by leaving a gap. Our notion of conscious dishonesty essentially aligns with that of Akhtar and Parens. We take the position that omissions and lies are two pieces of a broader whole: moments in which clients are not willing or able to share their reality with the therapist. It is the deliberate, conscious choice to be nontransparent itself that is most relevant to the therapeutic process.

There are several ways in which researchers have attempted to assess the magnitude of client deceit in psychotherapy, and it is to this research that we now turn.

PREVALENCE AND TOPICS OF CLIENT DISHONESTY

It is difficult to determine precisely the numbers of clients who are dishonest with their therapists—definitions, methodologies, and samples are diverse in this relatively new field of research. But it is nevertheless useful to provide some estimates of this behavior. Thus, on the basis of the extant research, somewhere between 20% and 54% of clients acknowledge having concealed information from their therapist—that is, been passively dishonest (Baumann & Hill, 2016; Blanchard & Farber, 2016; Hill, Thompson, Cogar, & Denman, 1993; Hook & Andrews, 2005; Kelly, 1998; Kelly & Yuan, 2009; Pope & Tabachnick, 1994). If we include "things left unsaid" during sessions—client thoughts and feelings that remained unstated—that number might be as high as 65% (Hill et al., 1993). As for outright fabrications or lies, in our recent research (Blanchard & Farber, 2016), 13% of our respondents acknowledged having made up facts in therapy sessions, but in Martin's (2006) study, 37% of respondents reported having lied to their therapist. In general, then, clients seem more likely to withhold or gloss over the salient details of their lives rather than create new untruths. Still, in Baumann and Hill's (2016) work, fully 90% of their respondents acknowledged either having a secret or disclosing a secret to their therapist, a figure consistent with our recent statement that a liberal definition of lying yields a client deceit rate of 93% (Blanchard & Farber, 2016). Dishonesty in psychotherapy is thus somewhere between widespread and nearly ubiquitous.

However, this last statement has to be deconstructed somewhat. That is, although nearly all clients have some secrets or tell some lies, most clients are quite truthful most of the time. Although they sometimes hide from or otherwise deceive their therapists, they tend to do so infrequently and in a limited, focused manner. Hill et al. (1993) found that clients reported only one thing they failed to say to their therapists within a given session. Over several studies encompassing several hundred respondents (see Farber, 2006), clients' average responses to the question, "Overall, how self-disclosing have you been to your therapist?" have ranged between 5.5 to 6.2 on a seven-point Likert-type scale (where 1 = *minimally*; 7 = *greatly*). Similarly, when asked to rate the accuracy of the question, "I tell my therapist even the most shameful aspects of my life," clients' mean scores were 5.0 on a seven-point scale ($SD = 1.9$). And last, in response to the statements "I have omitted or avoided discussing important information with my therapist" and "I have not been entirely truthful when discussing some important aspects of my life," clients' mean scores were 1.9 ($SD = 1.3$) and 1.7 ($SD = 1.4$), respectively. All of which is to say that patients are for the most part highly self-disclosing even as they do occasionally lie or conceal significant information.

Among the earliest efforts to empirically investigate questions about clinical dishonesty, Yalom (1970) analyzed written statements by college students participating in an encounter group exercise and identified three major themes of secrecy: basic inadequacy, feelings of interpersonal alienation, and sexual secrets. On the basis of the reports of another group of participants (359 undergraduates) in an encounter group, Norton, Feldman, and Tafoya (1974) derived 17 categories of secret content, predominated again by sexual secrets (27%), personal failure (16%), and *masking* (9%), the felt discrepancy between one's private and public selves. Although the scope of this early work is limited by its study of encounter groups—which many would argue do not even legitimately fall within the domain of true psychotherapy—and by decidedly nonrepresentative samples, it provided a foundation for later, more sophisticated efforts. Moreover, the results of this research proved to be somewhat prescient; the major themes identified have tended to be confirmed in subsequent studies of "actual" therapy.

One of the first efforts to classify the prevalence and topics of information that psychotherapy patients do not disclose came out of M. F. Weiner and Schuman's (1984) questionnaire study of 79 individuals who were in outpatient psychiatric treatment for a median duration of 3 years. Although these questionnaires were completed anonymously, they were initially distributed to clients by the psychiatrists themselves, introducing the possibility of some selection bias regarding the chosen sample. Of the sample, five of 21 males (24%) and 28 of 57 females (49%) were classified as nondisclosers; that is, they had withheld one or more topics of information from their psychiatrist. Results indicated that women more commonly withheld topics about sexual acts (37%) and sexual thoughts (30%), whereas men were more likely to report withholding topics related to violence toward self or others (30%), with sexual acts and thoughts ranking a nearby second (20% each).

Continuing in the vein of elucidating the type of material that is withheld in therapy, Regan and Hill (1992) found that both clients and counselors tended to withhold negatively valenced material. Clients indicated that they had left out approximately equal amounts of emotions, thoughts, and behaviors from their sessions. The authors also found that counselors were only able to identify 17% of what clients had withheld from them, attesting to clients' ability to keep much of their innermost selves private. Intriguingly, though, when counselors were more accurate at perceiving withheld reactions, clients rated those sessions as being less satisfactory, and counselors rated them as being rougher. According to the authors, it could be beneficial for clients to keep some things secret because doing so might function to enhance their sense of power or control in an essentially asymmetrical therapeutic relationship.

These findings are consistent with B. Thompson and Hill's (1991) earlier study that found that when therapists were able to perceive clients' negative reactions correctly, their subsequent interventions tended to be rated lower by clients on a measure of helpfulness. The authors suggested that therapists may become anxious when they sense that the client is dissatisfied, leading to a lower ability to be helpful. Clients, too, may become threatened by their sense that the therapist has recognized their negative reaction; in turn, they may become less involved in pursuing their own goals in therapy, contributing to their sense that the subsequent therapist intervention is less useful. It may be that clients want to express difficult thoughts but that they also want their therapists to "lay low" after doing so, a sequence that may enable clients to regain a sense of safety before returning to the work.

In the service of replicating the findings of Regan and Hill (1992) and B. Thompson and Hill (1991), Hill et al. (1993) studied *covert processes* in long-term individual therapy. Although eliding consideration of overt lies per se, the authors designed a categorization system that has achieved great currency as a means of organizing the types of information clients keep from their therapists. The three types of covert processes studied within this system include (a) hidden reactions in response to therapeutic interventions, (b) things left unsaid (i.e., the thoughts and feelings that occur during a particular session), and (c) secrets—that is, major life experiences, facts, or feelings that go unshared. These three interrelated processes differ regarding time frame, with things left unsaid taking place within a specific session, hidden reactions arising from specific therapist interventions that may span across sessions, and secrets occurring over a longer period that do not necessarily relate to events within the therapy.

The authors found that 65% of clients left at least one thing unsaid during sessions, often some discomfort they felt in reaction to some therapist behavior (Hill et al., 1993). In addition, 46% of clients (12 of 26 in the sample) indicated that they were keeping a relevant secret. Consistent with previous research, these secrets were most often sexual in nature (27%). These clients reported that feelings of shame, embarrassment, and fear of rejection prevented them from being more open. Those who acknowledged significant concealment reported lower satisfaction with therapy, suggesting that secret keeping could serve as a roadblock for therapeutic process or, conversely, that client dissatisfaction with therapeutic progress could increase the likelihood of secret keeping.

Pope and Tabachnick (1994) surveyed 476 clients who were therapists themselves about their experiences in treatment. In this sample, 20% reported that there was something important that they had not disclosed to any therapist. Of the 49 types of secrets, which fell into seven major categories, sexual secrets were again the most commonly reported type of content withheld (51%), followed by feelings about the therapist (10%), personal history of abuse (8%), substance abuse (6%), an eating disorder (4%), the identity of people mentioned in therapy (4%), and miscellaneous secrets (16%). Consistent with Hill et al.'s (1993) study, Pope and Tabachnick found that the higher the ratings of therapy helpfulness, the less likely it was that clients would withhold significant information. This seems to reinforce the notion that client disclosure is often a function of the perceived safety and support of the therapeutic relationship.

In a similar vein, Fedde (2009) found that clients' scores on a working alliance measure were significantly associated with keeping fewer relevant secrets in therapy and lower levels of self-concealment. In this study, the most frequently reported secrets included sex, habits, discrepancies between private and public self, failure, loneliness, and relationship issues. Notably, too, clients reported keeping an average of three relevant secrets from their therapist.

Martin (2006) queried 109 psychology graduate students who had been in therapy themselves about the lies they told in therapy. The specific attention in this work on lies per se distinguishes it from previous research. Lying was defined in this work as "statements (written or spoken) . . . which you knew at the time were not true" (p. 57). This captures a sense of intentionality on the part of the client and the need for the lie to have been overtly communicated, leaving out instances of avoidance, omission, and any other covert behavior. In this sample, 40 (37%) indicated that they had previously lied to a therapist and 11 (25%) reported that they had lied to every therapist they had ever seen.

Perhaps as a result of this study's shift in defining lies (i.e., restricting the definition to explicit statements of nontruth rather than concealment), sexual topics were significantly less prevalent (7%) than in previous research. Lies about relationships (13%) were at the top of the list, followed by substance use (11%), symptom severity (9%), feelings and thoughts generally (7%), and abuse-related lies (5%). This study also brought to light certain themes that did not emerge in previous literature, including lies related to medication (5%), self-injury (5%), completion of homework assignments (4%), and suicide (4%). Another focus of lies noted in this research—feelings or thoughts about the therapist—had been reported by Hill's (1993) research team and also by Pope and Tabachnick (1994). Here, in Martin's (2006) sample, it was endorsed by a surprisingly low 4% of respondents.

The motives for the majority of lies in Martin's (2006) study were classified as self-oriented; that is, lying allowed clients to accrue some personal benefit, whether this was psychological (e.g., the ability to manage the therapist's impression of them or to avoid uncomfortable feelings such as shame or embarrassment) or an actual concrete reward, such as a lower fee. Although other-oriented lies occurred more rarely, they concerned clients' efforts to protect their therapist from being worried or concerned about them. Although some clients had largely negative perceptions of the therapists they had lied to, citing characteristics such as having a "cold demeanor" or being "too judgmental," others highlighted a different sort of relational pattern that impacted their deception: lying that resulted from their deeply valuing the alliance and wanting to preserve it.

Returning to the realm of secrets rather than overt lies, Baumann and Hill (2016) surveyed 101 clients in individual psychotherapy about both their concealment and disclosure of secrets. About half (52%) of this sample reported concealing at least one secret from their therapist, whereas 85% had revealed at least one secret in therapy. Furthermore, 46% acknowledged that they had both previously revealed a secret and were also currently concealing a secret from their therapist, indicating that disclosure and concealment of secrets often co-occur in therapy. Only 10% of clients in this sample reported having no secrets that they had disclosed or concealed. According to the authors, although these clients may indeed be truly open with everyone in their lives, including their therapist, it is also possible that this group is less aware of or more defensive about what they have, in fact, concealed, and are thus making efforts to avoid the distress of confronting their secrets. Notably, too, Baumann and Hill found a significant gender difference, such that men were more likely to conceal a secret than women.

Although the majority of clients (71%) stated that they would be more likely to reveal their secret if they felt it was impeding their progress in therapy, it is not fully clear how clients assess whether secret keeping is an impediment to treatment. In managing the dialectic between wanting to be as truthful as possible and wanting to avoid feelings of shame or discomfort, some clients may choose to continue to withhold material if they do not believe it will negatively affect their treatment. A large portion (64%) of clients also reported that they would be willing to share their secret if the therapist were to inquire directly, suggesting a more active role of therapists in initiating a discussion of sensitive issues. Farber et al. (2004) suggested much of the same in their qualitative study of client disclosure, noting that most clients would welcome their therapists' active inquiry into difficult-to-discuss topics.

Baumann and Hill (2016) found a considerable amount of overlap between the types of topics that were concealed versus disclosed. The most common secrets were related to sex and substance use, supporting previous findings that these domains are more likely to contain high levels of difficult-to-discuss material. However, sexual secrets were also among the most frequently disclosed topics, indicating the particular salience of this subject in therapy. As we later discuss, Farber and Sohn (2007) found a similar pattern in their study; more specifically, they found that sexual issues, although typically discussed to at least a moderate extent, generated one of the largest discrepancies between perceived salience (importance) and extent of discussion among a great variety of topics discussed in therapy.

The most commonly disclosed secrets in Baumann and Hill's (2016) study were about relationship difficulties and failure. This type of content was less likely to be kept concealed, perhaps because these areas may generally be considered less sensitive, private, or taboo compared with material about sex or substance use. It may also be the case that these clients' therapists were more comfortable discussing and inquiring about relational difficulties than they were about sexual issues or substance abuse problems.

These findings highlight the degree of complexity that is involved for clients navigating the act of disclosure. It is not an all-or-nothing process but, rather, an ongoing, challenging, and multifaceted negotiation about what to reveal and when to reveal it. Baumann and Hill (2016) suggested that even those clients who have previously disclosed secrets may still find it difficult to be fully disclosing about all the important aspects of their experience. Clients are actively making a decision when they choose to disclose, one that may involve a weighing of the costs and benefits of sharing their secret with the therapist—an issue to which we devote considerable attention in the next chapter. Consistent with Farber's (2006) and Farber et al.'s (2004) finding that clients often experience ambivalence leading up to the decision to disclose about a difficult topic, clients in this sample endorsed heightened levels of both positive and negative emotions at the time of the disclosure itself, indicating that the process of sharing secretive material is highly charged and often quite difficult. The authors suggested that it would be beneficial for therapists to address this conflict and the mixed feelings that may arise directly with clients, inviting them to consider the pros and cons involved in the act of disclosure as an entry point to openness even if they do not feel ready to share the secret at that time.

A research perspective that reflects the fact that disclosure and deception are not all-or-nothing phenomena is one adopted by the senior author of this book (BAF) and his research team. Over the span of several studies, they have investigated the extent of client disclosure across multiple frequently discussed topics in therapy (e.g., Berano & Farber, 2006; Farber & Hall, 2002; Farber & Sohn, 2007; Hall & Farber, 2001; Pattee & Farber, 2008). These studies have provided a means for understanding the extent to which certain issues in psychotherapy are shared or avoided. Aggregate findings indicate that the individual issues most extensively discussed in therapy include aspects of one's personality or one's parents that are disliked; feelings of desperation, depression, or despair; feelings of anger toward one's parents; feelings about personal achievements; feelings about how to balance one's needs with the needs of others; expectations and hopes for the future; feelings about friends; and reactions to others' criticisms. More to the point of the focus of this book, and consistent with previous literature, these studies found that clients were least likely to extensively discuss topics about sexual and body-oriented experiences, including sexual feelings about the therapist; interest in pornography, masturbation, and sexual fantasies; nervous habits (e.g., nail-biting); and (ironically) tendencies to lie or distort one's experiences to other people.

However, there are two important caveats to be made about this line of research. One is that we cannot be sure to what degree these topics that are most extensively discussed are discussed honestly. Although a high degree of overlap is possible and even likely, it seems equally plausible that even among those topics most extensively discussed, there is still a fair amount of concealed or even distorted material. As the essayist Megan Dunn (2014) aptly acknowledged, "While some of the details I include may suggest that I'm spilling my guts, I can assure you that for every one of those details, there are hundreds I've chosen to leave out" (p. 7).

The second caveat is that there is an important distinction to be made between extensive disclosure and extensive disclosure of relevant information. That is, it is not hard to imagine a scenario in which clients share extensively about a topic that is not especially relevant to their most profound concerns (i.e., so-called "B" material). Thus, what the original research on "most and least discussed topics" omitted was a consideration of relevance or personal salience. It is crucial to know whether clients are actively avoiding (or discussing) a personally significant issue or whether they are addressing (or avoiding) topics that are essentially insignificant.

As a means of addressing the issue of salience, Farber and Sohn (2007) investigated the following question: For which issues do the greatest discrepancies exist between client-perceived importance or salience and the extent to which they are discussed in therapy? Results of this study indicated that there were some issues for which clients reported speaking more extensively than the perceived salience of these topics would seem to warrant. These included feelings of wanting to seriously harm someone, fantasies of revenge, and feelings of self-loathing. The authors suggested that these topics are "of the moment important," the kinds of issues that clients discuss in therapy in thinking about the events of the week, also the kinds of topics that clients, in retrospect, feel could have been discussed less extensively, leaving more time available for discussion of more enduring and significant issues.

The more important results here, though, at least in terms of understanding more about client concealment, are those that indicate large discrepancies in the opposite direction—topics for which clients reported less extensive discussion than their perceived salience would predict. These included the nature of sexual experiences, experiences of being sexually abused as a child, experiences or feelings about masturbation, concerns about sexual performance, and feelings of inadequacy or failure. Although it is important to remember that these issues, mostly sexual in nature, are discussed to a moderate extent, it is noteworthy that clients appear reluctant to explore them more fully with their therapist. As previous literature (Baumann & Hill, 2016; Hill et al., 1993; Martin, 2006; Pope & Tabachnick, 1994) has found, discussion of sexual and abuse-related issues seems to frequently involve some degree of concealment, though the degree of concealment may abate over time. Still, we imagine that for many clients this is the kind of difficult-to-discuss material that will always result in some discrepancy between importance and disclosure.

Further addressing both the question of salience and individual personality variables that influence dishonesty in therapy, Kelly (1998) asked outpatient clients at a community hospital, "What secrets have you not told your therapist that *seem relevant* [emphasis added] to your therapy?" Of the 42 clients in her sample, 25 reported that they were keeping no therapy-relevant secrets, whereas 17 clients (40.5%) acknowledged a secret of this sort, including secretly desiring the wrong person ($n = 7$), sexual secrets ($n = 4$), health problems ($n = 2$), and experiences with drugs or alcohol ($n = 2$). Using a multiple regression model that included secret-keeping scores as well as social desirability and self-concealment ratings, Kelly found that clients who were keeping a clinically relevant secret had lower symptomatology scores than those who were not keeping one, even after controlling for personality variables and therapy duration. Kelly used these findings to support her self-presentational view of secret keeping (more fully described later in the chapter), arguing that client secret keeping may be beneficial in that it preserves the therapist's positive view of his or her client. The small, nonrandom sample and the correlational nature of the design suggest that there are problems with this conclusion; it may be that healthier clients are simply better able to keep relevant secrets without experiencing repercussions. In addition, measuring symptomatology only addresses a single dimension of the potential ramifications of keeping secrets from one's therapist—dishonesty may impact the therapeutic alliance and treatment progress more broadly. Nevertheless, Kelly's work provides a useful counterpoint to the generally held assumption that secret keeping is ostensibly and usually negative, introducing the possibility instead that clients can derive some psychological benefits from the ability to self-regulate the flow of information in therapy and control how they are being perceived by the therapist.

Taken together, the clinical and empirical literature on topics of dishonesty in therapy—encompassing a variety of methodologies and definitions, from secret keeping to things left unsaid to important topics under-discussed to outright lies—gives an intriguing, if complicated, picture of what it means when a client chooses not to be fully honest with his or her therapist.

MOTIVES FOR DISHONESTY

As we have noted, a useful distinction can be drawn between external and internal motives for dishonesty. Dishonesty in therapy can function as a means of avoiding unwanted external events, such as being hospitalized for intense suicidal ideation; it can also serve as means for gaining external rewards, including monetary awards (e.g., compensation for emotional distress or military service-connected benefits). But most often, client dishonesty in therapy, especially in the form of secret keeping or minimal disclosure, reflects internal motives, protecting clients from experiencing strong, dysphoric emotions, especially shame (Farber, 2006; Hill et al., 1993; Kelly, 1998).

Shame comes up repeatedly in clinical and research reports on reasons for client deceit in psychotherapy. In their study investigating client and therapist covert processes, Hill and colleagues (1993) found that about half the instances of client secret keeping were motivated by shame and embarrassment. In a study of depressed clients by Hook and Andrews (2005), of all the reported reasons for nondisclosure, shame was by far the most frequently endorsed. The word itself is Indo-European in its origins, coming from the root *skam* or *skem*, meaning "to conceal," from which the words *skin* and *hide* are also derived (H. B. Lewis, 1971). Shame is often manifest as a global condemnation of the self, not being limited to thoughts, feelings, or actions, but rather associated with a great sense of inadequacy, unworthiness, and of simply being "no good" (Gans & Weber, 2000; H. B. Lewis, 1971). Common elements involved in the shame experience are intense emotional discomfort, hurt, and even anger, which accompany an overpowering desire to hide.

The therapeutic process is, by its nature, shame inducing. Clients are expected to lay bare their shortcomings, failures, and otherwise carefully concealed flaws and admit to their inability to independently resolve the problems or symptoms that have brought them to therapy—they have been unsuccessful in overcoming their depression, they are interpersonally or romantically inept, they need help picking up the shattered remains of their lives following a bitter divorce, they cannot stop drinking. Some find it terrifying to reveal their inner nature to another.

A common response to shame is the desire to hide to escape from further scrutiny and devaluation (Tangney, Miller, Flicker, & Barlow, 1996). Movement toward withdrawal and escape can be observed in numerous client behaviors, including concealment of relevant material and termination from therapy. Alternatively, the experience of or anticipation of shame may lead clients to attempt to construct desirable images of themselves for both the therapist and themselves. It might be said that some combination of avoiding shame and seeking the therapist's approval is, for many clients, at least as important as getting better.

Though perhaps intermingled with shame, there are other motives for clients' deception, many related to a fear of disrupting the therapeutic relationship. Thus, among the list of reasons collected by Kelly (1998) for why clients keep secrets was their fear that the therapist would see how little progress had been made. And in Hill et al.'s (1993) study, clients reported keeping secrets out of a concern about the fragility of their therapist, essentially foreshadowing the line made famous years later by Jack Nicholson in the movie *A Few Good Men* (D. Brown, Scheinman, & Reiner, 1992): "You can't handle the truth." Being fully honest with the therapist may feel too risky, endangering whatever equilibrium has been established in the relationship (Kelly & Yuan, 2009). By its very nature, the therapy relationship has a degree of formality and asymmetry, with the therapist occupying a higher position of power. It is also a vitally important relationship, and clients may fear that being fully honest about feelings of discontent—particularly about the therapy itself—could jeopardize the relationship. This also bears on psychodynamic ideas about transference—that to "talk back" or express disappointment or anger to an authority figure could lead to loss of love.

Rennie (1994) emphasized the role of clients' deference to their therapist in explaining their tendency to withhold relevant information. In his model, client deference arises from the conflict between the inherent asymmetry of the therapeutic relationship and the importance of that relationship. In a grounded theory analysis of 14 clients' experience of therapy, he found that they were most frequently silently deferential, holding back their dissatisfaction or criticism.

Rennie's (1994) sense was that clients are deferential for two primary reasons. First, they realize that the therapist is a "real person," and as such, they want to avoid hurting his or her feelings. Thus, clients present themselves in a manner that could be perceived as tactful and polite. T. Jacobs (2016) suggested much the same in noting that many clients conceal their fears about their aging therapists' health. Second, clients are reluctant to challenge the therapist's authority, believing that it is not their place to do so or that criticism might jeopardize the relationship or the therapist's positive view of them (a position later adopted by Kelly, 1998, as well as by Martin, 2006). Clients also seek to enhance that authority by making efforts to understand and accept the therapist's frame of reference. This seems to result from the nature of the client role, which can be conceived by many—especially perhaps new clients—as requiring acquiescence to treatment rather than challenges to it; this process of privileging the therapist's perspective may also result from the client's desire to experience the therapist as powerful and knowledgeable. Furthermore, in this study, clients suggested that it might be unfair to share negative reactions when the therapy was generally helpful and/or the relationship was strong. In some instances, they also described feeling indebted to the therapist, which can be a particularly powerful concern in subsidized or reduced-fee therapy situations.

According to Rennie (1994), clients manage to retain their sense of agency in these encounters, though covertly: They feel skeptical but still comply, pay selective attention to the therapist, and say one thing while thinking another. Another group of researchers (Rhodes, Hill, Thompson, & Elliott, 1994) extended this idea, suggesting that some clients conceptualize dubious or even unhelpful therapist behavior as intentional and part of the treatment plan. They do so, according to this hypothesis, to confirm their view of the therapist as a trusted expert who is not to be questioned or challenged.

A new aspect of client concealment is one that has been occasioned by the extraordinary growth of the Internet and social media. We are referring, of course, to the near inevitability these days of new clients, especially younger clients, googling their therapists to find information about them either before or soon after treatment has begun—and typically not revealing to their therapist what they find out.

Thus, multiple reports have indicated that many clients are in multiple ways, and for multiple reasons, not fully honest with their therapist about many of their problems and concerns, including their feelings about their therapy and what they know about their therapist. We have more to say in our concluding chapter about the ways in which therapists can deal in a proactive manner with client concealment, secrets, and lying, but for now it is sufficient to note that therapists can often attune to early indications of client disengagement and/or lack of candor, inquiring (even somewhat persistently) about the client's feelings about disclosure of specific topics or the general state of their work together. We now turn to a consideration of the multiple factors affecting the likelihood, process, and consequences of client disclosure and deception.

4

FACTORS UNDERLYING THE LIKELIHOOD, PROCESS, AND CONSEQUENCES OF CLIENT DISCLOSURE AND CONCEALMENT: "IT'S COMPLICATED"

It is both thrilling and threatening to be laid bare.

—Anatole Broyard,
Men, Women and Other Anticlimaxes

In the previous chapter, we addressed several aspects of client lies and secrets, including their types and overall prevalence. In this chapter, we delve into factors that influence the likelihood, process, and consequences of client disclosure and dishonesty, addressing several complicated questions (or rather, questions with complicated answers): What are some of the most significant variables affecting clients' tendencies to disclose clinical information honestly? What are the costs and benefits of such honest disclosure? What is the process by which clients decide to disclose rather than deceive? What is the relationship between disclosure and various forms of deception? What are the clinical consequences of keeping secrets and/or telling lies in therapy?

http://dx.doi.org/10.1037/0000128-005
Secrets and Lies in Psychotherapy, by B. A. Farber, M. Blanchard, and M. Love

FACTORS AFFECTING DISCLOSURE AND DISHONESTY IN THERAPY

There are multiple factors that affect the extent to which clients will disclose clinically important information to their therapist—to dig deeply into one or more core issues (*depth*) or to expand the range of topics about which they discuss in therapy (*breadth*)—or whether they will instead conceal or lie about their lives. We describe some of the more notable factors next; for a more in-depth discussion about some of these factors, the interested reader may consult the senior author's book on self-disclosure in psychotherapy (Farber, 2006).

The Nature of the Material

The content of the material itself may be the most consequential factor affecting clients' willingness to disclose honestly. Deeply personal issues are, for most people, simply harder to talk about because they often contain what feels like ugly or shameful truths. As noted earlier, research has consistently implicated certain topics as especially difficult for clients to discuss honestly. These include sexual issues, abuse, substance use, romantic feelings for and/or disappointment in one's therapist, and fears of failure.

The Client's Comfort Level in Revealing Personal Material

Some clients are simply more comfortable than others about sharing personal information, sometimes as a consequence of growing up in a family or community that shared a good deal with each other (e.g., Kahn, Achter, & Shambaugh, 2001; Macdonald & Morley, 2001; Mikulincer & Nachshon, 1991). Kahn et al. (2001) used the term *distress disclosure* to refer to the general tendency of individuals to disclose rather than conceal personally distressing information.

In a related vein, Larson, Chastain, Hoyt, and Ayzenberg (2015) investigated the construct of *self-concealment*, arguing persuasively that self-concealment can be considered a motivational construct, whereby an individual's need to remain hidden mobilizes the use of strategies to keep others at bay and regulate emotional distress. Their model, one that is consistent with our own theorizing, emphasizes a crucial clinical paradox: the approach and avoidance of clients who yearn to be known but remain painfully aware of the perceived adverse consequences of sharing intimate thoughts and feelings. Client self-concealment has, in fact, been found to be significantly correlated with keeping therapy-relevant secrets (Fedde, 2009).

In our research, high and low self-concealers held strikingly different positions when queried about the possibility of disclosing about a relevant topic they had previously avoided in treatment. Although low self-concealers indicated that they would be willing to disclose if they felt it was blocking their progress in therapy or if the therapist simply inquired directly, high self-concealers more frequently focused on their relational needs and concerns: They wanted their therapist to be warmer and more trustworthy, to believe that their therapist would not overreact, and to be assured that their disclosure would not ruin the therapeutic relationship (Love, Blanchard, & Farber, 2016).

The Client's Shame-Proneness

Shame-proneness, a trait, is distinct from momentary (state) feelings of shame that occur in all of us. Shame-proneness has been found to be a significant predictor of client disclosure on a cluster of items associated with negative affect (Hall & Farber, 2001). That is, clients with a greater tendency to shame were shown to be less likely to discuss their feelings of self-loathing, perceptions of personal failure, personality aspects they dislike, and events in their past about which they feel most ashamed. Reinforcing these findings, higher levels of shame-proneness among depressed clients were found to be significantly associated with a withholding of symptoms and behavior-related information (Hook & Andrews, 2005). Similarly, clients' nondisclosure of distressful feelings (e.g., guilt, hatred, disgust) has been found to be related to the belief that telling would engender shame (Macdonald & Morley, 2001). Moreover, secrets that are considered more shameful are associated with lower levels of anticipated support from a counselor (DeLong & Kahn, 2014). In short, shame—both the state and trait varieties—makes it more difficult for clients to reveal distressing information.

The Client's Attachment Style

Individuals' attachment styles, originally formed in childhood, reflect implicitly held assumptions about how relationships function, including expectations for how close others will respond to interpersonal needs (Bowlby, 1969, 1973). Therapy clients' "working model" of the extent to which their therapist will be available and responsive to distress has been found to be positively related to greater disclosure in therapy as well as the level of positive emotions (e.g., safe, proud, and authentic) experienced following disclosure (Mallinckrodt, Porter, & Kivlighan, 2005; Saypol & Farber, 2010). In short, clients who are securely attached, who harbor a representation of their therapist as caring and responsive, are more likely to disclose honestly and less likely to conceal and/or lie. Conversely, clients who are avoidant in their attachment style may conceal or lie to keep their therapist at arm's length.

The Strength of the Therapeutic Alliance

Among its many benefits, an effective therapeutic alliance facilitates an atmosphere in which increased disclosure occurs. Clients who report better working alliances with their therapists tend to report less of a discrepancy between the extent of their discussion of typically important psychotherapeutic issues and the importance they assign to these issues (Farber & Sohn, 2007). In short, a good therapeutic alliance makes disclosure easier; a tenuous or impaired alliance is likely to lead to greater instances of secret keeping and lying. Many clients need to establish an effective therapeutic alliance before revealing their most difficult issues. Some will test their trust and faith in their therapists by working on less toxic issues at the beginning of therapy before they reveal the "hard stuff." Even clients who are securely attached may need this gradual buildup of trust to disclose their most personal material.

An opinion contrary to the idea that a well-established alliance facilitates intimate disclosure has been offered by the noted psychoanalyst Nancy McWilliams. She wrote,

> I am not convinced that allowing a relationship to develop will create a climate of trust in which all pertinent material will eventually surface. Once the patient feels close to the therapist, it may become *harder* for him or her to bring up certain aspects of personal history or behavior. (McWilliams, 1994, p. 8)

Her point is that once a good relationship has been established, clients may be especially loath to speak about potentially shameful issues out of fear of rupturing that alliance. She suggested too that transferential issues may make the process of sharing personal information harder for some patients:

> Most adults can answer questions about their sexual practices with relative frankness when talking to a professional who is still a stranger. But once the therapist has started to feel like a prudish mother or moralizing father, the words flow anything but easily. (McWilliams, 1994, pp. 15–16)

Our sense, however, is that the impediments to disclosure that are posed by fears of disrupting a strong therapeutic relationship and/or by transference-based phenomena are more than balanced by clients' increasing trust in their therapists' acceptance of them.

The Extent to Which a Problem Feels Pressing

Some clients come into therapy or a specific session with an urgent need to discuss a particular issue. There may be a crisis at work, within the family, or in a specific significant relationship. In some respects, the crisis may facilitate honest disclosure—information that has been previously unexpressed or concealed now demands expression in the service of resolving or attenuating the crisis.

However, the crisis does not guarantee honest disclosure. We imagine that many therapists have had the experience of working, say, with a male client who wants immediate advice about how to best resolve an awful child-rearing disagreement between himself and his ex-wife. The client is angry about his ex-wife's perceived intransigence and fearful that she will obtain a court order to restrict his visitation rights to their children. The client is willing and even eager to focus on their differing philosophies about raising children, but it is several months later that he acknowledges that "maybe our arguments about this are partly the fallout of my 'fooling around,'" a circumstance that he had consistently denied—lied about—to that point.

The Extent and Type of Patient Resistance

Resistance in this context refers to the tendency to hold back in therapy, to not be honest, truly present, or amenable to change. Resistant behaviors may reflect a client's attempts to avoid painful feelings, especially shame or the vulnerability of closeness or, more generally, fear of significantly altering one's characteristic patterns of living. Resistance can be conceptualized as a more permanent character trait or as a temporary, situation-specific state (Beutler, Moleiro, & Talebi, 2002). In the latter case, resistance may reflect a rupture in the therapeutic alliance, often a client's "to hell with you" reaction to a perceived empathic lapse or frustration with therapeutic progress. Resistance is not, however, a pathological phenomenon but rather a normal means by which patients defend their sense of self and assert their need to be autonomous and separate from others, including the therapist (Messer, 2002). There are multiple forms of resistance, including "acting out" by coming late or missing appointments. But some clients resist by actively keeping secrets and/or lying about their experiences.

In a related vein, clients come to therapy with differing levels of motivation to change. Some are eager to enter therapy, highly motivated to do the work, and prepared to open up fully in the service of change. But others enter therapy with a lesser sense of urgency, neither fully "owning" their need to be there nor believing fully in the process; as such, they disclose reluctantly, concealing some of the basic truths of their experience. These are individuals who may be in therapy on the advice, urging, or insistence of others, perhaps via a spouse who has insisted on psychological treatment as a basic condition for continuing the marriage, perhaps via legal mandate. In the movie *Antwone Fischer* (Black, Haines, & Washington, 2002), the protagonist, a navy man, is mandated to see a psychiatrist. Among his first words to the well-meaning doctor: "You may be able to make me come here, but you can't make me talk." Here, we are in the domain of the empirically supported stages of change model (e.g., Krebs, Norcross, Nicholson, & Prochaska, in press) that posits that individuals may be at one of six very different motivational stages in terms of their attempts to change their undesirable behavior (e.g., smoking) and that therapists should not expect the same kinds of behaviors or degree of honesty from clients at these different stages.

Patients' Goals, Type of Therapy, and the Nature of the Therapeutic Contract

Some clients do not embrace or value a psychodynamic perspective that emphasizes the importance of extensive disclosure in therapy. They do not want to go deeply into the etiology of their issues nor their core conflicts. They simply want to feel better (i.e., experience symptom relief) as soon as possible. This, of course, is not an unreasonable position. But to the extent that a client adheres to this perspective, disclosure of personal material may be minimal (i.e., reluctantly shared, if at all) and secrets more likely.

Closely related to the influence on disclosure of a client's goals are the effects of a client's engagement in specific types of therapy. That is, different therapies tend to reinforce different types of disclosures, with some therapies, like cognitive behavior therapy, focusing on the specific nature of symptoms, and others, like contemporary psychodynamic psychotherapy, privileging discussions of early relationships as well as the here-and-now of the therapeutic relationship. In short, what clients disclose about as well as what they conceal and/or lie about is partially determined by the theoretical focus of the work.

A third, related variable here concerns the nature of the therapeutic contract—that is, whether therapy has been established as short-term and focused or long-term and relatively open-ended. Clients in short-term therapies are, generally speaking, not purposely concealing information; rather, they often do not have the time to disclose all relevant issues to their therapist. But the intense focus on defenses in some short-term therapies may affect secret keeping and lying in quite another way: For some patients, highly active, even aggressive inquiry on the part of the therapist facilitates more rapid and deeper disclosures about a specific issue than in longer term, open-ended therapies; for other patients, however, the same therapeutic stance may lead to resistance, a refusal to give up one's most private information.

In short, the temporal parameters of specific types of therapy are likely to influence the range and depth of disclosures as well as the inclination of clients to stay hidden or dissemble.

Length of Time in Therapy

Over time, and as the therapeutic alliance typically deepens, most patients broaden the domain of issues broached with their therapist and intensify the depth of discussion of those topics that are most relevant to their lives. This intuitive assumption has been empirically confirmed by studies that have shown a positive association between the extent of client disclosure and length of time in therapy (e.g., Hall & Farber, 2001).

Some clients, though, may become more fearful of revealing shameful truths over the course of therapy—fearing less their therapists' reactions (as per McWilliams's, 1994, ideas, discussed earlier) than their own. That is, as they fear that increasingly intimate disclosures will get them more in touch with feelings, thoughts, or behaviors that they find unacceptable. Clinicians see this situation most often with those who have been abused—as these clients continue to remember awful details, disclosure becomes more difficult and halting. Under such circumstances, concealment becomes more likely; lying ("I don't remember") may also feel like an option. In this regard, and counter to previous research indicating that greater disclosure is positively associated with length of treatment, Fedde (2009) found that the number of secrets clients acknowledged did not differ as a function of duration of treatment. Clients in longer treatment had, on average, as many secrets ($n = 3$) as those in those in treatments of lesser duration. Although some secrets may never be told to one's therapist (or anyone else), the evidence is strong that, in general, disclosure increases and concealment decreases as a function of treatment length.

The Nature of a Client's Problems

A client's symptom picture inevitably influences the nature and depth of self-disclosure and deceit. As McWilliams (1994) wrote, acknowledging and discussing difficult truths is easiest for healthier people because their self-esteem is essentially intact. Other clients, however, may struggle mightily to reveal themselves honestly. As noted earlier, those with insecure attachment patterns are more likely to withhold, distort, and lie as part of their symptom picture. Clients with a history of abuse or suicidality and/or those with eating disorders, gambling, substance abuse, or serious legal problems (including immigration issues) are also likely to struggle with full and honest disclosure. They are more likely to be prone to shame (Ferrari, Groh, Rulka, Jason, & Davis, 2008; Radcliffe & Stevens, 2008; Wallhed Finn, Bakshi, & Andréasson, 2014), to fear breached confidentiality (Gentilello, Samuels, Henningfield, & Santora, 2005; Newman, 1997), and to have concerns regarding legal consequences of honest disclosure (N. S. Miller & Flaherty, 2000; Newman, 1997).

Acknowledging that one is a substance abuser—or dealing with any socially unacceptable compulsion—is extremely difficult for most individuals. In fact, the first step in the 12-step Alcoholics Anonymous (and other 12-step programs) is to end the denial—to admit that one is powerless over addiction and that one needs help. In addition, substance abusers may be reluctant to admit to their use in therapy because they may equate discussing such behavior with having to take steps to stop it (Hyman, Malenka, & Nestler, 2006; Treeby & Bruno, 2012). Even nonaddicted individuals who use alcohol or other drugs to deal with depression or anxiety may be reluctant to reveal these behaviors, fearing that doing so could lead to discussions or pressure to find new ways of coping with their emotions or life stresses.

Clinical reports also suggest that clients with personality disorders tend to be more deceitful than other clients. We next briefly focus on the relationship of antisocial personality disorder (ASP), borderline personality disorder (BPD), and narcissistic personality disorder (NPD) to client tendencies to be deceptive in psychotherapy.

According to the *Diagnostic and Statistical Manual of Mental Disorders* (fifth ed.; American Psychiatric Association, 2013), one of the features of ASP is "deceitfulness, as indicated by repeated lying, use of aliases, or conning others for personal profit or pleasure" (p. 659). Individuals with ASP typically lack empathy for others, have no experience of inner guilt, and display a disregard for social mores and the law. As such, their deception does not seem to produce the typical sort of anxiety that emanates from a guilty conscience. Lies can be in the service of avoiding punishment or can generate a feeling of "contemptuous delight" in duping another (Akhtar & Parens, 2009; Ekman, 1992). Not surprisingly, the same dynamics tend to play out in psychotherapy: Clients with ASP manipulate the truth in an attempt to obtain some advantage vis-à-vis their therapist—for example, lying about their financial situation or availability, fabricating parts of their personal history, or concealing criminal behavior.

Yalom's (1997) book, *Lying on the Couch*, is an intriguing novel about this very situation. The book features a seemingly earnest and quite articulate client, a successful businessman, who is apparently committed to the spirit and value of intensive psychodynamic/existential psychotherapy. In fact, though, he is a con man and manages to convince—or, as it is perfectly set up, reluctantly allow—his too-trusting therapist to invest a great sum of money in a "sure thing." Needless to say, the con man/client disappears after receiving the therapist's money, leaving no trace of his whereabouts or true identity.

Clinicians and researchers writing about clients with BPD have invariably noted the frequency of manipulative behavior in this population. Often lacking the ability to emotionally self-regulate, these individuals look to others to fill this role and will often go to extremes—including fabricating stories and exaggerating experiences—to get their emotional needs of the moment met. Clients with BPD are almost always a significant challenge for clinicians, testing the boundaries in the inevitably elusive attempt to feel close enough or good enough. In this regard, we are reminded of Bill Murray's character in the movie *What About Bob?* (Touchstone Pictures & Oz, 1991), who, desperate for an appointment with his vacationing therapist, lies in multiple ways to get his therapist (Dr. Marvin, played by Richard Dreyfuss) on the phone: He works his way from unsuccessfully pretending to be Dr. Marvin's sister to presenting himself as a detective to Dr. Marvin's answering service, asserting that he needs his therapist's vacation address to continue his investigation of the suicide of Dr. Marvin's patient (i.e., Bob, himself). After finally tracking down his therapist in his vacation town but being rebuffed in his efforts for an appointment, he (Bob) cries out, "Gimme, gimme, gimme, I need, I need, I need, I need, gimme, gimme, please." Dr. Marvin relents (i.e., allows for a phone appointment later that day) but only after making Bob promise that he will immediately buy a bus ticket to go home afterward. Needless to say, that promise is broken, more boundaries are crossed, and mayhem ensues.

In clients with NPD, deception occurs in the intense pursuit of protecting a fragile inner self. Individuals with NPD tend to lack empathy, view others as "less than," and view their deception as a legitimate means of attaining the power and validation they so crave. They exhibit minimal concern for how others might view their exaggerations and lies, in this sense sharing some overlap with antisocial features (Kernberg, 1975).

One of us (BAF) worked with a client with NPD—let us call him Jim—for several years, which was unusual in that most such individuals do not seek out therapy because this situation often makes them feel vulnerable, a nearly intolerable experience. But his wife insisted on therapy as a condition for staying in the marriage. Jim was in some ways quite likable. He was quick to please, eager to ask how I was, and prone to tell engaging stories. But when it came time to "get to work," to talk about his life, his problems, and his history, two patterns colored our sessions: a consistent exaggeration of his "accomplishments" and consistent dissembling (e.g., half-truths, vague details, off-topic evasions) when discussion of any interpersonal relationship ensued. Minor administrative tasks morphed into significant, even newsworthy events; accomplishments completed within a group format became signature events for which Jim took almost sole credit; conflicts with important people in his life, especially his wife, were always their fault; and his feelings about me (when asked) were solely complimentary, indeed over the top—nothing whatsoever could be improved about our work. To get him to acknowledge his ambivalent (at best) feelings for me and his penchant to embellish events to make himself seem special took years, with many therapeutic ruptures that had to be resolved when he began to be frighteningly aware of his inauthentic presentation.

The Therapist's Attitudes Toward and Responsiveness to Disclosures

A major influence on honest patient disclosure is rooted in a large constellation of "therapist factors," including the therapist's tendency to self-disclose, the nature of his or her responses to patient disclosures and to apparent half-truths or lies, and the extent to which he or she takes an active role in pursuing more in-depth disclosures.

Clients are more likely to self-disclose if their therapists do; evidence suggests that therapist self-disclosure serves as a model for client disclosure (Henretty & Levitt, 2010). Moreover, the nature of the therapist's response to client disclosures inevitably affects the nature and likelihood of subsequent client honesty. Therapist attentiveness and/or overt statements of affirmation (e.g., "That was courageous of you") make it more likely that clients will continue to disclose honestly. In contrast, when therapists appear to be uncomfortable with certain disclosures—most often because certain disclosures (e.g., suicidality) catalyze anxiety in the therapist—clients are likely to conceal information to protect both themselves and their therapists. Similarly, therapists who are overly inquisitive or confrontational (i.e., not tactful in pursuing sensitive material) run the risk of having clients conceal or lie.

Although "overpursuit" of client information may lead to client secrecy or deception, earlier studies by our research team (e.g., Farber, Berano, & Capobianco, 2004) found that many clients wish their therapists would more actively push them toward greater disclosure of hard-to-discuss issues. In the absence of a therapist's active pursuit of difficult disclosures, it becomes too easy for clients to conceal information that could be of therapeutic value. Here is where therapeutic tact comes into play, the need for encouragement and empathy rather than aggressive pursuit: "I'm wondering if you could say more about that" or "I sense that it's difficult for you to speak about your parents' divorce, but it feels to me important that we continue to try to understand that."

Demographic Variables

Somewhat surprisingly, there have been few consistent findings linking demographic variables to client disclosure or deception. Take gender, for example. Recently, Baumann and Hill (2016) found that men were more likely to have kept secrets from their therapist than women. But in an early study by M. F. Weiner and Schuman (1984), men were found to disclose more than women in therapy. And Farber (2006) found that except for some minor differences regarding most extensively discussed issues (e.g., women disclose more about their sexual experiences and men more about their interest in pornography), there is extensive overlap between what men and women most often discuss in their therapy.

However, gender dyads have been shown to influence client disclosure, though not in the directions that might be expected. Rather than the more expected effects on disclosure of female clients with male therapists, or perhaps vice versa, one research study found that women with female therapists have greater difficulty discussing intimate topics in therapy than either men with female therapists or women with male therapists (Pattee & Farber, 2008). That study also found that female clients working with female therapists reported significantly greater concern about the impact of their disclosures on their therapists' feelings toward them. Extrapolating from these data, we might imagine that female clients working with female therapists are more likely to conceal information or, relatedly, harbor significant secrets.

Whereas most studies have found no significant age effects on disclosure in therapy (Farber, 2006), our recent research (Blanchard & Farber, 2016) indicated that older clients scored higher on a measure of honest disclosure than did younger clients. There is also considerable theoretical and clinical literature supporting the hypothesis that client and therapist racial, ethnic, and cultural differences affect disclosure patterns (e.g., Sue & Sue, 1999). As one respondent in Farber et al.'s (2004) study of client perceptions of disclosure noted, "It's easier to talk to someone of the same race" (p. 342). Others have suggested that therapists should be aware of and sensitive to the fact that some minority clients may need extra "warm-up time" in sessions before they begin to discuss deeply personal information. According to one of our colleagues at Teachers College, Marie Miville,

> In the Western way, the self is the basic unit of analysis, but under the Latina/o way, it's the community and the family. So while Whites might not think that beginning a session with five to ten minutes of humor and chitchat has a healing impact, it's essential when you're working with Latinas/os. (2016, para. 10)

Surprisingly, however, there is little in the way of empirical data to confirm assumptions about the effects of client ethnicity or race (or client–therapist match on these variables) on disclosure. One study, however, did find that ethnic minority clients did not self-disclose suicidal ideation as readily as their nonminority peers at a university counseling center (Morrison & Downey, 2000).

THE BENEFITS AND COSTS OF DISCLOSING IN PSYCHOTHERAPY

There is at least one more quite significant set of factors affecting the likelihood of extensive and honest client disclosure: clients' consideration of whether it is "worth it," whether honest disclosure is likely to feel more valuable than problematic. Although clients are unlikely to weigh the advantages and disadvantages of disclosure methodically, we assume that on some level there is some sense, some calculation of what can and should be said to one's therapist (including the possibility of explicit deceit) at this moment, in this session, in this course of one's therapy.

We start with the possible benefits, but it should be evident that the benefits as well as the costs that may accrue from honest disclosure inextricably overlap with the benefits and costs of therapy per se.

- *Feelings of intimacy*. Honest and meaningful disclosure about the client's concerns and/or the therapeutic relationship per se often leads to experiencing a sense of closeness and connection to one's therapist.
- *Experiencing the validation and affirmation of a respected figure*. Being affirmed and validated by one's therapist, especially when one is beset with shame or other distressing feelings, can lead to powerful feelings of being good enough (Suzuki & Farber, 2016).
- *Increased insight and self-awareness*. Disclosure may contribute significantly to a client's self-understanding, to a greater awareness of multiple aspects of his or her life, including feelings, thoughts, behaviors, fantasies, coping mechanisms and defenses, relationships, identifications, and pathogenic beliefs (McWilliams, 1994).
- *Strengthening one's sense of self*. Through disclosing, clients may experience a more cohesive as well as more complex sense of self, merging newly uncovered material with older, more familiar self-representations—in doing so, clients become aware of

attributes, roles, or experiences that had not previously been part of their self-definition.

- *Increasing one's sense of authenticity.* Sharing deeply personal aspects of experience leads to a greater sense of genuineness and authenticity, of clients' feeling more "real" and less fraudulent.
- *Experiencing catharsis.* Disclosures of deeply personal material may lead to clients' experiencing relief from the often overwhelming physiological and emotional burdens of keeping painful memories, thoughts, and feelings to themselves. This notion is consistent with Stiles's (1987, 1995) "fever model" of disclosure—that distress increases disclosure and disclosure reduces distress. In Farber, Berano, and Capobianco's (2006) qualitative study of client disclosures, it was this sense of unburdening that most respondents cited as their primary reason for disclosure: "It's like a release, a weight off my shoulder" (p. 466). In one of Yalom's books, *When Nietzsche Wept* (1992), the protagonist (a fictionalized Friedrich Nietzsche) said, "It seems to me that the more I am able to tell of my innermost feelings, the more relief I will gain" (p. 159).

And what of the costs of disclosure? Or perhaps more accurately, what are the factors or client fears that inhibit disclosure and/or increase the possibility of concealment and overt deceit? The importance of some of these factors—including the extent to which many are tied to the central consideration of shame—mandates our going into some degree of detail in explaining or illustrating their salience.

- *Fear of or actual rejection by one's therapist.* Clients are frequently apprehensive about how their therapist will respond to a disclosure that they feel puts them in a bad light. One study participant whom we interviewed noted quite explicitly that her fear of disclosure would only abate if she "knew for sure that he [my therapist] won't look down on me for these thoughts." Or, as T. S. Eliot (1920) once wrote about history's depravities, "After such knowledge, what forgiveness?" ("Gerontion," stanza 5).

  It is also unfortunately true that some patients have experienced not just a fear of rejection but also rather an actual rejection or some other form of disapproval or punitive action following a disclosure. Although this certainly could occur anywhere, including a private practice or clinic setting, it is more likely to take place in a hospital or forensic setting with an overwhelmed, burned out, or simply incompetent therapist. Some examples follow from *A Fan's Notes*, by Frederick Exley (1968).

The author, writing about his experiences as an involuntarily committed patient at a state psychiatric hospital, described the consequences of being belittled for his articulated thoughts and beliefs: "I knew how to beat the bastards; I had beat them before and the way was simple—one didn't tell them about one's devils" (p. 79). Later, writing about his experiences at an expensive private hospital, he provided a harrowing illustration of the price he paid for baring his soul to his weak and ultimately infuriating therapist:

> [But] then I proceeded to tell him something from my past that I had told to no one before him, nor will ever tell again. My eyes avoiding his, I spoke in the fitful, hesitant monosyllables of grief. When, finally finished and exhausted with relief (as one is with the ultimate confession), I looked up to make sure that he had understood me utterly, the room drifted away beneath me, the dizzying blood rushed to my head, something in me snapped: I broke. On his face was written the unmistakable legend of distaste. (pp. 84–85)

A prime subset of disclosures that breeds apprehension about therapist rejection includes those that reflect a client's feelings toward his or her therapist—for example, feelings of disappointment or anger or, conversely, love or sexual attraction. In the latter instance, the disclosure of strong positive romantic or erotic feelings toward one's therapist, when not reciprocated or somehow accepted, often leaves the client feeling "stranded," in turn leading to feelings of frustration, anger, disappointment, or shame. In short, the anticipation or previous experience of an untoward reaction on the part of therapists is why such feelings are often concealed or lied about.

- *An expectation that the therapist will feel burdened by or incapable of understanding certain issues.* Clients may fear or perceive that their therapist may be overwhelmed by hearing difficult material because he or she may also have "been there" (e.g., experienced divorce). Of course, sometimes this assumption, leading to concealment, is more about protecting one's self from anticipated shame than it is about protecting one's therapist.

  A related client concern is that the therapist is too naive, fragile, or inexperienced to either understand or handle especially raw (e.g., intensely sexual or aggressive), psychotic, or existentially tinged (e.g., related to death) material or specific life-stage issues (e.g., raising children, dealing with retirement or infirmity). Beginning therapists may not be privy to the full range and intensity of some clients' problems for just this reason.

- *Fear of creating undesirable impressions of oneself.* Clients may have an apprehension that speaking exclusively or nearly so about problems or shameful aspects of one's life will lead one's therapist to form impressions and judgments entirely on this basis. A patient of one of us (BAF), after weeks speaking about how fragile she constantly felt, plaintively said, "I fear I'm the sickest patient you see."

  Consistent with this notion, Kelly (1998, 2000) has argued that clients might benefit from concealing shameful aspects of their lives; doing so, she contended, serves to maintain their therapist's positive appraisal of them. Although most researchers (e.g., Hill, Gelso, & Mohr, 2000) believe otherwise—that therapists are generally quite respectful of their clients' admissions—some clients may nonetheless conceal or lie about aspects of their lives they fear will lead to a negative therapist appraisal of them.

  Analogously, some clients fear that certain disclosures will alter their sense of self. And now they are once again in the realm of shame. A client of the senior author (BAF) had intense difficulty in coping with the changes in her self-image ("I'm perverted") following disclosure of her sexual excitement when she was sexually abused by her brother. As many novelists and poets have suggested, we are what we remember.

- *Regret for hiding so long.* Some clients have spent a good part of their lives concealing or denying the importance of some significant experiences (e.g., a spouse-abusing or incarcerated family member, a bout with poverty or homelessness, academic or occupation failure). There is often a feeling of great relief—the cathartic effect noted earlier—and pride in ultimately acknowledging previously undisclosed but significant personal events. But sometimes embedded in the otherwise positive effects of finally discussing what had been suppressed or minimized for so long is a great sense of regret, one that may be tinged with shame: "I should have talked about this years ago." And yes, the therapist might well reassure this client that she was just not ready until now and that she should be giving herself credit for having gotten to this place at all. But the client might still be left with a terrible awareness of wasted years and wasted opportunities.

- *Feelings of increased vulnerability*. Patients may feel great apprehension about some disclosures—a sense that old traumatic experiences will flood them and lead to irreversible pain, vulnerability, and/or nightmares. "Disclosure," noted Terry Wise (2012) in her powerful book about her own therapeutic experiences, can be thought of as "taking a leap across the most terrifying chasm between trust and self-destruction" (p. 76). One person we interviewed for our current research had the following to say about her willingness to disclose certain frightening thoughts: "I'd need to be shown that I'm not the only one having thoughts like this no matter how unhealthy or destructive and that people have recovered from such modes of thinking in the past."

  Some may also fear a different type of vulnerability: that their therapists may respond to a disclosure with advice they may not want to hear (e.g., "Perhaps you should tell your husband why you're so unhappy and why you're considering leaving," "Maybe you need to consider another type of job").
- *Fear of practical (e.g., legal) consequences*. Some disclosures, including those that relate to child abuse, criminal behavior (including parole violations), immigration, and suicidal thoughts or behaviors may have significant legal or logistic consequences. Acknowledging child abuse to one's therapist, a mandated reporter of such behavior, may lead to an investigation by child welfare authorities. Acknowledging substance abuse may lead to termination from group therapy, partial hospitalization, or alternative-to-incarceration programs. Acknowledging suicidal thoughts, or especially suicidal intention, may lead to hospitalization—a common motive for client avoidance of this topic in therapy (see Chapter 7). For some clients, the cost of any of these admissions may feel disproportionate to the rewards of honesty.
- *Feelings of shame*. With the exception perhaps of the potential legal consequences of certain disclosures, virtually all other factors that potentially inhibit honesty in therapy reflect some aspect of shame. As we have noted, shame is a frequent antecedent, concomitant, and consequence of disclosure in psychotherapy (H. B. Lewis, 1971; Livingston & Farber, 1996; Wurmser, 1981), affecting greatly the nature, timing, depth, and honesty of what is revealed. Simply put, the anticipation of shame is likely the greatest single deterrent to truth telling in psychotherapy.

THE PROCESS OF REVEALING THE TRUTH (OR TELLING LIES) IN THERAPY

Positive and negative consequences of honest disclosure can and often do co-occur. A research study by Farber et al. (2004) asking clients to rate the extent to which they experienced several discrete emotions following "difficult disclosures" found that the five most highly rated emotions were "relieved," "vulnerable," "authentic," "safe," and "proud." Moreover, the balance between the overall benefits and costs of disclosures invariably changes as a function of the type, timing, and intensity of the disclosure, as well as the therapist's response to the disclosure. Nevertheless, we sense that clients' intuitive awareness of many of these cost–benefit issues affect deeply what they do or do not reveal to their therapists, including the possibility of outright lies.

So, how does all this play out in the here and now of a therapist's office? Something perhaps like the following: The client enters the therapist's office or perhaps has been in session for a few minutes, and the thought enters his or her head: "Maybe I should tell my therapist about this feeling or memory I've been having." Or instead, the therapist might have just asked the client a probing question about what they have been discussing. Now it gets complicated. The client may invoke an image of his or her "best (client) self" and, as honesty as possible, reveal fully what he or she is thinking. But many other possibilities present themselves. The client, on considering a new topic or a significant elaboration of an old topic, may instead say nothing. Or, on such consideration, he or she may essentially repeat old material with minor variations on the same often-played notes. Or, on consideration, or in response to the therapist's question—perhaps "What's on your mind right now?" or "You seem troubled," or "Do you have any thoughts about harming yourself?"—he or she may make something up. "I was thinking about a friend of mine who's coming over for dinner" rather than the truth, "I was thinking that we're not getting much done here" or "No, I'm fine, was just replaying what you just said to me" rather than the truthful thought, "I was thinking about how attractive you are and what it would be like to have sex with you" or "No, a bit sad, but nothing more than that" rather than the true sentiment of the moment, "I can't stand living anymore and wish I could just take those pills I've stashed away." As the great American novelist Saul Bellow once suggested, "Many common lies and hypocrisies are like that, just out of the harmony of the moment" (1953/2006, p. 217). And as the rock group REM once sang in *Losing My Religion*, "Every whisper of every waking hour I'm choosing my confessions."

Let us deconstruct this complex process a bit more, a task enabled by research on the very issue of clients' decision-making process regarding disclosure (Farber et al., 2006). According to the model laid out there, most clients in therapy hold a generally favorable view of the value of honest disclosure (e.g., "The more you disclose, the more helpful it is") and, conversely, an unfavorable view of the role of concealment and secrets in therapy (e.g., "If you start holding back important issues, you have to lie in therapy because you can't tell the whole story"; p. 466). Nevertheless, most clients are ambivalent about actually disclosing. That is, when their general attitude toward disclosure comes face-to-face with the actual decision-making moment, things get a lot more uncertain. As per the previous section on costs of disclosure, anticipatory shame and, relatedly, a fear of the therapist's reaction often act in tandem to make clients somewhat hesitant to act in concert with their positive attitude regarding the value of disclosure. It is at this point, at the juncture of "should I" or "shouldn't I," when doubts creep in and the possibilities of minimal disclosure, concealment, or outright deceit appear to strengthen.

But let us imagine that some combination of the client's courage, her experience of a positive therapeutic relationship, her sense that the value of a significant disclosure outweighs the risks at this moment, and the therapist's verbal and nonverbal encouragement come together and this client does, in fact, begin to disclose some significant clinical information. What then? Do the costs—the shame, vulnerability, and fears—vanish as the client begins to reveal some significant information, much as an amateur athlete's anxiety dissipates as soon as he or she throws that first pitch or returns that first serve? In fact, no. As noted previously, disclosure, although primarily a positive, relieving experience, is often accompanied by distressing affective experiences.

And now another choice point for clients. They begin a significant narrative, one replete with important clinical material and likely infused with some painful feelings, and now have to decide whether to go on and probe deeper or whether to round off the edges and go back to a safer emotional place—perhaps pretend they remember no further details or even provide details contrary to their remembered experience or current awareness. Over the course of multiple sessions, most clients will do both at times (i.e., continue with their open and honest narrative, edit their experience), though most clients most of the time opt for the former (honest) option. For the most part, this turns out to be a good choice: After a deeply personal disclosure, most clients tend not to regret their decision to disclose (Farber et al., 2006).

Perhaps as a result of this vulnerability, most clients report wanting their therapists' approval after their disclosures—and the data indicate that, in fact, most receive such approval in the form of either verbal ("You've done some good, hard work") or nonverbal ("looking kindly") expressions. This positive feedback, in conjunction with internally experienced feelings of pride and relief, increases the probability and ease of future honesty.

But this model also allows for pathways that lead to secrets and lies. Each step in the direction of disclosure comes with potential pitfalls: For example, clients may not have a generally positive attitude toward disclosure when they begin therapy, their sense of vulnerability during disclosure may be overwhelming, the emotions they experience after disclosure may be marked far more by negative emotions (e.g., shame, sadness, anxiety) than positive ones, and their therapists may be less forthcoming with approval than clients need to continue the process. Any of these situations increase the likelihood of client deception.

THE COMPLEX RELATION OF DISCLOSURE TO SECRETS AND LIES

Client disclosure is related to client secret keeping and lying, though this is not a simple inverse relationship. That is, the opposite of disclosure is not necessarily lying or permanent secret keeping; clients can and do take their time in revealing important information to their therapists in ways that do not constitute deceit.

We might think of a continuum of disclosure–deception among clients in psychotherapy, ranging from (a) those who consistently disclose highly personal details of their lives with a minimal degree of lies and secrets to (b) those who disclose a moderate amount of personal information but also conceal and/or distort significant parts of their lives to (c) those whose narratives are low on honest disclosure but replete with secrets and/or egregious misrepresentations. This is a fairly intuitive notion, with the simple assumption that as honest disclosures increase, lies and secrets decrease. Sidney Jourard, who pioneered the study of self-disclosure in the 1960s and 1970s, held this assumption. More recently, Kahn and Hessling (2001) proposed a continuum with distress concealment (i.e., rare or minimal disclosure) at one end, and distress disclosure (i.e., rare or minimal concealment) on the opposite end.

Several problems with this idea may be evident. One, noted briefly earlier, is that concealment (the absence of disclosure) may not reflect deceit as much as the need for some, even most, clients to establish a trusting therapeutic relationship before they reveal deeply personal material. In a related vein, some clients may be highly sensitive to changes in the therapeutic relationship, shutting down or ramping up their communicative output in response to perceived shifts in the therapist's attentiveness or helpfulness. Such individuals might be hard to place on this continuum. But such criticisms do not undermine the fact that people do differ in their general tendencies to disclose distressful information (Kahn et al., 2001; Larson et al., 2015).

That is, clients may fluctuate across the continuum over time but still be located at a general or most typical point on the scale. Our research also confirms the general truth of this proposition—we found that clients who score high on a measure of distress disclosure tend to score low on a measure of self-concealment in psychotherapy.

But there is another problem with a continuum that assumes an inverse relationship between disclosure and deceit. It does not allow for accurate representation of some interesting combinations of deception and honest disclosure, including those clients who are both highly disclosing and highly deceiving. For example, in our studies, about 10% of typically highly disclosing clients avoid (or are less than honest) about several highly charged, personally relevant topics, including their sexual fantasies and practices, experiences of trauma or abuse, substance use, suicidal thoughts, and the extent to which therapy is helping them. This pattern may manifest in regard to a specific topic such that clients reveal a good deal of relevant information (e.g., about their substance use or their feelings about their therapist) while simultaneously concealing some of the more shameful aspects of this part of their lives (e.g., instances of blackout drunkenness, sexual feelings toward a therapist). It may also manifest across topics, in a pattern wherein clients speak openly and fully about most aspects of their lives but keep other significant parts of themselves (e.g., their suicidal thoughts) completely secret.

In fact, several such patterns may manifest in therapy. In this vein, Figure 4.1 offers a potentially useful if imperfect perspective on the complex relationship between honest disclosure and lying and secret keeping. The 2 × 2 window here suggests four patterns. These are prototypes, of

	High disclosure	Low disclosure
High lies/secrets	Clients with borderline personality disorder	Clients with antisocial/psychopathic personality disorder
Low lies/secrets	Healthy clients	Introverted clients

Figure 4.1. Prototypes of psychotherapy clients with different combinations of disclosure and deception.

course, meaning that many individuals will not fit neatly into one of these patterns. Moreover, as the therapeutic relationship evolves and strengthens or enters a period rife with therapeutic ruptures, clients' disclosure–lying profiles may shift.

The top left box of this figure indicates that some individuals may be high on the dimensions of both disclosure and deception. This group is primarily, though not exclusively, composed of those who would be diagnosed with a personality disorder, especially BPD. These clients can often be expected to be both quite revealing about many aspects of their lives, even details of early abuse, and quite deceptive about many others—for example, their drug or alcohol use or their role in conflicts with others.

Another category in this figure (bottom left) refers to individuals who are high on disclosure and low in deception. These are the healthier clients who tend to consistently (though not invariably) speak the truth about their experiences, at least to the best of their current ability. They may have secrets—again, we all do—and there may even be pockets of lies about topics that exceed their generally high capacity to endure shame, but for the most part, they are reliable narrators.

There are two other categories noted in this figure. One represents clients (top right of the figure) who are low on honest disclosure but high on lies and concealment. This configuration and that noted previously are the patterns that several researchers have posited as normative—that is, reflecting an inverse relationship between honesty and concealment. The prototype here (top right) is the client with psychopathic tendencies, from whom it is difficult to obtain an honest story. As many theorists and clinicians (e.g., McWilliams, 1994) have documented, psychotherapy with individuals with psychopathic tendencies means working with a great deal of lies and, at least initially, few truths.

The last category in this figure (bottom right) refers to those clients who are low in terms of both disclosure and deception. These are people whom clinicians might label as introverted, though they might view themselves as simply private. These are individuals who reveal little of their lives to others but tend not to lie either, especially if asked direct questions about their lives. This is an especially imperfect category because although such individuals tend not to lie, their introversion can lead to concealment and secret keeping. The conceptual problem here stems from combining lies and secrets into one constituent element within this figure. Whereas secrets and lies may overlap as forms of deceitful concealment of relevant personal information, for some individuals, keeping secrets or at least seeming reluctant to share information is more functionally linked to privacy than deceit. They are not truly dissembling but rather making it difficult to be known. Per the singer–songwriter Neil Young ("Only Love Can Break Your Heart"):

"I have a friend I've never seen." Such clients often struggle to reveal themselves in therapy but may do so eventually in the context of a patient, caring, and gently inquisitive therapist.

Thus, both these templates—a single continuum reflecting clients' tendency to disclosure and a four-category matrix of disclosure and deception—offer a partial understanding of the relationship between disclosure and deception. They are simple models inasmuch as they do not reflect the multiple variables affecting either the tendency to disclose or to lie, nor do they allow for possible differences in motives between lying and secret keeping. But, as noted earlier, there is both empirical evidence and intuitive reasonableness underlying the assumption that clients who tend to speak openly and honestly about their concerns are generally less likely to lie extensively or keep secrets.

THE COMPLEX RELATION OF DISCLOSURE (AND LIES) TO TREATMENT OUTCOME

Although full disclosure in the vein of Freud's *fundamental rule* (1913/1958)—that clients should discuss every thought that comes to mind—is surely an unattainable ideal, it is a widespread clinical belief that honest communication is a critical part of what makes therapy beneficial (Stiles, 1995). The very structure of the therapy process, which places a premium on protected boundaries and confidentiality, is meant to encourage what Stiles (1995) termed *expressive disclosure*—that is, revealing one's important thoughts and feelings for nonstrategic purposes.

It has been difficult to find empirical evidence that greater client disclosure leads to better treatment outcome or, conversely, that more client secret keeping and lying leads to poor treatment outcome. This is at least partially because, as Stiles (1995) noted, more-distressed clients (i.e., those for whom better outcomes are more difficult to obtain) often produce more in-depth personal disclosures than less-distressed clients.

But if dishonesty does tend to exert a negative effect on therapeutic outcome, what is the pathway by which this occurs? Whether the deception is verbalized or hidden—manifest actively (through lying) or passively (through secret keeping)—it often has significant consequences for the process of therapy, As Newman and Strauss (2003) noted,

> Clients sometimes knowingly give false or misleading information, maintain counter therapeutic hidden agendas, and deliberately obscure clinically relevant facts. Such factors likely will obstruct the process of case conceptualization, strain the therapeutic relationship, and result in disagreements about proper interventions. (p. 241)

Dishonesty can also be distressing to clients. As several researchers (e.g., Jourard, 1971; Lane & Wegner, 1995) have postulated, keeping secrets goes beyond the lack of disclosure; it involves a constant conscious struggle to avoid becoming known by another. Maintaining the facade of dishonesty, especially about an important topic, requires effort that can siphon involvement away from the therapy process, including the possibility of a positive therapist response to a difficult disclosure (Slepian, Masicampo, & Galinsky, 2016).

When discovered, client dishonesty can also effect highly negative reactions in the therapist (Gediman & Lieberman, 1996), evoking feelings of frustration, futility, sadness, or even rage at being tricked or betrayed. Omitted information may be experienced less intensely than active lying because it represents less aggression toward the therapist and because undisclosed material may be discussed by clients at a later, seemingly more propitious time. In any case, the sense that something is awry can cause the therapist to overcompensate, actively trying to ferret out the client's dishonesty by "playing detective," or to withdraw defensively, becoming so overcome by the possibility of being deceived that he or she will pretend not to know what is happening.

The inconsistency in the empirical literature on the effects of dishonesty on psychotherapy also reflects the underlying methodology of the various inquiries. The definitions of the variables attempting to capture client dishonesty share some overlap but are still somewhat distinct; secrets, things left unsaid, hidden reactions, and overt lies all capture certain portions of the spectrum of client dishonesty, but each, to the extent that they exist in a "pure" state, are likely to have different effects on the therapeutic process and outcome. Concealment may be forever (becoming a never-revealed secret), or it may gradually dissipate; a nondiscussed topic may eventually become a discussed topic. Nevertheless, what does seem clear is that different clients with different histories, symptom pictures, and therapeutic goals have different needs, including different time frames, for truth telling and that lack of disclosure does not always reflect a wholly dysfunctional therapeutic process. Some clients may share excessively as a way of creating a barrier from the information that matters, whereas others may keep secrets as a way of establishing safety or autonomy until they become more comfortable. But ultimately, the ability to share as honestly as possible about the issues and feelings that truly matter to a particular client is likely to be facilitative in creating the conditions for positive process and outcome.

Before focusing more extensively on our research and specific types of client lies and secrets (Chapters 6–11), we next turn to an examination of lies and secrets of the other member of the therapeutic dyad, the therapist him- or herself.

5

THERAPIST DECEPTION

> Since we demand strict truthfulness from our patients, we jeopardize our whole authority if we let ourselves be caught by them in a departure from the truth.
>
> —Sigmund Freud, "Observations on Transference-Love," *Collected Papers*, Volume XXXIII

In some ways, we are faced with the same dilemmas in describing therapist lies (broadly defined) as we were in discussing the nature of client lies. In both cases, it is difficult to distinguish among such overlapping categories as secrets, hidden reactions, things left unsaid, partial disclosures, obfuscations, and overt lies; in both cases, motives can stem from such diverse sources as the wish to preserve the therapeutic relationship, the need to avoid shame, the wish to enhance oneself in the eyes of the other, and perhaps most commonly, the wish to be tactful (i.e., not hurt the other).

Still, as noted in the senior author's (BAF) previous book, *Self-Disclosure in Psychotherapy* (Farber, 2006), although client and therapist disclosures and nondisclosures share some common features, they are not truly complementary phenomena. In large measure, clients are in therapy to reveal themselves openly and honestly in the service of being helped; the same cannot be said of the therapists. The communicative imperatives of client and therapist are

http://dx.doi.org/10.1037/0000128-006
Secrets and Lies in Psychotherapy, by B. A. Farber, M. Blanchard, and M. Love

informed by quite different role expectations. Although their honest reactions to their clients' words and behaviors are often instrumental in facilitating an effective therapeutic relationship and ultimately effecting change, and although therapist genuineness is prized in many therapeutic traditions (e.g., humanistic psychotherapies, dialectical behavior therapy), therapists are not expected to share their innermost thoughts about their lives, only those (selective) thoughts that might be helpful to the client. According to Rogers (1957), the extent to which the therapist's feelings are shared with clients is a complex matter but is essentially based on two related principles: that therapist disclosure is appropriate and necessary to the extent that it facilitates the therapeutic relationship, and that such disclosure is guided by the need to avoid the possibility of a therapist being perceived by the client as disingenuous. Regarding this last point, Rogers offered the following: "Certainly the aim is not for the therapist to express or talk out his own feelings, but primarily that he should not be deceiving the client" (p. 242).

It is often difficult for therapists to determine how much personal information they should share with clients. Therapists may feel swayed by the allure of genuineness; they may be aware that some of their clients seem to feel more connected when some personal information is shared (though, of course, this can be a slippery slope), and they may also sense that some clients disclose more readily about their disorder when therapists acknowledge that they have experienced similar feelings or thoughts themselves. Regarding this last point, nearly a quarter of the respondents in one of our studies indicated they would be more willing to disclose honestly about a difficult topic if they knew their therapist had a similar problem. Carl Rogers, while working with a quite depressed, suicidal young man said to him,

> I don't know whether this will help or not, but I would just like to say that—I think I can understand pretty well—what it's like to feel that you're just no damn good to anybody, because there was a time when I felt that way about myself, and I know it can be really rough. (Rogers, Gendlin, Kiesler, & Truax, 1967, p. 405)

Judiciously acknowledging their own struggles with addiction is something that substance abuse counselors routinely do. But exceptions aside, therapists who share excessively about their experiences or personal lives are typically acting improperly and nontherapeutically and are insufficiently aware of their own narcissistic needs. Therapists who conceal the nature of their sex life or family relationships are not acting deceptively but rather appropriately. Far more often than not, therapists have no warrant for disclosing intimate personal information to their clients.

We know then that there are distinct differences in the meaning and appropriateness of disclosure, secrets, and lies for therapists compared with clients. But we also know that therapists do sometimes conceal and lie about significant therapy-related issues, including their feelings about their client's diagnosis or therapeutic progress, their availability, their mood or feelings, and their memory of what they have been told. Furthermore, we know that at times it can be difficult to distinguish between seemingly appropriate therapist nondisclosure—either of personal information or therapy-relevant information (e.g., relating to a client's diagnosis or a therapist's personal feelings)—and seemingly inappropriate concealment or outright lies. It is relatively easy to distinguish these categories at their extremes, but there is often a good deal of middle ground. Influenced by the perceived need for clinical *tact*—typically some combination of sparing the client (at least at this particular moment) some hard-to-process information and wishing to maintain an effective therapeutic alliance—therapists withhold and/or distort information—perhaps about feelings about the client—that some would consider clinically appropriate and others (clients included) would consider deceitful. Even seemingly appropriate nondisclosure of personal information—for example, not telling a client where one is going on vacation—can feel like a significant, hurtful secret to some patients. Note the following post from a therapy client:

> He asked me what I was doing for Xmas and I told him. I then asked him and he told me where he was going. But a few months later he was due to go on holiday again. I then took it for granted that he would tell me again but he didn't and was so vague and said he was going overseas. And I was devastated that he didn't want to tell me this time. And for the whole 3 weeks he was away I just cried and cried. When he got back it was one of the hardest sessions that I ever had. (Johnson, 2013)

More pointedly, when a therapist moves from nondisclosure of personal information to active deceit (e.g., lying about where he or she is going on vacation), a typically "discussable" situation becomes one in which there is great potential for serious and enduring clinical consequences. Although it is relatively easy to state that a therapist should never outright lie to a client, it is far more difficult to state with any certainty rules about therapeutic tact—about if and when and to what extent it is appropriate to reveal one's feelings (positive or negative) about a client or to acknowledge one's emotional or physical limitations (either of the moment or those of a chronic nature) or to let a client know what his or her working diagnosis is. In this regard, Gabbard and Wilkinson (2000) wisely observed,

> Unloading our feelings on the patient simply because those feelings are difficult to bear is certainly an abuse of psychotherapy . . . [but] failure to disclose powerful affects will also influence the patient. . . . The real issues for the therapist are to what extent feelings should be

> articulated and what mode of communication will maximize tact and minimize hurt. (p. 170)

They added the following caveat:

> Certainly there are some statements a therapist must never make to the patient. In addition to "I hate you," it is never productive to say "You bore me," because the therapist has not contracted for entertainment when a psychotherapy process has begun. (p. 170)

Among others, Gabbard (2014) noted that therapists constantly make judgments about what patients say or do, and although they sometimes share these thoughts and feelings with their patients, often they do not.

Thus, as is so often the case with clinical material, so much of what is appropriate for the therapist to reveal or not—even perhaps to tactfully lie about—is context dependent. The classic *specificity question* posed about the effects of psychotherapy (Paul, 1967) is, which types of therapy administered by which kinds of therapists to which kinds of clients having which kinds of problems produce which kinds of effects? The analogous question here about therapist concealment and lies might be, which kinds of omissions and lies told by which kinds of therapists at which point in therapy to which kinds of clients have what kinds of immediate and enduring effects on therapy and the therapeutic relationship? As with the first question, the number of variables in this second question makes definitive answers virtually impossible.

Answers to even basic questions about the nature or consequences of therapist concealment or lies are difficult to obtain because the literature on the topic is remarkably sparse. The great preponderance of what has been written about this area focuses on therapist self-disclosure, a topic that has engaged researchers and clinicians for decades (for reviews, see Farber, 2006; Henretty & Levitt, 2010; S. Knox & Hill, 2003). This literature has affirmed the value of therapist disclosure (broadly defined): Clients tend to prefer therapists who disclose, viewing them as warmer, and also tend to disclose more to therapists who disclose (i.e., "disclosure begets disclosure"). But as we noted earlier, disclosure and lies are not antithetical. Therapist disclosure may well be a good thing, at least in moderation (see especially S. Knox & Hill, 2003, in this regard), but the fact that about 90% of therapists tend to be somewhat self-disclosing tells us little about how many or on what issues or with what consequences therapists tend to lie or conceal therapy-relevant thoughts or feelings.

Our research lab has begun collecting data on the nature and extent of therapist deception (see the next section), but what has been written so far about this topic is primarily contained in several therapist blogs that include follow-up comments posted by other therapists and clients. Although this hardly constitutes a sound scientific basis for understanding this phenomenon, these accounts do provide material for generating hypotheses about patterns or norms.

THERAPIST CONCEALMENT AND LIES: WHAT WE CAN LEARN FROM ONLINE BLOGS

Many of the most telling stories and quotes about therapist lies and significant concealment of therapy-related material comes from the online journal of Joseph Burgo (AfterPsychotherapy.com).[1] The following is part of his entry on the blog dedicated to the topic "Lying to Our Clients" (first posted April 12, 2013):

> In thinking back over my years in practice, I can identify several instances where I lied to my clients, all of them involving shame or feelings of embarrassment. These were lies of omission. In my early years as a therapist, if a client accurately observed that I looked sleepy or stressed, rather than acknowledging the truth, I'd usually address their anxiety concerning what they perceived about my health or state of mind. In one sense, this is a perfectly valid therapeutic approach because it is the client's feelings, after all, that are the focus of the work. On the other hand, such interpretations can subtly imply that what the client accurately perceives is "only" a projection; sometimes, it can feel crazy-making, not to have your perceptions validated.
>
> What about deliberate falsehoods? I can't remember any instances when I consciously and intentionally lied to a client, but it's possible I may have forgotten. To me, this type of lying seems much more serious . . . it's inevitable that we will commit unconscious (and sometimes barely conscious) lies of omission. We're only human. But when we tell deliberate falsehoods, we betray our profession and undermine the very nature of the work we do. (para. 8)

Burgo (2013) nicely pointed out here the important distinction between therapist lies of *omission* and *commission*, contrasting the inevitability and typically benign nature of nondisclosure with the far more infrequent and more toxic nature of a deliberate falsehood. Although we believe he is essentially right—that lies of omission, of concealment, are typically without great consequence, we believe this is not always the case, especially with clients with borderline personality disorder or, more broadly, those with borderline features. These clients are often acutely aware of what is being left out of the dialogue—of what therapists have left unsaid—especially if such omissions

[1]From "Lying to Our Clients," by J. Burgo, 2013, on *After Psychotherapy*. Retrieved from http://www.afterpsychotherapy.com/lying-to-our-clients. Copyright 2013 by Joseph Burgo. Reprinted with permission.

touch on their need for affirmation or, worse, feel like a proxy for their therapist's disappointment or disapproval. These clients have a pronounced tendency to rejection sensitivity (e.g., Staebler, Helbing, Rosenbach, & Renneberg, 2011), to overreact to perceptions of interpersonal hurt. Even subtle rejection cues may trigger anger and fear and cause disruptions in the therapeutic relationship. Thus, perceived omissions on the therapist's part (e.g., "She's not telling me what she really feels"; "Even though she's not saying it, I know she's angry") or, similarly, perceived incongruity between a therapist's statements and his or her emotional tone or body language (e.g., "I hear what she's saying, but she doesn't look like she means it") may be clinically problematic, at least for some patients some of the time.

The following is an example of this scenario from a client who posted a response to Burgo's (2013) blog. We do not know, of course, and do not at all presume that this client has features of borderline personality disorder. This response reinforces our point that certain forms of therapist deceit do not have to rise to the level of overt lies to have significant therapeutic consequences:

> I do catch therapists, let's call it—contradicting themselves. I listen very intently to everything being said so it is easy for me to recognize a false statement. . . . What annoys me more than being lied to is hearing from a therapist or anyone that tone where you know that they are simply agreeing with you because they think that's what you want to hear. Then later on when the situation changes then they go back on what they originally said in agreement with you. (Does that make sense?) It is in those moments when you lose all faith in that person and wonder what else they have been lying to you about. (Sheila A., 2013)

More generally, although it is a valuable contribution to this understudied topic, this short piece by Burgo (2013) on therapist lies focuses on only one fairly specific area—a therapist's disavowal of feeling sleepy or stressed—and one general motivation—shame. Responses to this blog, primarily from therapy clients, suggest that there are multiple ways in which therapists sometimes lie and multiple motivations for their doing so. The following are some examples:

> Yes I think a therapist lied to me. She was away for a period of time and I had to see someone else until she returned and she told me when she did return that she had broken her foot. I did not believe her. (Pridham, 2013)

> When I was in therapy I wrote down a list of about 6 or 7 subjects I wanted to talk about. Months later most of them remained unaddressed so I told the therapist about it. She told me we had talked about them

> all. She would read out a subject I had written down on the list like "Teacher bullying" and then she would claim that we had talked about this subject and she would even attempt to recall the story, clearly making it all up. This broke my trust in her completely. (Gordon, 2013)

> I have been seeing a therapist for four months and he has lied to me at times. It is silly things like where he went to college (all that info is online) bragging kind of things. (Molly, 2014)

> I had a therapist who was very kind and supportive. He was working for a community health team but had a private practice on the side where he only sees people on Saturdays. He told me that he closed that up, that he was no longer doing it. Then at a much later date he said that he wasn't able to attend something because he had a client coming to see him. I didn't question him about it and was only mildly irritated because he had been so accommodating of me and my major depression. However, I wonder if there was anything else that he wasn't honest about. (Sheila A., 2013)

> My former therapist looked like he was going to fall asleep, and when I asked if he was tired he looked down at his cup and said, "I have my tea." I told him, "I just want you to know it's unnerving." He didn't reply. I felt angry and distant from him. I couldn't understand why he didn't feel safe enough to admit he was tired. (Sarah, 2013)

All therapist lies, of course, are not equally damaging. Some are never picked up on by clients. Some that are caught may be readily forgiven by clients intent on preserving the relationship. But some lies may lead to ruptures in the relationship that necessitate a good deal of subsequent negotiation and repair. And some therapist lies may never be forgiven by clients, leading either to immediate termination or an impaired relationship that ends with frustration at some later point. The following is an example of the damage that can be done by lying—or, more accurately, denying one's true feelings—to clients:

> If the therapist is angry at the patient but denies it, such a response compounds the difficulty. In addition to the knowledge that the therapist is angry, the patient also knows that the therapist is dishonest. The patient will then wonder, "If the therapist lies in this situation am I also being lied to in other situations?" (Gabbard & Wilkinson, 2000, p. 169)

Although written specifically to note the difficulties in working with patients with borderline disturbance, this caveat is relevant to clinical work with a wide range of clients.

With the caveat that clients who post about their experiences with therapist lies are likely those who are angriest about or least forgiving of them, the following are two further examples posted on Burgo's (2013) blog of the potential adverse consequences of therapist lies:

> On the few occasions that there might have been "lies from omission" it has significantly disrupted our communication as I have had a sense of something going on, but . . . my experience hasn't been validated. . . . I definitely feel that I can read him quite well—certainly well enough to know when there is something not being said. (Lizzie, 2013)

> Being lied to by a therapist is not a good feeling. It is betrayal of the trust we place in the therapist and trust doesn't come easy. It makes me feel like I can't be trusted to hear the truth—at times this may be true but that is my issue not theirs. And I feel it is just downright disrespectful. (Sheila A., 2013)

To this point, all client posts we have quoted have referenced therapist lies or omissions that were hurtful and/or destructive to the relationship. But several other posts on Burgo's (2013) blog acknowledged that certain therapist omissions were, in retrospect, warranted and helpful. These omissions seem to have been motivated by general considerations of tact or, similarly, therapists' sense that some hard truths about clients would be better revealed at later points in treatment—one example: "There are times as a client I have been grateful when I later learned my therapist did not tell me the whole truth because I would not have been able to handle it at the time" (John, 2013). The following is another reflection on the same theme:

> I have been out of therapy for a long time but from what I remember, she never told me an outright lie or at least I didn't pick up on it. However, I know (now) that she told many, many "lies" of omission. I think she had to—I couldn't have coped with "the truth." I think she told me as much of the truth as she thought I could bear at the time. Sometimes when I remember how deluded I was at that time, I cringe. I truly was obtuse and I thought I was an insightful, wise person. I often wonder (now) what she thought as she sat there listening to another deluded story or statement. I did get there in the end—I'm grateful for her patience and that she didn't face me with the truth too soon. (Fiona, 2013)

In response to Burgo's (2013) acknowledgment of his denial of stress and sleepiness, some (though not many) other therapists admitted to their own lapses of honesty. One therapist wrote the following:

> Like all people, we engage in lies too. These can be small, like sitting in our client's experience while de-centering from our own authentic experience, or can be bigger, like telling a client that we are not bothered by something when they ask us if we are bothered. (Jessica, 2013)

On another blog with a similar focus (http://www.quora.com/Do-psychologists-lie-to-their-patients), several therapists provided motives for their omissions and lies. According to one therapist, "Psychologists lie, much the same as some people lie. They lie for the same reasons—feeling there are things they have to hide; insecurities; not trusting patients" (Dillard, 2013). Another contributor to this last-cited blog, perhaps a therapist, perhaps not, wryly noted the following anecdote:

> During a discussion about telling people what we think of them (which I do way too much), a very good therapist asked me, "Do you think if I told my clients what I really think of them they would come back?" (Kutappa, 2013)

EMPIRICAL STUDIES OF THERAPIST DECEIT

Our perusal of the literature revealed no published empirical studies focused specifically on therapist deceit—no studies of either client perceptions of their therapists' presumed lies or deceptive behavior, nor of therapists' reports of specific lies told to clients. The one published investigation that touched at all on the issue of therapist lies featured a clever title: "Pinocchio's Nose in Therapy: Therapists' Beliefs and Attitudes Toward Client Deception" (Curtis & Hart, 2015). Although this study focused mostly on therapists' reactions toward clients' lies—not surprisingly, they tended to trust and like such clients far less after discovering the lie—one part of this work did investigate therapists' lies. Among a sample of 112 clinical and counseling psychologists, 96% acknowledged deceiving their clients by intentionally withholding information when these therapists thought to do so protected their clients. Furthermore—and this is the more startling figure—81% reported that they had directly lied to their clients. On the 7-point Likert scale used in this study (where 1 = *never* and 7 = *very often*), therapists' mean score for intentionally omitting information to protect clients was 4.0, whereas the mean score for lies per se was 2.3, suggesting that although most therapists lied occasionally, omitting information from clients was far more common. Unfortunately, the nature of therapist lies was unreported in this study.

Other data about therapist lies come from two unpublished studies. One of these is a study of disclosure among 34 clients in our clinic at Teachers College, Columbia University. One of the items presented to respondents (a rephrased item from Larson & Chastain's [1990] Self-Concealment Scale) was, "I believe my therapist doesn't always tell me the truth about me or my therapy." On the basis of a 7-point Likert scale (where 1 = *strongly disagree* and 7 = *strongly agree*), the mean score on this item was 1.2 (SD = .65), suggesting that most clients believe strongly that their therapists are consistently honest with them. This data point, in conjunction with the results of the previously mentioned Curtis and Hart (2015) study, suggests that clients are more convinced of their therapists' honesty than therapists are themselves. However, it may also be the case that when clients assess their therapists' honesty, they mainly consider the frequency or intensity of actual lies rather than what the therapist has presumably concealed. As one therapy client wrote on a blog, "Lying is a bit harsh. But they definitely mask the truth many a time" (Kutappa, 2013). If this latter hypothesis is right, clients and therapists are in agreement in believing that outright therapist lies are a rare phenomenon. Therapists, however, are more aware of what they have concealed from clients and have thus "lowered their grade" (i.e., rated themselves more severely) regarding their self-perceived honesty.

The second source of data about therapist deceit derives from an ongoing investigation of this topic by our research team at Teachers College (Jackson & Farber, 2018). From our reading of the clinical literature on therapist deceit and online blogs devoted to this issue, we constructed a survey (PATCH: Psychotherapists' Assessment of Truth, Candor, and Honesty) to investigate therapists' perceptions of the extent to which they believed they were dishonest about 23 clinical situations. This list includes only those instances of deception that take place directly between the therapist and client. Thus, for example, insurance-related instances of deceit (e.g., reporting a different fee than one is charging, reporting a diagnosis more likely to be reimbursed) are not on this list. Among the situations we included in our survey were those that reflected therapist acknowledgment of nonalertness or inattention, forgetting something a client mentioned previously in therapy, reason for lateness, the extent of clinical progress, client diagnosis, one's physical or emotional state, liking or disliking a client, feelings of frustration, and romantic or sexual feelings toward a client.

The survey was designed to assess multiple aspects of therapist deceit. For example, for one of the items—"Forgetting something a client said"—we posed the following scenario: "Sometimes it's tempting to avoid acknowledging that we've forgotten something a client has previously told us." We then asked respondents three questions about this situation, in each instance using the same 7-point Likert scale (1 = *never*, 4 = *sometimes*, 7 = *frequently*):

- How often, if ever, have you been less than completely honest when talking to a client about whether you remember something he or she previously mentioned in session?
- To what extent has this involved saying you remember something when you really didn't?
- To what extent has this involved not correcting a client's misperceptions that you remember something when you didn't?

This procedure allowed us to calculate an index of overall dishonesty for each of these 23 situations as well as separate indices of both active and passive dishonesty. At the time of writing this book, we had collected data on 271 therapists with a mean age of 39.2; on average, they had been seeing clients for 11.4 years. The sample was primarily female (80%), Caucasian (87%), heterosexual (86%), PhD or PsyD psychologists (88%) working in clinics or hospitals (59%) and/or private practice (53%); most endorsed either cognitive behavior therapy or dialectical behavior therapy (57%) or psychodynamic therapy (31%) as their primary theoretical orientation.

What did our preliminary findings indicate? First, there were several items on which fairly substantial numbers of therapists indicated that they were at least "sometimes" deceitful (i.e., had scores of 4 or higher on the 7-point scale), including feelings of frustration (49%), liking or disliking clients (45%), and deception about one's physical or mental state (43%). Another perspective, however, is offered by the fact that on none of the 23 items on the survey did the overall mean dishonesty score—or the mean scores for either passive or active dishonesty—exceed 4.0 on the 7-point scale. The items with the highest mean scores were those that were just noted: feelings of frustration ($M = 3.3$, $SD = 1.4$), liking or disliking clients ($M = 3.1$, $SD = 1.7$), and one's physical or mental state ($M = 3.1$, $SD = 1.5$).

As for items for which respondents reported overall low degrees of deception, therapists apparently are rarely deceptive about their training or credentials ($M = 1.3$, $SD = 0.8$), their fees ($M = 1.5$, $SD = 1.1$), their reasons for terminating therapy with a client ($M = 1.7$, $SD = 1.1$), and their reasons for being late or absent from sessions ($M = 1.7$, $SD = 1.2$).

When looking specifically at instances of overt therapist dishonesty (i.e., lies rather than concealment), the data indicated that expressing frustration or disappointment ($M = 2.4$, $SD = 1.4$), stating one's availability ($M = 2.3$, $SD = 1.5$), and making statements regarding one's liking or disliking a client ($M = 2.3$, $SD = 1.5$) are the three items with the highest mean scores, suggesting that although these are not egregious problems, there is something about each of these situations that provokes some degree of active dishonesty on the part of some therapists. In each case, this behavior is seemingly in the service of not engaging honestly with clients who are in some way difficult. In terms of *covert dishonesty*—allowing clients to believe that which is not true—the items with the highest mean scores were liking or disliking clients ($M = 2.8$, $SD = 1.7$) and expressing one's personal beliefs or values ($M = 2.8$, $SD = 1.7$). In the first case, this would usually mean that a therapist would not correct a client's inaccurate perception that he or she is liked by the therapist; in the second case, it would mean that the therapist would allow the client to believe something about the therapist's beliefs or values (e.g., political stance) that is not true.

Did some type of therapists tend to be more deceptive than others? In fact, yes, and in a somewhat surprising way. Nonstudent therapists who were older than 30 and in private practice for more than 5 years tended to have higher scores on these deception scales—perhaps because most (assumedly) were no longer being supervised and perhaps, as they became more experienced, were more likely to judge certain types of deception as "allowable," falling within the range of therapeutic tact.

A FIRST-PERSON ACCOUNT OF AN INSTANCE OF THERAPIST DISHONESTY

Therapist blogs, in tandem with a few sources of preliminary quantitative data, have allowed us to begin to map the domain of therapist dishonesty. Clearly, though, far more data are needed for us to more fully understand the nature of therapist lies of commission and omission, including the factors that affect the likelihood of certain types of therapist dishonesty. One factor, for example, that may increase the likelihood of some types of therapist deceit is the clinician's status as a beginning therapist. In this regard, we turn to a blog-like anecdote from one of us (MB), one self-entitled "Confessions of a Doctoral Trainee."

She was my first training client: A tough little woman from the Bronx whose paranoid and narcissistic personality features got her fired from job after job. She was a qualified paralegal with a long work history, yet she struggled to pay her electricity bill. At each new job, she would find someone on staff whose behavior was "unprofessional," someone who "has no respect," someone who was "out to get" her. With her proud bearing and hair-trigger temper, she made more enemies than friends. It was never long before people on staff really were out to get her. And she would be let go. In session, she watched me like a hawk. Her eyes on my eyes, watching for any sign of judgment or even dissent from what she was telling me. I often felt pinned in place, with little room to move. Nonetheless, we developed a real bond and made real progress.

About 7 months in, she had a conversion experience in her living room and was "born again" as an evangelical Christian. Our work took on a whole new cosmological cast. She became a veritable crusader. She was gifted with prophetic visions and could hear the Holy Spirit, yet was hounded by the devil at every turn. She joined a street-preaching church in Times Square, handing out pamphlets, picketing abortion providers, and protesting gay pride parades.

I knew what was coming. For months I tried to prepare for the day when she would try to evangelize me. I figured it would start with a question like "Are you religious?" but progress rapidly to a full-blown effort to save my soul. I spent many hours with my supervisor trying to figure out what I would say. You see, I was baptized into the Catholic Church, but I have been an atheist most of my life. Although I respect religion, I prefer not to make claims about the nature of reality beyond what is demonstrably knowable, and the existence of a deity is just too big a leap for me. I can write about my atheism now with perfect calm, but back then I was panicked that my client would find out. Keeping our alliance alive for so long had involved a lot of nodding along with her religious claims and getting quite deep into certain biblical verses. I left several sessions feeling like a chaplain. If she knew I had been a godless atheist the entire time, I could not imagine the response. I had watched her abandon half a dozen friends just for failing to believe The Word in the way she did.

For months in supervision, I tried to plan the proper response for when the day came. I was desperate for some strategy, some words to protect me. Half-heartedly, I settled on a variation on a classic psychodynamic rejoinder: "I'll be happy to tell you about my religious thoughts, but first perhaps you could tell me what makes you ask?" Yet I had almost zero confidence in this line. I felt like a soldier marching out to battle with a wooden sword. She had proven herself impervious to any number of similar interventions. She would blow through the old "what makes you ask" trick without batting an eye. I felt like a soldier marching out to battle with a wooden sword. Nonetheless, it was all I had.

It came one day in June 2015. My client was playing me a video on her iPad. It was a YouTube clip of a Southern Baptist pastor in his pulpit, decrying those falsely religious types who study the Bible just to prove how smart they are. "Do not associate with these people!" he cried. Then, as the video came to a quiet part, I saw she had turned to look at me, her lips moving. She was asking me something:

Client: So you're Jewish, right?

Therapist: Huh?

Client: You're Jewish, right? I mean, you've got some Jewish in your background?

The moment had arrived. I did not even think of the wooden sword or any of the other possible responses I had cooked up in supervision. Feeling the heat of her eyes on me, I just said, "Uh . . . yeah!" and made a sort of gesture as if tossing something over my shoulder, which I think was meant to indicate, Sure thing! I am Jewish from way back!

My client seemed inwardly pleased with my fabrication. "I thought so," she said while smiling to herself. She explained that the Holy Spirit had hinted to her that I had at least some Jewish heritage. Mortified to hear myself lying, I attempted to recover my wooden sword: "So what is it like for you to ask me about my background?" She stared back at me. What's-it-like questions never worked with this client. I tried to clarify, but my attempt to process was badly muddled, and she finally said, "Well, it's good because the Lord wants you to be saved. And I think that, while I've come to you for help, you have also learned a lot from me."

Yes, yes of course! This point I was eager to concede. Certainly, I had learned a lot from her. And in a few more heartbeats, the topic changed and the moment had safely passed. I was now Jewish in her eyes, part of an ancient religion from which her faith had sprung. I was Jewish and, therefore, off limits for conversion.

Some days after, I realized that the Jewish solution was what we both wanted. There was no doubt that I wanted to be protected from her relentless Christianity, the force that had really taken over her entire life at that point and would certainly swamp our therapy if unleashed directly into our relationship. But I think she, too, had wanted me to be Jewish because it would mean I was someplace safe from the overwhelming force of her faith and the demands it seemed to place on her. And, by her estimation, the Holy Spirit wanted it, too.

I cannot help but cringe as I tell the story, of course. Yet I find myself a bit blurry about what precisely makes it so cringeworthy. I would not say my transgression was an ethical lapse, per se. The client had no particular right to know anything about my background. Neither did it end up being a clinical error. The lie escaped notice, the client made progress, and she and I parted with genuine affection after a successful run of work. And yet I do cringe, perhaps because I took the easy way out. Faced with the messy, gutsy task of bringing my real self into the room, I decided instead to warp a bit of reality for a client whose grip on reality was not always the tightest.

Again, further research is needed to understand the nature, extent, circumstances, and motives of each type of therapist lie, their detection by clients, and perhaps most importantly, the consequences for therapy and the relationship. We end this chapter, though, with a quote from Mark Twain (1882/2009), one that we think has great relevance for the practice of psychotherapy, from his essay, *On the Decay of the Art of Lying*:

> The wise thing is for us diligently to train ourselves to lie thoughtfully, judiciously; to lie with a good object, and not an evil one; to lie for others' advantage, and not our own; to lie healingly, charitably, humanely, not cruelly, hurtfully, maliciously. (p. 24)

To the extent that Twain's wry observation holds true for therapists, we may be overestimating the consequences of many therapist untruths, privileging moral judgments over clinical judiciousness. Our colleague, Jesse Geller, has spoken of this clinical tendency as the "fetishization of honesty" (personal communication, March 22, 2017) By this, he means that obsessive adherence to the moral call to absolute honesty may be understandable and even well-meaning, but it is also frequently a short-sighted strategy and one that comes with unintended consequences. For example, I do not have to tell my patient that I was 5 minutes late for our appointment because I had forgotten about our new time to meet. I may well have to think about why this occurred and may even have to consult a peer or therapist about this lapse, but to tell my patient I had forgotten about her would likely have significantly damaged an effective long-term relationship. It is likely clinically advantageous to tell her instead that I had not left enough time to arrive at my office on time and apologize for this. This would serve as a mea culpa of sorts, acknowledging that I had not privileged our time well enough, making that mistake more acceptable and serving to protect our relationship. To be sure, this would be a lie, but one that, arguably, is clinically indicated.

In the following chapter, we return to the topic of client omissions and lies, presenting an overview of our research on this topic—our two large-scale survey studies aimed to address multiple dimensions of the phenomenon of client dishonesty, framed by the following fundamental questions: What do clients lie and keep secrets about? How prevalent are secret keeping and lying among psychotherapy clients? What do clients perceive as their most egregious secrets and lies? Why do clients lie and have secrets? What factors affect their tendency to keep secrets and lie? And finally, what do clients see as the consequences of their concealment and lies?

6

THE COLUMBIA PROJECT ON LYING IN PSYCHOTHERAPY: WHAT DID 1,345 PSYCHOTHERAPY CLIENTS TELL US?

> Lying is man's only privilege over all other organisms. . . . Not one truth has ever been reached without first lying fourteen times or so; maybe a hundred and fourteen, and that's honorable in its own way.
>
> —Fyodor Dostoevsky, *Crime and Punishment*

Whenever we present our research on client dishonesty, no matter how large or small the audience, there is always someone who challenges the direction of our questioning. Why would we survey and interview clients about lying? Are we out to catch them? Surely clients have a right to share what they want to share in therapy and to conceal what they do not feel ready to discuss. Is there not something accusatory, something at the very least shame inducing, about the entire thrust of our research?

These questions are good ones. The answers—the real reasons we study client dishonesty—can be found in poignant stories shared by clients like Sarah, a woman in her mid-20s who sought psychotherapy to deal with post-traumatic stress disorder–like symptoms after a traumatic assault. Throughout her 2-year individual treatment, she found herself concealing the fact that the trauma had ever happened. Sarah had plenty of good reasons for concealment: She feared becoming too upset to keep her composure, too upset

http://dx.doi.org/10.1037/0000128-007
Secrets and Lies in Psychotherapy, by B. A. Farber, M. Blanchard, and M. Love

to advocate for herself if she wanted to stop the discussion, too upset and ashamed to even remember what she wanted to tell her therapist, and too upset to allow herself to believe that her therapist could understand or help. Yet she also left therapy frustrated and feeling more alone. "I couldn't be honest about the main reason why I was seeking therapy, so I feel that it prevented me from making any real progress at all." The other side of this story, though not as poignant or consequential as Sarah's side, would reveal the frustration and pained helplessness of her therapist, someone who truly wanted to help but did not have the means to do so.

Few of the 1,345 clients we surveyed liked being or feeling dishonest. Like Sarah, they were often conflicted, frustrated, or confused and decided concealment or outright dishonesty was their best option. Yet also like Sarah, they frequently wished their therapist could have helped them be more honest, helped them make a tough disclosure or reveal a secret, or somehow freed them to stop perpetuating a lie. The real reasons we study client dishonesty have nothing to do with "catching" clients or making moral judgments. We study dishonesty not to end dishonesty, which we see as the right of all clients, but to learn how to better foster honesty when our clients need it. Our research suggests that most clients want to discuss the important secrets of their lives, but that they often need our help.

In this chapter, we discuss in greater detail than in previous chapters what we have learned about client dishonesty from two national surveys conducted by the Psychotherapy, Technology, and Disclosure Lab at Teachers College, Columbia University (overseen by the senior author [BAF]). Our first major survey asked 547 clients what they had lied about in therapy, with our choice of the word *lying* being a deliberate one. Our goal was to capture the client's felt experience of being dishonest, and pilot testing showed that *lying* was the clearest way for respondents to get this and understand that we were not simply asking about topics that had not come up in their therapy. Study 1 collected hundreds of examples of both active dishonesty (telling a lie) and passive concealment or avoidance (lying by omission). As it happened, and as we noted previously, 93% of all respondents could recall at least one time they had lied during psychotherapy, and most could recall lying about two, three, four, or even eight, 12, or 20 different topics. Study 1's online delivery platform allowed hundreds of clients to type in personal stories about a time when they had lied, what their motive was, and how it had affected them.

Although the Study 1 findings were intriguing, we knew we had captured only one angle of a wide phenomenon. Study 2 would help us see client dishonesty in several additional dimensions. For starters, there was the dimension of time. We knew that the vast majority of clients could recall moments when they lied about at least one topic with their therapist. But beyond single-incident lies, how many clients would report a more ongoing or routine pattern of dishonesty? How many would say that they are generally not honest about certain topics? As expected, when we asked about the sense of being dishonest on a continuing basis, the prevalence of dishonesty fell somewhat to 84% of the 798 clients queried in Study 2 but clearly remained quite high. Study 2 also allowed us to experiment with semantics. What would happen if we dropped the word *lying* and instead asked people to rate how *honest* they were with their therapist? As it happened, this positive spin appeared to have little effect on the type of material offered by respondents. And finally, Study 2 broached what might be the most important question of the project: "How could your therapist make you feel more comfortable being honest about this?" Thanks again to the online platform we used for Study 2, hundreds of clients could offer their perspective on changes to clinical practice that might foster honesty on a wide range of topics.

We set out to remedy some of the limitations of previous research. First, much of the best-known work on client dishonesty had been conducted with small samples. For example, Hill, Thompson, Cogar, and Denman's 1993 qualitative study of "covert processes" was designed to capture subtle "hidden reactions" and "things left unsaid" between client and therapist and so understandably involved only 26 clients. Larger sample quantitative studies also had limitations. Pope and Tabachnick (1994) queried 476 people in therapy, but all were psychotherapists themselves, suggesting a level of education, income, and psychological sophistication well above the general therapy-using population. Similarly, a study by Martin (2006) drew a sample of 109 clients, all of whom were graduate students studying to become psychologists.

Our instinct was to cast the widest possible net, distributing our first online survey via Craigslist volunteer opportunities sites to 13 large metropolitan areas in the United States: New York, Los Angeles, Chicago, Boston, San Francisco, Houston, Philadelphia, Atlanta, Miami, Seattle, Phoenix, Denver, and Washington, DC. We added 28 smaller cities and rural areas for our second survey. This enabled us to reach 547 clients with our first survey and 798 with the second; less than 20% of respondents had a job or training in the mental health field. Our respondents ranged in age from 18 to 80 (mean age was 35), and they tended to be quite well-educated, with 57% having a college degree. In terms of gender and race, our sample was 22% male and 24% nonwhite, which although not representative of the general population, resembles the subset of the population that uses mental health services in the United States, as captured in annual surveys by the federal government's Substance Abuse and Mental Health Services Administration (2011, 2014).

A subtler limitation of previous studies we sought to address had to do with survey design. Previous studies tended to start out by asking respondents a single question to separate those who had been dishonest in therapy from those who had not. Such *filter questions* can take on outsized importance in a survey, at a single stroke ruling some people in and other people out, so they must be used with caution. For example, the filter question in Martin (2006) asked, "Since your 18th birthday, other than in an intake session, have you ever lied to a therapist during a therapy session?" (p. 44). To answer such a question accurately would require quite a lot from the survey taker. It could mean mentally reviewing years of therapy, a task that is likely beyond the cognitive capacity or commitment level of most respondents. Not surprisingly, only 37% of Martin's sample reported having ever lied to their therapist, a far lower number than that suggested by the body of research on lying in everyday life (e.g., DePaulo, Kashy, Kirkendol, Wyer, & Epstein, 1996; Serota, Levine, & Boster, 2010), where we see at least 40% of people having told one or more lies in just the past 24 hours. The approach in our first survey was to skip the filter question altogether to avoid overtaxing our respondents' memory. Instead, we presented a diverse list of 58 topics that respondents might have lied about—from "times I cheated on a partner" to "why I was late or missed a session" or "my use of drugs or alcohol." Respondents had only to click the box next to any lie that jogged their memory. Alternatively, they could respond, "No, I have never lied to my therapist," which only 7% did. Our memory-jogging approach gave us access to small but fascinating lies that could have otherwise been forgotten.

That goal, to capture big and small acts of dishonesty alike, also propelled us to break down a long-standing semantic barrier in the field between "secrets" and other types of dishonesty such as "lies." Up to now, secrets have been the main preoccupation in studies of client dishonesty. Beginning with Norton, Feldman, and Tafoya in 1974, psychotherapy researchers have used filter questions asking whether there was "something important they had kept secret" (Pope & Tabachnick, 1994) or whether there were "any secrets that you have not disclosed to your therapist that seem relevant to your treatment" (Baumann & Hill, 2016). The focus on secrets is understandable. Secrets are by definition at least moderately important. It is not quite a secret if you do not mention getting intoxicated on a Friday night, for example, but it becomes a secret if, while intoxicated, you totaled the family car or relapsed from a long period of sobriety. Secrets also get "kept" for periods of time and are thus at least moderately persistent features of a client's experience. The danger of focusing on secrets, then, is precisely that you get the seemingly important and persistent topics of dishonesty at the expense of the seemingly minor and ephemeral. And as we see in the next section, this can be a major limitation indeed. To our great astonishment, the number one most commonly reported topic of dishonesty found in our first study was not something most people would consider a secret at all, but yet its importance goes right to the heart of the therapeutic experience.

WHAT PEOPLE LIE ABOUT IN THERAPY

Predictions based on the mostly secrets-focused past research led us to include the classic topics such as sex, substance abuse, and suicidal thoughts—each of which ended up being important findings for us and are prominently discussed in this book. But we also included some innovative items, one of which was by far the most common lie being reported. It was "I minimized how bad I really feel," and it was endorsed by 54% of all respondents (see Table 6.1). That so many therapy clients selected this topic out of dozens of possible topics was striking. This "minimizing" was nearly twice as common as other types of dishonesty we imagined would be almost universal, such as "Why I missed appointments or was late." In addition, the second most common item was similar: "I minimized the severity of my symptoms," which was reported by 39% of the sample. Both items had originally appeared mixed among all the other 57 options, each paired with its opposite (e.g., "I exaggerated how bad I really feel"). These opposites, which asked about exaggeration rather than minimizing, were endorsed by only 6%. Clearly, the idea of minimizing one's suffering had struck a chord with our sample.

We came to call this type of client dishonesty *distress minimization*, and it appeared that taken together, 62% had endorsed one or both of these lies about their level of suffering in therapy. What is more, this distress minimization was not an area of subtle downplaying or slight shading of the truth. When asked to what extent they felt they had minimized their suffering, three fourths of these individuals reported "moderate" or higher levels of dishonesty. Further, the types of distress they minimized were highly relevant to their progress in therapy. When asked how important their minimization had been to their therapy, slightly more than 80% said it was either "important" or "very important."

Overall, the survey collected a total of 4,616 lies from all respondents. As noted in Chapter 1, the average number of topics lied about was 8.4 (range 0–39, $SD = 6.6$), with no difference observed between men and women or between income or education levels or based on the gender of the therapist. A small but significant correlation with age ($r = -.16$, $p < .001$) suggests that younger clients are more likely to report a greater number of topics about which they had lied. The majority of topics were selected by between 5% and 25% of respondents, including lies about eating habits, self-harm, infidelity, violent fantasies, experiences of physical or sexual abuse, religious beliefs, lies to get a certain prescription, and many more.

TABLE 6.1
Lies Reported by Therapy Clients in Study 1 ($N = 547$)

Topic	n	Percent reporting lie
1. How bad I really feel—I minimized	295	54
2. The severity of my symptoms—I minimized	212	39
3. My thoughts about suicide	172	31
4. My insecurities and doubts about myself	167	31
5. Pretending to like my therapist's comments or suggestions	161	29
6. My use of drugs or alcohol	159	29
7. Why I missed appointments or was late	157	29
8. Pretending to find therapy more effective than I do	156	29
9. Pretending to be more hopeful than I really am	145	27
10. Things I have done that I regret	141	26
11. Pretending I did homework or took other actions suggested by my therapist	140	26
12. My sexual history	119	22
13. My eating habits	113	21
14. My real opinion of my therapist	100	18
15. My feelings about my body	99	18
16. My sexual fantasies or desires	93	17
17. Not saying that I want to end therapy	86	16
18. Self-harm I have done (cutting, etc.)	85	16
19. What I really want for myself	83	15
20. Things I have done that were illegal	81	15
21. Things my parents did that affected me	81	15
22. Secrets in my family	75	14
23. How I really act outside of therapy	73	13
24. The state of my sex life these days	72	13
25. Basic facts about my life	71	13
26. My real feelings about my parents	71	13
27. My masturbation habits	69	13
28. That my therapist makes me feel weird or uncomfortable	67	12
29. How I really act in relationships	62	11
30. The way I give in to others' demands	61	11
31. Experiences of sexual abuse or trauma	56	10
32. My attempts to commit suicide	55	10
33. My real feelings about my friends	55	10
34. My desire for revenge	54	10
35. How I am mistreated by others	54	10
36. A sexual problem I have had	53	10
37. My real feelings about my spouse or partner	53	10
38. Times I cheated on my spouse or partner	52	10
39. Violent fantasies I have had	51	9
40. My use of pornography	50	9
41. How I really act with my friends	45	8
42. What I can afford to pay for therapy	45	8
43. Placing blame on others when much of it lies with me	44	8
44. My accomplishments (academic, professional, etc.)	39	7

TABLE 6.1
Lies Reported by Therapy Clients in Study 1 ($N = 547$) (*Continued*)

Topic	*n*	Percent reporting lie
45. Unusual experiences (e.g., seeing things, hearing voices)	39	7
46. Experiences of physical abuse or trauma	35	6
47. How bad I really feel—I exaggerated	34	6
48. Religious or mystical beliefs that I hold	33	6
49. The severity of my symptoms—I exaggerated	33	6
50. My romantic or sexual feelings about my therapist	27	5
51. Lies to get a certain prescription	26	5
52. Cruel things I have done to people or animals	25	5
53. Racist feelings I have had	25	5
54. Not saying that I am seeing another therapist	16	3
55. Political beliefs that I hold	15	3
56. Lies to get a certain diagnosis	15	3
57. The way I treat my children sometimes	12	2
58. My real feelings about my children	9	2

In addition to the high prevalence of distress minimization, the results contained genuine surprises. For example, we found that 31% of the sample had lied about having suicidal thoughts, a sobering number given the potential consequences. We also found that six of the 20 most common lies were about the patient's experience of therapy itself, including pretending to like a therapist's comments or suggestions, which was endorsed by 29% of the sample. In subsequent chapters, we discuss in depth several of the most common lies, including those related to suicide and distress minimization (Chapter 7) and those related to therapy and the therapist (Chapter 11). Other surprises included the relatively small proportion of the sample that endorsed certain topics, including one's behavior in relationships (11%), feelings about one's spouse or romantic partner (10%), and romantic or sexual feelings about one's therapist (5%). We had imagined that these relational issues would have been endorsed by greater numbers of our sample.

Back to the issue of distress minimization—therapy is supposed to be the one place where it is safe to explore the depths of one's psychological pain. Indeed, the special confidentiality of therapy is designed to foster this honesty. Could it be that clients routinely downplay the extent of their suffering? Could the majority of clients be acting happier and healthier during therapy sessions than they really feel? If so, why? Is it to please their therapist? To avoid seeming too needy or hopeless? To avoid seeming too disturbed or pathological? To avoid therapist overreaction? Could such minimizing be a personal trait? Or perhaps the result of something about the therapeutic relationship?

The mystery of distress minimization provides a chance to describe the design of our first round of research further. Endorsing any one topic of dishonesty led to opportunities for clients to tell us to what extent they were dishonest about this topic and how important this topic was to their therapy. Data were also collected about clients' level of trust in their therapist and their tendency toward self-concealment generally (Self-Concealment Scale; Larson & Chastain, 1990). Finally, participants could choose one of the topics they found it hardest to be honest about to answer a set of detailed follow-up questions, including open-ended essay-box questions where they could write about their experiences in their own words. Their narratives provide a quite vivid picture of the circumstances and consequences of their dishonesty, though it is also important to keep in mind that these are descriptions offered by those who struggled most to be honest about a given topic, and their responses may not be typical of all clients who have lied about this topic.

Our distress minimizers tended to be younger and less satisfied with therapy. They were less likely than other respondents to endorse the statement "I trust my therapist" and had a higher tendency to self-conceal in general. They tended to feel regretful, guilty, and frustrated about downplaying their distress, and they reported negative effects on therapy of doing so, with most saying that this particular form of dishonesty had hurt their progress (68%) and prevented them from addressing real issues that brought them in. Distress minimizing looked like a major problem. So why did they do it?

Essay responses written by clients could be analyzed qualitatively. A substantial subset ($n = 52$) elected to write about their motives for minimizing emotional distress, and two basic motives emerged. The first was a desire to manage the therapist's emotions, primarily to protect the client from some truth he or she imagined the therapist would find disappointing or overwhelming. Several respondents said they were anxious not to worry their therapist or be seen as a complainer. As one client wrote,

> She has worked very hard on me and is proud of my good progress. It's important—to me—to not be such a downer in our sessions after such a positive breakthrough. . . . She has become that missing maternal figure to me and sometimes I try to spare her the distress/disappointment of my life. I don't want her to feel like she'd failed or I'm hopeless.

A second basic motive behind distress minimization was to protect the self, often from the painful realization of precisely how bad things are. Clients shared reasoning such as "Talking about how I am really doing makes me feel more depressed," and "I can't admit it to myself, let alone say it out loud. I want to tell her everything, but I can't bring myself to do so." As with so many types of client dishonesty, respondents' ambivalence about the choice to hide their distress was laced through their descriptions. Respondents often seemed to weigh the pros and cons of dishonesty as they wrote, "I waste my own therapy by not getting to the core as I know I should, but I maintain a comfort zone because 50 minutes would never cover the depth. So keeping it mostly buried works."

As evidenced by clients' narratives, our studies generally indicated that clients use dishonesty to actively tailor the therapist's experience of their problems. When it comes to being deceptive about the extent of felt distress, this tailoring is motivated by the avoidance of painful feelings and fear of interpersonal consequences should the depth of their suffering be known. As we see later on in this chapter, the motives driving concealment and lies tend to vary somewhat according to what is being lied about or concealed.

ONGOING DISHONESTY IN THERAPY

As noted earlier, our second survey provided a somewhat different perspective on client dishonesty. Rather than asking about *lies*, we wondered what would happen if we asked clients how *honest* they typically were while discussing important topics in therapy. Further, if they did not discuss certain material, was it because it just did not apply to them? Or were they deliberately avoiding it? Respondents were presented with a reduced list of 33 topics and asked whether they discussed or did not discuss each topic in therapy. They were then asked to rate their typical level of honesty when talking about topics they discussed. Respondents were also asked whether they were deliberately avoiding any topics they did not discuss. This approach was designed to help us move beyond single-incident lies told in therapy and capture some sense of the magnitude of routine or ongoing dishonesty and concealment in therapy. By asking about ongoing dishonesty, this approach also brought us closer to the secrets-based research tradition. We also got an opportunity (see Table 6.2) to compare the prevalence of active lying (i.e., speaking dishonestly) with passive avoidance (i.e., never bringing this topic up).

Just as in Study 1, respondents in Study 2 were given the opportunity to select one topic that was "hardest to be honest about" and about which they were willing to answer a series of follow-up questions. These follow-up questions covered their motives for dishonesty, their feelings about lying, and whether and under what circumstances they could imagine being more honest about the topic. We also asked about their perceptions about how dishonesty had impacted their progress in therapy and what their therapist could do differently to help them disclose. The sheer volume of data generated by Studies 1 and 2 is too much to cover even in a book-length format, so

TABLE 6.2
Most Commonly Reported Topics of Ongoing Dishonesty in Psychotherapy, With Breakdown of Active Lying and Passive Avoidance: Study 2 ($N = 798$)

Topic	Total percent reporting dishonesty	Percent who speak dishonestly	Percent who deliberately avoid
1. My sexual desires or fantasies	34	4	30
2. Details of my sex life	33	7	26
3. Suicidal thoughts	21	10	11
4. My real reactions to my therapist's comments	20	6	14
5. My sexual orientation	17	7	10
6. Times I treated others poorly	16	7	9
7. Secrets in my family	16	5	11
8. Whether therapy is helping me	16	7	9
9. Trauma or abuse experiences	15	7	8
10. Self-harm (cutting, etc.)	13	5	8
11. Feelings of despair or hopelessness	13	8	5
12. My eating habits or eating disorder	13	5	8
13. Times I was mistreated by others	13	8	5
14. Habits I know I should break	13	6	7
15. Things my family did that hurt me	13	7	6
16. My feelings about the cost of therapy	12	4	8
17. Past suicide attempts	12	6	6
18. Why I missed a session or was late	12	7	5
19. My religious or spiritual beliefs	12	6	6
20. My financial situation	12	5	7

in the chapters that follow we have focused our discussion on certain key data points. A chart of the major domains of inquiry and how we studied them is provided in Table 6.3.

As predicted, our study of ongoing dishonesty returned lower prevalence rates than those seen in Study 1's assessment of lifetime prevalence. It should also be noted that, for various reasons, Survey 2 included no items that captured pure distress minimization. We introduced the topic "Feelings of despair or hopelessness" to see whether it might account for the bulk of distress minimization, but with 13% of respondents endorsing it, it appears that distress minimizing applies to a broader set of experiences.

In keeping with previous studies (e.g., Baumann & Hill, 2016), the results reported in Table 6.2 suggest that sexual matters, both the details of one's sex life and one's sexual fantasies or desires, are the most commonly endorsed topics of ongoing dishonesty. Just as in Study 1, suicidal thoughts were disturbingly prevalent, with 21% endorsing ongoing dishonesty. Also

TABLE 6.3
Overview of Variables Investigated in Studies 1 and 2

Domain	Study 1 ($N = 547$)	Study 2 ($N = 798$)
Prevalence of dishonesty	Assessed lifetime prevalence of dishonesty on 58 topics: "Have you ever lied to your therapist about any of these topics?"	Assessed current levels of honesty, dishonesty, and avoidance on reduced list of 33 topics: "Have you discussed this topic with your current or most recent therapist?" (yes/no) If yes, "How honest are you when discussing these topics?" (1 = *not at all*, 2 = *a little*, 3 = *moderately*, 4 = *a lot*, 5 = *completely or totally*) If no, "What is the main reason you have not discussed this?" (Options: "It does not apply"; "I would discuss this if it came up"; "I try to avoid this topic")
Techniques of dishonesty: Active versus passive		Active dishonesty attributed to those who discussed a topic but reported being "not at all honest" or "a little honest." Passive dishonesty attributed to those who reported they do not discuss it in therapy because "I try to avoid this topic."
Extent of dishonesty	Assessed extent of dishonesty on all topics lied about: "To what extent did you misrepresent the truth about this topic?" (1 = *a tiny bit*, 2 = *a little*, 3 = *a moderate amount*, 4 = *a lot*, 5 = *totally or extremely*)	
Motives for dishonesty	Respondents from both surveys provided short essay answers to the question "Please tell us more: What makes it hard to be honest about this?" Content analysis conducted to identify major themes.	
	Assessed motive with multiple choice question with 28 options (e.g., "I was being polite"; "to avoid hospitalization"; "to direct the conversation").	Assessed motive with multiple choice item: "Which of these describes your reason for not being more honest?" (Options: "Practical consequences"; "My therapist would be upset, hurt, or disappointed"; "I didn't want this to distract from other topics"; "I doubt my therapist can help or understand"; "Embarrassment or shame"; "It would bring up other overwhelming emotions for me"; "Other reason")

(*continues*)

TABLE 6. 3
Overview of Variables Investigated in Studies 1 and 2 (*Continued*)

Domain	Study 1 ($N = 547$)	Study 2 ($N = 798$)
Importance of the topic	Assessed with 7-point Likert scale item: "How important was this topic to you?" (1 = *not important*, 7 = *very important*) Assessed with 7-point Likert scale item: "How important was this topic to your therapy?" (1 = *not important*, 7 = *very important*)	
Timing of dishonesty	Assessed with multiple-choice item: "How much consideration did you give this lie before you told it?" (Options: "None, it was spontaneous"; "I planned to lie beforehand"; "I often lie about this to others"; "I can't remember") Assessed with multiple-choice item: "About when in your therapy did you first tell this lie?" (Options: "During the first session"; "During the early sessions"; "After I knew my therapist well"; "Towards the end of therapy")	
Attitude toward future honest disclosure		Assessed perceived likelihood of future honesty with multiple choice item: "Is this a topic you would ever be more honest about?" (Options: "Yes with my current therapist"; "Yes but with different therapist"; "Yes, but only with family or friends"; "No, not with anyone")

TABLE 6. 3
Overview of Variables Investigated in Studies 1 and 2 (*Continued*)

Domain	Study 1 ($N = 547$)	Study 2 ($N = 798$)
Perceived facilitators of honesty		Assessed clients' ideas about how therapists could foster honesty with short essay response: "How could your therapist make you feel more comfortable being honest about this?" Content analysis conducted to identify major themes. Assessed clients' ideas about what could help them be more honest with multiple choice item: "Under what circumstances would you be more honest about this topic?" (Options: "If I trusted my therapist more"; "If my therapist was warmer"; "If my therapist was more skillful"; "If my therapist asked me about it directly"; "If I knew my therapist had a similar problem"; "If my therapist understood my culture or class"; "If I knew my therapist would not over-react"; "If I knew it wouldn't ruin my relationship with my therapist"; "If I felt like this was blocking my progress in therapy"; "Under no circumstances would I be more honest")
Feelings after being dishonest		Assessed with a multiple-choice item: "How did you feel after being dishonest about this?" (Options: "frustrated," "guilty," "worried," "regretful," "satisfied," "safe," "in control," "true to myself," "neutral," "confused," "conflicted," "unconcerned")
Perceived impact of dishonesty on therapy		Assessed with a multiple-choice item: "Has not being honest affected your therapy?" (Options: "It hurt my progress"; "It helped my progress"; "No effect") Assessed with short essay question: "Can you tell us how not being fully honest affected your therapy?" Content analysis conducted to identify major themes.

(*continues*)

TABLE 6. 3
Overview of Variables Investigated in Studies 1 and 2 (*Continued*)

Domain	Study 1 ($N = 547$)	Study 2 ($N = 798$)
Disclosure and detection of lies	Assessed with multiple choice item: "Does your therapist know that you were untruthful?" (Options: "I don't know," "definitely not," "probably not," "maybe," "probably yes," "definitely yes") Assessed with multiple choice item: "How has the lie been acknowledged in therapy?" (Options: "It has not been acknowledged"; "I told my therapist I lied"; "My therapist said he/she knew"; "I was called out about it"; "The lie eventually unraveled on its own"; "The lie itself wasn't discussed, but some of the details were") Assessed with multiple choice item: "When was the lie acknowledged in therapy?" (Options: "never," "within the same session," "after a few sessions," "months later," "years later")	
Self-concealment	Self-Concealment Scale (Larson & Chastain, 1990); 10-item measure	Self-Concealment in Therapy Scale (adapted from Larson & Chastain, 1990); 10-item measure
Therapeutic relationship	Assessed with five 7-point Likert scale items: • *I like my therapist.* • *I respect my therapist.* • *I feel that my therapist is honest with me.* • *I feel that my disclosures are confidential.* • *I trust my therapist.* • (1 = *not at all*, 7 = *to a very great extent*)	Short Revised Working Alliance Inventory (Hatcher & Gillaspy, 2006); 16-item Likert scale measure

common was the routine concealment of real reactions to comments made by the therapist, endorsed by 20%. As expected, asking about routine dishonesty returned lower levels of prevalence than did asking about lying. For example, whereas 29% could recall being dishonest about why they missed a therapy session in Study 1, only 12% reported regular or ongoing dishonesty about this topic in Study 2.

TECHNIQUES (ACTIVE VS. PASSIVE) OF CLIENT DISHONESTY

We have argued in earlier chapters that deception can be seen on a spectrum from active to passive. When clients decide not to be honest with their therapist, they can choose from a range of strategies, from actively exaggerating or making up wild fabrications to passively avoiding, omitting, or concealing information. Our research suggests that passive strategies are clearly dominant in psychotherapy, as they are believed to be in everyday life.

A glance at Table 6.2 shows that for almost every topic presented in Study 2, passive techniques of avoidance and concealment were more prevalent than active lying. For example, although 33% of the sample reported dishonesty about their sexual fantasies or desires, a mere 4% reported actually speaking falsely (telling a lie) on this topic. This confirmed something we had previously observed in Study 1. Even though that survey asked about *lying*, the nature of the dishonesty shared by clients was still heavily weighted toward passive dishonesty (e.g., concealment) and away from active dishonesty (e.g., fabrication). Specifically, whereas 50% of respondent lies involved minimizing, only 8% involved exaggeration. And although 42% involved omitting important information, only 12% involved making up facts.

Interestingly, the most common topic of active lying was suicidal thoughts, with 10% of our respondents reporting this. It is ironic, considering that lies to conceal suicidality are probably those most feared by therapists, and surprising because only about 4% of the general nonclinical U.S. population has reported experiencing "serious" suicidal thoughts in a given 12-month period (Substance Abuse and Mental Health Services Administration, 2014). Ours being a clinical sample, the proportion of suicidal respondents would certainly be higher. But we were curious: Why would suicide be associated with more active lie telling than other topics? One explanation has to do with the routine suicide assessments conducted in most hospitals and clinics. While being assessed, patients who wish to conceal suicidal ideation are confronted with direct questions to which they must actively verbalize a response. If they choose to conceal, they must at least say "no." Passive avoidance is less of an option when being assessed. Therefore, suicide tops the list of topics about which clients tell active lies.

Evidence supporting this explanation comes from Study 1, in which suicide concealers were three and half times more likely than all other respondents to describe the nature of their dishonesty with the following statement: "I denied something that was true."

MOTIVES BEHIND CLIENT DISHONESTY

Our assumption, which our studies confirmed, is that when patients decide not to be honest, their reason for doing so depends to a certain extent on the topic. For Sarah, the client concealing a past trauma whom we introduced at the opening of this chapter, several emotional and relational motivations were in play: a fear of being emotionally overwhelmed, a sense of shame, and uncertainty about whether her therapist would understand. By contrast, another female client, whom we will call Dana, lied to her therapist based on a motive that was entirely practical. Although Sarah hid her experience of being a victim, Dana hid the fact that she had committed a crime and lied to keep her therapist in the dark: "I was afraid she might tell the police." Different secrets, different motives. Dishonesty in each of several clinically important areas—suicidal thoughts, sexual issues, substance abuse, trauma, and lies about therapy and feelings about one's therapist—appears to be associated with distinct patterns of motivation and is addressed separately in subsequent chapters.

We must also acknowledge the complexity of motivations that can be present in any one example of client dishonesty. When a painful truth threatens to emerge, there are fears about what might happen inside the therapy room, such as upsetting the therapist. These fears can sometimes interlock with fears about possible consequences outside the therapy room, such as the police being notified. And both types of fear are often accompanied by fears of what might happen inside the client him- or herself, such as intense or overwhelming feelings of guilt or shame. Such feelings can be the product, at the same time, of feeling judged by a therapist and judged by oneself. Many clients in our research reported this complex and overlapping array of motivations. One young woman, a victim of childhood sexual assault, was beginning to feel sexual urges toward young children and also animals, but she did not breathe a word of it to her therapist:

> I lied because I felt that the truth would land me in heavier-duty therapy, which I didn't have the emotional fortitude or the time for. I also felt shame and wondered what my therapist would think of me. I also felt that maybe the whole mandated reporting thing might cause me some trouble. I was basically a teenager and thought that just having pedophile-type urges, even if I never acted on them, was enough to put me on a watch list to ensure I never made it to offender status.

This client struggled with her feelings of shame and was concerned too with what her therapist would think and how this would impact her therapy. In fact, emotional, practical, and legal motivations for concealment are all present in her narrative, each playing a role in the difficult choices she made about what to share and what to conceal in therapy.

With this complexity in mind, however, there is still something appealing about having an overall answer to the question "Why do clients lie?" And so, in addition to collecting written narratives, we asked respondents to select from among six possible motives, generated in great measure from previous research in this area (Farber, 2006; Hill et al., 1993; Hook & Andrews, 2005; Kelly, 1998). Table 6.4 provides responses from Study 2, drawn from the 84% of respondents who reported dishonesty on at least one topic.

Consistent with prior research in this area, shame and embarrassment were the most frequent motivators for dishonesty in therapy, cited in 61% of the situations shared by our respondents. Also of interest is that the desire to not "distract" the therapist and thus control the direction of therapy was the second most common motive, cited in 27% of cases. This makes sense, given the complaint frequently lodged by clients in our data set that therapists "overreact" to certain material (e.g., disclosures about substance use). Lying and concealment is an effective way to keep such hot-button issues off the table.

We also learned that Dana was not alone: Nineteen percent of reported motives had to do with practical consequences, such as legal problems or unwanted hospitalization. That suggests that, rightly or wrongly, nearly a fifth of clients in this sample feared therapists would feel professionally obligated to break confidentiality and begin to take actions that could impact their lives outside the therapy room. A closer look at these 127 clients reveals the reason why: Fifty were concealing suicidal thoughts or behaviors, 16 lied about drugs or alcohol, 10 were concealing eating disorders, and nine concealed homicidal thoughts, with smaller numbers reporting dishonesty about

TABLE 6.4
Most Commonly Reported Motives for Ongoing Dishonesty on All Topics: Study 2 (*N* = 672)

Reported motivation for dishonesty	*n*	Percent
Embarrassment or shame	410	61
I didn't want this to distract from other topics	179	27
I doubt my therapist can help or understand	161	24
Practical consequences (e.g., legal problems, hospitalization)	127	19
It would bring up overwhelming emotions for me	120	18
My therapist would be upset, hurt, or disappointed	109	16

issues such as self-harm or being the victim of sexual abuse. Clients concealing these aspects of their lives appear to be making hard calculations about the impact of their disclosures: If I tell my therapist I have a drug problem or have had homicidal or suicidal thoughts, what might he or she do and who else will be told? It is a reminder that clients may be quite aware that the confidentiality of therapy has limits, a point which becomes paramount for clients concealing suicide and self-harm, as we discuss in Chapter 7.

THE "BIGGEST" AND "SMALLEST" LIES

The most common lies are not necessarily the biggest or most dramatic. Our research suggests there are a number of topics about which clients are inclined to be totally dishonest. Most of these "big lies" were relevant to only a small subset of respondents. Indeed, the topic that was associated with the most extensive dishonesty—romantic feelings about the therapist—was something that, as noted earlier, only applied to 5% of respondents. Our method for identifying these "biggest" (i.e., most extensive) lies was to ask in our first study about the extent to which clients felt they were dishonest on a 5-point scale, ranging from 1 = *a tiny bit* dishonest to 5 = *totally or extremely* dishonest. Table 6.5 shows the top 10 topics on which respondents reported a 5 on this scale.

Four of these topics involved therapy itself, with respondents reporting extreme dishonesty about romantic attraction to their therapist, their desire

TABLE 6.5
Topics on Which Dishonesty Was Most Likely to Be Extensive: Study 1 (*N* = 547)

Topic	Percent of sample reporting	Percent of those who endorsed "total or extreme" dishonesty
1. My romantic or sexual feelings about my therapist	5	46
2. Not saying that I want to end therapy	16	37
3. Experiences of sexual abuse or trauma	10	33
4. My masturbation habits	13	32
5. My use of pornography	9	31
6. That my therapist makes me feel weird or uncomfortable	12	30
7. Times I cheated on my spouse or partner	10	29
8. My real opinion of my therapist	18	27
9. Racist feelings I have had	5	26
10. My past attempts to commit suicide	10	26

Note. "Total or extreme" dishonesty was defined as a score of five on a five-point dishonesty scale.

to end therapy, their real opinion of their therapist, and their sense that their therapist makes them feel uncomfortable. Experiences of sexual abuse are also on the list, as are pornography and masturbation. Racism and infidelity were also subjects of extensive dishonesty for the small subset of respondents who reported lying about them. One young woman who acknowledged extreme dishonesty (i.e., reported a score of 5) regarding her habit of watching violent pornography reported, "I'll never explicitly tell her any of this, even though I think it is probably deeply relevant to have a serious violent pornography addiction."

On the opposite end of the spectrum, we can identify the "smallest" lies, topics that are subject to only slight levels of dishonesty. The data reported here are for those who reported concealing or distorting the truth on these topics (in Study 1) but reported only doing so "a tiny bit," with scores of 1 on a 5-point scale: "The way I treat my children sometimes," "Lies to get a certain prescription," and "What I can afford to pay for therapy." Each is an easy subject for fudging and minor distortion: putting a positive spin on the sometimes-chaotic process of child-rearing, shading the truth about symptoms to ensure a certain prescription, and downplaying one's ability to afford the therapist's fee.

WHO LIES?

To reiterate, 93% of clients surveyed were able to recall being dishonest with their therapist on some topic in the past, and in a second survey, 84% reported being dishonest or deliberately avoiding at least one topic on an ongoing or routine basis. These prevalence estimates are the highest yet in the literature on client dishonesty in psychotherapy; previous studies have arrived at estimates between 20% and 46% of clients admitting to the specific act of "secret keeping" in therapy (e.g., Hill et al., 1993; Pope & Tabachnick, 1994). The difference is likely due to our broader definition of dishonesty that includes twisting the facts, minimizing, omitting, or pretending to agree with the therapist, all smaller acts that do not rise to the level of secrets but are nonetheless relevant to the psychotherapy process. Because subtle dishonesty such as the "white lie" is woven into the fabric of social communication starting in middle childhood (Talwar, Murphy, & Lee, 2007), we might ask why fully 100% of our participants did not endorse lying to their therapist. The answer? Research into everyday lying outside of therapy appears to support the near but not total ubiquity of dishonesty, with polls of the general public suggesting that 90% to 96% of adults can recall specific instances of lying in the past (Kalish, 2004; J. Patterson & Kim, 1991). We also imagine, though we do not know for sure, that at least some of our respondents were less than totally honest with us about the extent of their dishonesty with their therapists.

This question aside, we were interested in knowing how much lying people would report and how it was distributed. Recall from Chapter 2 that a fascinating body of recent research (Levine et al., 2011; Serota et al., 2010; Serota, Levine, & Burns, 2012) has demonstrated that dishonesty does not follow the bell curve. That is to say, the distribution of dishonest communication appears to be deeply skewed toward a small number of "prolific liars," perhaps 5% of the population, whereas as much as 60% of the adult population will go through the average day without telling any lies at all. The skew was so dramatic in these studies that, within a given 24-hour period, the prolific 5% were responsible for 50% of all lies recorded.

Did we find the same prolific liars in psychotherapy that Serota et al. (2010) found in everyday life? Although our surveys were not designed to replicate that other work, the results are intriguing. Turning to our findings from Study 1, we see that about 60% of respondents reported dishonesty on between zero and eight topics over the course of their psychotherapy treatments (see Figure 6.1). In contrast, it was possible to identify a small group of about 6% who reported 20 or more topics of dishonesty.

Who were these prolific therapy liars? We found no racial or gender differences, but they were, on average, about 5 years younger ($M = 30$, $SD = 12.5$) than the mean age of the rest of the sample ($M = 35$, $SD = 13$). They not only lied about more things but also were more likely to tell bigger lies—that is, to distort the truth more extremely—and they reported a greater general tendency toward self-concealment. Most interestingly, this group was more than twice as likely to cite "traumatic experiences" as a reason they had entered therapy (55% of them did, compared with 22% of the rest of the sample). Other reasons for entering therapy that prolific liars were significantly more likely to give included suicidality, self-harm, social anxiety, mood problems, depression, and anxiety or panic attacks. To our surprise, the prolific liars had not been in therapy for a longer time. Nor had they had more sessions; therefore, it was not simply a matter of having had more time to exhibit dishonesty on more topics. Rather, prolific liars in our sample appeared to be more symptomatic, with at least some characteristics and problems often associated with borderline level pathology.

TIMING AND PLANNING

Everyday experience gives us two possible models for imagining when in the therapeutic relationship a client is likely to be dishonest about a given topic. The first we might call the "stranger on a train" hypothesis, which

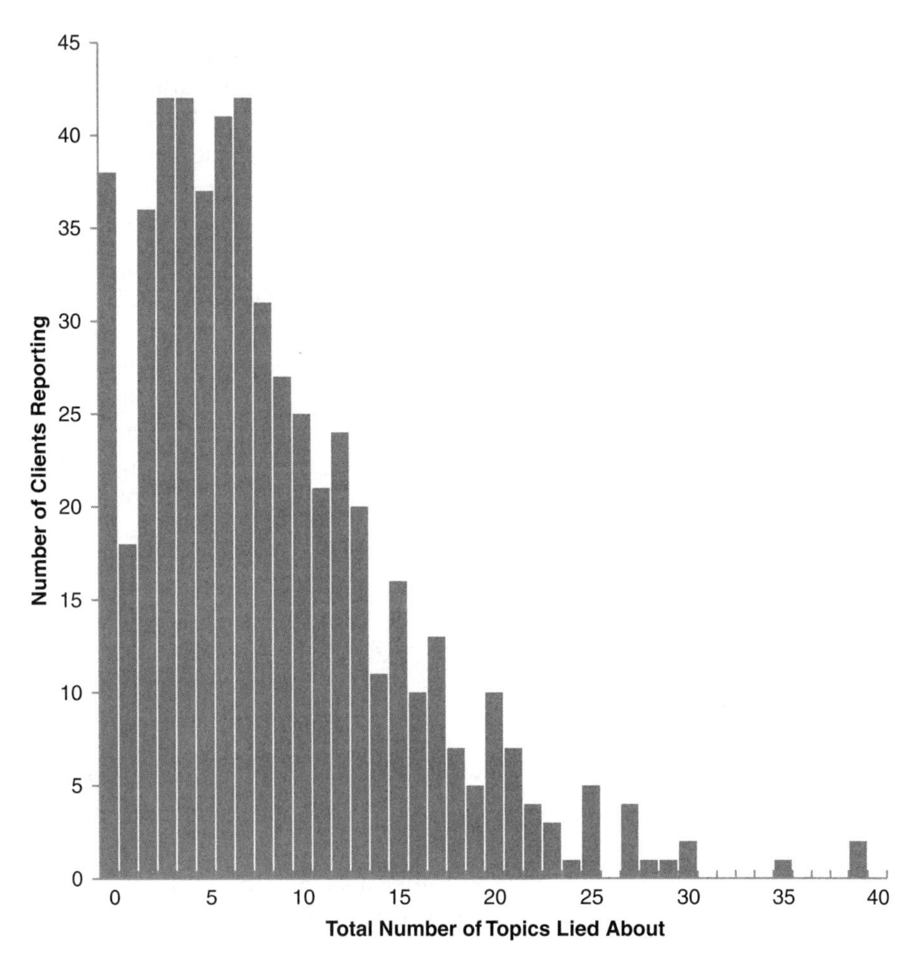

Figure 6.1. Distribution of topics lied about (Study 1). Mean = 8.4, Std. Dev. = 6.6, N = 547.

suggests that clients are likely to be more honest early in therapy because, just as when unburdening ourselves to a stranger on a train, the client barely knows the therapist at the start of therapy and therefore should have reduced sensitivity to shocking or upsetting them. A new therapy is, by this theory, a clean slate on which patients can honestly and freely write without the kind of embarrassment that can creep in later when their therapist has become someone they actually know, someone with assumptions and expectations about them, someone whose image of them patients might want to protect. The alternate model we might call the "first date" hypothesis, which suggests that dishonesty and concealment would actually be at their highest during the initial meetings, when the client, like someone on a first date, would be most preoccupied with making a good impression and thus most likely to use strategies such as concealment. The first date model suggests that honesty is more likely in later sessions, when presumably a level of mutual trust has been established, and secrets can safely be disclosed.

Our first study included an item that allowed us to gauge which model is correct. At first glance, the findings appear to favor the first date hypothesis over the stranger on a train by a substantial margin. Among all Study 1 respondents, 71% of client dishonesty incidents occurred in the early sessions, with about a quarter of that coming in the first meeting with the therapist. The remaining 29% of client dishonesty incidents we captured happened in later sessions, "after I knew my therapist well." We could conclude that the first date hypothesis prevails. This picture changes, however, when we account for the fact that many of our respondents may only have had 10 to 20 sessions of therapy, necessarily limiting their lies to the early sessions. When we narrow the focus to just those clients with 20 or more sessions of psychotherapy with their current therapist, we see the proportion of lies first told during the early sessions drop to 57%, with an increase to 43% of those happening after client and therapist knew each other well. First date or stranger on a train? Our research suggests something close to an even split.

Most client lies were not specifically planned. They were either spontaneous (45% of the time) or part of a general habit, something the person generally conceals from others in most settings (28%). In only about 16% of cases did respondents describe a premeditated effort to deceive their therapists. What kind of lies do clients plan beforehand? Three topics were clear winners: concealing suicidal thoughts, hiding alcohol and drug use, and lying about the reasons why they were late or missed an appointment.

For the most part, then, clients appear to lie without great forethought and, to a great degree, early on in the therapeutic relationship. For clinicians interested in fostering disclosure, these findings could indicate a need to "circle back around" to topics about which honesty is important, providing opportunities for clients to reconsider disclosure at various points in the course of therapy.

FEELINGS ABOUT HAVING BEEN DISHONEST

Although it has been argued that some types of client dishonesty can help clients to manage their self-presentation and construct desirable identities by avoiding shameful disclosures (Kelly, 2000), respondents in our first study reported overwhelmingly negative feelings after telling a lie. In that study, they were allowed to select as many emotions as they liked from a list of 13; on average, they selected three emotions that characterized their feelings after being dishonest. Of the emotions reported, 58% were explicitly negative, including guilt, regret, frustration, and shame. Only 7% of all descriptors were positive emotions such as pride, relief, powerfulness, or satisfaction.

In our second study, we asked respondents to choose just one dominant feeling they had after being dishonest, providing an equal number of positive and negative options from which to choose. Again, negative emotions (e.g., frustrated, guilty, worried, regretful) were the most commonly cited, by 31% of this sample; another 22% of the sample reported feeling primarily confused or conflicted. Only 20% reported positive emotions (e.g., satisfied, safe, in control, true to myself). Those who felt neutral or unconcerned made up 27% of the sample. Among those reporting positive emotions, few endorsed feelings of "satisfaction" about dishonesty; instead, positive feelings were more in the realm of feeling "in control" (assumedly of the therapeutic process) and "safe" (assumedly from various perceived dangers, such as feeling an emotion they wanted to avoid or being hospitalized involuntarily). These findings are in keeping with those of Baumann and Hill (2016), who noted higher levels of negative emotions about concealment among 61 clients who had kept a secret from their therapist.

Again, we were curious: Would some topics buck the negative feelings trend—that is, topics for which lying more often led to positive feelings? As can be seen in Table 6.6, there were indeed a handful of subjects for which positive emotions were more commonly reported than negative. These topics

TABLE 6.6
Topics That Elicited the Highest Percentage of Positive and Negative Emotions Following Client Dishonesty

Topic	Respondents' reported emotions: Percent positive	Respondents' reported emotions: Percent negative
Topics that elicited the highest percentage of positive emotions		
Suicidal thoughts ($n = 64$)	37	27
Times I treated others poorly ($n = 28$)	28	6
Trauma or abuse experiences ($n = 66$)	27	24
Topics that elicited the highest percentage of negative emotions		
Habits I know I should break ($n = 25$)	20	60
My insecurities or doubts about myself ($n = 32$)	14	59
My real reactions to my therapist's comments ($n = 30$)	13	53

Note. Rows do not equal 100%; remaining respondents reported either neutral or conflicted emotions. The *n*'s noted in this table reflect the number of respondents who chose that topic as the "hardest to be honest about."

included suicidal thoughts, times the respondent treated others poorly, and trauma and abuse experiences. As we see in later chapters, each of these topics comes with different reasons why concealment or dishonesty may be experienced more positively—or at least with greater satisfaction and less regret—by clients. Topics for which dishonesty triggered mostly negative emotions were far more common, and each of these were subjects that clients wanted to discuss honestly but for various reasons could not.

DETECTION OF DISHONESTY

Does the truth ever come out? Apparently not, or at least rarely. In our first study, we asked a series of multiple-choice questions about the eventual disclosure and detection of various lies reported by respondents. Across all topics, 73% of respondents said the truth about their lies had never been acknowledged in therapy. Only 3.5% came clean and told their therapist about the lie. Another 9% were essentially discovered, either because the therapist called them out or because the lie unraveled on its own. According to our clients, then, less than a tenth of client lies were detected in any way by therapists. This is somewhat of a worse track record than might be predicted by previous literature. In their detailed study of the "hidden reactions" of clients to events in session, Hill et al. (1993) found that experienced therapists had a hit rate of about 45% in detecting these reactions. There is a chance, of course, that our study might have shown a higher rate of detection for dishonesty had we been able to query therapists as well as clients.

What sort of deceptions do therapists detect? According to clients, by far the most common type of deception detected involved the minimizing of symptoms and distress, which accounted for about four out of every 10 detected lies. This suggests that therapists have some ability to notice when clients are faking good during a session, and their actual hit rate (per client report) was not too bad. As we can see in Table 6.7, for clients who minimized the severity of their symptoms, the truth came out in about 41% of the cases recorded in our research. By comparison, deception regarding alcohol or drug problems was reversed only 11% of the time and among those concealing suicidal thoughts only 6% of the time. One explanation for the higher levels of eventual truth about distress minimization is that it involves events occurring in the therapy session itself. In that sense, minimizing distress is akin to the hidden reactions studied by Hill et al. (1993). This would be unlike, for example, the client who conceals something that by its nature happens outside therapy, such as self-harm, for which the rate of reported detection was 0%. The overall picture, however, is that clients

TABLE 6.7
Rate at Which Therapists Eventually Detect Dishonesty on Selected Topics, per Clients' Perception: Study 1 ($N = 547$)

Topic	Rate of detection
I minimized the severity of my symptoms	41%
I minimized how bad I really feel	20%
Pretending to find therapy more effective than I do	16%
Not saying that I want to end therapy	14%
My use of drugs or alcohol	11%
My sexual history	8%
My thoughts about suicide	6%
My insecurities and doubts about myself	0%
Self-harm I have done (cutting, etc.)	0%
All topics combined	9%

who desire to hide facts and feelings from their therapist generally believe they have been quite successful in doing so.

THE IMPACT OF DISHONESTY ON THERAPEUTIC PROGRESS

It may be impossible to know what impact dishonesty has on the effectiveness of psychotherapy, especially given the variety of possible topics and situations involved. As we noted in the case of Sarah at the start of this chapter, concealment can be an important way for emotionally fragile clients to protect themselves. We were nonetheless curious to see what clients would say when we asked them how being dishonest impacted their progress in therapy. Respondents in both surveys were asked to assess the likely impact of their dishonesty as helpful, harmful, or as having no effect on their therapy. Because we asked the same question in both studies, we are able to report the answers of well over 1,000 clients.

As Table 6.8 indicates, across both surveys, 42% of respondents felt their dishonesty was harmful, having a negative impact on their therapy, and they often expressed this with palpable regret. Dishonesty made their therapy "useless" and "moot" because they never got to the "real issue" and ended up "not really doing therapy." Many looked back ruefully at the progress they could have made if they had only been honest. As one client wrote: "I wasted years in therapy when I could've been 100% upfront and truthful about my situation. I could have spent that time working on myself and learning what a healthy relationship is." Clients were more likely to see dishonesty as harmful if they were lying about certain topics. For example, a large majority of distress minimizers (68%) felt their dishonesty was harmful to their progress in therapy.

TABLE 6.8
Perceived Impact of Dishonesty About Selected Topics

Topic	Hurt my progress	Helped my progress	No impact
Minimizing level of distress (*n* = 52)	68%	5%	27%
Traumatic experiences (*n* = 80)	48%	5%	47%
Use of drugs or alcohol (*n* = 80)	41%	3%	57%
Why I missed a session or was late (*n* = 21)	33%	0%	67%
Sexual topics (*n* = 158)	28%	5%	67%
All topics combined (*n* = 1,130)	42%	5%	54%

Note. Samples noted are drawn from both studies, with the exception of the item "Minimizing level of distress," which was only investigated in Study 1.

By contrast, only 5% of respondents felt their dishonesty had been helpful for therapy. For these clients, dishonesty often helped them avoid unwanted interventions by their therapist, who they felt would overreact to the truth. As one male patient with posttraumatic stress disorder and bipolar disorder wrote,

> My personal experiences with the mental health field has taught me that it is BEST that I don't always disclose how I am really doing. . . . [Dishonesty] has kept me from being thrown into a state institution, I am sure of that.

Many of these clients appear to be experiencing more severe symptoms, including suicidality. There was, however, no single topic for which lying was more commonly seen as helpful. For example, clients concealing suicidal thoughts to avoid hospitalization were four times more likely to describe their dishonesty as harmful rather than helpful.

Victims of physical or sexual abuse may have particular sensitivities about how and when they reveal their traumas in psychotherapy (Farber, Feldman, & Wright, 2014). We might imagine that controlling the timing of trauma disclosures could be seen as helpful by patients in this category. Nonetheless, among those who concealed physical or sexual trauma in therapy, only 5% found concealment to be helpful, whereas 48% found it harmful, and the remaining 47% felt it had had no effect. As one client wrote, "I have made little progress. The pain and fear is so overwhelming that I can't bring myself to talk about the abuse."

Finally, 54% of clients across all topics found their dishonesty or concealment had no serious impact on their therapy, either negative or positive. Substantial numbers of clients on a wide range of topics reported no impact on their therapy of lying about matters such as family secrets, use of drugs and alcohol, or self-harm. According to our research, the area in which lying was most likely to be seen as irrelevant to psychotherapeutic outcome was sex, including topics such as sexual fantasies, one's sexual history, masturbation, or the use of pornography, with 67% reporting that dishonesty had no effect. For some, sex just seemed out-of-bounds for their particular psychotherapeutic relationship or irrelevant to their primary problems, so a smattering of passive dishonesty is used to prevent awkward conversations or fend off therapist curiosity about topics clients believe are tangential to their core concerns. Even when clients allow that there could be serious issues in their sex lives, they are often happy to dodge questions about sex. As one client put it, "I just move around this topic and we work on other areas."

HOW CAN THERAPISTS HELP CLIENTS BE MORE HONEST?

As we noted, a major goal of studying client dishonesty is to find ways to help clients become more honest about topics that matter to their progress. Perhaps it was the arrogance of assumed expertise, but we had been studying this problem for several years before it occurred to us to simply ask clients directly "Under what circumstances would you be more honest about this?" The results shown in Table 6.9 come from our second study. They should not be taken as gospel for clinical practice because respondents had to choose from among 10 answer choices chosen a priori by our team. But we also asked respondents to write short narratives in response to the related question "How can your therapist help you be more honest?" A good number of respondents offered unrealistic ideas, and another subset frankly said they did not know how their therapist could help—as one client put it, "Don't ask me. I'm not the doctor!" Yet the majority of respondents did have workable

TABLE 6.9
Circumstances Under Which Clients Would Be More Honest About a Topic About Which They Had Been Dishonest ($N = 672$)

Circumstance	*n*	Percent
If my therapist asked me about it directly	311	46
If I felt like this was blocking my progress in therapy	218	32
If I knew my therapist would not overreact	169	25
If I trusted my therapist more	168	25
If I knew my therapist had a similar problem	157	23
If I knew it wouldn't ruin my relationship with my therapist	124	18
If my therapist was warmer	99	15
If my therapist was more skillful	96	14
Under NO circumstances would I be more honest	79	12
If my therapist understood my culture or class	76	11

ideas, which provided a useful illustration of their multiple-choice responses. Where possible in the chapters that follow, we apply content analytic techniques to these open-text responses to derive the major themes. These analyses were performed per Neuendorf's (2002) protocol, with a research team of psychology graduate students overseen by the senior author.

One major takeaway from this could be summed up in two words: "Just ask." Nearly half (46%) of clients reported that they would be more honest if their therapist asked direct questions about the topic at hand. Across a wide range of secrets, from self-harm to feelings about therapy, clients expressed a desire for therapists to bring up things they do not feel ready to bring up themselves. In some cases, this sounded like an unrealistic wish that the therapist could read their minds; as one client wrote, "He'd need to bring up the subject without me mentioning it." But more often, the desire for therapists to ask direct questions seemed to reflect a need for the clinician to take leadership of the discussion, to walk the client down the very path he or she is most afraid to tread. Sarah, the young female client concealing a traumatic past that we have returned to several times in this chapter, was among those who felt this way. She wrote about powerful, fearful words and about wanting her therapist to take the lead by "saying the words" and about allowing her to respond with only "yes" or "no," if that was all she could manage.

> I think it would be helpful if my therapist asked me direct questions about it, especially yes/no questions. This would make it less embarrassing for me. I think that if I'm asked open-ended questions about this topic, I'm so focused on avoiding things that would be uncomfortable for me to say, that anything I do say probably isn't honest or fully honest. Words have a lot of power, so if the therapist is the one saying the words that are difficult to say, and my job is only to say yes or no, then it lifts away a lot of the burden for me. I really wish that therapists did this more often, or at least asked whether I prefer open-ended questions or yes/no questions. I feel that I would have made a lot more progress in therapy.

A variant of "just ask" was the hope that therapists would "just ask again," circling back to ask about things that may have made the client balk the first time they came up. One client, who said she concealed her struggle to find a "healthy sexuality" in relationships due to shame, wished her therapist had gone back to reopen that door. She wrote,

> It did somehow come up one time near the end of a session, but we never came back to it. . . . If she would have brought it up again after the first time it came up I think I could have talked some more about it.

For others, the "just ask" wish took the form of wanting the therapist to ask on a regular and routine basis. One client who engaged in occasional acts of nonlethal self-harm decided to completely conceal this from her therapist, rather than bring it up and trigger a big response. She felt that honesty could have been possible if her therapist had made asking about self-harm a routine part of their weekly sessions. As she explained, "It would be easier if she asked every week. Then she could see that it doesn't happen all that often and it's not necessarily a sign of me completely falling apart. It's just a thing that happens sometimes." Routine asking like this is built into several manualized therapies, for example, dialectical behavior therapy, in which a weekly diary card is used to capture incidents of suicidality, self-harm, or substance use that may occur, without relying on the client to bring them up. Our research suggests that when topics are brought to the table and kept on the table in this way, clients find it easier to be honest.

Asking direct questions was not the preferred tactic in all situations or for all clients. A majority of clients who were concealing sexual infidelity, for example, reported feeling in control of their decision not to disclose. Few reported a desire to be asked about it. Similarly, clients who were concealing alcohol or drug abuse, suicidal thoughts, or homicidal urges were more inclined to be honest if they could be guaranteed that disclosure would not lead their therapist to "overreact." At times, a strong therapist reaction can be clinically or legally necessary. Nonetheless, clients concealing these serious issues saw no reason to be honest if honesty would land them in hot water. Often, they wanted to know where the boundary line was between things one could safely say in therapy and things that would have to be reported. A client concealing violent urges wrote that he would be honest if his therapist could "assure me that I will be completely in control of my freedom as long as I only talk about, and don't act upon, homicidal ideation." A different client saw some chance for honesty through "discussing what is and isn't grounds for immediate hospitalization." We discuss this link between certainty and disclosure in our chapter on suicide and self-harm (Chapter 7), where our respondents speak of wanting to know precisely how therapists will react to certain disclosures before they risk being honest.

One surprise in Table 6.9 is that trust appears to be only a second-tier factor in fostering honesty. When asked under what circumstances they might be more honest, only 25% of our sample selected the option "if I trusted my therapist more." This number is partially composed of clients concealing certain topics for which trust was valued by a mere 10% of respondents (e.g., anxiety symptoms, labile moods). However, trust appeared to play a much larger role for clients concealing depression symptoms; 42% of respondents saw it as a way to foster honesty. Increasing trust was also important to clients concealing mistreatment in relationships and even for those lying about self-harm. The reasons for the uneven importance of trust are not immediately obvious. It may well be that many clients already believe they have a good level of trust with their therapist and therefore do not see increasing trust as a way to foster honesty. As one client with a binge eating disorder remarked,

> She really already does everything that she could possibly do to make the subject more comfortable. Sometimes certain things are simply difficult to talk about, because they are repressed or show a darker side of yourself, and all a therapist can do is listen and clarify your own thoughts, ask questions, be understanding and not judgmental.

The importance of trust can also be examined through the *therapeutic alliance*, a popular and highly influential concept in psychotherapy research that captures the client's felt sense of being in alignment with his or her clinician on the tasks and goals of therapy, as well as a sense of having a solid bond with that clinician. The alliance is often measured with a standardized scale called the Working Alliance Inventory; we used its short form in our second study (WAI-SR; Hatcher & Gillaspy, 2006). We were interested in seeing how the strength of the alliance would affect the amount of honesty reported by clients, so we also developed and validated our own measure, the 15-item Honesty in Therapy Scale (HITS), also used in our second study. Results showed a significant correlation between the WAI and the HITS ($r = .54$, $p < .01$), suggesting that greater trust between therapist and client does indeed co-occur with greater honesty by clients. In a similar vein, those with higher alliance scores were significantly more likely to predict that they could one day "come clean" and be honest with their current therapist. This effect was found irrespective of the topic being lied about.

There were also circumstances in which clients felt they could be honest if their therapist had a similar problem or had some clearer understanding of their culture or class. These "I've been there, too" factors were notably important to clients concealing a handful of specific subjects, such as eating disorders, and also for those who felt unable to be honest about their religious or spiritual lives in therapy and those whose experience of being a racial minority was largely avoided or concealed in their therapy. Showing a client that you have "been there" was seen as effective for between 44% and 83% of clients in these categories. But it can also involve significant self-disclosure by the therapist, which some clients say is exactly what they want. Respondents frequently mentioned a desire to "know my therapist better." One respondent reported concealing a particular erotic interest out of shame but said she was willing to disclose provided her therapist could meet her halfway. Her particular fascination was with vampires, and she hoped for some hint that her therapist might understand. "The thought of talking about what I like makes me feel like I'm going to explode from total embarrassment," she wrote. "He'd have to share something personal about himself that involved his fantasies, sexual thrills, etc." Unfortunately, this might be a place where the client's wishes and clinical prudence diverge.

Finally, there were two topics for which the prevailing feeling was that under no circumstances would the client be more honest, no matter what the clinician might do. Fittingly, these were "my romantic or sexual feelings about my therapist" and "how much I can afford to pay for therapy," two topics for which clients were most likely to see no benefit to honesty and believe the truth was better left unexplored.

In this chapter, we have been able to highlight only some of the fascinating nuances of when, why, and how clients in psychotherapy decide to conceal their true feelings and the true facts of their lives. It has been a whirlwind tour of our research that might seem a bit overwhelming unless one was taking copious notes. In the following chapters, we slow things down a bit and provide more focused discussions of client dishonesty and concealment on several of the most critical topics that clients bring to treatment: suicide and self-harm, the broad field of sex and sexuality, substance abuse and trauma, and finally, the client's feelings about therapy and about their therapist, too.

7

COMMON CLINICAL LIES: SUICIDAL THOUGHTS, SELF-HARM, AND EMOTIONAL DISTRESS

> I blamed her for not seeing the bruise so I wouldn't be blamed for hiding it from her.
>
> —André Aciman, *Harvard Square*

In terms of their suicidality, Cindy and Rebecca are very different women. Cindy is a 30-year-old with bipolar disorder and a history of suicide attempts and psychiatric hospitalizations. When she took part in our research, she was frank about her philosophy on disclosing suicidal thoughts:

> I've found it's best never to be honest about wanting to commit suicide, plans to do it, or attempts, because therapists see that you are going to harm yourself and can have you hospitalized. Everyone I've met with experience in the mental health system knows exactly what to say and how to act around therapists. Lying about everything is easier than dealing with med changes, therapist reactions, hospitalizations and ECT [electroconvulsive therapy] treatments.

Rebecca is about the same age, 32, but has never been hospitalized. She has never attempted to kill herself and has never seriously considered

http://dx.doi.org/10.1037/0000128-008
Secrets and Lies in Psychotherapy, by B. A. Farber, M. Blanchard, and M. Love

doing so. Nonetheless, she decided to entirely conceal her occasional suicidal thoughts from her therapist—for reasons not so different from Cindy's:

> My therapist asked me if I had ever had suicidal thoughts, but I didn't feel I could be truthful. I was afraid that might qualify as a situation where she would have to violate doctor–patient confidentiality, and I didn't want to frighten my family. I was also concerned that honesty might result in the situation being blown out of proportion: that I might be placed on some kind of watch or forced to get additional treatment.

Cindy and Rebecca are two different patients with the same concern. Rightly or wrongly, they conceal their suicidal ideation because they believe honesty would put them at risk—not only of feeling ashamed or upsetting their therapist but also of triggering a response that would have repercussions outside the therapy room. Both women fear losing control of their treatment or, for a time, losing their freedom. Moreover, both women told us they were content with their decision to conceal; as Rebecca put it, "it was for the best" that she never shared her suicidal thoughts. According to the accounts we collected from psychotherapy clients who acknowledged concealing or actively lying about their suicidal ideation, such responses are not at all uncommon.

Cindy and Rebecca illustrate the special problem of fostering honesty with patients who are potentially suicidal or prone to self-harm. Unlike every other topic covered in this book, suicide, and to some extent nonsuicidal self-injury (NSSI), introduce dramatic new pressures into the therapeutic relationship. As Jobes and Ballard (2011) pointed out, suicidality is a game changer, injecting fundamental issues of interpersonal control and power into psychotherapy and kicking up strong emotions for all involved:

> Because suicide implicates a potentially life versus death scenario, the therapeutic stakes are raised to the highest possible level. Indeed, both parties (clinician and patient) may feel vulnerable, powerful, scared, angry, worried, wary—and sometimes all at the same time. (p. 51)

Resnick (2002) noted that although mental health professionals would like to imagine themselves as allies in treating depression and suicidality, seriously suicidal patients often see their therapist as a potential adversary, wielding the power of involuntary hospitalization or civil commitment. Mildly suicidal clients like Rebecca are also well aware that professional ethics and legal precedent mandate action by therapists if a client is deemed a risk to themselves or others. For clinicians, too, these legal and moral pressures can feel intense (Bongar & Sullivan, 2013). The stress may trigger an avoidant dismissal of the client's suicide risk or, alternately, an overreaction to suicidal material, following a policy of "better safe than sorry" that can seem like the only option when suicide risk is elevated or unclear (Bryan & Rudd, 2006).

Nonsuicidal forms of self-harm such as cutting or burning, although recognized as a clinically distinct phenomenon from suicidality, are easily confused with a desire to die and have indeed been found to be a strong predictor of eventual death by suicide (Hawton & Harriss, 2007; Whitlock et al., 2013; Zahl & Hawton, 2004). Thus, self-injury raises many of the same alarms on both sides of the therapy dyad. In addition, encountering the physical results of cutting, burning, scratching, scab-picking, and other forms of self-inflicted tissue damage can produce in a therapist precisely the sort of responses that self-harming clients may be desperate to avoid: shock, disgust, confusion, anger, and fear (Walsh, 2014).

One result of these pressures is that many clients simply lie about or conceal their suicidal thoughts and self-injury for a range of reasons that both overlap and diverge. We first consider suicidal thoughts; respondents in our studies sent a clear message about why they are dishonest and how they would like to see clinical practice change. Subsequent sections of the chapter address the concealment of self-injury and the client's minimization of distress in general. For the most part, we use the term *concealment* to describe dishonesty on these matters because hiding this painful material—avoiding speaking about it—is almost always the preferred means to keep these thoughts and behaviors away from the therapist.

CONCEALING SUICIDAL THOUGHTS

The prevalence of suicidal thoughts in the U.S. population is believed to be about 3.9% in any given 12-month period (Centers for Disease Control and Prevention [CDC], 2018), which amounts to nearly 13 million Americans in 2017. The prevalence of suicidal thoughts among clients in psychotherapy is not known, however, nor is the rate at which clients honestly disclose about this issue.

In our first study ($n = 547$), we were struck to find that 31% of the sample reported having lied about their suicidal thoughts while in psychotherapy, making it the third most common topic of dishonesty among a diverse set of 58 topics presented, behind only two related forms of distress minimization, "I minimized how bad I really feel" (54%) and "I minimized the severity of symptoms" (39%). It is likely not a large leap either to imagine that some of those reporting distress minimization were, in fact, specifically concealing suicidal ideation. Our second study ($n = 798$) was expected to return a lower prevalence of concealment of suicidal thoughts because it asked about dishonesty that was routine or ongoing, and indeed, we found that 21% of the sample endorsed either active dishonesty (i.e., speaking dishonestly) or passive dishonesty (i.e., deliberate avoidance) about their suicidal thoughts on an ongoing basis with their current or most recent therapist.

To what degree can these numbers help us gauge the prevalence of suicide-related concealment among clients we encounter in clinical practice? Our sample bears a good overall resemblance to a national mental health services-using population reported by the National Survey on Drug Use and Health (Center for Behavioral Health Statistics and Quality, 2015), but it was not designed to be statistically representative of the population in psychotherapy. In particular, our sample included a higher proportion of young adults aged 18 to 25, a group which is thought to experience serious suicidal thoughts at a higher rate than older age groups (Centers for Disease Control and Prevention [CDC], 2018). Therefore, the ballpark prevalence figure of 21% to 31% offered here may be on the high end for suicide-related concealment in the clinical population, which can also vary widely by the type of patients being served in a given clinical setting (e.g., veterans, college students, psychiatric inpatients).

Nonetheless, these findings are in accord with research that has suggested that concealment of suicidal thoughts is fairly widespread. One study of 355 students at a college counseling center, for example, found that 13.8% denied suicidal ideation when asked on an intake questionnaire but later disclosed it during a face-to-face suicide assessment by a counselor (Morrison & Downey, 2000). There is no way to know how many more of these students continued to conceal it during assessment. Indeed, hiding suicidal ideation is believed to be at least as common as disclosure. A CDC study of 9,032 completed suicides in 16 states found that only about 33% of victims were known to have disclosed any intention to take their lives (CDC, 2012). Further, in a sample of 1,321 college undergraduate and graduate students who reported serious suicidal ideation in the previous 12 months, 46% said they had told no one about their thoughts (Drum, Brownson, Burton Denmark, & Smith, 2009).

Such high rates of concealment are troubling when we consider the many thousands of suicidal ideation concealers (or *SI concealers*, as we shall call them) who will eventually attempt suicide. It is also troubling for the far larger number of concealers who will never attempt, a group that may number in the millions. The psychotherapy clients in our sample had likely crossed multiple barriers to treatment and had access to a counselor trained and ready to help them. Yet these clients chose not to reveal their thoughts about wanting to die, arguably one of the hardest possible emotional experiences. So, what drove them to conceal? Our findings on this matter rely on two interrelated samples (Blanchard & Farber, 2016, 2018). We were able to gather short narratives from 107 psychotherapy clients across both our studies who had reported that suicide was the topic that was "hardest to be honest about." We asked them to explain in their own words what motivated them to conceal, and they did so, often at great length. Sixty-six of these respondents came from Study 2, which went on to present them with a host of additional multiple-choice and essay questions. How did they feel about being dishonest? What impact did concealment have on their progress in therapy? Did they envision ever telling their therapist? Or did they imagine only telling a different therapist, only family or friends, or no one at all? Last, how could their therapist help them be more honest?

MOTIVES FOR CONCEALING SUICIDAL THOUGHTS

Suicide stands out from other topics of dishonesty in that respondents overwhelmingly express concern about practical consequences—events they fear will affect their lives outside therapy should they disclose. Among six multiple-choice options for motives offered to respondents in our second study, 73% selected practical consequences, and 62% indicated embarrassment or shame. This prevalence of practical concerns is five times higher than that for all other nonsuicide topics combined.

To get a better understanding of respondents' motives, we turned to qualitative research methods, specifically content analyses of respondents' (n = 107) short essay responses to the question, "What makes it hard to be honest about this?" A total of 21 separate motives were identified which could be grouped into four basic thematic categories (see Table 7.1).

The headline finding is just how dominant the practical fears of patients like Cindy and Rebecca were. As Table 7.1 indicates, a large majority of respondents reported one or more motives for dishonesty relating to the practical, real-world consequences of disclosing suicidal ideation, including fears

TABLE 7.1
General Categories of Motivation for Concealing Suicidal Thoughts in Psychotherapy (n = 107)

Categories	Number of individuals reporting	Percent of sample
Concealment to avoid certain practical outcomes (e.g., hospitalization, medication, career impacts, family members becoming aware)	78	73
Concealment for reasons specific to therapy or therapist (e.g., to control the course of therapy, because of an insensitive therapist)	43	40
Concealment to avoid certain emotional experiences (e.g., shame, frightening thoughts)	36	34
Concealment due to beliefs about self or about suicide (e.g., "I would never do it," "No one can help me," suicide is taboo)	33	31

of involuntary hospitalization, unwanted medication, family members finding out, impacts on their career or education, impacts on others (e.g., dependent children), and in a few cases, the loss of autonomy to commit suicide if they choose to die.

Among these practical fears, avoiding inpatient hospitalization was by far the dominant motive, spontaneously cited by 52% of all respondents who provided narrative accounts of their reasons for nondisclosure of suicidality. Many fell into the Rebecca category: mildly suicidal clients who nonetheless believed that by merely mentioning suicidal thoughts they would be subject to forcible hospitalization. One respondent noted that she never came close to attempting suicide but was "afraid my therapist would commit me so I lied and said I didn't have thoughts about suicide." The belief that mentioning suicide was risky drove some to conceal it from everyone in their lives. As one respondent wrote, "I was scared of telling my therapist, or anyone, the truth. I was scared that would get me placed in some sort of intensive inpatient therapy." Or as another succinctly explained, "Talking about suicide is never okay." Another respondent expressed fears based on the experience of a friend:

> I was terrified that if I talked about just how bad I felt, the topic of suicide would come up, which would lead to me admitting thoughts about killing myself, which for whatever reason makes me think I will be Baker Acted [subjected to an involuntary and emergency psychiatric examination] and held against my will in a hospital gown (like my best friend was just over a year ago). And if there is one thing I can't deal with, it's losing my control over my circumstances.

As Hom, Stanley, Podlogar, and Joiner (2017) predicted, many clients in this sample seemingly do not understand the triggers for hospitalization. They imagine the worst and take steps to avoid it. This fear of hospitalization was, for many, a fear of the unknown. Although a few respondents in our study indicated that they had been hospitalized in the past, the majority of those reporting hospitalization fear did not give an indication of having that experience. Many reported that they simply did not know what would happen and did not want to take the chance. Our findings provide support for Ganzini et al. (2013), who found that one reason veterans did not disclose suicidal thinking on routine screenings was a desire to avoid unwanted hospitalization or medication. Our findings are also consistent with recent work that found that two thirds of college students who reported nondisclosure when probed by therapists about suicidal thoughts were motivated by concerns about being hospitalized (Hom et al., 2017).

Other respondents endorsing fear of hospitalization fell into the Cindy category, having personal experience of psychiatric hospitalization triggered by suicidal disclosures and perhaps representing a more chronically symptomatic population. One patient with bipolar disorder and a history of sexual abuse shared the following account:

> When I was a child, I threatened suicide after experiencing a traumatic sexual event. I was sent to a psychiatric hospital, and that in itself was also a traumatizing experience. The hospital was incredibly unwelcoming, I was very scared the whole time, and a nurse there told me that I should be ashamed of the traumatic sexual experience I'd had. Fearing going back there, since then I've never told anyone when I've felt like suicide was a valid option, and I've definitely thought about it since then.

Even among these clients, however, none described active suicidal planning or intent. Thus, despite having experience with this part of the mental health system, they may still be overestimating the likelihood that their therapist will react in ways they would find overwhelming. Both the Cindys and Rebeccas in our sample end up in a similar situation: They are afraid of crossing a certain line without a clear sense for where that line is and thus stay well back of the border by concealing even mild suicidal symptoms. Sadly, by hiding suicidal thoughts, they are concealing precisely the sort of painful emotional material that therapy is designed to help with.

There were several other participant motives for concealment of suicidal thoughts or feelings. Reasons specific to therapy or the therapist were mentioned by 39% of our follow-up group of respondents. Chief among these was a desire to control the direction of therapy, essentially to work on other issues in therapy. Other respondents within this category essentially blamed their therapist for their concealment, lodging complaints such as "It seemed he was concerned about his liability more than how I felt."

Concealment motivated by a desire to avoid painful emotions was reported in 34% of these follow-up responses. Most commonly, the feared emotion was shame or embarrassment. As one respondent remarked: "I know [talking about suicidal thoughts] is supposed to be good for me and protect me from myself, but it adds more shame and self-loathing that just exasperates everything." Also notable in this category was a small subgroup of respondents who frankly stated that they conceal to further their denial or suppression of these thoughts. One client, the victim of a past sexual assault, said she conceals the full scale of her suicidal thoughts in therapy because to tell the whole truth would force her to face the full impact of the assault. As she explained,

> It's hard to be honest because it means admitting that the trauma of the sexual assault had such an impact on me that now I'm in this scary space where these thoughts even come into my head, and it scares me.

Several respondents noted that to speak about suicidal urges makes them more real.

Finally, a total of 31% of respondents suggested that their relatively low level of suicidality necessitated avoiding or lying about such feelings. Most commonly, this took the form of a belief that they were at low risk for actually committing suicide and feared being considered for hospitalization. One respondent wrote: "Since I wouldn't really do it, I don't want to talk about it."

DISHONESTY AS A DOUBLE-EDGED SWORD

How do SI concealers view their dishonesty on this issue? In our second study, we asked, "How did you feel after being dishonest about this?" and provided 12 multiple-choice options partially derived from previous research on secret keeping, asking respondents to select one primary feeling that they experienced following dishonesty on the topic they felt was most difficult to discuss. SI concealers were most commonly "conflicted" (18%) about their dishonesty on this issue and also reported feeling "frustrated" (15%), "guilty" (13%), "in control" (15%), and "safe" (10%). Only 5% reported feeling "satisfied" about their dishonesty; fewer still (3%) reported feeling "regretful." At first glance, these results may seem confusing, but the overall picture supports an interpretation that clients view suicide as a complicated issue about which they would prefer to be honest if they felt honesty was a viable option. Dishonesty could be described as a double-edged sword, protecting clients from unwanted outcomes, yet denying them the opportunity to speak freely and openly with their therapist about a profound issue. Motivated by concerns that seemed real to them, they did not regret concealment, yet were not happy about it either.

Arguably the most discouraging finding here was from the question posed in our second study: "Is this a topic you would ever be more honest about?" to which respondents could choose one of four options: with a different therapist, with their current therapist, only with family or friends, or not with anyone at all. A majority (55%) of those who acknowledged lying about or concealing suicidal thoughts or feelings said they had no intention to share their experiences with anyone at all, whether inside or outside of therapy. In addition, only a third of these respondents anticipated that they would be willing to honestly disclose about suicide to their current therapist or any other therapist. Perhaps because of the potential consequences, SI concealers were substantially less likely to see themselves ever disclosing honestly about this issue than respondents who reported dishonesty about other topics. This suggests that clinicians may have to initiate discussions of suicidality, perhaps repeatedly, and especially with clients with symptoms of depression or self-injurious behaviors; on the basis of our findings, they may face well-entrenched reluctance from many SI concealers.

FOSTERING HONESTY FOR SUICIDAL IDEATION CONCEALERS

In our second survey, we asked respondents who considered thoughts of suicide the hardest topic for them to discuss honestly to imagine what their therapist could do to make it easier. Reading their short essay responses, we were struck that relatively few respondents cited the foundational aspects of psychotherapeutic work, including trust, validation, and the therapeutic relationship. As shown in Table 7.2, only 9% of these respondents mentioned normalization or validation as something that could help foster honesty, and only 8% cited a closer or more trusting relationship.

Instead, responses to this question were again overwhelmingly focused on the fear of therapists breaking confidentiality. The largest percentage (48%) of suicide-concealing clients told us they would be more honest only if the threat of hospitalization were somehow reduced or controlled. These clients

TABLE 7.2
Themes in Open-Text Responses to "How Could Your Therapist Make You Feel More Comfortable Being Honest About Your Suicidal Thoughts?" ($n = 66$)

Themes	Number of individuals reporting	Percent of sample
Provide assurances about reporting my suicidal ideation	32	48
"Explain what would happen if I talked about my suicidal thoughts."		
"Allow me to decide if I needed to be hospitalized."		
There is nothing my therapist can do	13	20
"I honestly would not share it with a therapist. As much help that they may be giving me, I trust my friends and family a whole lot more."		
Ask me direct questions about my suicidal thoughts	10	15
"If my therapist asked me frankly about it, I think that could make me finally open up about it."		
"If she asked about specific time frames, for example, I would probably tell her directly."		
Normalize my suicidal thoughts or validate my experience	6	9
"If he assured me very clearly . . . that I am normal for having these feelings, and that they can coexist with healthier feelings, then I might discuss them."		
If my therapist and I had a closer, more trusting relationship	5	8
"I would have to be more comfortable with them."		
Don't know	10	15
"I honestly don't know."		

Note. Quotations taken from survey responses. Sample percentages refer to proportion of 66 suicidal ideation concealers from Study 2 who reported each theme.

said they would feel more comfortable being honest with their therapist if they received some form of assurances, explanations, or certainty about the chances of being hospitalized as a result of their disclosure. Some wanted a frank promise not to report the ideation. Others wanted to be educated about the triggers for hospitalization so as to control their disclosure strategically. And still others wanted to be included in a collaborative decision about hospitalization and other treatment interventions. One respondent went so far as to propose that their therapist "contract" with them not to overreact to their disclosure, implying that nervous therapists, rather than suicidal patients, were the appropriate focus of a suicide contract.

This desire for predictability and control was well-illustrated by a 34-year-old female respondent who remarked that although she has learned much about the rules and procedures for hospitalization, her full honesty would only come with yet more certainty about how those rules would be applied:

> I am concerned they will force me into a hospital. I am less concerned about this than I first was as I learned that it [suicide] can be discussed to some degree if they realize you are not impulsive and at immediate risk. But still I don't know how much people know that or what their view of what "immediate risk" means. A week, a month, a year?

A similar point was articulated succinctly by another respondent: "Inform me what the protocol is when I am having these feelings, before it occurs, so I can decide how comfortable I am sharing."

Our findings suggest a possible new focus for the already extensive literature on suicide assessment. If suicidal clients are silenced by a fear of triggering unwanted interventions, it is imperative for clinicians to take seriously clients' fears about hospitalization and their uncertainty about the limits of confidentiality. After all, it is almost always the client who controls disclosure and therefore it is the client who must believe he or she will not be misunderstood or incorrectly assessed based on a therapist's overreaction. This might imply a new emphasis on "informed consent," specifically on the aspect that involves educating clients ahead of time about precisely what is likely to happen—as well as what is not likely to happen—if the client reports experiencing various levels of suicidal thoughts, urges, and behaviors.

Transparency about treatment goals, methods, and the expectations of therapist and patient already play a central role in several newer treatment modalities for psychological conditions that involve suicidality, including dialectical behavior therapy (Linehan, 1993), collaborative assessment and management of suicidality (Jobes, 2006), and cognitive therapy for the prevention of suicide attempts (G. K. Brown et al., 2005). Further, a strong case has been made for a suicide-specific process of informed consent, with the aim of educating suicidal patients and their families about the risks and benefits of treatment, as well as the risks of opting out of treatment (Rudd et al.,

2009). Yet recommendations for managing suicidal risk (e.g., Jobes, 2006; Maltsberger, 1986) often proceed from the point after a patient has been identified as a known suicide risk—for example, advocating that the clinician come to the emergency room after a suicide attempt.

As for patients who are entirely concealing suicidal ideation, the many excellent guides to assessing suicidal ideation have surprisingly little to say about the very real practical concerns raised by clients in our research. For example, Shea's (1999) comprehensive *Practical Art of Suicide Assessment* contains three insightful chapters about uncovering suicidal ideation but only includes one brief mention that clients may hold beliefs and fears about being "locked up" for revealing suicidal ideation to a clinician (p. 112). Methods of assessment have been developed to minimize the patient's anxiety by easing into the subject of suicide in a step-by-step fashion (e.g., the "hierarchical approach"; Bryan & Rudd, 2006). Yet clients who believe—correctly or incorrectly—that they will have their lives upended if they disclose suicidal ideation may remain strongly motivated to conceal no matter what method of assessment is used.

The question then arises, to what extent should therapists explain the "rules of the game" when it comes to confidentiality and reporting? Although treatment settings often require clients to read and sign consent documents, it is not clear how often clients receive detailed explanations about the triggers for hospitalization. Neither is it clear whether these explanations get remembered. Inpatient treatment remains a critical tool in protecting suicidal patients, but it is not required in the vast majority of cases. Thus, as our participants suggested, careful and slowly paced explanations of the real triggers for hospitalization can bring predictability to discussions of suicide, fostering greater honesty by clients who feel less afraid because they have a measure of control. Possible clinical interventions are not, as they say, rocket science. They may be as simple as pausing the normal discussion of confidentiality to say,

> When it comes to suicide, there may be extreme situations in which I recommend hospitalization or even am required to involve others, but the vast majority of situations won't call for any of that. Suicidal thoughts are common, happening to about 13 million Americans each year, so I want you to feel comfortable bringing experiences like that into therapy. Talking about suicide in therapy is normal. It won't make me think less of you, and it doesn't mean you'll be automatically taken to a hospital.

Our focus on clients' voices in this chapter precludes a full accounting of many other insights into working with suicidal clients. We especially recommend the recent work of the Aeschi Working Group detailed in *Building a Therapeutic Alliance With the Suicidal Patient* (Michel & Jobes, 2011).

SELF-HARM

Dishonesty about self-harm behaviors in our research was less common, with about 16% of respondents reporting having lied about this to their therapist in our first study and 13% reporting ongoing or routine dishonesty about self-harm in our second study. The prevalence of self-harm in the general population has drawn widely different estimates, but a recent meta-analysis (Swannell, Martin, Page, Hasking, & St John, 2014) suggested it is most common among adolescents (where lifetime prevalence estimates range from 8% to 26%), followed by young adults (from 4.5% to 22%); it is least common among adults (from 2% to 16%).

Part of the variance in these figures arises from the wide continuum of possible behaviors that can be called self-harm. These range from acts of direct self-harm, such as cutting, burning, or self-hitting, to indirect acts of self-harm where the intent to self-injure is ambiguous, such as starting fistfights in bars or punching walls, and finally to high-risk behaviors such as reckless driving or unsafe sex, where there may be no conscious intent to self-harm (Green, Hatgis, Kearns, Nock, & Marx, 2017). The term, one we introduced earlier, that best describes our interest here is NSSI; this has been included in the *Diagnostic and Statistical Manual of Mental Disorders* (fifth ed. [*DSM–5*]; American Psychiatric Association, 2013) as a condition for further study. In our research, we simply asked respondents about "self-harm I have done (cutting, etc.)," and this terminology generated narrative accounts matching the *DSM–5* definition of NSSI: intentional self-inflicted tissue damage done without suicidal intent and not for a socially accepted purpose such as tattooing or piercing.

As we discuss later, confusion over the nature and significance of self-harm plays a key role in how self-harmers justify the decision to conceal the behavior from their psychotherapists. When razor marks are found on adolescent arms, the reaction of parents and teachers can be frantic. Clinicians, too, are not immune to quietly panicking about the potential for suicide—a response that many young self-harmers may both crave and ridicule. Self-harm concealers in our sample were prone to express themes of being misunderstood or to dismissively contend that self-injury was not the "real" problem in their lives but merely a symptom they saw no need to discuss. The sense that authority figures do not understand self-harming behaviors is palpable in responses such as this one from an 18-year-old respondent:

> It feels like it's my own private thing, like it shouldn't be shared with ANYONE. People tend to misunderstand when I say I cut myself recently. One time in therapy my therapist asked me when the last time I did it was (in front of my mom) and I told the truth (two weeks before).

> And my mother took that to mean that I've BEEN cutting for a long time and do it ALLLL the time and am CONCEALING THINGS from her. . . . Yeah basically it's easier to avoid all that. . . . People, even those who have studied it and even fellow self-harmers, tend not to understand other people's self-harm practices.

In truth, researchers and theorists are still evolving their understanding of self-harm practices, particularly as they relate to how anxious clinicians should be about the risk of death. When Walsh (2006) published the first edition of his acclaimed book *Treating Self-Injury: A Practical Guide*, he was keen to draw a sharp distinction between self-injury and suicidality, urging readers to recognize what he called the most important point: "Self-injury is separate and distinct from suicide. Self-injury is not about ending life but about reducing psychological distress" (p. 3). This point indeed holds for the majority of self-harm cases, in which the most common individual goals include releasing the emotional pressure of bad feelings or, in the opposite direction, breaking through emotional numbness to "feel something" (Klonsky, 2011). Self-harm may also serve to satisfy the urge to punish oneself for perceived transgressions or to communicate one's distress to important others (Klonsky, 2011). Nonetheless, recent studies have shown that self-harm is not unrelated to suicide but ranks among the strong predictors of suicide risk. This is perhaps because the practice essentially serves as a "gateway" behavior, habituating individuals to hurting themselves in a way that reduces barriers to more lethal self-harm (Whitlock et al., 2013). Thus, by the time Walsh (2014) published the second edition of *Treating Self-Injury*, the wording of the most important point had changed to reflect the evolving, and at times confusing, current understanding of self-harm: "Self-injury is a conundrum. In many ways it is separate and distinct from suicide, and should be managed as such. Yet self-injury is also an important risk factor for suicide attempts" (p. 3).

MOTIVES FOR CONCEALING SELF-HARM

Among the 192 respondents who endorsed dishonesty about self-harm behaviors in therapy, a subsample of 30 provided us with both short essay responses and multiple-choice responses explaining what motivated them to be dishonest. This group was primarily female (73%), which may reflect in part the greater presence of females in psychotherapy and the greater use among women of the one self-harm method we mentioned by name, cutting (Bresin & Schoenleber, 2015). The group was also considerably younger than those reporting dishonesty on other topics (mean age 27 compared with 35 for all other topics). It is important to note that adolescents younger than

18 were excluded from both studies. Two thirds (67%) listed depression as a reason they entered therapy, and about 40% noted anxiety. They tended to use passive strategies of dishonesty, with 82% reporting they sought to avoid discussion of the topic altogether.

A simple multiple-choice question in our second survey, "Which of these best describes your reason for being dishonest?" gives us a sense for how motives for concealing self-harm may differ from the concealment of suicidal ideation. From among six options, nearly three fourths selected "embarrassment or shame," whereas only around a third selected the "practical consequences" that motivated so many SI concealers.

Just as with the SI-concealing group, our most comprehensive understanding of the motives for concealing self-harm comes from content analysis of their short essay responses, the dominant themes of which are shown in Table 7.3. As with the suicidal group, fear of involuntary hospitalization was present for self-harm concealers, although here reported by only 23% of respondents. The other six motives for self-harm concealment seen in Table 7.3 often appeared together in client narratives. They fall into two basic constellations, one of which we might call *dismissive reasoning* and the other *shameful reasoning*.

Clients who expressed dismissive reasoning said that their cutting, burning, or self-choking habits did not merit discussion because they were not the real problem (37%) or because therapists misunderstand the purpose of their self-harm (27%) or because therapists are likely to overreact and overfocus on self-harm (17%), either by devoting too much time to the issue or by becoming emotional or making "too big of a deal" out of it. These respondents downplayed the impact of their concealment, making remarks such as "I'm not in any immediate danger" and "Keeping it to myself hasn't bothered me." One 19-year-old female client experiencing recurrent major depressive disorder said she had been honest with her therapist for the first few months but began to hide it even as she continued to self-harm:

> I knew that if I brought it up, we would end up talking about it the whole session, or at least it would be in the back of her mind. I considered my self-harm an extension of other larger issues that I wanted to talk about. . . . I felt like talking about it more would be beating a dead horse—I understood why I did it, but I wanted to talk about bigger things.

For this client, self-harm was seen as a distracting hot-button issue that would prevent her from addressing the "deeper problems" underlying both her depression and her self-harm. She expressed "no regrets" about nondisclosure.

Other respondents were more circumspect about their motives. The client who initially remarked that she concealed because she was "not in any immediate danger" also said there were "plenty of other topics" she would

TABLE 7.3
Reported Motivations for Concealing Self-Harm in Psychotherapy ($n = 30$)

Motive	Number of individuals reporting	Percent of sample
Embarrassment or shame	14	47
"I am ashamed and kind of embarrassed that I still cut myself and I don't feel comfortable talking about it with anyone."		
"Self-harm has such a juvenile reputation. It is the exclusive domain of teenagers and borderliners."		
Self-harm is not my real problem	11	37
"I wanted to talk about bigger things."		
"I knew that it wasn't escalating and wasn't a problem that was getting in the way of my daily life."		
People don't understand self-harm	8	27
"Even those who have studied it . . . tend not to understand other people's self-harm practices. I think it's very idiosyncratic."		
"That's how most people think of self-harm—strictly in terms of the physical harm being done."		
Fear of being hospitalized	7	23
"If I were to share this with my therapist, I would be hospitalized, which would disrupt my life."		
"I didn't want him to put me in the psych ward against my will or on a psychiatric hold for being a danger to myself."		
Fear of disappointing therapist	6	20
"I felt like I was letting my therapist down if she knew to what extent I was inflicting myself with harm."		
"It would've been like telling my mother. She'd have felt HURT. Sad. Sad that I was hurt."		
Fear of therapist overreaction (excluding hospitalization)	5	17
"Therapists will look shocked or express pity, and I do not like that at all."		
Speaking about self-harm will trigger me	3	10
"If I talked about it I'd go down the path of all the things I hate about me and spiral into a self-pity, loathing, hopeless pit."		
"It would make me want to hurt myself."		

Note. Sample percentages refer to proportion of 30 self-harm concealers who reported each theme.

benefit from talking about in therapy. But she went on to admit that she may merely be dodging the issue:

> It is easy for me to convince myself to avoid it and talk about other things. I feel that talking to my therapist about this will help, but I don't think I want to deal with it, and this contributes to my avoidance.

Clients who expressed what we are calling shameful reasoning for concealing self-harming behaviors made up the larger proportion of concealers. They mostly referenced embarrassment or shame (47%) but also a fear of disappointing the therapist (20%). The narrative of an 18-year-old respondent illustrates the role of shame, and perhaps of fear and ambivalence, and is worth quoting at length:

> The first time I did it was in middle school, and I was doing it because I wanted someone to notice, to reach out and help me. But even when they asked or noticed I would hide and deny it. I don't know why. The most recent time was because I felt so overwhelmed with everything, like I was going to explode, that I needed some release and relief. So I did it, and I could focus on the pain. For a second it did help to calm me down. But then I felt regret, because I know I'm better than this. . . . I've seen my therapist 3 times since then and still haven't told anyone. I feel ashamed that I broke so hard. I want it to be in the past. But honestly I don't think I'll ever get past it unless I talk about it. But I'm too afraid. I'm trying hard to love myself, but if I talked about it, I'd go down the path of all the things I hate about me and spiral into self-pity, loathing, a hopeless pit. That's why it's too hard to be honest face to face about this.

The power of shame to silence some self-harming clients stands in contrast to more dismissive clients who believe they have the situation under control. Shame-motivated respondents spoke of needing to build up the courage and confidence to talk about self-injury in therapy. One client said she would wait to see how her therapist reacted to the disclosure of trauma before she broached self-harm. Respondents felt they "should have grown out of this by now" and worried that their self-injury was "strongly suggestive of borderline personality disorder." For shame-driven concealers, the moment of disclosure was feared primarily because of what else it might reveal or suggest about them, their weakness, or their immaturity, such that concealment becomes a way to protect a fragile self-esteem. One is reminded of Kelly's (2000) contention that an important purpose of secret keeping in therapy is the maintenance of a desirable identity. If the therapist serves as the audience for the rehearsal of a healthier self, revealing self-harm may threaten this performance too much. Several respondents mentioned wearing long sleeves to therapy sessions, and one remarked: "I did not want my therapist to really see my moments of weakness."

The distinct split in motives for self-harm concealers was also reflected in how respondents said they felt about having been dishonest. Unlike our SI concealers, almost none felt "conflicted." Instead, 31% reported feeling neutral and unaffected by the decision to conceal, whereas 41% reported feeling purely negative emotions such as "frustrated" or "guilty." The same split could be discerned when we asked them to assess how their dishonesty had affected their progress in therapy. On this question, 50% claimed no effect on their progress, and 40% reported that concealing self-harm had hurt their progress.

There was, however, one issue on which our sample of self-harmers was nearly unanimous: In our first study, more than 90% said the truth had never been acknowledged in their therapy. In our second study, roughly the same percentage said that as things stood now, they did not predict ever telling their current therapist. As one respondent tersely explained: "I don't think she would be very helpful." As we discuss later, however, clients did see some relatively simple ways they could be encouraged to open up.

FOSTERING HONESTY ABOUT SELF-HARM

Excellent resources on fostering honesty with patients who self-harm are available through the Cornell Research Program on Self-Injury and Recovery, as well as in the work of Walsh (2006, 2014) and Klonsky and Lewis (2014), among others. In our second study, we asked respondents to give us their sense of what their therapist could do to help them be more honest. The results, based on short narratives from 19 self-harming clients, are largely confirmatory of best practices recommended by experts in the assessment of self-injury and nicely illustrate some of the key principles of clinical practice.

Some respondents in our sample (37%) suggested that simply being asked direct questions about self-harm could be enough to foster honesty. In fact, clients who had a known history of self-harm asked for regular check-ins on the topic, chiefly to help them fight their tendency to avoid it but also so the therapist would have an accurate sense for how often they did or did not engage in self-harm. As one client remarked, "It would be easier if she asked every week. Then she could see that it doesn't happen all that often and it's not necessarily a sign of me completely falling apart." Clients whose self-harming was entirely unknown to their therapist still hoped that their therapist might take the initiative in bringing it up. One particularly articulate respondent explained the feeling as follows:

> It's possible that direct, but nonaggressive, questioning, with a strong basis in fact-based discussion of the issue, would help. I know there's a lot of emphasis on calm, quiet waiting for the patient to have their own emotional insight. But if I'm anxious, terrified, and ashamed, sometimes I do just need to be asked. Not interrogated. Just probed. Give me an opening, rather than making me make the first overture.

How can we know to ask? It may not be realistic to expect psychotherapists to intuit behaviors being diligently concealed by clients, yet numerous warning signs have been identified. These include burns, cuts, scars on areas opposite the client's dominant hand, frequent unexplained bandages, the tendency to keep the body covered even in warmer weather, and evasive or incomplete explanations for injuries (Cornell Research Program for Self-Injury Recovery, 2018). The use of routine screening instruments is recommended (Klonsky & Lewis, 2014), and these can also provide inspiration for the types of language one might use in the flow of a psychotherapy session. The Suicide Attempt Self-Injury Interview (Linehan, Comtois, Brown, Heard, & Wagner, 2006) and the Self-Injurious Thoughts and Behaviors Interview (Nock, Holmberg, Photos, & Michel, 2007) are two validated options.

Importantly, the manner and style of asking were of particular concern to our sample, with 26% asking for a nonjudgmental stance and 21% asking that their therapist not react with strong emotions to the disclosure or otherwise make a "big deal" of it. A male respondent with a history of self-inflicted burns spoke of wanting to avoid a shocked or concerned response from his therapist, which he would find "mortifying." Demeanor is, in fact, one of the best practices highlighted by major writers on self-harm. Walsh (2006), for example, provided half a dozen principles for how to act when assessing self-harm, focused on the notion of a "low-key, dispassionate demeanor" (p. 77). Walsh argued that any emotionally laden response to disclosures of self-injury could carry a therapist offtrack. Negative responses such as shock, horror, or emotional backing away are destructive to clients who may have already dealt with considerable rejection. At the same time, effusive, supportive responses run the risk of reinforcing the behavior. As Walsh explained,

> On the one hand, the nurturing, overly solicitous response may be immensely gratifying for people who have been neglected, ignored, or abused. On the other hand, condemnation and recoil may be paradoxically rewarding, especially for adolescents who take some gratification in provoking strong reactions from adults. (p. 77)

Walsh (2006) recommended avoiding the use of suicide terminology to prevent misunderstandings; he also recommended, when possible, using the same language used by clients to describe their behavior as a means of signaling respect and willingness to enter their world of experience. Citing Kettlewell's (1999) memoir of self-injury, he made the point that therapists should not convey an eagerness to "solve" the problem of self-harm but rather continue a low-key approach with a respectful curiosity about the causes and functions of the client's behavior. Clients in our sample made direct reference to this dynamic, saying that others' eagerness for them to "get better" had a silencing effect. Of course, in attempting a low-key demeanor, therapists are encouraged not to underreact to evidence of medically serious self-mutilation (Heath & Nixon, 2009; Walsh, 2006).

Finally, a few clients wanted assurances about not being hospitalized (16%), with one respondent describing some dramatic experiences with this particular part of the disclosure dilemma. A 27-year-old client struggling with addiction and depression reported that she had been goaded into talking honestly about her cutting with assurances that, she claimed, were later betrayed. As she explained,

> I've had some therapists tell me that if I was honest they would not lock me up, and lied and tried to lock me up for cutting. She ruined it for me. I can never really trust a therapist after that experience.

Just as with suicidal clients, handling the limits of confidentiality here is a delicate matter but one that should be approached with up-front and comprehensive informed consent (Klonsky & Lewis, 2014).

MANAGING OUR RESPONSES

Suicide and self-harm can trigger intense reactions for those who practice psychotherapy, from revulsion at the sight of another's self-mutilation to the cold fear of potential legal liabilities should a client walk out of the consulting room and take his or her life. As we have seen, clients report that it is most often our responses—what clients imagine therapists might feel or say or do—that push them to choose concealment over disclosure, to choose suffering (albeit with some degree of relief as well) over reaching out for help. The definition of trust, for many of our respondents, is the certainty that a clinician would react with a clear head and in a measured fashion based on an accurate assessment of the client's real condition.

To that purpose, it is valuable to highlight Walsh's (2006) injunction that part of the therapist's job is to "unlearn normal reactivity" (p. 223), to train ourselves out of our unhelpful automatic responses. Negative thoughts, including that our suicidal or self-harming clients are malicious, manipulative, or attention seeking, can be challenged using the same cognitive restructuring practices we might apply to them. Our intense affective experiences (e.g., fear, revulsion, or anger) can be channeled into focused attention to the client's struggle and a passionate commitment to helping with recovery. Although the client ultimately decides whether to disclose, much of our work may consist of making ourselves truly ready to receive these disclosures.

MINIMIZING DISTRESS IN THERAPY

As noted previously, dishonesty about experiences such as suicidal thoughts and self-injury is related to a broader tendency we observed among therapy clients we call *distress minimization*. As reported in Chapter 6, distress minimization came to our attention in our first survey on lying, in which the two most commonly reported lies told to therapists were "I minimized how bad I really feel" and "I minimized the severity of my symptoms." The obvious question is why so many would make an effort to undertake psychotherapy only to downplay the problems that brought them in.

A subsample of 52 respondents elected to provide short essay responses about their motives for minimizing emotional distress. Most of these clients wrote about hiding either the depth of their depression or the heights of their anxiety, whereas smaller numbers concealed the occurrence of anger outbursts, manic episodes, or other symptoms that contributed to their unhappiness. In this sense, distress minimization is a far more diverse phenomenon than suicide or self-harm concealment, and so we interpret our findings on it in broad strokes. Content analysis of their short narratives suggests two major (though not mutually exclusive) categories: minimizing to protect the therapist and minimizing to protect the self.

The larger number of distress minimizers (56%) sought to protect themselves from a range of experiences such as shame or having to face the full weight of their unhappiness or lack of progress in therapy. One respondent wrote that she hides her symptoms because "I don't want to FEEL crazy. I feel that by verbalizing my symptoms they become more real." A smaller group (27%) reported minimizing their distress to protect the therapist from being disappointed or feeling that therapy was a failure. They often sought to maintain the illusion of progress. As one respondent wrote, "I don't want to make my counselor's job any harder than it already is." Here again, we are in the realm of Rennie's (1994) ideas about clients' tendencies to defer to their therapists' authority or needs.

Two additional, less common themes are no less interesting. Twelve percent of distress minimizers were motivated by a belief that expressing the full depth of their unhappiness would make them seem like complainers or even "drama queens." As one such respondent wrote, "I don't like to appear overly dramatic or attention seeking." Finally, 6% of respondents voiced a theme familiar from previous topics addressed in this chapter: a desire to control the conversation in therapy and steer it toward areas they believe will be more productive. One respondent wrote, "I didn't want to take time away from talking about other issues so I minimized the way I felt in order to change the topic."

Further evidence of the tendency to downplay one's distress comes from the fourth most commonly reported topic of dishonesty in our first study, "my insecurities or doubts about myself," about which 31% of respondents reported having lied to their therapist at some point in the past. All of those who answered in-depth questions on this topic ($n = 22$) described either minimizing or omitting material about their insecurities; none reported exaggerating.

Embarrassment was the most common motivating factor for self-acknowledged lies about this topic, reported by 64% of this group. From their short essay responses, we can distinguish several forms of embarrassment. Some were motivated by a fear of appearing to be weak or whiny. One respondent described carrying attitudes picked up from regular life into the therapy room:

> I always found it difficult to express myself honestly about my doubts and insecurities to my therapist because I didn't want to seem like I was whining. . . . I was used to hearing from my friends that I just needed to "suck it up and get over it."

Similarly, other respondents reported not wanting their therapist to think they were a "loser" or that they were failing to make progress in therapy. More poignant, a few respondents spoke of experiencing self-hate that they could not find the words to express or did not believe the therapist could ever understand. A married female client in her 30s anticipated that disclosing to her therapist would only lead to disbelief: "It's hard to tell people how much I hate myself sometimes. Mostly because the general reaction is always one of disbelief and that I shouldn't feel that way because other people love me."

The most notable feature of all these forms of distress minimization may simply be how common they are. Taken together, 67% of all respondents in our first survey admitted to lying (in some form) to downplay their symptoms, insecurities, or how bad they felt. In this regard, distress minimization calls to mind Goffman's (1959) notion of *self-presentation*, the nearly constant work we all do to maintain the performance of being a person who is outwardly coherent, believable, respectable, and "normal." To admit that one is dramatically in distress—even to one's therapist—may violate the basic social rules that Goffman observed. Our results provide evidence that the struggle of self-presentation is highly relevant to what happens in the therapy room. Despite the confidentiality and supportive atmosphere of psychotherapy—which is designed to limit the need to manage self-presentation—clients, often under the weight of considerable shame, at times carry on the performance of their public self in therapy, just as they would in any other situation. Still, clients' ambivalence about their tendency to minimize their distress is apparently considerable: As we noted in the previous chapter, distress minimization is notable among all the topics of dishonesty dealt with in this book in being the lie most likely to be eventually detected by therapists, a phenomenon we suspect is abetted by clients' growing awareness during the course of their therapy that downplaying their distress is antithetical to their needs to be known, understood, and helped.

8

COMMON CLINICAL LIES: ALL THINGS SEXUAL

> I don't try to write an archaeology of sexual fantasies. I try to make an archaeology of discourse about sexuality, which is really the relationship between what we do, what we are obliged to do, what we are forbidden to do in the field of sexuality, and what we are allowed, forbidden, or obliged to say about our sexual behaviour. That's the point. It's not a problem of fantasy; it's a problem of verbalisation.
>
> —Michel Foucault,
> "An Interview With Stephen Riggs"

Erica has a fetish she cannot talk about with anyone—not even her partner. She has played out the fantasy in her head of how her therapist would react if she told her: "I feel like she'd act like she was okay with it, but she would really be judging me. That's the human thing to do." Tom has been cheating on his wife with multiple women for nearly 30 years. It makes him regretful, but the idea of disclosing to his therapist fills him with dread. "It's hard to admit that I'm capable of doing something so wrong," he said. "Avoidance is easier than acknowledging the issue." Josie is a young woman working with an older therapist who she describes as a "mom" figure in her life, which has made it feel impossible to disclose that she is a lesbian: "It just feels like a very adult subject. I feel huge shame about sexuality in general, but it is also hard with her in particular."

All three of these clients offer compelling reasons for concealing sexual material from their therapist. And yet, they also share a sense of being

http://dx.doi.org/10.1037/0000128-009
Secrets and Lies in Psychotherapy, by B. A. Farber, M. Blanchard, and M. Love

distressed over their inability to be more open about this intimate, important information. For Josie, for example, being dishonest about her sexuality seemed necessary as a way of avoiding the intense shame that disclosure provoked, but it also made her feel guilty afterward and stalled her therapeutic progress. "No work really gets done if I can't bring the issues to the table," she said. "It's like I want the naked truth to come out so I can actually address the issue, feel the feelings, and move on. But it's never all the way uncovered because I'm too ashamed." Josie's conflict captures a common clinical dilemma. Although clients often have the desire to navigate this area, talking openly about sex can feel too taboo, sensitive, or fraught with the possibility that the therapist will react negatively. Avoiding the topic protects clients from these negative feelings, providing relatively effective relief from the possibility of embarrassment or judgment. But in the long term, for clients like Josie, this short-term solution can serve to intensify shame and impede meaningful therapy work.

The empirical literature has indicated consistently that sexual topics are the most frequent theme of nondisclosure in therapy (Baumann & Hill, 2016; Hill, Thompson, Cogar, & Denman, 1993; Martin, 2006; Pope & Tabachnick, 1994). Even when clients discuss sexual issues in therapy, they tend to do so partially, leaving out a great deal of information. In Farber and Sohn's (2007) study of client disclosure, some of the largest discrepancies between client ratings of salience (i.e., perceived importance of a topic) and extent of disclosure emerged in the domain of sexual issues, including such topics as "the nature of my sexual experience," "my feelings about masturbation," and "concerns about sexual performance."

Even therapists who are psychotherapy clients themselves find it hard to talk about sex. In Pope and Tabachnick's (1994) study of 476 clients who were therapists, the highest percentage of secrets concealed in treatment concerned sexual issues (51%). Among a sample of 109 psychology graduate students, Martin (2006) found that material most often lied about in their therapy was about relationships (13%) and sexual behavior (7%). Years spent learning to be self-reflective and to negotiate the most challenging of interpersonal situations are apparently insufficient in overcoming some therapists' reluctance to discuss sex in their own therapy.

In our surveys of dishonesty in therapy, sexual and relationship topics were among those most subject to various forms of dishonesty. As noted earlier, in our first survey of 547 outpatient therapy clients, we asked clients "What have you lied about in therapy?" and instructed them to select as many topics as were relevant out of 58 possible options. Table 8.1 indicates the prevalence rates for all topics related to sex and relationships.

On the one hand, we were somewhat surprised that sexual and relational issues were not reported more frequently as topics about which clients

TABLE 8.1
Prevalence of Lies About Sexual Topics in Psychotherapy:
Study 1 (*N* = 547)

Topic	*n*	Percent reporting lying
1. My sexual history	119	22
2. My sexual fantasies or desires	93	17
3. The state of my sex life these days	72	13
4. My masturbation habits	69	13
5. How I really act in relationships	62	11
6. A sexual problem I have had	53	10
7. My real feelings about my spouse or partner	52	10
8. Times I have cheated on a spouse or partner	52	10
9. My use of pornography	50	9

lied. In fact, as was noted in Chapter 6, several topics far exceeded the prevalence rate of lying about these specific sexually related issues, including minimization of distress, thoughts of suicide, personal insecurities, pretending to like one's therapist's suggestions, and use of drugs or alcohol. On the other hand, 48% of this sample reported at least one sexually related lie. Notably, too, three of the 10 "biggest" lies, defined in terms of a self-reported score of 5 on a scale where 1 = *tiny bit dishonest* to 5 = *totally or extremely dishonest*, were related to sex: "My masturbation habits," "My use of pornography," and "Times I cheated on my partner." And two other of the top 10 "biggest" lies—"Romantic or sexual feelings about my therapist" and "Experiences of sexual abuse or trauma"—are not about sex per se but have a sexual component. In short, many of those who acknowledge lying in therapy about some sexually related issues report being quite deceptive when doing so.

Our second study focused on ongoing dishonesty. The prevalence of ongoing dishonesty about sexual topics in psychotherapy, with the breakdown between active lying and avoidance, is presented in Table 8.2. For example, the 4% figure in this table in the row "My sexual desires or fantasies" refers to those 30 respondents (among the 798 in the sample) who indicated that they had discussed this topic in therapy but with a low degree of honesty (i.e., scores of 1 or 2 on a 5-point honesty scale); the 30% figure refers to those 238 respondents in the overall sample who indicated that they had not discussed this topic in therapy because they were deliberately avoiding it. The 34% figure derives from simply adding these two percentages. This approach was designed to help us get a clearer sense of the "style" of dishonesty—and as can be seen, and is true for almost all topics, psychotherapy clients prefer passive dishonesty (avoidance) to active lying in regard to sexually themed issues. In this sample, 48% of respondents were dishonest about one or more

TABLE 8.2
Prevalence of Ongoing Dishonesty About Sexual Topics in Psychotherapy, With Breakdown of Active Lying and Passive Avoidance: Study 2 ($n = 798$)

Topic	Total percent reporting dishonesty	Percent who speak dishonestly (active lying)	Percent who deliberately avoid
1. My sexual desires or fantasies	34	4	30
2. Details of my sex life	33	7	26
3. My sexual orientation	17	7	10
4. Times I have cheated on a partner	9	3	6

Note. Total dishonesty comprises those who speak dishonestly (active lying) and those who deliberately avoid (passive dishonesty). Speaking dishonestly defined as 1 or 2 on a 5-point scale where 1 = *not at all honest.*

sexually related topics in therapy, a percentage identical to the percentage of respondents in Study 1 who reported at least one sexually related lie.

It is also notable that although sexual issues were not particularly high on the list of topics respondents acknowledge having lied about in psychotherapy at least once, two sexually related issues—sexual desires or fantasies and details of sex life—are at the top of the list of those issues in therapy that are the subject of ongoing dishonesty. In short, clients may not overtly lie about sex a great deal, but they sure do avoid talking about it, even when they acknowledge its relevance to their lives.

In our second survey, we also gave a select group of respondents—those who indicated that one of these topics had been the "hardest" to discuss in their therapy—a checklist of six common motives identified in the literature and allowed them to select as many as were relevant to that particular topic. Table 8.3 presents the top three most endorsed responses to the question "Which of these describes your reason for not being more honest?" among those in our sample who found each of four sexually related topics most difficult to discuss. For example, the first row in this table comprises only those 55 respondents among the sample who indicated that "details of my sex life" was the most difficult topic for them to discuss in therapy—and 82% of this group reported that "embarrassment or shame" was a reason for their difficulty in being honest about this topic. The respondents who endorsed a specific topic as most difficult to discuss were also given the opportunity to respond at length to the open-ended question "What makes it hard to be honest?" These open-text responses, along with the responses derived from our investigation of client motives in our first study, are discussed further in each topic section.

TABLE 8.3
Most Prevalent Motives Endorsed for Dishonesty About Specific Sexual Topics

Topic	Top three motives		
Details of my sex life ($n = 55$)	Embarrassment or shame: 82%	I doubt my therapist can help or understand: 20%	I didn't want this to distract from other topics: 15%
Sexual desires and fantasies ($n = 44$)	Embarrassment or shame: 82%	I doubt my therapist can help or understand: 32%	I didn't want this to distract from other topics: 23%
My sexual orientation ($n = 18$)	Embarrassment or shame: 77%	I doubt my therapist can help or understand: 35%	My therapist would be upset, hurt, or disappointed: 23%
Times I cheated on a partner ($n = 17$)	Embarrassment or shame: 94%	My therapist would be upset, hurt, or disappointed: 35%	I didn't want to look bad: 24%

Although the open-text responses provided by our respondents suggest that clients' motivations for dishonesty on specific sexual issues are topic dependent, the data in Table 8.3 indicate substantial overlap. For each of these four sexually related topics, the most commonly endorsed motive for dishonesty—by far—was "embarrassment or shame." Moreover, for three of these topics, the second most widely endorsed motive was "I doubt my therapist can help or understand." Thus, among those who feel that sexual issues are the most difficult topics for them to discuss in therapy, there is a consistent two-prong attribution for this behavior: a sense that this issue is inextricably linked with shame and an accompanying sense—or perhaps rationalization—that the therapist could not understand this problem or issue anyway.

For both sides of the dyad, it is all too easy to avoid the discomfort of talking about sex, but our findings suggest many clients experience real costs for this avoidance. When we asked those who were dishonest about a sexually related topic in their therapy, "How has not being honest affected your therapy?" it was common to report "no effect"; more than half of respondents tended to compartmentalize sexual matters as simply not what they sought therapy for and not what they needed help with (see Table 8.4). But substantial numbers reported that dishonesty actually hurt their progress in therapy, ranging from 39% to 61% depending on the topic. They perceived themselves as less honest about other topics or less connected with their therapist due to this avoidance. Clients concealing their sexual orientation were most likely to report negative treatment effects, with those concealing infidelity not far behind. By contrast, clients who struggled most with dishonesty regarding their sexual desires or fantasies were more likely

TABLE 8.4
Perceived Effect on Therapy Progress of Client Dishonesty About a Sexual Topic

Topic	No effect	It hurt my progress	It helped my progress
1. My sexual desires or fantasies ($n = 44$)	61%	39%	2%
2. Details of my sex life ($n = 55$)	56%	44%	0%
3. Times I have cheated on a partner ($n = 17$)	47%	53%	0%
4. My sexual orientation ($n = 18$)	39%	61%	0%

to report that this behavior had no effect on their treatment than those acknowledging struggling with dishonesty about these other sexually related topics. Importantly, almost no respondents reported that dishonesty about sexual topics helped their progress. Even those clients who described how dishonesty served a protective function for them did not find that their choice ultimately conferred any benefit overall.

With these considerations in mind, we turn to individual discussions of four sexually related issues that clients struggle to discuss honestly in therapy, looking at the complex reasons they have for being dishonest, their feelings about their dishonesty, and the perceived effects of their dishonesty on the therapy process.

DETAILS OF ONE'S SEX LIFE

Sheila entered therapy wanting to target symptoms of emotional dysregulation, including self-harm and feelings of aloneness. Working with her older female therapist, however, she found that it was nearly impossible to discuss some of the associated issues she most desperately needed to address, including problems in her sex life: "When I've tried to talk about sex in small ways, she was very supportive, but I felt tremendous discomfort and wished I'd never brought it up." As a result of this impasse, Sheila felt "trapped by shame." Yet the idea of bringing this up with her therapist made her want to "run away from her, to crawl under a rock, or just disappear—anything so I wouldn't have to look at her."

Shame or embarrassment emerged as the most prevalent motivation—cited by 82% of the follow-up sample—for dishonesty about the details of their sex life. In comparison, across every other topic of dishonesty in our survey, shame or embarrassment was a motive for 58% of clients. When it comes to discussing their sex lives, clients seem especially likely to imagine their therapist's reaction, often one that is far more judgmental and shame inducing than is likely to be the case.

In addition to being seen as judgmental, therapists may also be seen as ineffective: Twenty-eight percent of our follow-up sample reported that they had been dishonest about their sex lives because they doubted the therapist could help or be able to understand. These concerns were often related to features of the therapist, such as their demographic identity, knowledge base, or warmth. In the words of a male client whose sexual life involved BDSM, "I'm not in therapy so that I can spend 20 minutes providing sufficient context for her to understand my sex life." Indeed, the anticipation of therapist ignorance or even bias about certain sexual topics may not be unfounded: In a study of self-identified BDSM enthusiasts, Kolmes, Stock, and Moser (2006) found that over half reported experiencing "biased care" such as being lectured about BDSM being "unhealthy," needing to provide therapists with education on the topic, or being told to discontinue kink activities as a condition of receiving further treatment. Acknowledging the possibility that being open would do more harm than good, the male client continued by saying, "Even knowing that her job is to be nonjudgmental, I still have a sense that it would affect how she sees me and other kinksters if I gave her the details."

Several clients also suggested that their inhibition around disclosing details of their sex life was related to poor clinical technique on the part of their therapist. These perceived problems ranged from subtle empathic failures to truly troublesome behaviors. According to one of our female respondents, "She [my therapist] let me know more than once that sexual details were not really the point of our work. She avoided my every attempt to talk about this." In what sounds like an especially ethical breach, one female client who used to act in X-rated movies reported that her male therapist "started asking me questions about it that were not of therapy value but eventually led to him asking me out on dates."

Another theme that emerged in our follow-up questions was that dishonesty about sexual details is sometimes related to a client's desire to protect a romantic or sexual partner. As one married woman commented,

> This is between a man and a wife and I don't want to bring a third party in. There are issues that I would like to talk about, but I don't want to say anything to bring shame to my husband. It feels like I'd be going behind his back, so I just smile and shrug.

Thus, one's sexual life—even if it is a cause of distress—is seen by some as sacred and intimate, a topic that is off-limits even with one's therapist.

In general, though, clients were 5 times more likely to experience negative emotions (e.g., "conflicted" or "frustrated") than positive ones (e.g., "safe" or "in control") as a consequence of being dishonest about their sex lives. Although 56% of this follow-up group indicated that dishonesty regarding details of their sex lives had no effect on their treatment, about 44% reported that this dishonesty negatively affected their treatment course. One client, for example, felt that being dishonest "prevented me from reaching any insight or improvement about this issue, and has only made me more afraid to discuss the topic."

Importantly, though, over half of these clients could imagine themselves being more honest in therapy about this topic, either with their current therapist or in a different treatment. When asked what would help facilitate their honest disclosure, many (53%) felt that it would be helpful if the therapist would just "ask me about it directly." The therapist's curious, neutral inquiry into this area can often set the right tone for clients to feel that this is a discussable and welcome part of the therapy dialogue. Another significant portion of this group of respondents (33%) felt that they would be more willing to address this topic if they had a sense it was blocking their progress in therapy, suggestive of a significant link between honest disclosure and client-perceived treatment goals. Interestingly, another third of clients felt it would be more comfortable speaking honestly if they knew the therapist had experienced a similar problem. Of course, with rare exception, this is not going to happen. But although it is well beyond the bounds of appropriate self-disclosure for therapists to share the details of their sexual experience—and has been both before and after a small "anything goes" period in California in the 1960s—it could be facilitative for therapists to acknowledge that they have dealt clinically with similar material in their practice, or more broadly, to empathize with and thus normalize the client's concerns regarding the difficulty of discussing sexual details.

SEXUAL DESIRE AND FANTASIES

Over the course of her therapy, Jennifer has wanted to broach the topic of her sexual desires multiple times, particularly her worry that she and her husband are not sexually compatible. As she put it,

> I suppress my sexual desires because I'm not satisfied with my sexual relationship with my spouse. I feel like I've tiptoed around the topic with my therapist. I think she would have a fuller understanding of how I relate to my spouse if she knew this and would be able to help me more.

And yet, Jennifer has routinely been dishonest about this topic, consistently avoiding discussion: "She has asked me about my fantasies, but I don't feel comfortable telling her about this. I only talk to close friends about it, if ever." Jennifer's story highlights some of the unique characteristics of disclosure about sexual fantasies; perhaps even more so than the actual details about one's sex life, talking about sexual desires or fantasies can be seen as especially taboo and beyond the pale of the therapy room. Indeed, about 80% of our Study 2 sample reported that they did not address this topic in their therapy at all, and as Table 8.2 indicates, for a third of those clients, it was because they were engaging in what they perceived as ongoing and total avoidance.

A total of 44 clients selected "sexual desires and fantasies" as the topic that had been most difficult to discuss in therapy and then completed a series of follow-up questions. Their motives were similar to those clients who were dishonest about the actual details of their sex life: shame and embarrassment predominated (82%), a sense that the therapist would not be able to understand or be helpful (32%), and feeling concerned that the therapist would be upset, hurt, or disappointed (9%)—such as the client who described her fantasies as "kind of offbeat" and imagined that if she had been more honest "my therapist would think less of me."

When asked how they felt about being dishonest, these clients endorsed a range of emotions: A quarter reported being "conflicted," whereas another quarter indicated a positive emotion such as "safe" or "in control," which was over three times the rate of those who felt positively being dishonest about the details of their sex lives (7%). Another quarter felt "neutral" or "unconcerned" about leaving this material out of the dialogue. For some clients, discussion of certain sexual material is simply seen as elective, especially if it is not causing any particular stress or problem—hence the finding that 61% of the follow-up sample reported that dishonesty about sexual desires or fantasies had "no effect" on treatment overall. As one client noted, "I think it could be important for me to discuss this topic, but there is so much more to work on at this time that it doesn't seem like the highest priority." With other clients, it would take experiencing a specific problem in the area of their sexual desires or fantasies for them to feel more inclined to disclose.

When asked whether this was a topic they would ever be more honest about, about 41% of the follow-up sample indicated that they would be willing to do so either with their current therapist (34%) or in a different treatment (7%), suggestive of the possibility that more effective clinical strategies (e.g., the therapist "just asking") could facilitate greater honesty in this realm. In contrast, 43% of this follow-up sample indicated that they would not feel comfortable disclosing their sexual desires or fantasies to anyone, ever, under any circumstances.

Moreover, dishonesty about sexual desires or fantasies seems to be especially bound up in wanting to protect the therapeutic relationship. Compared with the rest of the sample, the "sexual desires" follow-up group was three times more likely to report that they would only be more honest if they could be assured that doing so would not ruin the therapeutic relationship. In this regard, McWilliams (2004) described a pattern in which discussion of sexual issues in therapy may become increasingly difficult rather than easier as clients develop strong, positive emotional reactions to the therapist. But it is not just a strong therapeutic relationship that must be protected against the "encroachment" of sexual material; rather, all therapeutic relationships, even, and perhaps especially, vulnerable ones, seem to be regarded by clients as needing safeguarding. One of our study respondents, who described his fantasies as "bad and dishonest" feared that disclosing this material would result in his therapist respecting him less and altogether ruining what was already a less than ideal relationship.

INFIDELITY

John is a married man in his 40s who has seen multiple therapists since he was a young adult to target issues related to childhood sexual abuse, including severe depression and a history of suicide attempts. But he was also hiding what he called "serious and large-scale infidelity and sexual addiction" in his current relationship: "Infidelity is wrapped up in my sexual shame and repression. I simply can't bring it up without dramatically changing the therapeutic relationship." He described a wide spectrum of emotions about his concealment, including vulnerability, regret, and frustration but also pride and power. John noted too that he preferred to change therapists "each time I feel like I can reveal more of my story. It's frustrating, but I only feel comfortable starting fresh."

John's experience just begins to capture how multifaceted discussions of infidelity can be. One has to understand the history (including sexual history) of the original relationship and the extra-relational encounter, the personality dynamics of each of the involved parties, the possible diagnoses of the offending partner, and the presence of co-occurring factors such as alcoholism (Bagarozzi, 2007; Blow & Hartnett, 2005; Duba, Kindsvatter, & Lara, 2008). But one of the most difficult aspects of this topic for a clinician is the fact that many clients are unwilling to disclose about it. (As a note, because our sample is composed exclusively of clients in individual therapy, we cannot say as much as we would like about concealment or lies about infidelity in couples therapy, often the primary arena for treatment for this topic—and also one in which clients are often more inclined or encouraged to address this issue.)

Across both our studies, 8% to 9% reported being dishonest about infidelity. In Study 2, this proportion of self-acknowledged dishonest clients consisted of 2.5% of the sample who reported that they discussed the topic but with a low degree of honesty (1 or 2 on the 5-point scale) and 6.5% who avoided the topic entirely. As one client succinctly put it, "I can't imagine being more honest about this; it's hard to talk about something so cunning, dishonest, and disloyal."

When considering the factors that motivate clients to conceal infidelity from their therapists, it is not surprising that shame emerged as the predominant theme, endorsed by all but one client in our follow-up group. Infidelity is both highly prevalent and morally condemned in most societies (Linquist & Negy, 2005), often creating feelings of untenable internal conflict. Relatedly, several respondents in the follow-up sample reported that their dishonesty was motivated by a desire to avoid their therapist's judgment or disapproval. Said one client, "I didn't want her to think of me as a terrible person. I feel like I know what she'd say if I told her. Being dishonest helps me cope without the fear of being judged." Some clients also just concluded the therapist would not be able to understand due to generational differences, such as the young woman who disclosed to her therapist about being involved in multiple relationships but felt like a more thorough discussion of these interactions would be too much for her older female therapist to handle. Therapists can easily become pulled into serving as representations of clients' social proscriptions against infidelity. However, as we discuss later in this chapter, therapists can also end up communicating their feelings or biases about relationships either covertly or overtly, which can stifle any willingness the client might have toward disclosure.

Another theme that emerged from respondent narratives was a desire to lie about or conceal this information among those clients who planned to keep cheating: "I knew what I was doing was wrong, but I was going to do it anyway," said one married male client who had been cheating for 3 decades, sometimes with multiple women. "As I see it now, I never really wanted to solve my problems. It was all a fake to satisfy someone else." Another respondent, a young woman, acknowledged feeling unhappy in her "illicit" relationship, yet did not want to admit it to her therapist: "Sometimes you can't say it out loud without realizing how bad it really is, and I wanted to ignore that. I didn't want my therapist to tell me to break up with him."

Concealment about infidelity reflects the fact that these experiences involve another person, someone to whom the client may feel a sense of loyalty. Affairs occur in the shadows, insulated from the outside world, and some clients feel the need to protect that other person, including their shared secrets. In our open-text data, several clients made specific reference to feelings about the affair partner as motivating their choice to be dishonest: "This is between me and the person I cheated with," said one married woman who felt "satisfied" about keeping this secret and felt there was absolutely nothing her therapist could do to make her more inclined to share.

On the whole, our follow-up sample had complicated feelings about their choice to be dishonest about infidelity. They reported mostly negative feelings, predominately guilt, regret, and shame. Some, however, indicated that they felt "conflicted" or that their dishonesty had helped them feel "safe." About half of this group stated that it had "hurt their progress" in therapy overall. As one respondent, a woman who had a history of cheating on every boyfriend she had been with, acknowledged, "If I were more honest, I might be able to work out why these things happen." However, about half stated that being dishonest had "no effect" on their treatment.

Infidelity emerged as one of the few topics in our research which clients did not state that they would be more willing to disclose if the therapist just asked. Of the nine follow-up respondents, only two reported that they would be responsive to such direct inquiry. In addition, none of our follow-up sample felt that having a more trustworthy, skillful, or warmer therapist would make a difference. Four of nine respondents in this small follow-up group could only envision being more honest if they felt their progress in therapy was being blocked, and even then, they would still find it quite difficult to do so. As noted, many feared that disclosure might entail being encouraged by the therapist to make actual behavior changes.

SEXUAL ORIENTATION

"I'm gay, I'm Christian, she's a Christian counselor," Carla said when asked what made it difficult for her to be honest about her sexual orientation with her older, heterosexual, religious therapist.

> I know her stance is that it's "wrong," but she accepts that I'm struggling with it and is open to talking about it. But it's hard to discuss having sex with women with a woman who hasn't. I don't want to weird her out and I don't want her to think badly of me. Even though my heart literally aches over the topic, I just avoid it for now.

In Carla's pained story, we get a sense of just how effortful it felt to bring the topic of her sexual orientation—both her conflict around it and her sexual thoughts and attractions to women—into therapy due to feelings of shame as well as worry that doing so would jeopardize what she felt to be a valuable therapeutic relationship. Carla was young and gay, her therapist was older and straight (and explicitly represented heteronormative Christian values), and these dynamics made her wonder whether her therapist could truly understand or accept where she was coming from. Although Carla was quite satisfied with other areas of their work together addressing her anxiety and depression, she felt guilty about concealing this, one of the most fundamental truths about her identity, and believed being dishonest ultimately hurt her progress in therapy:

> I'm trying so hard to be honest in therapy; I know that no work gets done if I don't bring the issues to the table. And I've got trust issues anyway, so it would be great to feel like at least one person could be trusted.

Of 136 clients in our second study who indicated that they had been overtly dishonest or avoidant about their sexual orientation in therapy, 18 highlighted this topic as being the most difficult to talk about in their treatment overall and answered a series of follow-up questions.

Even as the dominant culture has become far more accepting of lesbian, gay, bisexual, transgender, queer, or questioning (LGBTQ) individuals, shame or embarrassment still affects many in this community who seek therapy; these emotions served as motives for lying or concealment for 77% of our follow-up sample. Downs (2006) captured this dynamic in a succinct phrase, meant to describe the experience of gay men but that is likely applicable to the broader LGBTQ community: "The avoidance of shame becomes the single most powerful driving force in . . . life" (p. 29). This sense of shame is assumedly even more intense for those who are concealing their sexual identity. I. H. Meyer (2003) found that concealment (and the attendant dishonesty it requires) was a primary cause of mental health problems in gay individuals. Other highly endorsed motives for dishonesty about sexual orientation in our study included client doubts about whether their therapist could help or understand (35%) and whether disclosure would upset, hurt, or disappoint the therapist (23%).

Nearly half of our follow-up sample pinpointed feeling "conflicted" about the choice to be dishonest about their sexual orientation to their therapist, a finding that speaks to an ongoing internal struggle in which there is both the desire to disclose more fully but an equally powerful sense of paying an emotional price for doing so. In terms of therapy progress, 11 of these 18 clients viewed their dishonesty as having a negative impact on therapy progress overall. A female client in her 30s who felt dishonest about identifying as "straight" on her therapist's intake form when "bisexual was closer to the truth" referred to "a feeling of heaviness when we talked about anything that had to do with relationships because I wasn't as open as I should have been."

Almost half (47%) of clients who concealed their sexual orientation reported that they were willing to be more honest about this topic but only with a different therapist. This number greatly exceeds the relatively small proportion (17%) of clients who reported this sentiment in regard to all other topics. Other respondents who described struggling to be honest about their sexual orientation reported a need to feel more trust in the therapeutic alliance (50%) and to believe that the therapist understood their culture or class better (33%) before they could disclose more openly—often, this was described in terms of a desire for their therapist to share their sexual and/or gender identity. "I don't feel like my therapist understands my orientation," said one client who identified as asexual. "I'd be more comfortable if I knew she was the same orientation." For therapists who do identify as nonheterosexual, a certain degree of self-disclosure can be quite transformative for their nonheterosexual clients, leading to higher levels of reported connection to the therapist (Kronner, 2013). Another significant portion (39%) of clients in our follow-up sample of those reporting dishonesty about their sexual orientation indicated that they would only disclose more honestly if they could be assured that doing so would not ruin their relationship with the therapist. Still, the majority of clients (61%) felt that they would be able to navigate this topic more willingly if the therapist simply asked directly. Capturing some of the difficulty of initiating what could be an awkward conversation, one client stated, "I would answer the question if she asked. I just can't bring it up without the prompt."

Although for the most part our subsample of clients seemed quite willing to disclose further under the right circumstances, several respondents felt certain that they could not be more honest about their sexual orientation with anyone. One young woman was in a new romantic relationship with her first same-sex partner but was closeted from her family members: "Since it's something that's being kept a secret in other domains of my life, it's difficult for me to say the words out loud to my therapist." Charles, a male client in his 40s, called himself a "closet bisexual" but felt he could not talk about this with his older male therapist without "a firm vow of silence. I know they keep notes, and they discuss things with colleagues and probably sit around and laugh at people's problems." For Charles, the homophobic derision he had likely received from too many others during his life was now assumed to be his therapist's attitude as well.

WHAT IS GOING ON HERE? WHY ARE DISCUSSIONS ABOUT SEX SEEMINGLY SO DIFFICULT?

Stigma about sex is inextricably wound with the attitudes of one's family of origin and the broader culture. In some cultures, sexual expression is normal and even encouraged, whereas in others it is so uncommon that individuals rarely even talk to their partners about it; they like to have sex but not talk about it (Findlay, 2012). One of our respondents, an Asian female client in her late 20s, described why she avoided discussing her sexual desires or fantasies:

> This subject was never talked about in my upbringing and culture because it was taboo, so my natural inclination is to shy away from talking about it. If I did talk about this, I think I would feel really awkward and uncomfortable.

Another of our respondents, a woman from an Indian American background, was brought up in a culture where arranged marriages were the norm and sexual education was sparse, leading her to feel "bad and guilty for wanting to explore sexuality. I find it too personal to discuss now—maybe because my mother said it was wrong to talk about. My parents barely even held hands in front of us."

In general, American culture tends to present a paradoxical attitude toward sex and sexuality. Although popular culture often is highly sexualized, American parents tend to dramatize the topic of sex and focus their efforts on controlling and deterring children's sexual behavior, leading to a tendency for American teenagers to disclose less to their parents and to hide their sexual identities (Schalet, 2011). Ultimately, though, this culminates in an attitude toward sex that is fraught with tension, whereby sexuality is both prominent and sensed to be prohibited. Thus, a certain amount of avoidance of this topic in therapy may stem from the fact that many clients are never socialized to talk about sex, leaving them lacking adequate language to express sexual concerns clearly or confidently. As Gochros (1986) noted, "The sexual vocabularies provided by our society are either from the depths of the gutter or from the highest reaches of academia. . . . Thus, when discussing sex with a therapist, clients may become literally speechless" (p. 11).

Talking about sex can make some clients feel like they are exposing themselves. "I feel like my therapist would know too much about me," one client admitted. And for some, this sense of exposure is interwoven with past experiences of trauma. One woman concealing porn addiction and violent rape fantasies from her therapist was loath to explicitly address this in therapy, "even though I think it is probably deeply relevant to the fact that I was once gang-raped." Speaking about her sexual fantasies would mean speaking about her sexual trauma. For this client and others concealing this sort of abuse, disclosure may feel like entering a minefield of history and intense affect. Once they go in, they are not at all sure what shape they will be in when they come out.

Gender roles and expectations may also help explain why so many clients struggle to talk openly with their therapist about sex. Both men and women in our culture have strong, if distinct, culturally influenced attitudes about such disclosure. Even now, in the 21st century, many women feel bound to traditional gender-based norms that discourage the free expression of female sexual behavior, desire, or problems. Researchers and theorists alike have indicated that women fear judgment if they show sexual desire or communicate too much interest in sex, leading to a pervasive reluctance to openly engage with these topics, even with same-gendered peers (Hamilton & Armstrong, 2009; Muise, 2011; Tolman, 2002). Results of an interview study of 95 heterosexual women aged 20 to 68 indicated that, despite describing sex as important in their relationships and their lives, few women saw it as relevant or appropriate for discussion with others (Montemurro, Bartasavich, & Wintermute, 2015). As the authors noted, "Sexual selves appear to be private selves" (p. 150).

For men, too, frank discussion of sexuality can be problematic. In a study of sexual health communication in men aged 15 to 24, Knight et al. (2012) found that men primarily talked about sex as a way of demonstrating masculinity. Their conversations about sexual health centered on sexual encounters that represented their sexual prowess and virility. Discussions about health or illness were typically avoided out of fear that initiating such dialogue would be perceived as feminine or weak.

Speaking about sex can pose a particular difficulty for individuals whose sexual identity does not adhere to a traditional binary model. Modern sexual identity is better understood as a spectrum and can often be quite fluid rather than categorical and fixed. Especially in younger clients, sexual identity can feel confusing and complex, a phenomenon that contains more nuance than older therapists learned in their clinical training. Fluidity regarding both gender and sexuality is now seen as more common than has previously been thought, and the therapist's acknowledgment of this, as well his or her understanding of the relevant terminologies, is likely a crucial first step in helping clients feel safe enough to share their worldview. Although some therapists seek continuing training to become better acquainted with these newer sexual and cultural norms, younger clients can be skeptical that their experience will be understood, and some may never be able to believe or trust that their therapist can truly appreciate the complexity of their experience.

Although our quantitative data did not yield any significant differences in nondisclosure (across all topics) based on any demographic characteristics other than age—younger clients lied more than older clients—an analysis of the qualitative responses of our participants who acknowledged dishonesty about sexual topics suggests that some of these variables may be more relevant (at least in individual cases) than our earlier statistical analyses indicated. In this regard, some clients cited the intersection of multiple demographic factors as influential in their choice to be dishonest, as in the case of Erica, whose story opened this chapter. Her identity as a young woman and a lesbian made it too difficult to imagine connecting with her older, heterosexual therapist on the topic of sex, and she wondered whether it would have been easier given a greater level of demographic similarity.

Capturing the effects of dyadic demographics on disclosure is a complicated enterprise, influenced not only by how client and therapist overlap and diverge demographically but also by the degree to which each member of the dyad identifies with those aspects of self-identity. In the words of one 25-year-old Caucasian male client who was dishonest about his sexual orientation, "I think the age gap is a huge issue. My therapist is around 70, and the generational differences make it difficult to discuss certain things. He also seems somewhat arrogant and self-absorbed." Here, we get the sense that personality factors may have played as much of a role as demographic variables for this client in his consideration of disclosing something of personal or sexual significance to his therapist. (Alternatively, from a psychodynamic perspective, we might consider the possibility that these factors are transferentially linked—that this young man views his older therapist in ways consistent with his view of his parents.) A female respondent in her mid-20s provided another example of how demographic differences can affect disclosure on sexual topics:

> I think that the only thing his age and gender affected was that I never, well not never, talk about sex, but I would never, like, linger in that area. Like, if I was in a relationship with someone I would say whether we were sleeping together or not, but I would not feel comfortable going into a conversation about sex. But that also wasn't something that I had issues or concerns around. But for sure there was like a sense of "oh, I don't want to talk to a middle-aged man about my sex life." . . . to me it was like telling my dad.

Client disclosure around sexual topics may be affected too by the fact that psychologists and other health care professionals tend to lack sufficient didactic or supervised clinical training in sexual health. In Reissing and Giulio's (2010) survey of 188 clinical psychologists, 50% of respondents reported that their lack of training either moderately or very much affected their comfort in addressing sexual topics with clients; perhaps relatedly, 60% either did not ask or asked only infrequently about their clients' sexual health. Moreover, given that much of the clinical and empirical literature on sex and marital therapy is conducted from a Western heterosexual perspective, there is a particular dearth of understanding of how therapeutic treatments can be adapted to more diverse populations: "The majority of therapists are ill-equipped to work with lesbian, gay, and bisexual clients, having had little training on the topic of sexuality, and often expressing a lack of knowledge about such clients" (Evans & Barker, 2010, p. 375).

CLIENTS' DECEPTION ABOUT OTHER RELATIONSHIP ISSUES

What clients tend to speak most about in therapy are their experiences of intimate relationships with others, including characteristics of their parents they dislike and feelings of anger toward parents and spouse or partners (Hall & Farber, 2001). The question, then, is whether they are also dishonest about relationally oriented topics, including nonsexual aspects of relationships with family, friends, and romantic partners. As noted in Table 6.2, four of the 20 most endorsed topics regarding ongoing dishonesty in therapy were about relationships: times I treated others badly (16%), secrets in my family (16%), times I was treated badly by others (13%), and things my family did that hurt me (13%). Our findings thus suggest that although most clients are generally open and honest in discussing family and romantic relationships in therapy, there is a modest percentage—somewhere between 9% and 16%—who do lie about or conceal information about their relationships. Notably, these numbers are well below the numbers of clients who are dishonest about sexually related issues per se.

We now briefly examine one of these topics, "secrets in my family." Although it is possible that many of these secrets are related to issues of abuse (i.e., child physical or sexual abuse or domestic abuse), the way we framed this topic makes it impossible to know precisely what secrets are being lied about or concealed in therapy. With this in mind, we touch on some of the motives and major themes that clients reported about this broad topic.

Of the 32 clients in Study 2 who provided more information about their reported dishonesty on this topic, slightly more than 40% selected "embarrassment or shame" as a motive, whereas slightly more than 20% reported concerns about whether the therapist would be able to understand or be helpful. In their open text responses, many clients referred to another motive that was not captured by our multiple-choice checklist. As was the case with deceptions about sexual desires and fantasies, and about affairs, clients who were dishonest about family secrets suggested that because these types of issues were inherently relational—involving not just themselves but others close to them—the information was not theirs to disclose. As one client succinctly put it, "It's not my truth. It belongs to someone else, I'm just troubled because I know." Ultimately, then, family loyalty was an important force that protected this material from being disclosed. In the words of another client, "Family secrets are not to be shared. Whether you hate each other or not, it is an unspoken law." In this sense, family secrets have a good deal in common with secrets about infidelity: For some, there is the perception of a private and closed system, the details of which are not to be shared even with one's therapist. Moreover, this was not a topic clients felt especially willing to discuss further in therapy, and the majority indicated that being dishonest had "no effect" on their therapy.

CLINICAL IMPLICATIONS

Because many clients have difficulty bringing sexual material into the room, it often falls on the therapist to initiate discussions about the function and benefit of disclosure about sex. But there are multiple risks of doing so. There is the risk that talking about sex with clients will be interpreted as being seductive or voyeuristic, something that therapists are bringing to the therapy room for their own prurient interest. There is the risk of communicating an attitude of embarrassment or ambivalence that stifles openness on the part of the client. There is the risk that the therapist's anxiety about sexual issues—for example, sexual identity issues—may be misread as disinterest, or worse, judgment and antipathy (Eubanks-Carter, Burckell, & Goldfried, 2005). However, with increasing levels of education and sexual knowledge, therapists are more likely to engage confidently in conversations about sex with their clients (Byers, 2011), suggesting the necessity for more comprehensive training in the form of didactics, routine discussion, and extensive supervision to increase clinician competency about and comfort with sexual issues.

In particular, therapists' efforts to educate themselves about sex and sexuality frequently involves overcoming their discomfort or unfamiliarity with such dialogue. Findlay (2012), for example, recalled

> how nervous I was at starting to "talk about sex" in therapy. My start was not in isolation. I began with the support of the peer supervision group and trusted friends. I persisted and my knowledge, practice and comfort improved. (p. 31)

However, he also noted that "the fear that comes with 'talking about sex' has reduced, but it hasn't gone away" (p. 31). But by becoming attuned to one's own hesitations, the therapist can better understand the factors that make such disclosure feel forbidden for clients. It can be especially facilitative to check in with clients about their hesitancies or their sexual attitudes more generally, normalizing the fact that talking about sex in therapy can seem challenging or even taboo. As Berry and Lezos (2017) noted, too, clients often look to the therapist to know whether discussion of this topic is acceptable or not and may have to be assured that they are not unique in their sexual concerns or identities.

Eliciting disclosure about the prospect of disclosure rather than jumping directly into talking about sexual material is also useful as a means of gradually increasing clients' sense of ease. Findlay (2012) recommended the value of questions such as, "Does 'talking about sex' fit with you or not?" "Does it fit in your background, family, or community, or your religious or personal values, etc., or not?" "Am I creating an issue to talk about, or are we getting around to discussing something that needs discussion?" (p. 15)—each of which may serve as an entry point into the domain of sexuality.

Findlay (2012) wisely noted too that although therapists have to bring the topic of sex to awareness in the therapy space, they still have to grant clients the autonomy to decide what is most important to their treatment. Especially for clients whose sexual history includes activities that could be considered beyond mainstream social norms or involve a high degree of secrecy or shame, disclosure may seem entirely out of the question. In fact, when the 120 clients in our second study who indicated that sexual topics ("details of my sex life," "my sexual desires or fantasies," "times I have cheated on a partner," and "my sexual orientation") had been the hardest to address in their psychotherapy were asked, "Is this a topic you would ever be more open about?" slightly over a third endorsed the response "No, probably not with anyone." As Gochros (1986) framed it, "What we call 'resistance' may reflect the client's wisdom about what concerns, problems, or issues he or she is ready to talk about" (p. 12), asserting that it is always within clients' rights to direct the course of therapy as they see fit.

When asked what might allow them to feel more comfortable disclosing about sexual topics in therapy, clients in our studies focused on the potential of several therapeutic techniques. About half the respondents who elected to discuss more about any of the four sex-related topics reported that they would disclose if their therapist asked them about these issues directly, suggesting that the therapist's curious, nonjudgmental stance could facilitate greater client openness. Another portion of clients identified more relationally based prerequisites to feel comfortable disclosing sexual material: Approximately 40% described needing to trust the therapist more or to be assured that disclosure would not ruin the therapeutic relationship. And 30% also indicated that they would be more disclosing about sex if they felt that being dishonest was blocking their progress in therapy. One of our respondents had this to say: "If my therapist brought the topic up, then I might be more honest about it. However, I would not initiate the conversation." Another client in our sample suggested that it would be helpful if her therapist would ask "very specific questions using the words I have trouble with." In this regard, Gochros (1986) recommended using *invisible language*—words that are invisible in that they do not distract and that strike a balance between being too explicit or too removed or clinical. Whenever possible, Gochros suggested, it is helpful to frame inquiries using the same language that clients use; for instance, clients who talk about "fucking" may feel shamed if the therapist responds by reframing their words as "making love." It can also inadvertently signal the therapist's discomfort or judgment on the topic, which can preclude further exploration.

Therapists should be prepared to welcome questions from nonheterosexual clients about their gay-affirmative attitude and understanding of the population (Burckell & Goldfried, 2006). In a related vein, McWilliams (2004) pointed out the particular ambivalence that gay and lesbian clients have when working with a heterosexual therapist as distinct from the typical inhibitions about talking openly about sexuality that the majority of clients feel. These clients, she wrote,

> want me to be able to identify with their sexual nature, but they do not want me to presume to define it by simple analogy to my own experience. They want to be understood as struggling with lust, aggression, dependency, and longing the same way everybody else does, but they need to know that I will not simply pass off their *particular* sexuality as a matter of minor consequence. (p. 206)

Ultimately, as Berry and Lezos (2017) contended, clients yearn to be understood for their specific experience of sexuality as well as for their experience as a whole person, of which sexuality is a critical piece but not all encompassing of their identity. The implication is that doing so will make it far easier for all clients, LGBTQ or otherwise, to openly disclose these aspects of their lives in therapy.

Meeting clients where they are at and communicating an attitude of acceptance are also crucial ingredients in increasing honest disclosures among those clients involved in extramarital affairs (Linquist & Negy, 2005; Snyder & Doss, 2005). For many therapists, especially those trained in the United States where cultural attitudes tend to favor conventional monogamy (Van Den Bergh & Crisp, 2004), there is a lack of exposure to topics such as consensual nonmonogamy, polyamory, or other expressions of sexual minority identities. This can result in a range of covert or overt stigmatization and pathologizing of clients, which reduces the likelihood of disclosure or puts clients in a position where they feel they have to justify or explain their choices. In a convenience sample survey of self-identified polyamorists, Weber (2002) found that 38% of clients who had been in therapy at some point did not disclose to their therapist that they were consensually nonmonogamous, and 10% who had revealed it received a negative response.

Talking honestly and openly about sex and sexuality is not always easy for the therapist or the client. It frequently involves the unlearning of deeply ingrained prohibitions and the powerful sense that one is directly flouting societal rules by doing so. We can see why it often feels easier or seemingly necessary to avoid these topics entirely in therapy. And yet, being able to talk freely about such a deeply personal and profoundly influential part of life can be an unburdening for clients, a way of integrating those aspects of themselves that feel shameful by being witnessed through the eyes of another. Although some clients who view talking about sex as a distraction from their main issues of concern are likely genuine in their belief (e.g., they want to want to work on other, more pressing issues), our sense is that many times such declarations reflect a defense against the anticipated anxiety of disclosure about sexually charged issues. Our feeling then is that, in general, but especially in longer term, open-ended therapies, therapists should "check-in" with clients who have not yet addressed sexual issues, presenting them with the opportunity to engage with these important but difficult topics as they see fit.

9

COMMON CLINICAL LIES: SUBSTANCE USE AND ABUSE

> Most liars are tripped up either because they forget what they have told or because the lie is suddenly faced with an incontrovertible truth. But Cathy did not forget her lies, and she developed the most effective method of lying. She stayed close enough to the truth so that one could never be sure.
>
> —John Steinbeck, *East of Eden*

Few topics are so inextricably wound with dishonesty as substance use. Addiction has long been considered "the disease of denial" (Freimuth, 2005, p. 47), a phrase meant to capture the notion that substance abusers will engage in self-delusion and lying to others to avoid unwanted consequences, especially those that would entail ending this behavior. And although advocacy efforts have attempted to portray those affected by substance abuse in a more sympathetic and less condemnatory light, many psychotherapists believe that clients presenting with substance use issues are especially difficult, impossibly resistant, or even hopeless to treat. Some who work with this population exhibit notable patterns of avoidance, demonstrating less empathy and adopting a more task-oriented approach to care (Peckover & Chidlaw, 2007). Many also feel ill-equipped to address substance problems: Health care professionals consistently report low levels of knowledge and skill for treating such patients, issues that serve to compound already-existing negative attitudes toward working with these individuals (V. Howard & Holmshaw, 2010;

http://dx.doi.org/10.1037/0000128-010
Secrets and Lies in Psychotherapy, by B. A. Farber, M. Blanchard, and M. Love

van Boekel, Brouwers, van Weeghel, & Garretsen, 2013). Not surprisingly, then, clients with substance addictions have often been considered inappropriate for traditional psychotherapy and instead referred to more intensive medically based treatments, self-help programs, or addiction counseling.

Before examining the data on the extent to which and ways in which clients are deceptive about their substance use or abuse, it is important to note, albeit briefly, the role of the psychotherapist in "allowing" or even colluding with this behavior. Even experienced clinicians may harbor stereotypes of what problematic substance use or users look like, leading to a reluctance to directly inquire about the topic out of fear of upsetting seemingly well-mannered, well-behaved clients. Research has shown that substance abuse is most frequently undetected or misdiagnosed when the patient is employed, married, white, insured, female, or either an older or younger adult (Finkelstein, 2011; Harris et al., 2012; Schottenfeld, 1994; Widlitz & Marin, 2002). In a related vein, clinicians may fail to properly inquire about drug or alcohol use because their tendency is to attribute noticeable behavioral or emotional difficulties to more "acceptable" diagnoses, a position made easier as substance use problems tend to be comorbid with or mimic other diagnoses—for example, bipolar disorder (Henn, Sartorius, Helmchen, & Lauter, 2013). In short, routine assessment about substance use is not a "given" among health care providers, including therapists, making it that much easier for clients to gloss over potentially serious substance problems.

The clinical literature suggests that for substance-abusing clients, dishonesty—either in the form of failing to report or underreporting use—is typically in the service of impression management, self-deception, avoidance of shame, or as noted previously, circumventing behaviors on one's own part or those of others that might result in discontinuation of the behavior (e.g., Ferrari, Groh, Rulka, Jason, & Davis, 2008). Because substance use may provide pleasure, social connection, and/or relief of negative feelings, users may feel highly ambivalent about acknowledging their use, fearing subsequent efforts on the part of others for them to give up what they deem to be a necessary or even reasonable way of coping. In addition, some authors have found that self-report of substance use is most likely to be valid (honest) when individuals are assured that there will be no negative consequences to disclosing, including practical consequences, such as discharge from treatment, or interpersonal consequences, such as negative judgment from others (e.g., Weiss et al., 1998). Notably, too, many substance users will make no connection between their pattern of use and their reported reason (e.g., anxiety, marital problems) for seeking treatment (Khantzian, 1985; 1997), thus keeping this part of their lives outside the treatment room.

Consistent with work on the "stages of change" model (e.g., Krebs, Norcross, Nicholson, & Prochaska, in press; Prochaska, DiClemente, &

Norcross, 1992)—a way of categorizing clients' readiness to make substantial changes in their lives—there appear to be some characteristic patterns of disclosure about substance use that clients display at different stages of readiness. There are those who enter treatment to target issues of addiction or problematic use and are ready to fully and honestly disclose the history and current extent of the problem. There are others who enter treatment with substance abuse issues but who struggle to stay sober and then feel compelled to conceal their use to avoid shame and/or an anticipated negative reaction from their therapist, such as disappointment or disapproval. Other clients enter treatment ambivalent about substance use, recognizing to some extent that their use might be problematic, and although they muse about making changes, they are not quite ready to address the topic. And some clients are unwilling or uninterested in addressing the topic. This can span the spectrum from casual users who do not want to devote "valuable therapy time" to something they deem to not be an issue, to those who know it is an issue but refuse to deal with it right now right here, to clients who are fully in denial about their use being problematic.

Take the case of Marsha, a woman in her 30s who began therapy to address feelings of depression. Throughout her treatment, she kept silent about a major aspect of her life—her habitual pot use since the age of 14. Although she classified pot as "part of my lifestyle," adding that it was something she enjoyed and had a legal prescription for, she still viewed her drug use as an area to work on in treatment "to cut back somewhat, and get my usage down into the more 'moderate' category." But Marsha has concerns about disclosing the full extent of her use:

> Therapists are so gung-ho about sobriety, and everyone seems to think that in order to treat depression or anxiety, you have to abstain completely from drugs and alcohol. I'm just not ready to give it up entirely, so I tend to downplay the amount that I smoke. I don't want people to label me as an addict. I'm a highly functioning individual and my drug usage doesn't negatively impact my career or my ability to raise my daughter. But most people don't see these things as compatible.

Although Marsha viewed this area as one she could benefit from addressing more openly, she resisted doing so, fearful of how her therapist would react, both regarding possible interventions and judgments about her usage. Marsha was clearly in the "contemplative" stage of change, having identified a goal of reducing use, though she was yet uncommitted. The barrier to moving toward action had everything to do with disclosure; she was fearful of how her therapist would react, both in terms of possible interventions and judgments about her usage. She concealed her use so as not to lose control of the direction of therapy, yet this concealment prevented her from taking action on a reasonable therapeutic goal.

Our study sample contains a high degree of dishonesty on the topic of substance use. In our first study, which simply asked 547 clients "Have you ever lied about this in therapy?" 29% reported having been dishonest about their use of drugs and/or alcohol at any point in their treatment, making it one of the most commonly endorsed topics (see Chapter 6). When we asked these clients what lying actually looked like in the therapy setting, they were most likely to describe minimizing the behavior, omitting key details, or avoiding speaking about it entirely.

The results from our second study confirmed this finding in terms of style. Of our 798 clients in that study, 92 (11.2%) reported that this was a topic of ongoing dishonesty in their therapy. (We sense that the much higher prevalence in Study 1 reflects the difference in focus between our two surveys—that is, dishonesty about substance use at any point ever in therapy, and routine, ongoing dishonesty.) The 92 clients were evenly split between those who indicated that although this topic had been addressed in their treatment, it was discussed with a low degree of honesty (i.e., they classified themselves as "not at all" or "a little" honest) and those who indicated that they did not address this topic in treatment because they were avoiding it entirely.

Of our follow-up sample—which represents the 80 clients across our two studies who elected to answer in-depth questions about "my use of drugs or alcohol"—about 19% entered therapy specifically endorsing substance use as having been an explicit presenting concern in their therapy; the balance of these clients entered outpatient treatment citing depression (50%), anxiety (43%), or relationship problems (34%), suggesting that substance use is often intertwined with but sometimes seen as secondary to other presenting concerns. Among all 1,345 clients involved in our research, only 7.5% reported seeking therapy to deal with drug or alcohol use. This is consistent with other literature that suggests that patients often do not disclose having problems with substances and will instead present to treatment citing other mental health or physical concerns (Substance Abuse and Mental Health Services Administration, 2011).

Given that much of the literature has been geared toward the assessment and treatment of clients for whom addiction is an explicit part of the referral question, how should clinicians inquire about substance use for clients who do not present actively wanting to target this as an area of concern? Highlighting the experiences of a heterogeneous sample of clients who have acknowledged dishonesty about substance use (and who have found this topic to be among the hardest of all issues to disclose honestly about in therapy) may help therapists facilitate increased disclosure for those clients for whom this issue is relevant.

MOTIVES FOR DISHONESTY

As we noted, across our two surveys, a subsample of 80 elected to provide both short essay responses and multiple-choice responses explaining why they chose to avoid or lie about their "use of drugs or alcohol" in therapy. Table 9.1 represents the multiple-choice selections from the respondents in our Study 2 sample who were presented with a list of six possible options of motives and instructed to click as many as applied.

These findings provide an overview of the concerns that clients have when navigating the topic of substance use—namely, wanting to avoid embarrassment or shame, to direct the course of therapy to what they deemed to be more relevant topics, and to steer clear of possible real-world consequences (e.g., hospitalization, legal issues). Of course, it is possible that even on surveys about dishonesty on which respondents were assumedly willing to provide honest (and anonymous) answers to difficult questions, some may have still been influenced by considerations of impression management and/or the press to avoid acknowledging painful emotions (e.g., shame). We imagine, then, that there were some respondents—most likely those who were engaging in substantial substance use rather than say, occasional users of marijuana—who rather than acknowledging shame as a motive for a lack of honest disclosure about this topic, instead indicated their avoidance was motivated by a wish to focus on other topics.

To further understand the motives that drive dishonesty about substance abuse, we analyzed clients' open-text responses regarding their reasons for this behavior. The major themes, derived from coding clients' qualitative responses from both Study 1 and Study 2, are presented in Table 9.2. Note that narratives from any one client often included multiple themes; thus these numbers total to more than 100%. As can be seen in this table, no one motive dominated in client narratives, but four of the major themes related to either internally or externally, imposed shame.

TABLE 9.1
Multiple-Choice Motives for Dishonesty
About Substance Use ($n = 37$)

Motive	n	Percent reporting
1. Embarrassment or shame	24	65
2. I didn't want this to distract from other topics	18	49
3. Practical consequences	16	43
4. My therapist would be upset, hurt, or disappointed	9	24
5. I doubt my therapist can help or understand	6	16
6. It would bring up overwhelming emotions	2	5

TABLE 9.2
Reported (Open-Text) Motivations for Dishonesty About Substance Use, With Examples ($n = 80$)

Motive	*n*	Percent reporting
Avoiding being judged, stereotyped, and/or labeled "I didn't want to be judged."	20	25
Fearing real world consequences "Because I don't want to go to rehab."	20	25
Fearing that the focus of therapy would change "I'm more focused on improving my anxiety and depression."	18	23
Shame or embarrassment "I'm embarrassed and ashamed at how much and how frequently I drink."	15	19
Denial "I didn't want to discuss it, I wasn't ready, I was being resistant." "I was unwilling to admit the frequency of my use."	15	19
Fearing a negative impact on the therapeutic relationship "I told her that I quit, but I started again; I know better, and she knows I know better. I don't want her to be disappointed in me."	13	16
Wanting to preserve a useful coping mechanism "I'm afraid of how to fill the void of not using right now." "He would tell me I have to stop using, but marijuana helps manage my depression."	12	15
Having it under control "I'm not sure I consider it a problem. I could stop at any time." "I'm a highly functioning individual, and my drug usage doesn't affect me."	6	8

Note. Sample percentages refer to proportion of 80 respondents who reported each theme.

A quarter of respondents cited fear of being judged, stereotyped, or labeled as an addict by their therapists, situations that involve a painful loss of status and the potential for others to respond based solely on that label (e.g., "I'd only be seen in these terms"). One client in our study was fearful that his therapist would view him as a "low-life addict"; another believed that his therapist would see him as either "stupid or a drug addict because I use pot once or twice a year for spiritual purposes." Feelings of shame were cited by 19%, who sought to avoid experiencing their feelings of being damaged or flawed, and defensive denial was cited by 16% who, looking back, reported that their dishonesty with their therapist stemmed from dishonesty with themselves. Many with substance abuse problems struggle with the stigma of this behavior (Wallhed Finn, Bakshi, & Andréasson, 2014), and varieties of shame appear to be at play even once clients have overcome the barrier to enter therapy. Indeed, once they are in therapy, clients face the temptation to conceal relapses for fear of harming their relationship with their therapist; 16% of our respondents cited this concern as a reason for lying. One of them, a recovering crystal meth addict, expressed the following concern: "I'm insecure about my therapist's opinion of me, and afraid he'll get frustrated with me because I can't follow his 'simple' advice."

These findings echo the research literature in highlighting the powerful emotional experiences many clients predict if they disclose their substance use, particularly early in therapy (Forrest, 2010). Kirsten, a woman in her 50s who sought treatment for depression and trauma, told us that she felt unable to disclose to her therapist that she had relapsed after 18 years of sobriety. She explained,

> I went to treatment but have had trouble staying clean and sober since that time. I had two recent surgeries requiring prescription medication and I've started getting "slippery." I am ashamed by my lack of control and embarrassed to tell my therapist.

The expectation of shame and therapist judgment in response to disclosure, particularly about relapse, was a theme that also emerged in work by Lovejoy et al. (1995), who interviewed 17 patients enrolled in a relapse prevention treatment program for cocaine dependence and found that patients expected to be shamed by therapists for speaking honestly about their feelings, actions, or failure to achieve treatment goals. Although relapse is an almost inevitable part of the healing process for substance users (Witkiewitz & Marlatt, 2004), some will feel like a failure following relapse, resulting in resistance to thinking about or discussing the possibility of renewed attempts at change.

One wonders whether all this fear of therapist judgment is not a bit unrealistic, given that a nonjudgmental stance is close to a universal role requirement for therapists. Yet our respondents describe plenty of therapist behaviors that were far from nonjudgmental. One female client in her 40s in our sample who sought therapy for depression concealed her alcohol use because her therapist would regularly disparage "alcoholics" and/or praise her for not drinking. "I believe," said this client, that "my therapist had a bias against drug/alcohol users and that she was unable to separate out her own feelings in order to be open to mine."

Another prominent theme was that of clients fearing that their honesty about this issue would lead to "real-world consequences," meaning practical impacts such as job loss, legal consequences, changes in psychotropic medications, or forced hospitalization. In the words of one young woman, "I worry that I'll be thrown back into an inpatient program that I can't afford (time or money-wise)." Another client felt that disclosing her alcohol use would make her therapist think her current prescriptions were insufficient and try to increase her dosage or change medications. A college student who was abusing her prescription for Adderall stated, "It's hard to be honest about this because I feel that they will hold it against me, or not offer me medications that will help me." Another client had the sense that disclosing might lead to "getting in trouble, or cause my therapist to talk to my doctors."

Some clients also saw dishonesty about their substance use as a means of managing the course of therapy. As noted earlier, some imagined their therapist would start to overfocus on this topic, making it harder to devote time to what they really wanted to target: "I omitted my use of medical cannabis because I didn't want my therapist to dwell on it. It wasn't why I was there," said one client. For those clients who described using drugs or alcohol casually, it could seem like more trouble than it was worth to address it with the therapist, especially if they felt it did not impair their functioning in a meaningful way. A few clients also indicated that their nondisclosure emerged from the sense that the therapist could not be helpful or would not understand; these clients referred to wanting to avoid an unwanted intervention, such as being told to stop using or getting a lecture on how substances were unhealthy for them. One recent college grad admitted that she concealed binge drinking from her older therapist because "while I know that it's unhealthy, I also know that I don't have a problem; it's hard for older people to see that sometimes. I didn't want her to get concerned about the wrong thing."

All the reported reasons in this previous paragraph regarding dishonesty—that substance use is irrelevant to treatment or that such use does not impact functioning or that the therapist could not help anyway—are quite likely confounded with out-and-out denial—of clients protecting themselves from the shameful awareness of the self-destructiveness nature of their behavior. One client reported the following:

> I started seeing a therapist since I felt like I was unraveling. I blamed circumstances and people for my unhappiness. When she asked me about my drinking—what my habits were—my gut reaction was to lie. I didn't even think to myself, "Hmm, I should tell the truth, I could get help." I defensively lied and minimized how much I drank; I was in denial about what a problem it had become.

A related theme reported in our open-text data was that dishonesty regarding substance use was a means to keep the therapist sufficiently far away from a problem the client did not want to be modified, a motive reminiscent of what some clients said about their dishonesty regarding infidelity. For some clients, figuring out other, non-substance-using ways of coping with depression or anxiety can seem too daunting. Or in the words of one of our respondents, "I'm afraid of how to fill the void of not using right now."

In short, many clients expressed multiple, intersecting motives for their dishonesty about substance use—a wish to protect a more ideal image of themselves in the minds of their therapists, a need to avoid the shame of acknowledging substance use, and/or a fear that honest discussion could lead to significant therapeutic, behavioral, or legal consequences. As we explore in the next section, clients tend to believe that the wish to disclose their substance use along with a concomitant fear or reluctance to do so can have significant personal and therapeutic repercussions.

CLIENT FEELINGS ABOUT DISHONESTY AND PERCEIVED EFFECTS ON THERAPY

Our follow-up respondents in Study 2 ($n = 37$) were asked, "Which of these best describes your primary feeling about avoiding or being dishonest about this topic?" and were presented with 12 possible options. Our analysis indicated that the most common emotions identified were "guilty" (24%) and "conflicted" (22%). If they did endorse a positive emotion, it was "safe" (5%); not a single client felt "satisfied" afterward. About 27% of clients felt "neutral" or "unconcerned" about their dishonesty; we imagine these might be the more casual users who do not feel that disclosing use is particularly relevant or those whose problematic usage has not been incorporated fully into awareness.

In addition to stimulating negative feelings in the client, dishonesty about substance use appears to have detrimental effects on treatment progress more generally. The majority (59%) of our subsample of respondents in Study 2 who were asked, "Has not being honest affected your therapy?" and given three possible responses ("It hurt my progress," "It helped my progress," "No effect") indicated that not disclosing about their substance use "hurt their progress." For the 41% of clients who believed that dishonesty had "no effect," their rationale tended to be that drug or alcohol use was a separate part of their lives that was not treatment relevant. Not a single client felt that their dishonesty had been helpful or had beneficial impacts.

Dishonesty about substance use can sometimes be so taxing as to require the client to constantly redirect therapy away from what is being hidden. Take Jim, who was hiding his substance use from his family and therapist. Even though he was seeing his therapist for addiction counseling, he managed to maintain the facade that he was sober for 3 years despite multiple relapses. He felt he needed to avoid the loss of financial and familial support that would inevitably occur if anyone found out. Noting his intense feelings of self-loathing and guilt, he described how the need to maintain the illusion was detrimental to his treatment:

> It led to me searching for things to work on that did not really matter, or chatting about random bullshit in order to avoid being asked too many questions about my drug use. It certainly hindered my progress, as I did not talk about what was probably at the root of many of my anxieties and problems in my life.

Another client highlighted how being dishonest "keeps my guard up. I constantly feel like I'm avoiding questions I'm too conflicted to answer, which causes more irritability." And according to another respondent, "I don't even know how to bring this up now since I've been lying to her since the start."

FOSTERING HONESTY ABOUT SUBSTANCE USE

When we queried our 37 follow-up respondents about whether they would ever be more honest about their substance use, 46% indicated that they would be willing to disclose about this topic in therapy, either in their current treatment (30%) or with another therapist (16%). What did they imagine might help them do so? We asked this follow-up sample to provide both quantitative and qualitative data, providing them a checklist of 10 possible motives from which they could select as many as were relevant in response to the question "Under what circumstances would you be more honest?" and an open-text section to write in additional thoughts about how the therapist could make them feel more comfortable addressing their use of drugs or alcohol.

The two most widely endorsed checklist responses were "If I knew my therapist wouldn't overreact" (24%) and "If I knew it wouldn't ruin my relationship with my therapist" (15%). In the open-text data, the most common response (reported by 35% of respondents) was "If I knew my therapist would not judge me." Other common responses included "If I knew more about possible consequences of my honesty" (24%), "Nothing would help" (16%), "I would need more time to become more comfortable and develop greater trust" (13%), and "Just ask me directly" (11%).

When clients said they could be more honest if they knew their therapist would not "overreact," they were hoping to avoid two types of overreaction. The first is emotional and may involve disappointment, pity, or judgment. For example, one client felt that for her to be honest, her therapist would have to "understand why I act that way and help me solve that problem rather than making me feel like it's all my fault." The second type of overreaction is clinical; clients want assurances their therapist would not push to escalate their level of care. As one client stated, "I would need my therapist to reassure me that I would not be thrown in rehab and that we could take other steps to deal with the issue." Although in some cases the revelation of substance abuse could lead to a therapist's recommendation for a higher, more restrictive level of care, the reality is that except in the most severe cases (i.e., when the client is actively suicidal), a therapist could not mandate hospitalization. However, many clients are likely unaware of the legal and ethical obligations of therapists in such cases, which suggests that the therapist's explicit communication of the possible clinical consequences of client acknowledgement of substance use or abuse might be a critical factor in fostering disclosure.

It is important for therapists to recognize that clients often need time to trust them before they are ready to disclose fully, let alone begin to take steps to address problematic usage. Clients may test the therapist with small disclosures, gauging his or her reaction, before fully owning the scope of their behavior and feelings about it. For example, one woman in her 20s in our study reported that she would sometimes leave out the specifics of her drug use, expecting judgment from her older female therapist, but was eventually able "to bridge the gap" in the presence of her accepting and compassionate therapist:

> Being honest helped me to give compassion to the self-shaming parts of myself that were inclined to conceal drug use in the first place. It also helped me to feel more trust after the reaction I got from my therapist.

How might therapists proceed given this set of possible impediments to honest disclosure about drug and alcohol use? There are a number of possibilities, although, of course, interventions are always idiosyncratic to the specific nature and needs of a specific client at a specific time in therapy. That said, therapists can negotiate explicitly with clients about the amount of information that is comfortable for them to discuss (Palmieri & Stern, 2009). They can also normalize the fact that disclosing about this issue can be difficult but valuable. Finally, when it comes to inquiring directly, therapists are advised to take a neutral, curious, and open-minded stance. They are also advised to make a routine assessment of substance use and other factors that increase the risk of misuse (i.e., past trauma, medical conditions, psychiatric disorders) a part of every intake, regardless of age, gender, presentation of the client, or referral question. A comprehensive assessment can help uncover clients who are early in the addiction cycle or make potentially problematic use an area of increased awareness. Regularly checking in with clients to see whether anything has changed in this domain can be fruitful, especially for those who may not have felt comfortable disclosing fully at an earlier time.

Finally, in working with any client contemplating behavior change, but especially those working toward addressing substance use, a review of

W. R. Miller and Rollnick's (2012) book on motivational interviewing can be of great help. Their work highlights the crucial importance of the therapist's stance in guiding clients toward developing thought processes that will result in identifying a salient reason to help them commit to change, rather than simply following the client's direction, which can be insufficient to elicit disclosure, or by directing the client, which can result in defensiveness.

In the words of one of our survey clients, a middle-aged woman who sought treatment for her anxiety symptoms but who ultimately was able to reveal that substance use was a problem for her,

> It [my honesty] helped my therapist help me. She was able to treat someone now who wasn't just feeling down and stressed out, but was feeling the effects of alcoholism. It helped her to steer me toward getting help, and to have more trust in the relationship after the [accepting] reaction that I got from her.

10

COMMON CLINICAL LIES: TRAUMA

> If pursued, the truth withdraws, puts on one false face after another, and finally goes underground.
>
> —William Maxwell, *The Folder Leaf*

Two decades after his service in the U.S. Army, Clarence's life was practically ruled by posttraumatic stress disorder (PTSD). Loud noises in the neighborhood could send him into many hours of pacing the floor of his apartment, checking and rechecking the door locks, and planning his suicide. His medical chart suggested there had been an accident during live-fire training nearly 20 years previously. A stray bullet struck and killed a man in his unit. But over several months while he was a client in the care of one of the authors (MB), he would not go near the memory, often saying: "I don't need to be talking about that. Things are bad enough." His therapist and the therapist's supervisor essentially agreed. To confront his trauma at this point risked triggering emotional responses Clarence was not yet ready to handle. At this point, keeping this secret was part of keeping him safe.

Any discussion of trauma-related secrets must take into account the fact that disclosure at the wrong time or under the wrong circumstances may not

http://dx.doi.org/10.1037/0000128-011
Secrets and Lies in Psychotherapy, by B. A. Farber, M. Blanchard, and M. Love

be beneficial and can be counter-therapeutic (e.g., Depue, Banich, & Curran, 2006; Farber, Feldman, & Wright, 2014; Seery, Silver, Holman, Ence, & Chu, 2008). Even if a client appears motivated to dive into detailed descriptions of trauma, clinicians must proceed with caution. As Herman (1992) explained in her landmark book, *Trauma and Recovery*, clients and therapists alike may feel a certain drive to discuss traumatic secrets, unwittingly partaking of the fantasy that there could be a "violent cathartic cure which will get rid of the trauma once and for all" (p. 172). But exploration of traumatic material must often come only after the slow, preparatory work of ensuring safety and sobriety and of building up the client's ability to safely manage emotional distress. When we have asked psychotherapy clients about "secrecy," "dishonesty," or even "lying," we have done so with full awareness that these forms of nondisclosure can be protective for clients.

That said, honest disclosure is a major goal of most psychotherapeutic treatments with trauma survivors (Foa, Keane, Friedman, & Cohen, 2010). Disclosure-based interventions come in many forms, including imaginal exposure, cognitive reappraisal, two-chair techniques, eye movement desensitization and reprocessing (EMDR), and stress inoculation training. All assume that "reviewing and transforming trauma memories is a critical step in the treatment of abuse survivors" (Thomas, 2005, p. 31). Indeed, the client's past avoidance of traumatic memories through denial and secret keeping is seen as core to the pathology of conditions such as PTSD.

Thus, for example, prolonged exposure therapy for PTSD (Foa, Hembree, & Rothbaum, 2007) involves the deliberate, systematic confrontation with trauma narratives and other feared stimuli in a safe environment to alter the fear associations encoded in the brain during traumatic events. Disclosure is undertaken in such detail that the client almost relives the event, often flushed and sweating in a state of heightened autonomic arousal. Disclosure is repeated until the formerly terrifying traumatic experience is essentially "talked to death," with the client both habituating to the fear and having the chance to reevaluate distorted ideas about the trauma, such as blaming him- or herself for being made a victim. Some other trauma therapies bring honest disclosure out of the confines of therapy into real-life confrontations with former abusers (e.g., Arlene Drake's "carefrontation," 2017), in a sense completing the movement from traumatic secret to publicly acknowledged truth.

Our research focused on finding out to what extent and why clients in psychotherapy withhold or lie about the trauma that they have experienced. In our first study, we found that 13% of clients surveyed reported having lied to their therapist about sexual or physical abuse or trauma at some point in the past. Sexual abuse was somewhat more commonly lied about (10%) than was physical abuse (6%). We also asked respondents to gauge the extent of their dishonesty on this topic and found that the average response was a rating of

4 (*a lot*) on a 5-point scale. Our second study found that 15% reported ongoing dishonesty on these topics. Respondents were evenly split between those who had actively spoken dishonestly about their traumas and those who passively avoided the topic. Previous research on secrets in psychotherapy has provided little context for these prevalence numbers, except for Martin's (2006) study that examined 55 different lies told to therapists, only three of which were related to a history of trauma.

Prior research on the motives for concealing traumatic experiences is particularly robust in the areas of rape and sexual assault, where the major focus has been on the response victims expect to receive after making their disclosure. Negative social responses—such as blaming the victim, minimizing the assault, attempting to force the victim to tell others or go to the police, or treating the victim as damaged—have been found to have detrimental implications, delaying the victim's recovery (e.g., Campbell, Wasco, Ahrens, Sefl, & Barnes, 2001) and possibly fostering the development of PTSD symptoms (Ullman, Filipas, Townsend, & Starzynski, 2007; Ullman, Townsend, Filipas, & Starzynski, 2007). These experiences have been called *secondary victimization* (Campbell & Raja, 2005) and for some victims can feel just as violating as the original assault. The expectation of secondary victimization is particularly silencing for women of lower socioeconomic status, unmarried and childless women, and those who were assaulted by someone they knew rather than a stranger (Ullman, 1996). The experience of male victims of sexual assault, although distinct, suggests that similar fears of negative social response often block disclosure (Sorsoli, Kia-Keating, & Grossman, 2008; Vearnals & Campbell, 2001).

The circumstances of psychotherapy introduce new fears about trauma disclosure. Writing about survivors of childhood sexual abuse, Farber, Khurgin-Bott, and Feldman (2009) noted that the intimacy of individual therapy raises distinct fears for those who have been betrayed by close others in the past. Particularly in the early stages of therapy, "the shadow of the abuser's betrayal tends to haunt the therapeutic relationship" (p. 53). The victim fears that disclosure would again lead to exploitation or hurt, and this fear is only intensified by the power imbalance between therapist and client. The sexual nature of many traumas discussed in therapy also tends to magnify the shame and vulnerability involved in disclosure (Hill, Thompson, Cogar, & Denman, 1993; Kelly, 1998), as do the feelings of disgust and self-blame that often accompany certain types of victimization. The mix of revulsion, fear, and shame clouds the prospects of disclosure (Farber et al., 2009).

Our research provides the opportunity to hear from clients about the causes and consequences of concealing traumatic experiences from their therapist. A subsample of 80 respondents from both studies agreed to answer detailed follow-up questions. This group was 83% female and 21% non-White, with an average age of 33.2 years, making them broadly similar to the overall sample demographics. They entered therapy for a wide range of reasons, most commonly depression and stress. Only 20 respondents (25%) mentioned traumatic experiences as the reason they entered therapy, five of whom specifically mentioned PTSD. We did not ask respondents to describe their traumas, but some did. Sexual assault and childhood abuse were mentioned most often.

A good first look at their motives for dishonesty about trauma experiences comes from our second study, in which we asked respondents to choose from among six basic motives for this behavior. As Table 10.1 shows, our trauma respondents were most likely to cite embarrassment or shame, a common consequence of many types of traumatic experiences. Yet they were not more likely to cite this reason than respondents who were dishonest about all other topics, among whom almost precisely the same number (61% vs. 62%) cited shame as a motive.

The real difference with trauma respondents appears to be the nature of the emotions that they imagine experiencing during or after disclosure. They were 3.5 times more likely to report "It would bring up overwhelming emotions" as their reason for concealment, compared with respondents on all other topics examined in our research. The emotions they reported were numerous and intense. One respondent offered no less than 10 overwhelming emotions: "Powerless, violent, distraught, withdrawn, tearful, threatened, rejected, self-hating, agitated, alone." Among emotions offered by other respondents, sadness and self-hate were most common.

To get a better understanding of these emotions, we can turn to the short essay responses provided by respondents from both studies ($n = 80$), answering the question "What makes it hard to be honest about this?" Content analysis of these responses identified a set of six separate thematic categories of motive (Table 10.2).

A little over half of respondents (53%) spontaneously described overwhelming emotional impacts, often in great detail. More than being merely

TABLE 10.1
Multiple-Choice Motives for Dishonesty About Traumatic Experiences ($N = 66$)

Motive	n	Percent reporting
1. Embarrassment or shame	41	62
2. It would bring up overwhelming emotions	34	52
3. I didn't want this to distract from other topics	15	23
4. I doubt my therapist can help or understand	12	18
5. Practical consequences	7	11
6. My therapist would be upset, hurt, or disappointed	5	8

TABLE 10.2
Major Themes in Clients' Motives for Dishonesty About Traumatic Experiences ($n = 80$)

Motive	Number of individuals reporting	Percent of sample
To avoid being triggered or other emotional impacts	42	53
"Because when I talk about it, I tend to have flashbacks for a month or more."		
"I would cry and get upset then shut down and not be able to function. . . . Maybe even want to attempt suicide again."		
"Talking makes me feel like a terrible person and deeply upsets me."		
To deny the trauma's impact on me	19	24
"I don't want to talk about it because I don't want to think about it."		
"I didn't want it to happen so if I don't talk about it I can pretend it didn't."		
Fear of empathic failure by therapist	17	22
"They might not believe me or realize how bad it hurt."		
"She might pity me or look down on me."		
"I thought my therapist would judge me and be mad at me for not bringing it up a long time ago."		
To control the direction of therapy	13	17
"Avoiding this topic has helped keep my therapist on track with what I actually wish to deal with."		
"It would have become a distraction. Picking a scab that is long healed."		
Disclosure cannot help or is not needed	12	15
"I don't know how she could possibly help me."		
"Feels like it shouldn't be an issue. It happened so long ago . . . nothing can really be done about it."		
To prevent others finding out	9	11
"Therapist would have told my parents and it would have changed my relationship with them forever."		
"Police would have got involved."		
"I agreed not to ever discuss it."		

Note. Example quotations taken from essay responses. Sample percentages refer to proportion of 80 respondents who reported each theme.

embarrassed or uncomfortable, respondents reported strong, disorganizing experiences. As one 22-year-old woman explained it, had she attempted to address her sexual assault in therapy, "I would have either had a panic attack or dissociated." Respondents not only feared being overwhelmed in session but they also believed that by disclosing their traumatic experience they would be left with exacerbated symptoms—flashbacks, nightmares, self-blame, suicidal thoughts—that could continue for hours, days, or weeks afterward. These fears were vividly described by a respondent in her late 40s who entered therapy for help with her borderline personality disorder but had kept her traumatic past to herself. She did not believe in the idea of being triggered, yet her writing suggested this is exactly what she was afraid of:

> I don't believe in idiotic "triggering," but why re-live painful crap? Who needs or wants to cry? [There would be] a shit ton of crying and feeling bad for like the rest of the month, if not a FEW months. I would start having weird anger issues and I would inappropriately "act out" or behave badly with others. There would be distrust of people. I would act paranoid with strangers, etc. OK, maybe this does qualify as "triggering."

Not disclosing helped her feel in control, she explained, a perception which, as we noted earlier in this chapter, matches decades of clinical observations about how divulging trauma experiences may lead to an exacerbation of symptoms (Courtois, 1999; Depue et al., 2006; Herman, 1992; Herman & Harvey, 1997; Seery et al., 2008; Simha-Alpern, 2007).

A second group, 24% of respondents, stated that they were dishonest to suppress or deny the impact trauma had on them. This is poignantly described by a 32-year-old victim of relationship violence:

> It's hard to admit I put up with some things repeatedly and realize yet again, WOW I allowed this to continue. It's easier to detach and think of it like it happened to someone else. Like it never happened to me. To just let it go and pretend it doesn't exist. That wasn't me.

A second respondent with a similar trauma history stated simply, "I'm in denial." Her motivation to keep past traumas out of awareness was immediate. She was currently in another abusive relationship and was afraid to face the idea of leaving her abuser, which she was sure her therapist would try to convince her to do.

Still others described willful suppression of past trauma in a more positive light—motivated by a desire to focus their energies on the future. As one respondent wrote, "I believe it does not help to relive the past or define myself as a survivor or someone who has overcome instead of someone who is becoming more human each day." This approach calls to mind research on the repressive coping style, the tendency to direct one's attention away from negative emotional states. Repression has traditionally been seen as maladaptive. Yet studies of adults who have lost a loved one and studies of teenage and adult women with histories of sexual abuse have suggested that a repressive coping style may be associated with better psychological adjustment and fewer psychological symptoms for some people (Bonanno & Field, 2001; Bonanno, Keltner, Holen, & Horowitz, 1995; Bonanno, Papa, Lalande, Westphal, & Coifman, 2004). We cannot say whether our respondents qualify as true repressors—they were conscious enough of their repression to tell us about it—but it is notable that a quarter of our sample was committed enough to repressive coping to conceal a past trauma from their therapist. Although this may work for some, the use of suppression ("I don't want to think about it") and denial ("It did not happen") among psychotherapy clients does raise a question: If these defense mechanisms were truly effective, why would they feel the need for professional help? (Farber et al., 2009).

Another important theme was the fear of empathic failure by the therapist, reported by 22%, a theme that links strongly to the fears of negative social response described in the literature on rape trauma. Respondents in this group predicted that their disclosure would result in their therapist's disbelief, dismissal, or even anger regarding their previous secrecy. For some, the fear was backed up by actual experience of therapists reacting badly to trauma disclosures. One client recalled feeling comfortable enough with her therapist to begin to share deeper feelings of guilt and shame, but when she did so, the therapist laughed:

> I asked her if this was some sort of therapeutic technique I was not understanding, and she said, "no," she just thought I was "ridiculous" but would try to refrain from laughing at me. Next session, I shared again (although a less truthful and less significant fact), and she laughed again. She told me she knew it was wrong but didn't think she could control it.

The patient soon left therapy.

It was much more common for clients to report imagining, though not getting, a negative response from their therapist, with examples such as "They might not believe me" and "She might pity me or look down on me" and even "She might tell me to leave." One respondent imagined an angry, judgmental response to his disclosure that he knew was not realistic: "I didn't bring it up later because I felt that it had been too long and I irrationally thought my therapist would judge me and be mad at me for not bringing it up long ago."

These fears may be an accurate perception of the respondent's therapist—the field certainly attracts some imperfect practitioners. It is also possible, though, that after years of being met with judgment, disbelief, pity, or even anger by some in the outside world, those who have been traumatized expect and perceive similar reactions on the part of their therapists. Although understanding the risk here of "blaming the victim," it would not be surprising if even the most well-attuned and accepting therapists are experienced by at least some traumatized patients as rejecting, disparaging, or in other ways inadequate. More pointedly, those with the experience of being dismissed or blamed for their trauma would understandably be loath to risk further disclosure.

As with other topics discussed in this book, controlling the direction of therapy was a theme among trauma respondents, reported by 17%. Therapy time is sometimes seen as too precious to spend discussing a past trauma when what the client really wants to discuss is, for example, their depression or addiction—topics they may insist are unrelated to past traumas. And so, concealment is chosen as the easiest and most effective strategy to keep their clinician "on track." Several respondents expressed astonishment at the persistence of their therapist in asking about their past traumas. As one respondent wrote: "I sought therapy for help with my current self and my current struggles. However, therapists tend to think otherwise, and often wish to drag up old issues rather than focus on what I actually need help with."

Some respondents (15% of this subsample) also cited a related motive: Disclosure cannot help or is not needed. Most of these conveyed a despairing sense that they are beyond help with this issue, noting, for example, that "there is no possibility of closure" and "no one can help me." Others responded with an air of acceptance. Although they concealed it from their therapist, they believed they had made their peace with what happened and moved on. Whether this is wishful thinking is impossible to say. Further, a few stated that the initial trauma had never had an impact on them in the first place, so why discuss it? One respondent who reported having an eating disorder and self-esteem issues wrote that therapists kept asking about a sexual assault, even though it was not a big deal: "I have been to five therapists since the incident and each one attributes most of my problems to my sexual abuse. I don't feel like it affected me that much so I would rather just keep it from them."

Finally, 11% of respondents were motivated at least in part by a fear that telling their therapist would lead to others finding out. Those others were most often the police, whom clients worried would attempt to contact or arrest the perpetrator. Several noted "mandated reporting" by therapists as their reason for keeping quiet or said simply, "I did not want it documented." Respondents in this group expressed disbelief that therapy was actually confidential or would remain so after their disclosure. Another subset expressed what sounded like loyalty to their abusers, describing some unsettling motives for dishonesty, such as "I agreed not to ever discuss it" and "I was conditioned not to talk about it."

Looking broadly at the major themes, it is possible to discern a sense among concealers of trauma that they understood how disclosure could make them feel worse, but they were not entirely sure how it might help them feel better. As one respondent put it, "The consequences were not worth the benefits." As in so many areas of life, clients may make an implicit cost–benefit analysis: The clear costs of dredging up the past must be balanced against the uncertain benefits of disclosure (see Chapter 4). This finding suggests that clinicians may be able to impact disclosure by fleshing out the benefits side of the equation, perhaps explaining the role of disclosure in healing. It is also possible that the clients we surveyed about dishonesty were essentially correct: At their particular time and in their particular condition, nondisclosure could well have been their best and safest option.

FEELINGS ABOUT DISHONESTY

In our second study ($N = 798$), we asked clients to select just one word from among 12 options to describe their feelings about having been dishonest. Compared with other major topics of dishonesty covered in our studies, respondents who were dishonest about traumatic experiences showed an interesting pattern that highlights the perceived dangers of disclosure. They were more than twice as likely to say they felt "safe" (15% vs. 6% for all other topics). They were also far less likely to feel "guilty" (3% vs. 12% for all other topics), suggesting that they did not feel they owed their therapist honesty on this topic. There were also hints that the choice to conceal was more intensely felt by traumatized respondents: "Conflicted" was selected at a higher rate (26%) than any of the other major topics covered in this book.

Some of those conflicted feelings may arise from the sense that although secret keeping feels safe, being unable to disclose honestly about physical or sexual abuse has hindered progress in therapy. In our second study, respondents were asked to rate the impact on their therapy as either "hurt my progress," "helped my progress," or "had no effect." Nearly half of trauma respondents believed it had hurt their progress (48%), and only a small fraction believed it had helped (5%). Some respondents described a sense of defeat in not having disclosed, as one remarked: "I'm still giving power to the abuser." Another client, one who had already been in therapy for 10 years, wrote the following:

> I believe building trust and being able to be vulnerable with a therapist may help me in my personal life, but I am not ready to take this step. I have not been able to work through my anxiety/depression in a meaningful way without disclosing trauma, but it is something I don't want to ever talk about.

The strength of resistance to disclosure was evident when we asked clients whether trauma was a topic about which they would ever be more honest. Although about a quarter of clients said they could imagine someday being honest with their current therapist, more than half selected the choice "No, not with anyone" (53%). In this way, our trauma respondents most resembled those concealing suicidal thoughts, reinforcing the sense that trauma disclosure also carries real consequences—in this case emotional consequences—that strongly motivate concealment.

HOW THERAPISTS CAN FOSTER HONESTY

Our second survey asked respondents who acknowledged dishonesty about traumatic experiences to imagine the circumstances under which they might be more honest. Among the list of 10 possibilities, such as "If I trusted my therapist more" or "If I felt like this was blocking my progress in therapy," the most commonly endorsed response was "If my therapist asked me about it directly" (21%). In this regard, trauma respondents did not show a dominant trend or any real difference from clients who had been dishonest about other topics.

A more nuanced understanding of their feelings on this comes from their open-text essay responses to the question "What could your therapist do to help you feel more comfortable being honest?" which were coded for major themes. Of 66 respondents, 17 (26%) felt that either no help was possible or that the change had to come from within themselves, not the therapist. As one client wrote, "I am the one who has to make myself more comfortable." Another group (17%) felt that developing trust over time was needed to make honesty possible.

Some respondents also felt that 50-minute sessions were not long enough to allow them to get into traumatic material. One client feared becoming so distraught that she would not be able to drive home. She wrote that her therapist could help by "giving me more than 50 minutes to talk and making sure I am in a safe place after talking about it." This insight—that highly aroused patients need time to calm down—has shaped the design of exposure-based trauma treatments, which call for extended 90-minute sessions whenever trauma processing is on the agenda (Foa et al., 2007).

A substantial group (38%) expressed ideas on how they wanted the conversation to be handled. These ideas were diverse, but many imagined the therapist leading the discussion by asking direct questions, with one client remarking that even being handed a paper questionnaire would help her disclose. Another client specified that she would like to be asked only yes-or-no questions. She worried that with open-ended questions, her urge to avoid painful material would lead her to confuse and obfuscate the issue. She wrote, "I think that if I'm asked open-ended questions about this topic, I'm so focused on avoiding things that would be uncomfortable for me to say, that anything I do say probably isn't honest or fully honest." Some expressed a desire to have explicit control over the pace and extent of the conversation. One respondent noted that a session in which she talked in detail about her trauma would have to be planned in advance and "talked about slowly." Another asked her therapist to "only bring it up or talk about it when I say I want to," and yet another said she would be more comfortable disclosing if she could know that "all discussions on it were brief."

In short, there is something about patients' anticipation of discussing their trauma experiences in therapy that offers unique challenges to the clinician. Here, client concealment and outright deception are not just about the avoidance of shame and the anticipation of therapist rejection but often, and more so, the fear of being re-engulfed by overwhelming painful memories and feelings. Thus, perhaps more than any topic, therapists encouraging greater and/or more honest patient disclosure about traumatic experiences are likely to need to resort first to a *metaconversation*, a collaborative planning discussion about how the client would like to discuss (or not discuss) the relevant experiences and symptoms. What are the fears in discussing the topic? What level of therapist inquisitiveness feels right? How might this client signal to the therapist that, for now, this is enough? How can the therapeutic relationship as well as the inevitable time constraints of therapy be best fashioned for the client to feel sufficiently safe to broach terrifying events of the past?

11

COMMON CLINICAL LIES: CLINICAL PROGRESS AND FEELINGS ABOUT ONE'S THERAPIST

> I have stuck to facts except when facts refused to conform with memory, narrative purpose, or the truth as I prefer to understand it.
>
> —Michael Chabon, *Moonglow*

As we have noted in previous chapters, clients lie—or are less than fully forthcoming—about a great many things, including issues relating to their suicidal thoughts, experiences of abuse, trauma, addictions, and of course, sex and family matters. In this chapter, our focus is on the inability of clients to reveal honestly their thoughts and feelings about therapy itself, including the state of their relationship with their therapist and their sense of their progress. A good example of the type of problem we are addressing here is contained in the following quotation from one of our study participants:

> It's hard to talk about the interaction between us when things aren't great or when I think she's made a mistake because I think of the worst that could happen—that she feels bad and the dynamic between us doesn't feel right anymore and then I feel uncomfortable and then there are more things I feel uncomfortable about and then all of a sudden we get to a point where it is affecting everything and has ruined our relationship and I need to find a new therapist. . . . I don't think it could happen,

http://dx.doi.org/10.1037/0000128-012
Secrets and Lies in Psychotherapy, by B. A. Farber, M. Blanchard, and M. Love

> but if it did happen, that worse-case scenario is so much worse than me just not saying anything in the first place that I don't think it's worth bringing it up.

It is difficult for most people to talk about *process* (that which goes on between any dyad or group of individuals), typically because of concerns that doing so will irreparably harm a reasonably functional or "good-enough" relationship. Therapy clients are often fearful of upsetting the balance in their relationship with their therapist by addressing their concerns. Intuitively, they seem to know that the success of therapy is at least as dependent on the quality of the relationship as it is on any "technical" intervention.

Therapists, too, recognize that a good patient–therapist connection is critical to the success of the work. Virtually every contemporary psychotherapy, even those that are typically thought of as manual driven and symptom oriented, endorses the central importance of the therapeutic relationship. Practitioners of some therapeutic orientations (e.g., person centered) hold the relationship as primary, as the essential healing force underlying therapeutic progress; others (e.g., cognitive behavior therapy [CBT] providers) view it as the foundation for effective interventions; and still others (e.g., relationally oriented psychodynamic psychotherapists) see the therapeutic relationship as both healing in its own right and as the basis for understanding other prior and current interpersonal relationships. The significant association between an effective therapeutic alliance and treatment outcome (e.g., Fluckiger, Del Re, Wampold, & Horvath, 2019) provides further evidence of the importance of a good—and presumably trusting and honest—therapist–client relationship.

Clients' lies or concealment of any salient information may pose threats to the integrity and mutative potential of the client–therapist relationship. But lies or deception about the relationship itself may be especially troublesome, depriving therapists of information about the patient–therapist connection or clinical progress—or lack thereof—that could be so useful in allowing therapists to modify what they are doing in the service of more effective treatment. We imagine many therapists having thoughts such as the following about clients:

> I expect you to lie about, or at least conceal, aspects of your drug or alcohol problem or your affair or even the depths of your despair, but when you don't tell the truth for a long while about how we're doing or how you feel about me or how I've been responding to your needs or whether you're thinking about terminating therapy, it creates havoc, it feels unsettling and confusing, and my compass feels like it's struggling to find the right direction.

Or, similarly:

> It's often easier to tell when you're not being entirely truthful about some piece of your history or some event that you've just described than it is

> to tell when we are or are not in a good therapeutic place together. And yes, it's not hard to know something's gone awry in the relationship when you don't pay me or when you miss sessions, but when you do show up every week on time—or have a reasonable excuse for not being there on time—and when you do pay me regularly and when we do seem to be talking about something productively, I tend to believe that we're doing okay, that you're satisfied with our work together—and then I find myself feeling somewhat clueless and incompetent when I find out that you've been thinking my comments or suggestions have not really been that helpful or even that you've been thinking the last few months about terminating treatment. By keeping this kind of stuff to yourself, you haven't given me, or us, a chance to find a better way for us to work together.

Our speculations here are consistent with the findings of Hill, Thompson, and Corbett (1992) and Hill, Thompson, Cogar, and Denman (1993) that (a) clients tend to hide more of their negative reactions in therapy (e.g., feeling confused or misunderstood) than they do any other kind of reaction, and (b) therapists are not good at identifying when clients are hiding or what feelings they are hiding. Hill and colleagues (1992) also found that when therapists were aware of unarticulated negative client reactions, therapy may suffer. In short, there is something particularly important about lies or concealment about therapy per se. These deceptions have a strong potential to short-circuit the work. When "things left unsaid" or outright dishonesty about the relationship are not dealt with at some strategic point in a forthright manner—that is, when there is little or no opportunity for repair of a damaged alliance—therapeutic work is likely to become stale, confusing, and/or unproductive.

What, then, are the most common lies and concealed information in this realm? First, some reminders about context: The data here are primarily from our first study of 547 therapy clients who were primarily female, Caucasian, single, and working with female therapists practicing a variety of different psychotherapies. (The data we collected in Study 1 regarding therapy-related topics is more comprehensive than the comparable data collected in Study 2; thus, the great majority of the material in this chapter is based on Study 1 data.) There were 10 items on the survey we used with this group that referenced possible lies about therapy and the therapist (see Table 11.1). Surprisingly, and perhaps remarkably, nearly three quarters of our respondents (72.6%) in this study reported lying about at least one of these therapy-related topics. By comparison, only 46.8% of respondents reported at least one of seven sex-related lies in the survey. Four of the 10 therapy-related topics were each reported by more than a quarter of the sample, making them among the most widely endorsed items on the survey. These included "Pretending to like my therapist's comments or suggestions" (29%), "Why I missed therapy appointments or was late" (29%), "Pretending to find therapy more effective than I do" (28%), and "Pretending I did homework or took other actions suggested

TABLE 11.1
Therapy-Related Topics That Are Most Frequently Lied About in Psychotherapy ($N = 547$)

Topic	*n*	Percent reporting dishonesty	Extent of dishonesty	
			M	*SD*
1. Pretending to like my therapist's comments or suggestions	161	29	3.1	1.1
2. Why I missed therapy appointments or was late	157	29	2.8	1.2
3. Pretending to find therapy more effective than I do	156	29	3.5	1.1
4. Pretending I did homework or took other actions suggested by my therapist	140	26	3.0	1.1
5. My real opinion of my therapist	100	18	3.6	1.1
6. Not saying I want to end therapy	86	16	3.7	1.3
7. That my therapist makes me feel uncomfortable	67	12	3.3	1.4
8. What I can afford to pay for therapy	45	8	2.8	1.4
9. My romantic or sexual feelings about my therapist	27	5	3.7	1.6
10. Not saying I am seeing another therapist	16	3	2.9	1.6

Note. Extent of dishonesty was rated on a five-point scale where 1 = *very little*, 3 = *a moderate amount*, 5 = *totally or extremely*; these means are based only on the scores of those individuals who reported they were dishonest about this topic. From "Lying in Psychotherapy: Why and What Clients Don't Tell Their Therapist About Therapy and Their Relationship," by M. Blanchard and B. A. Farber, 2016, *Counseling Psychology Quarterly, 29*, p. 100. Copyright 2016 by Taylor & Francis. Reprinted with permission.

by my therapist" (26%). By comparison, the most commonly reported sex-related lie, "My sexual history," was reported by 23% of respondents.

Another three of the therapy-related topics were lied about or avoided by a smaller, but still notable, proportion of our participants. These included "My real opinion of my therapist" (19%), "Not saying I want to end therapy" (16%), and "My therapist makes me feel uncomfortable" (13%). To a great degree, then, our data further confirm the validity of the earlier findings of Hill and colleagues (1992, 1993; Regan & Hill, 1992). To put it colloquially, there is a fair amount of negative stuff about their therapy and their therapist that clients simply do not bring into the room, at least in any verbally explicit way. The remaining three topics among the 10 therapy-related ones in this survey were endorsed relatively infrequently, including "What I can afford to pay for therapy" (8%), "My romantic or sexual feelings about my therapist" (5%), and "Not saying I am seeing another therapist" (3%). Of note, though, and we have more to say about this shortly, client lies or concealment about their romantic or sexual feelings toward their therapist, although not among the most common of lies, are among the most extreme lies told in therapy—that is, a lie that many clients who acknowledge this specific instance of dishonesty report as 5 on a 5-point "extent of dishonesty" scale.

The likelihood of reporting at least one therapy-related lie was not significantly affected by client gender or race or number of therapy sessions attended. Similarly, there were no significant differences as a function of gender, age, or racial differences between client and therapist. However, those who reported at least one therapy-related lie were on average 4.7 years younger than those who did not (M = 33.4 years vs. M = 38.0). For the most part, then, lies about therapy or the relationship seem to be common across the whole spectrum of therapy clients.

EXTENT OF DISHONESTY ABOUT THERAPY

As Table 11.1 indicates, among the 10 therapy-related topics, seven had mean scores of 3.0 or higher on the 5-point "extent of dishonesty" scale. Topics with the highest mean score on this scale were "My romantic or sexual feelings about my therapist," "Not saying I want to end therapy," and "My real opinion of my therapist." In fact, the mean extent of reported dishonesty for each of these items was higher than mean scores for concealing or lying about sexual abuse, physical abuse, and suicide attempts. Furthermore, these three therapy-related topics were those that were most likely to occasion the most extreme degree of dishonesty (i.e., had the highest proportion of clients who rated the extent of their lies on these topics as 5, corresponding to *totally or extremely*). Lies about therapy, then, were not only among the most commonly reported lies—even more common as a category than lies about sex—but also made up a disproportionate percentage of those lies that were extreme in their degree of perceived dishonesty.

In general, clients are more likely to conceal from their therapists any indication that they are troubled by what is going on in their therapy than they are to conceal information about being sexually abused. It is the direct "in-the-room," face-to-face admission of a problem between one individual and another that derails so many people in all situations. We suspect that clients assume that their partial truths about sexual abuse (or other traumatic material) will be met with acceptance on the part of the therapist and willingness to proceed slowly and at the client's preferred pace of disclosure. By contrast, we suspect that clients assume that any statement of theirs that speaks to their perception that the therapeutic relationship is suffering or that therapy itself is not progressing well—or that they harbor strong romantic or erotic feelings toward the therapist—will inevitably and immediately lead to a deep, prolonged, and intense conversation, one in which the client will feel put on the spot to explain him- or herself and to reveal details, feelings, and specific examples and that such conversation will continue via therapist questioning in subsequent sessions.

Moreover, we suspect that a typical client, in comparing his or her choices about revealing feelings about sexual abuse (or any trauma) versus feelings about the current therapeutic relationship, is better able to justify the decision to say nothing at all about the therapeutic relationship, fearing that saying anything will jeopardize a good-enough relationship. Of course, invoking the "leave well enough alone" rationale is hardly unique to the therapist–client dyad; it is one that partners often use to circumvent hard talks and friends use to avoid letting the other know about a habit or characteristic that is off-putting. It is hard to resist the anticipated relief—technically, the immediate negative reinforcement—of not confronting a difficult, then-and-there interpersonal situation. Although most of us intuitively know that such honest talk, although anxiety provoking, typically leads to greater intimacy and interpersonal satisfaction, at the moment the perceived danger of such talk feels paramount, and thus, we conceal or lie about our feelings. Courage is needed for such discussions, and it often eludes many of us, including psychotherapy clients and psychotherapists themselves (Geller, 2014).

MOTIVATIONS FOR THERAPY-RELATED DISHONESTY

Motivations for dishonesty in Study 1 were initially assessed with a "clickable" checklist. As shown in Table 11.2, the most common motives selected for all instances of therapy-related dishonesty were "I wanted to be

TABLE 11.2
Common Motives for Therapy-Related Versus All Other Lies

Reported motive	*n*	Percent reporting
For therapy-related lies ($n = 106$)[a]		
I wanted to be polite	57	54
I wanted to avoid upsetting my therapist	44	42
This topic was uncomfortable for me	36	34
I wanted to avoid my therapist's disapproval	35	33
For all other lies ($n = 325$)[b]		
This topic was uncomfortable for me	162	50
I didn't want to look bad	148	46
I wanted to avoid shame	143	44
I wasn't ready to discuss the topic	122	38

Note. From "Lying in Psychotherapy: Why and What Clients Don't Tell Their Therapist About Therapy and Their Relationship," by M. Blanchard and B. A. Farber, 2016, *Counseling Psychology Quarterly, 29,* p. 101. Copyright 2016 by Taylor & Francis. Reprinted with permission.
[a]Represents 106 respondents (out of the total 547) who provided motives for any of the 10 therapy-related topics. [b]Represents 325 respondents (out of the total 547) who provided motives for any of the 48 topics that were not directly related to therapy.

polite," "I wanted to avoid upsetting my therapist," "This topic was uncomfortable for me," and "I wanted to avoid my therapist's disapproval." These motives seem related, coalescing into a broad category of not wanting to experience the discomfort and possible ramifications of confronting a somewhat difficult but still-manageable therapeutic relationship. These four motives can also be compared with the most common motives reported for all other nontherapy lies. As this table indicates, the somewhat generic phrase "This topic is uncomfortable to me" is on both lists. This is hardly surprising inasmuch as we would expect that most instances of concealment and lies are about discomfort in one form or another. Nevertheless, the remaining motives for nontherapy-related lies are different, including "I didn't want to look bad" and "I wanted to avoid shame." In short, there is something distinctive about lies about therapy and the therapeutic relationship per se; their particular interpersonal flavor adds an extra dimension of difficulty.

SPECIFIC LIES ABOUT THERAPY: PRIMARY MOTIVATIONS AND NARRATIVE ACCOUNTS

The following section provides more information about nine of the 10 therapy-related lies, including the primary motives associated with each lie and clinical examples of each lie, the latter drawn from the set of open-ended text-entry questions to which respondents could provide a short narrative explaining their dishonesty in their own words. For purposes of clarity, we report the checklist data as *motives* and refer to the open-text data as *narratives*. The one exception here is about the tenth topic, "Not saying I'm seeing another therapist," a lie about which no respondent provided a clinical example.

Pretending to Like My Therapist's Comments or Suggestions

As we noted, among the three most reported therapy-related lies, 29% of our respondents pretended to like their therapist's comments or suggestions. The overall mean was in the mid-range of the scale, indicating that the extent of lying about this topic was moderate; further, only 8% of respondents who lied about this topic did so with extreme dishonesty (i.e., chose 5 on the 5-point scale). The precipitants of this behavior varied, from unwanted advice or mistimed interventions to overlong personal anecdotes or what one respondent called "the premature focus trap," in which her therapist regularly latched onto the first thing she said, missing the important stuff.

As for motives for this form of dishonesty, "I wanted to be polite" was selected by 10 out of the 14 respondents who completed a checklist of motives. A larger number of respondents, 45 across both studies, provided narrative accounts of their reasons for concealing their "hidden reactions" (Hill et al., 1992) to their therapist's comments or suggestions. A large majority (71%) of this group wanted to be polite or avoid interpersonal friction with the therapist. As one client wrote, "I view my therapist as the expert and don't want to challenge what she says." Others said they could not bear the idea of upsetting their therapist:

> I just wanted to make sure the therapist felt like she was helping me, even when her comments did not help, or maybe made things worse. I was already feeling so bad about myself, that I didn't want the guilt of making someone feel bad at their job.

Others voiced fears that this interpersonal friction would lead to real consequences, such as abandonment by the therapist or withholding of the therapist's care. As one respondent explained: "I am afraid if she took things personally, then she would not help me as much in therapy." Thus, "politeness" as a motive here blends with issues of guilt, deference, and clients' perceived needs to preserve a functional therapeutic relationship.

The irony is that trepidation about giving feedback often arises from the client's reason for seeking psychological treatment. Depressed patients spoke of lacking the confidence to respond, anxious patients reported being too afraid, and a recently hospitalized patient described doubting her own perceptions:

> I've been told for years that I blow things out of proportion or "overreact," or that I'm too sensitive. So when she said things that hurt me I was too confused and scared to confront her. She's a professional; she's supposed to know best, right? I'd better just keep quiet about it. I'm probably reacting to this wrong anyway.

This type of dishonesty appears to carry significant clinical consequences for many clients; 24 of the 45 narratives we collected contained direct references to the progress of therapy or even termination of treatment. "It had the effect of totally neutralizing my progress" and "I was always unhappy when I left her office," noted two of our respondents. The client quoted in the previous paragraph, who wanted to make her therapist feel helpful, remarked: "I ended up leaving therapy. . . . It was a waste of time and money to continue to see her as I pretended to respond positively to her suggestions and observations."

That so many clients—almost a third of our sample—acknowledged concealing or lying about their reaction to their therapist's comments or suggestions leads us to ponder several questions: Are therapists not allowing enough room for disagreement in session? Have so many therapy clients learned in early life, through damaging experiences, to avoid honesty or conflict, even in the presence of those who care for them? Are therapists not explicit enough about the clinical value of a client's accurate feedback about the helpfulness of a therapist's comments or the client's perception of progress in therapy?

In the final chapter, we offer suggestions for how therapists can foster more honesty in the therapeutic relationship. Here, though, we share an intervention that one of us (BAF) learned many decades ago from a therapy supervisor. When receiving a compliment from a client, either about clinical progress or about something one has said or done, a good response may be as follows: "I appreciate your compliment about me and the work we're doing together, but what feels to me even more important is that you let me know when I or we are not doing so well." Therapists can also facilitate client honesty about these issues by contextualizing their insights, thoughts, or suggestions as preliminary—that is, as hypotheses that call for a client response. Beginning sentences with "I'm not sure, but it's possible"; "It feels to me as if this could be the case"; or "I'm wondering if," or ending sentences with "What's your sense of what I just said?" increases greatly the possibility that the client feels like a respected partner in the therapeutic dialogue, someone whose honest responses to the therapist's comments are warranted and important. Although no specific action is likely to eliminate some clients' needs to defer to their therapist's authority or perceived wisdom automatically, we believe that therapists who invite responses from their clients while acknowledging their own fallibility are more likely to elicit a greater degree of honesty. Respondents in our study generally agreed with these ideas, urging therapists to be truly inviting of negative feedback, to say convincingly that they will not take it personally, and to encourage clients to see the therapeutic value of speaking up. As one client put it, "I think just her acknowledging that it may be hard for me to be truthful would make me feel more comfortable doing so."

The Real Reason for a Missed Appointment

Clients' dishonesty about missing an appointment also appeared as one of the three most common therapy-related lies. The data show a modest extent of lying reported on this topic; the overall mean was slightly below the midpoint on the 5-point scale, and only 11% of respondents reported extreme dishonesty.

The 21 respondents who provided narrative details about this lie described a variety of real reasons for their missed sessions. Some overslept. Others forgot. Others contended they could not pay for the session. Some admitted to simply being "too lazy" to go to therapy, whereas a few felt they had been in no condition to undertake therapy that day, often due to the very symptoms (e.g., anxiety or depression) that brought them to treatment in the first place.

When asked why they could not be honest about missing therapy, 14 of the 21 respondents across both studies who provided narratives indicated a desire to avoid embarrassment ("I didn't want to look bad"), with smaller numbers reporting either a desire to "avoid my therapist's disapproval" or "simplify the conversation." Clients felt the truth would disappoint their therapist. As one client explained,

> My reason for being late or missing an appointment is usually just laziness or feeling like I don't want to go anymore and I feel embarrassed for being so flaky and irresponsible. . . . I feel so ashamed and disappointed in myself and don't want anyone else to feel that way toward me so I usually make up an excuse.

Respondents also noted that having a good excuse (i.e., "work emergency") decreased the likelihood of being charged a late cancellation fee.

Although most said this lie had little effect on their therapy, a few respondents noted that it seemed to feed a tendency to lie about other topics, serving as a sort of "gateway" lie. As one client noted with apparent alarm, "Overall it promoted my lying about other things."

Pretending to Find Therapy More Effective Than It Is

Similar to "pretending to like my therapist's comments or suggestions" is the phenomenon of "pretending to find therapy more effective than I do"—a kind of dishonesty noted by 28% of the sample. The average extent of dishonesty about this topic fell slightly above the midpoint of the scale ($M = 3.5$); 21% of those who pretended to find therapy more effective than they truly felt admitted to practicing total dishonesty on this topic.

Among the reasons for lying about this topic, the most cited (among the multiple-choice items) included the desire to be polite and the wish to avoid upsetting one's therapist. The narrative accounts provided by 38 respondents confirmed this finding, with 82% of this group noting that they worried about insulting or offending their therapist or otherwise "making her feel bad at her job"; a few admitted to spending many months in therapy to avoid a confrontation.

In several cases, clients felt they should not contradict the therapist's stated belief that they were making progress. The more dramatic examples were of clients feeling pressured to agree with rosy and self-serving estimates of their progress. As one respondent explained,

> Well, she kind of says things about how she can see improvement, she thinks I'm getting better, and I just kind of agree with her. I nod and say

> that I do feel better, more able to handle things, etc., when really I feel pretty much the same as when I started [six years previous]. I wanted to make her think she's helping, and it just didn't seem I could convince her otherwise.

Such stories suggest we should think carefully about the tone we use when offering encouraging feedback.

Along with the fear of upsetting the therapist, some respondents (24%) mentioned a fear of being judged or punished in some way if they complained. Because negative feedback about therapy might be seen as insulting to the therapist, some clients assumed the natural response would be payback, which could take the form of being criticized, blamed, or referred out to another provider. One respondent explained this reasoning: "No matter how enlightened someone claims to be, they'll always remember if you've personally insulted them. This can lead to hurt feelings and unfortunately, retribution from some."

Yet, concealing one's doubts about therapy was widely seen as harmful. More than half of the 38 respondents (20 individuals) felt dishonesty had "hurt my progress," placing it among the lies (broadly defined) most often seen as harmful in our research. One client indicated that telling this lie "made it [therapy] useless," and similarly, another stated that as a result of this deception, "I never dealt with my core issues." Another respondent described an extreme example of what these harmful implications might look like:

> When I was in short-term intensive dynamic psychotherapy, I was not happy with the outcomes. It was making me more anxious about seeing my family, and my mental state was increasingly worse. My therapist kept saying how much this therapy helps and can cure people, but I wasn't believing him. After I stopped seeing him, I became suicidal. Since I did not believe in the therapy when I said I did, I lied to him and myself. Thus, it made my mental state much worse.

Pretending to Do Homework or Take Other Actions

Over a quarter (26%) of the sample's respondents acknowledged that they had feigned having done their homework or other therapy-related tasks. Some assignments they pretended to have completed included keeping a journal, practicing meditation, and studying a book on anxiety management. Not surprisingly, 62.5% of the sample who had admitted to this type of deception were CBT clients. The extent of dishonesty about this topic was exactly at the midpoint of the scale, and only 9% of those who admitted to this kind of therapy-related lie indicated they were totally dishonest.

When asked about their motivation for this behavior, respondents suggested that they wanted to "make a good impression" or, conversely, "avoid my therapist's disapproval." Some also admitted to being in "secret revolt" against their therapist. As one client explained,

> I want advice from a therapist, not a complete takeover of my life. She is asking me to let go of all my life issues . . . and just fill out a stupid form whenever I have a feeling, or when I eat, drink, pee, or even "pleasure myself." I pretend to fill those sheets she gave me, to make it seem that I am improving.

Again, this raises the question, why is this person still working with his or her therapist? One would imagine, perhaps despite this therapist's shortcomings and despite this client's failure to voice opinions about her style, the client still found the treatment somewhat beneficial. Or, as Billy Joel so astutely put it, "I took the good times, I'll take the bad times."

Still, we believe that CBT therapists, in particular, have to be attentive to the possibility—in fact, strong likelihood—that at least some of their clients are pretending to complete their homework. One possibility is checking with their clients, early in therapy, as to their willingness to perform intersession tasks and/or evaluating their ability or willingness to honestly report those occasions when they could not or did not complete such assignments.

Overall, our participants tended to acknowledge significant consequences to this specific therapy-related lie: They reported feelings of guilt and a sense that this brand of dishonesty hindered their therapeutic progress, and they believed that they experienced a sense of diminished connection to their therapist.

My Real Opinion of My Therapist

There is clear conceptual overlap between this topic and two previous topics—"Pretending to like my therapist's suggestions" and "Pretending to find therapy more effective than it is." This topic, however, yielded a lower percentage of acknowledged lies but a higher percentage of extreme lies. As Table 11.1 indicates, only 18% reported having concealed or lied about their real opinion of their therapist. But the average extent of dishonesty on this topic surpassed the midpoint of the scale; moreover, 27% of those who were dishonest about this issue reported "extreme" dishonesty, a percentage among the highest of all topics. Respondents who offered explanations for this lie ($n = 15$) tended to depict therapists who either talk excessively, seem "too culturally different," struggle to stay alert during sessions, give "ridiculous" advice, are intimidating, or seem either overly supportive or not supportive enough.

Although, as we noted, some clients find it difficult to provide honest responses to their therapist's comments or suggestions, others struggle with a more challenging, perhaps more personal issue—telling their therapists what they really think of them. Some therapists are simply not as skilled as others, potentially lacking the "right stuff" in terms of technical or interpersonal competency (Castonguay & Hill, 2017); moreover, even typically effective therapists may not offer the right match for a particular client's style or needs. In either case, some clients experience great difficulties in providing honest feedback about the helpfulness of the person whom they are paying to be helpful.

Thirteen of the 15 respondents who explained their motives for lying about this topic attributed it to "politeness," though the narratives indicated that many were simply conflict avoidant. As one respondent revealed,

> She asked me if there was some feeling that this wasn't working, and I lied and said that it wasn't about her. I didn't want to have to deal with her feelings or my own about what it means for me to not particularly like her style.

Another client explained the predicament he had created as a result of disguising his real feelings about his therapist:

> I don't like the guy. . . . The sessions are horribly awkward and I don't feel like I'm representing myself accurately and I know he doesn't have a clear picture of what I'm really like. I can't think straight when I'm there so I over- and under-exaggerate all the time.

Most respondents acknowledged that this lie had unfortunate clinical consequences, including impairment of progress and early termination. The general sentiment clients expressed was along the lines of, "I'm not really that engaged in the work of therapy," "I'm only half there," "I'm always thinking about how and when to stop coming." Clearly, not allowing the therapist to know what one thinks about him or her provides no opportunity for the therapist to change, virtually inevitably derailing the possibility of a good outcome.

Not Saying "I Want to End Therapy"

Another frequent area of client dishonesty was clients' uncommunicated wish to terminate therapy. It should be evident, though, that lying about this issue may be related to lies about one of the previously mentioned topics—for example, clients' inability to be truthful about their real feelings about their therapist or pretending to find therapy more effective than they truly believe. When clients chose to be dishonest about this topic, they tended to do so with a high degree of dishonesty; indeed, 37% of respondents who endorsed dishonesty in this domain reported that they had been totally dishonest. The mean extent of dishonesty on this topic ("Not saying

I want to end therapy") was 3.7, making it among the two highest of all therapy-related topics (along with "Romantic or sexual feelings about one's therapist"). It is no wonder that so many clients terminate therapy with no warning. Apparently, many had been considering this, even planning to do it, without mentioning it to their therapists.

Among the respondents who reported motives for this lie, most said they either "wanted to be polite," wished to "avoid upsetting my therapist," or feared that they would "look bad" if they were honest about wanting to end therapy. These motives surely overlap. We imagine a client's self-statements in this regard to be something like,

> My sense of myself is of a nice person who doesn't want to upset others, and if I do, I'll look and feel bad about it. Thus, I'll just avoid letting my therapist know that I really don't want to continue the work. It's easier that way.

As one respondent explained in her narrative account, "I couldn't bring myself to tell my therapist I no longer wanted to continue sessions because I was afraid she would disagree or take it personally." Clients' reported consequences of being dishonest about wanting to end therapy were wide ranging, including a sense that progress had been stalled, they had wasted money, and they left without a sense of completion. As one young adult client framed it, being dishonest "prevented me from getting closure and figuring out what it was about therapy that did or didn't help me in my life." An unfortunate and all-too-likely possibility is that clients who feel they cannot talk about terminating will be less likely to seek out therapy again after they do terminate. Why risk entering another treatment when getting out is so hard?

My Therapist Makes Me Uncomfortable

Although not as common as the previously reported instances of client lying, 12% of our sample reported that their dishonesty in therapy was related to their therapist having made them feel uncomfortable. Apparently, what these respondents meant was that their therapist's response to something they said or did was "off" enough such that further honest disclosure about this issue seemed impossible, and telling the therapist about the discomfort itself seemed out of the question. Therapists, we were told, could be "off" in many ways: They could be a bit too casual or friendly, too focused on a client's body or appearance, too self-disclosing, too formal (stiff), too confrontational, too focused on money (fees), too unsure of him- or herself, or too "spiritual." Although they are not directly equivalent circumstances, the percentage of clients acknowledging a level of discomfort in therapy that occasioned dishonesty or concealment is somewhat comparable to the 10% or so of clients whose clinical course spirals downward (Mohr, 1995), a phenomenon attributed, among other things, to inappropriate therapist behavior.

About a quarter of respondents who selected this topic rated the extent of their dishonesty to be total or extreme. The respondents who provided more details most often reported that their decision to dissemble or stay silent was motivated by both their discomfort addressing this topic openly as well as out of a desire to avoid upsetting their therapist and to be polite. These reasons overlap considerably with previously noted client lies about therapy and the therapist. One female respondent explained,

> I brought up some sex-related anxieties and he asked LOTS of detailed questions and I got uncomfortable so I gave really vague answers and haven't brought up sex in sessions with him since. I don't know if I'm being overly paranoid or if he was actually being creepy.

Respondents were mixed in their assessment of the effects of this lie on their therapy: Three reported negative outcomes (e.g., "It makes me not want to go to therapy"), whereas three reported minimal impact. We speculate that the specific outcome here is based on several overlapping factors: the extent to which the therapist's response was discomfiting, whether the therapist's seemingly inappropriate response or behavior was a "one-off" incident or had happened previously, the extent to which the client wanted to be forgiving, and the extent to which the therapy had already proven to be at least somewhat successful.

Ability to Pay for Therapy

Payment issues are a common point of dispute and negotiation in therapy (e.g., Schonbar, 1967). In some modalities of therapy (primarily psychodynamic), these conflicts may be a useful entry point into discussing the client's interpersonal dynamics. Particularly when therapy is expensive or the client financially stressed, discussions about the fee can be intensely emotional. As one client remarked, "I find myself thinking about the finances instead of what I or my therapist is saying."

However, in our survey, dishonesty about "What I can afford to pay for therapy" was relatively uncommon, and the mean extent of dishonesty was among the lowest of the therapy-related lies; only 13% of clients who endorsed this lie rated their dishonesty as total or extreme. Not many clients seem to lie or conceal information in this realm, and among the few who do so, their dishonesty is self-perceived as mild to moderate. Reading between the lines, it seems they likely fudge their incomes to their therapist as they might to the Internal Revenue Service. We suspect the low rates of dishonesty here might be primarily because many clients' fees are set by their insurance companies and not negotiated with their therapists. Notably, though, a wording change in our second survey to "My feelings about the cost of therapy" resulted in 12.5% of respondents endorsing ongoing dishonesty, suggesting that dishonesty about the actual feelings about money spent on therapy may be moderately common, on a par with concealing an eating disorder or lying about why one missed a session.

Across the two studies, 16 clients provided narratives to explain their motives for dishonesty about fees or money spent on therapy. The majority (56%) were not honest due to fears of damaging the therapeutic relationship, offering explanations such as "I think her feelings would be hurt" and "Talk of billing creates emotional distance." It may be that discussing money can bring up questions about the real value of the services offered and, by extension, the skill of the therapist. A few in this group worried as well about appearing cheap or not sufficiently committed to therapy. One felt bringing it up would cause the therapist to believe she could not pay for treatment and in turn, urge termination: "It can be a deal-breaker conversation, like a bad omen for therapy. It's best to avoid it."

Smaller numbers of respondents acknowledged that their dishonesty in this realm was specifically about avoiding higher fees. To this end, they exaggerated their current financial hardship or lied about their current income. "I hold back from sharing the good financial things that happen," explained one client, "I tend to highlight more our struggles financially." Although money is often described as "the last taboo," most clients expressed a willingness to speak about it if the therapist took the lead or showed sensitivity to their financial position. When asked what their therapist could do to make them feel more comfortable, most said "If my therapist asked me directly" or "If my therapist understood my culture or class."

Romantic or Sexual Feelings About One's Therapist

Only 5% of our sample in Study 1 reported lying about romantic or sexual feelings about their therapist, though a somewhat higher figure (about 9%) was reported in Study 2. According to Sonne and Jochai (2014), who reviewed the literature in this area, when patients do disclose these feelings or enact sexual behaviors, therapists typically respond with discomfort, particularly if they experienced the disclosure as constituting a form of sexual harassment. We imagine that many clients anticipate this sequence, which may explain their reluctance to reveal these feelings in the first place.

In our study, dishonesty about romantic or sexual feelings about one's therapist emerged as one of the topics about which clients were most likely to be totally or extremely dishonest, ranking alongside "Not saying I want to end therapy" as receiving the highest mean extent of lying scores. In fact, among all the therapy-related lies, it elicited the highest proportion of respondents (46%) indicating that this lie was total or extreme. Thus, among those clients who lied about their romantic feelings toward their therapist, most attempted to keep these feelings totally out of the room. Although it is tempting to imagine that despite these clients' best efforts to deny or conceal, their therapists nevertheless must know something of these feelings, this may not be the case. As noted earlier, the work of Hill and colleagues (1992, 1993; Regan & Hill, 1992) suggested that therapists tend not to be able to discern clients' unarticulated thoughts and feelings. But whether therapists do or do not pick up on their clients' romantic or sexual feeling toward them—and perhaps the likelihood of this increases as a function of both time in treatment and intensity of feelings—it is still the case that the clients who have these feelings believe that their therapists do not know and that they themselves are harboring a significant secret.

Across both studies, the two most common motives for client dishonesty in this realm were avoiding shame and, relatedly, general discomfort. Still, there were some interesting thematic twists unique to the situation. Among the 20 narratives on this topic we analyzed, 11 made direct reference to it being simply too "weird," "awkward," or "unprofessional" to mention having romantic or sexual feelings for their therapist. For many, such feelings were not merely embarrassing but the most embarrassing topic. As one woman wrote, "I can talk about other embarrassing things in my life, but not this. . . . I'm sure he would have discussed it with me in a professional manner, but I would have been mortified."

What makes this topic so much worse? As several clients explained, embarrassment in this context takes on the quality of romantic rejection with all its unique pains but, moreover, rejection at the hands of an esteemed, helpful professional with whom one may want or need to continue a professional relationship. Clients fear "humiliation" and at the same time fear "offending" the therapist who has done so much to help them. Four of the 20 respondents believed their feelings were normal, even using terms such as *transference*, but still unspeakable. As a male client explained, "I understand that it's just a feeling that comes out of an intimate relationship. I don't feel it's abnormal or wrong, but way too embarrassing to admit."

Our findings also indicated a high level of concern among clients that acknowledging the truth of their romantic or sexual feelings would not only ruin the therapeutic relationship but could also result in forced termination. Five of the 20 narratives contained expressions of this fear, such as "I don't want to risk having to transfer to another therapist" or "If the lie got out,

I would likely be transferred or treated differently." One middle-aged woman was convinced that revealing her infatuation would end the relationship:

> I never told him how obsessed I became the first few years of therapy. I think he knew but we never talked about it. It was painful and I missed him between sessions and thought about him constantly. Even found out where he lived and drove past his house sometimes, hoping to see him. . . . I was afraid he would stop seeing me.

Perhaps for these reasons, the vast majority of clients did not see themselves ever bringing this topic up in therapy.

Surprisingly, however, the overall impact of this topic of dishonesty was seen as essentially insignificant. The most commonly reported impact on therapy was "none" (reported by 10 of 14 respondents to this question). Most interestingly, one young woman described her romantic feelings for a female therapist as ultimately quite helpful:

> Being able to see her while I'm attracted to her is beneficial to me, since it makes me want to always be on time for all my sessions and I try very hard to not slip-up or relapse in order to impress her.

SUMMARY

Our focus here on therapy-related lies produced several notable findings. First, the extraordinary prevalence of therapy-related dishonesty—over 70% of the respondents in our study acknowledged some dishonesty of this sort—appears to have been overlooked by many previous studies, partly because secrets have typically been defined as events occurring outside therapy or because these topics have been omitted or minimized in survey research. Our operationalization of therapy-related lies approximates Hill et al.'s (1993) notion of "things left unsaid," in a study in which the prevalence of this type of secret or lie was a roughly similar 65%.

Although younger clients were more likely to report therapy-related lies, no other significant differences were observed across demographic variables for the client, therapist, or dyad, suggesting that lying in therapy about therapy is nearly universal and that its occurrence has to be understood not in terms of individual characteristics but rather in terms of the structure and demands of the psychotherapeutic situation. That is, the expectation of revealing one's most profound thoughts and feelings in time-limited segments to a typically high status, nonreciprocally disclosing other, even in a context in which confidentiality is almost total and one's therapist is likely to be accepting and empathic, may inexorably lead to moments or instances of concealment and dishonesty. It is, at times, all too much; self-judgment and/or assumed external judgment leads most therapy clients to less-than-honest expressions of the truth about therapy and/or the therapeutic relationship.

Second, we found that some therapy-related topics occasion more extreme degrees of dishonesty than almost any other subject. Three topics—romantic or sexual feelings about the therapist, the desire to end therapy, and clients' "real opinion" of their therapist—elicited "total or extreme" dishonesty at a higher rate than any of the other 55 topics on the survey. Discussing here-and-now feelings, especially feelings that may seem off-limits or disrespectful, demands more intimacy and courage than many therapy clients can muster. We suspect that difficulties in discussing this cluster and other related items are a major factor underlying the tendency of great numbers of clients to terminate therapy without involving the therapist in the decision.

Third, we found that clients' motives for therapy-related dishonesty are often different from those associated with other subjects of dishonesty. Whereas shame and embarrassment motivate deception on many topics brought into therapy, therapy-related dishonesty is more often motivated by "other-oriented" psychological concerns (DePaulo, Kashy, Kirkendol, Wyer, & Epstein, 1996), such as a desire to be polite, avoid upsetting the therapist, and minimize the possibility of provoking the therapist's disapproval. This finding lends empirical support to Rennie's (1994) argument that clients' fears of criticizing their therapist, their eagerness to meet their therapist's expectations, and their attempts to avoid threatening their therapist's self-esteem are all part of an overall pattern of deference to the clinician. That said, some therapy-related lies, especially concerning clients' romantic or sexual feelings toward their therapists, are still heavily influenced by feelings of shame; furthermore, clients' desire to avoid their own discomfort, another prime motive for therapy-related lies, is almost certainly related to the anticipation of shame.

In addition, although some therapy-related lies are clearly motivated by the tendency for clients to be deferential, other lies or concealment seem triggered primarily by a poor therapeutic relationship—that is, by clients' dislike and/or distrust of their therapist, leading to their sense that honesty would be pointless. Although it has proven difficult to determine on an a priori basis the elements of an effective therapeutic "match," the data documenting the clinical importance of a positive therapeutic alliance in the first three to five sessions of therapy (e.g., Fluckiger et al., 2019) point to the fact that some therapeutic dyads simply do not work well from the beginning, providing a facilitative context for dishonesty.

That so many clients seem to struggle with being honest with their therapists about their relationship—and that so many who are dishonest in this realm perceive themselves as extreme in their deception—is a phenomenon the field has yet to truly recognize. Despite the trend toward relationally oriented practices (across multiple theoretical orientations), many clients are still unwilling to discuss honestly their thoughts about the therapeutic relationship and therapeutic process. Not doing so—not discussing the ways in which therapy is helping or the ways in which it is disappointing—has consequences for the client (including his or her commitment to therapy and self-image), the therapist (including his or her morale and feelings of self-efficacy), the therapeutic alliance, the likelihood of sudden or premature termination, and of course, the probability of positive therapeutic outcomes.

12

SECRETS AND LIES IN PSYCHOTHERAPY: SUMMARY AND CLINICAL IMPLICATIONS

It is a joy to be hidden, and disaster not to be found.
—Donald Winnicott, *The Maturational Processes and the Facilitating Environment*

What have we learned? That many, perhaps virtually all, psychotherapy clients are not entirely truthful about their thoughts, feelings, or experiences and that a good proportion of this dishonesty revolves around issues of sex, suicidal ideation, self-harm, minimization of distress, experiences of abuse or other trauma, negative or at least ambivalent feelings about therapy or the therapist (e.g., "My real reactions to my therapist's comments"), and drug and alcohol abuse. Our research gathered data on many other topics, from eating disorders to criminal offenses to racist feelings, that we have only had space to mention briefly. Our sense is that if it is spoken about in therapy, it is at least occasionally lied about in therapy.

We also learned that although these were the topics most commonly lied about or purposely avoided by clients, several other topics emerged as the focus of the most extreme lies—those that clients reported as "total or extreme." These included romantic or sexual feelings toward one's therapist,

http://dx.doi.org/10.1037/0000128-013
Secrets and Lies in Psychotherapy, by B. A. Farber, M. Blanchard, and M. Love

not acknowledging wanting to terminate therapy, and experiences of sexual abuse or trauma. Other, mostly sexually tinged lies, were also frequently in the "total or extreme" category, including masturbation habits, use of pornography, and infidelity. Suicidal feelings and self-injurious behaviors (e.g., cutting) constituted yet other topics on which there were significant indications of extreme dishonesty by clients. We learned too that most of the dissembling that occurs is in the form of concealment of information rather than overt lies and that, for the most part, client deceit in psychotherapy is not affected by gender or other demographic factors, except that younger clients are on average dishonest about more topics than their older counterparts. We found too that many instances of deceit come early in therapy, even in the first session, and that most lies are "of the moment"—spontaneous and not planned.

The results of our research indicate too that the predominant motives for client secrets and lies are shame (confirming what many other studies have found), a sense that the therapist would not understand the issue or be helpful (particularly in the case of sexual orientation), a fear that honest discussion would engender overwhelming emotions (particularly in the case of trauma), a fear (particularly in the case of suicidal feelings) that the therapist would overreact, and a fear (particularly in the case of providing negative feedback about therapeutic progress) that the therapist would be hurt or angry. Importantly, and as reflected in these examples, we found that the frequency of these motives differs markedly depending on the topic at hand.

Our data also show that patients who do conceal or lie in therapy tend to feel conflicted about it: Most acknowledged feeling guilty, frustrated, worried, and regretful, though many also reported simply feeling unconcerned, and some (especially those who were dishonest about their suicidal feelings or their history of being abused) reported feeling safe and in control because disclosure on those topics felt risky. Just about half the patients we surveyed felt their dishonesty had no effect on the therapy, though another quarter or so acknowledged that it negatively affected their clinical progress. It seems, then, that some lies and secrets are more easily compartmentalized than others, or perhaps some individuals are more capable of compartmentalizing their dishonesty, keeping certain areas of life unknown to their therapist while being essentially honest about most other parts. In this sense, our findings are more or less consistent with what the behavioral economist Dan Ariely suggested in his (2013) book, *The (Honest) Truth About Dishonesty*. His contention, based on laboratory studies, was that few people are grossly dishonest, but many people are willing to cheat or be "somewhat" dishonest. In his estimation, many people consistently "fudge" the truth—for example, lying on their income tax—but restrict their fudge factor to about 10%.

We also learned that those who are secretive outside of therapy (i.e., tend toward self-concealment) are more secretive within the bounds of therapy as well; apparently, the confidentiality accorded to therapy goes only so far for some people who are characteristically nondisclosing. We learned too that many—about a third of respondents—believe there is no one with whom they would ever be more honest about a lied-about or concealed topic, not with this therapist and not with family or friends either. However, another third or so of our respondents suggested that they could imagine disclosing more honestly about a particular topic with their current therapist, and an additional 15% indicated that they might be able to discuss the topic more honestly with a different therapist. Finally, most of our respondents believed that their dishonesty was never detected by their therapists; to the extent that there was an exception to this trend, it was in those cases in which clients minimized the extent of their distress. A bottom line of sorts is that clients who wish to keep themselves hidden from their therapists are quite able to do so.

Our focus in this final chapter is on how therapists can work with those clients who, under the right circumstances, could be helped to disclose, or disclose more honestly, concerns and experiences they presumably want to be part of the therapeutic conversation. This discussion presumes situations in which clients are consciously dishonest—that is, aware of what they are doing—rather than engaged in myriad types of unconscious self- and other-deception that are not the major focus of our research.

THE THERAPIST'S POSITION

Most clients come to us in some degree of pain, eager to be helped, seemingly earnest in telling their stories, and aware that honest accounts of their experiences will benefit their treatment. Knowing this, many therapists are thus susceptible to believing that their clients are telling them the truth. "Our default belief," contends social psychologist Robert Feldman (2009), is that those with whom we interact are telling the truth (p. 44). Furthermore, some therapists, reflecting the ethos of humanistically oriented therapists such as Carl Rogers, believe in the essential goodness of their clients. Others, perhaps especially those who are young or new to the work, may not yet have much experience with the rawness of the world or the desperation of some clients to falsify the world according to their needs. Still other therapists, including those who are more experienced, may assume (falsely) that a good working relationship essentially precludes the possibility of client deception. Nevertheless, all therapists experience the clinical reality that dishonesty, or at least evasiveness, is inevitable, even among the apparently healthiest and most trustworthy of clients.

Perhaps the most pervasive dynamic, however, the one that cuts across all types of therapists and is most responsible for not attending effectively to client secrets and lies, is that clinicians often do not want to know. "We don't notice lies because we don't want to notice them" (Feldman, 2009, p. 30). Or, in the wise lyrics of Paul Simon (in "The Boxer"), "Still a man hears what he wants to hear and disregards the rest." It is not only the client who may benefit (at least in the moment) from evading the truth; the therapist's obliviousness forestalls a good deal of his or her anxiety, including the fear of committing a potentially egregious clinical error by making a false assumption. We often convince ourselves that we stay clear of inquiring about certain material for the benefit of the client—we hold to the notion that they cannot handle the truth or that persistent or active inquiry will damage the therapeutic relationship—when in fact, this decision is primarily a self-protective maneuver on our parts.

But having the courage to address client evasiveness or apparent lies still leaves open questions of when and how to do this—questions reflecting the quite common clinical reality that it may be extraordinarily difficult for a therapist to distinguish between ongoing, problematic concealment and the not so problematic and not at all atypical case of the client just needing to proceed slowly in revealing difficult, perhaps shameful information. In this regard, the following is an example offered by one of our study participants, a cautionary tale about why immediately delving into a client's apparent concealment may not always be the appropriate clinical choice. This client, a divorced, professionally successful woman in her early 30s with self-reported symptoms of loneliness and depression, acknowledged having quite angry feelings toward her therapist of 2 years for his perceived lack of empathy in regard to her inability to actively seek out new people and engage more fully in the world. However, she reported that she did not let him know this at the time she became aware of these feelings:

> It's not that I'm dishonest, but sometimes it will take me longer to admit something to my therapist than I am usually comfortable with. . . . I'll think about it for a while and then in the next session I'll say hey, I think you were being really judgmental last time.

Some emotions, behaviors, or thoughts take longer to talk about, and the prudent therapist does not always push, even if he or she has a sense that something does not quite compute or that some feelings or thoughts are being concealed.

We imagine that some readers will now have the following thought or rejoinder: What if the therapist had some inkling of this client's anger when she first experienced it in session—would it not have been okay, perhaps even preferable, to have addressed it then? To this, our answer would be a cautious "maybe." Yes, of course, it is possible that an especially sensitive therapist could choose just the right words and tone such that this client's anger could have been discussed and understood and perhaps even alleviated right then and there. But we do not know from this narrative whether the therapist had any clue as to whether his client was angry at him. And just as in many other interpersonal situations wherein conversations about hot topics are often conducted with more reason and better resolution after a short perspective-taking interval, the therapeutic setting may work the same way. This client clearly needed or wanted a cooling off time; moreover, she did address this important clinical issue and relatively soon (i.e., the next session) after she became aware of it. Although she did conceal her feelings as they occurred in therapy, she also knew or felt that this should not turn into a long-term secret, one that could affect the therapeutic work. So yes, the therapist could have inquired as to his suspicions that something was amiss in this session and he would have been right, and it might have turned out just fine. But maybe too the therapist's immediate questioning would have led to defensiveness on the part of the client and a true therapeutic rupture. And maybe too this therapist considered asking his client about her feelings in this session but instead decided he would wait to see whether she would bring this issue up the next session and if not, he would then be more active in pursuing this.

Thus, part of the art of therapy is for the therapist to know or somehow intuit when certain partially disclosed information, partially expressed feelings, half-truths, or lies are to be accepted (at least at the moment) and when they should be pursued or challenged. Of course, it depends, as virtually all clinical decisions do, on multiple factors, including the specific character structure, problems, and goals of the client; on the state of the therapeutic alliance; on the nature and chronicity of the nonconcealment or lie at this time with this therapist; on the therapist's sense as to whether the client will provide more complete or more honest information at his or her own speed at a later time in therapy; on the therapist's clinical orientation and working model of therapeutic action; on the therapist's assumption about how the client might react to a clinical intervention at this particular point in the treatment; and likely on several other factors as well. What makes this process even more challenging is that therapists are neither well trained to detect secrets or lies nor to deal effectively with them (Curtis & Hart, 2015).

ONE CLINICAL PERSPECTIVE: THE TRUTH IS SACROSANCT (OR AT LEAST QUITE VALUABLE)

Clinicians have hard decisions to make about pursuing truth. But let us shift the argument somewhat, from considerations about when to pursue the truth—the now or later dilemma—to something perhaps even more basic: whether to pursue the truth at all.

Therapists are guided by different perspectives on the clinical importance of the phenomena of truth and deceit. One strand of thinking, one that resonates deeply with many clinical traditions but especially that of psychodynamically oriented psychotherapy, is that client avoidance or distortion of potentially significant clinical material is inherently problematic, an indication of resistance to the therapeutic relationship and/or the fundamental goals of treatment.

In fact, whether one uses the old clinical metaphor of "layers of an onion" to describe the increasing depths to which client disclosure should strive, the idea that clients should make themselves as known as possible to their therapists—and that therapists should facilitate that endeavor—is a fundamental axiom of those therapies that posit that healing and growth are inextricably connected to self-knowledge and self-awareness. The stance of the therapist, as well as the rules, setting, and assumptions of the many varieties of insight-oriented therapies and some varieties of cognitive behavior therapy too (e.g., exposure and response prevention), are primarily in the service of providing a safe enough space for clients to find the courage to disclose those parts of themselves that are most difficult to face and that they most fervently wish to avoid. Though there are distinct differences among a classic Freudian exhorting a patient to "say whatever is on your mind without censorship," a contemporary psychodynamic therapist urging a client to provide full descriptions about the history and current nature of his or her relationships, and a therapist trained in exposure therapy encouraging a patient to provide as much information as possible about the exact nature of his or her traumatic event(s), all assume that concealment and/or evasiveness are inimical to effective treatment. Many, if not all such therapists, have likely thought to themselves or said aloud to their clients variations on one or more of the following maxims: "We need to get to the bottom of this," "The truth is in the details," or "If you let me know more about that, it will be easier for us to do this work effectively."

From this perspective, the client's decision to not disclose openly about a significant life experience precludes the possibility of learning something important about him- or herself and of forging a deeper and more honest connection with the therapist. As the poet and essayist Adrienne Rich (1979) noted, a liar is someone who loses sight of the great alchemy that can exist between people.

To be evasive in therapy, then, is to not take advantage fully of the possibilities of knowing oneself or of communion with another. Furthermore, client evasiveness or misrepresentation may have a chilling effect on the therapist. Although therapists often assume honesty on the part of their clients, and although they also tend to acknowledge that this will not always be the case, a chronic pattern of concealment or deceit about a significant clinical issue (e.g., substance abuse, client feelings about the relationship itself) may deflate or even anger a therapist. It may lead to the therapist questioning his or her competence or clinical judgment. It may also critically impair the therapist's ability to continue to believe or trust the client. Though inaccurately attributed to Nietzsche, the following sentiment may accurately reflect the therapist's position: "I'm not upset you lied to me; I'm upset that from now on I can't believe you." Research has confirmed these clinical observations. Therapists do not like to be lied to; they are less enthusiastic about working with clients who lie, tend to trust them less, and view them as less likable, less successful, and less well-adjusted (Curtis & Hart, 2015).

For many reasons, then, it may be important to pursue the truth, even if in most cases there is no single, capital T-truth that will be found. But if there is no unvarnished truth, most therapists still believe there is still great value in pursuing successive approximations to somewhat more accurate and more complex versions of it. "I would like to think," wrote Arabella Kurtz, "that, on a good day, the trajectory of a therapeutic session is from a partial subjective truth to a great subjective truth" (Coetzee & Kurtz, 2015, p. 74). Similarly, Spence (1982) suggested that historical or objective truth (i.e., accurate rendering of the past) may well be impossible, and often the best we can do as therapists is to collaboratively construct with our clients an essentially subjective "narrative truth" that reasonably fits the facts and works for the client—that is, resonates with his or her emotional needs. A further variation on this theme was offered by Levinson (1991), who suggested that clients' truth is of the moment—appropriate to this time in therapy and subject to constant further modifications.

CONTRARY PERSPECTIVES

There is a strand of clinical thinking that holds that psychotherapy can be and inevitably is focused on and effective with a select number of issues and that unless a client is in psychotherapy forever (and even then), there will always be information, even potentially useful information, omitted from sessions. Adopting this perspective means the therapist essentially lets it go—that is, does not pursue (at least not with any urgency or persistence) information that the client seems to have left out of the narrative or even misrepresented. Therapists accept the fact that the constraints of time and the needs of clients result in the clinical reality that all data of potential clinical import will not be shared.

A participant in one of our studies remarked on this in her interview, reporting that time (or rather the lack thereof) was a major factor in her not sharing with her therapist one relatively significant part of her life. Specifically, she was asked whether there was anything her therapist could have done to have facilitated her sharing information on a topic she had concealed:

> I don't think it's a matter of something my therapist could have done. I think not sharing this particular piece of information [her mother's illness] had more to do with the amount of other issues to discuss, and this one being relatively low in priority.

More cynically, in response to some online discussion of the preliminary results of our work, a blogger wrote the following:

> There are lots of things I no longer bother trying to tell the one I pay about. Telling her about it never helped and so I stopped. The woman is useful in one narrow way but I would not bother with telling her about other things even if she asked. I tried it and it was worthless. (Anonymous, 2016)

Furthermore, as we have noted throughout this book, psychotherapy clients—or anyone for that matter—cannot be fully truthful all the time. Clients share what they can at any given time and only when they feel safe enough to do so; even then, some degree of impression management must be expected. Thus, it is fundamentally up to the client to decide which issues will be addressed at what level of disclosure and at what point in therapy, and even if some issues seem more pressing, clinically fruitful, or deeper than the one(s) chosen by the client, the therapist accepts this decision. In some ways, this is a person-centered stance, one that privileges the needs of the client and insists on no *conditions of worth* (Rogers, 1959)—no value judgment about what, when, how, or to what extent the client wants to pursue issues, just simply acceptance.

Moreover, as Langer (2010) contended,

> Often, the need to discover "the truth" of what our patients tell us, especially about the past, is more of a narcissistic issue for the therapist—frequently a need to make the patient's story fit our theories—than of any therapeutic importance for the patient. (p. 11)

In this regard, I (BAF) am reminded of a traditional psychoanalyst I had as a supervisor many years ago during my internship year. No matter what material I brought to our supervision—regardless of my concerns, the patient's concerns, or the clinical problems at hand—he had but a single, quite persistent recommendation: pursue the transference. All truths were to be discovered within the transference. All that the patient left unsaid, discussed vaguely, or evidently distorted were attributable to transferential issues, and my task was to find the truth within that paradigm. Nearly 40 years later I confess I rarely listened to his advice but told him otherwise (see Ladany, Hill, Corbett, & Nutt, 1996, for more about supervisees' lies to supervisors).

More significant, the therapist who pursues his or her own agenda is at risk of alienating patients. The following is an example, drawn from one of our interviews:

> My therapist went through this phase where I felt like he wasn't really understanding what it was I wanted to be working on and really had an idea of what he thought we should be working on . . . and we really butted heads, like passive aggressively for a few months and then um, eventually, it came to me that this was not OK. . . . I really wanted to do a lot of work around my mother dying and was like, this is really the time, and was really excited to start this work and he just had in his head that we were going to confront the issues I had around my father having left when I was really little and he was like always pushing that agenda . . . it just made the process really difficult—because he had the idea that we would be working on one thing and I was just showing up every week talking about something else and then he would relate it back to that. . . . I described it as I thought he was taking up too much space in the room. It was like "I come here and I feel like I deserve all of the space to belong to me and then I show up and you're taking up half the room and I don't like that."

Yet another perspective on deceit, arguably a more radical one, is that promoted by psychotherapy researcher Anita Kelley and more recently by the noted South African author J. M. Coetzee. This position holds that there is no particular virtue and value for clients to disclose painful truths, even those that are inarguably their own issues. We have noted Kelley's argument earlier in this book; the quick recap is that she contends that clients may be better off not disclosing their most shameful truths inasmuch as concealment protects their positive image in the eyes of their therapist.

Coetzee, recipient of the Nobel Prize in Literature and the author of several highly praised books that have dealt with issues of morality and truth (e.g., *Waiting for the Barbarians*, 1980; *Disgrace*, 1999) engaged in a 5-year correspondence with psychologist Arabella Kurtz, the result of which was a (2015) coauthored book, *The Good Story: Exchanges on Truth, Fiction, and Psychotherapy*. In one of the more provocative exchanges in the book, he asked Kurtz,

> What is it that impels you, as a therapist, to want your patient to confront the truth about themselves, as opposed to collaboration or colluding in a story—let us call it a fiction, but an empowering fiction—that would make the patient feel good about themself, good enough to go out into the world better able to love and work? (p. 3)

His question is this: Why seek out the truth—much less have that truth be vetted by one's therapist—if a series of lies will lead to better outcomes? Kurtz replied to Coetzee that in the real world the quest for truth and the value of practicality are not antithetical; they exist as complementary needs. Self-delusion, she contended, cannot lead to happiness. Not surprisingly, her psychoanalytically informed position is that it is necessary for patients to address harsh truths to achieve inner peace. Perhaps the mediated position here is that we seek out therapy when our normally functional self-delusions are no longer meeting our needs.

WORKING WITH CLIENT CONCEALMENT AND LIES: ACCEPTANCE, CURIOSITY, AUTHENTICITY, AND THE ESTABLISHMENT OF A SECURE BASE

There are, of course, multiple positions a clinician can assume between the poles of immediately assuming a significant problem when clients are seemingly avoidant or deceptive versus "simply" accepting their decision to conceal or dissemble. Most of these spaces are embodied in the stance of those many therapists who would be curious and openly reflective, inquiring of their client the reasons—including therapist–client relationship issues—this particular subject seems difficult to talk about, while simultaneously refraining from judgment or placing any pressure on the client to resume or redo his or her narrative. After all, virtually all clinicians use questioning as part of their therapeutic repertoire; that is, it is a quite natural aspect of the give and take in psychotherapy for therapists to want to know more about what the client is thinking or feeling. That kind of questioning might just expand somewhat more when a client's narrative feels incomplete, vague, or implausible. Not infrequently, such an intervention facilitates greater, more open client discussion of difficult topics, if not immediately then shortly thereafter. This idea, like many, can be traced back to Freud: "What was most helpful to patients like Gloria, Freud found, was not circumventing her defenses (through hypnotism) to discover her secrets, but exploring those defenses as they manifested themselves in the analytic situation" (Mitchell & Black, 1995, p. 8).

When respondents in our recent studies were asked, "Under what circumstances would you be more honest about this topic?" the most frequently endorsed answer was a straightforward, "If my therapist asked me directly"; nearly half indicated their willingness to be more open and honest if the therapist simply inquired. About a third of respondents reported, "If I felt like this was blocking my progress in therapy." About a quarter of respondents also pointed to therapist variables that would facilitate their disclosure, such as assurance that the therapist would not overreact or knowing that the therapist had a similar problem. In addition, nearly 20% reported that they needed to know that their honesty would not jeopardize the relationship with the therapist, indicating the way in which disclosure can feel fraught with relational consequences. Only about 10% of respondents indicated that they would not disclose under any circumstances, suggesting that most clients can envision the prospect of disclosing more openly.

It is important to note, though, that it is far easier to deal clinically with a client who is concealing or avoiding information—assuming that the therapist has a sense that this is what is happening—than it is to deal with instances of overt client lies. Encouraging a client to "say more" or stating matter-of-factly, "I don't think I understand," poses far less a threat to the therapeutic alliance (and to the client's sense of self) than does an intervention, even a tactful one, that implies the possibility of a client's overt deceit.

Perhaps the first task, though, of the clinician in dealing with clients who keep secrets or tell lies is to remember just how normative this is, both in and out of therapy (see earlier chapters). As Wiley (1998) cautioned, "Let us be careful not to pathologize what is so much a part of normal human behavior" (p. 871). Clinicians also have to keep in mind that everyone is not temperamentally suited or inclined to disclose all that is on his or her mind in therapy, even if such material seems significant. As we have noted previously, not only are there great differences in clients' self-awareness, self-concealment and distress disclosure tendencies (Kahn & Hessling, 2001; Larson, Chastain, Hoyt, & Ayzenberg, 2015), and degree of psychological mindedness (Farber, 1989) when they begin therapy, but there are also great differences in these individuals' motivation to further these capacities in themselves. It may be somewhat difficult for clinicians, most of whom are extraordinarily self-aware, self-disclosing, and psychologically minded, to appreciate the resistance to these ways of being in the world. Having experienced the advantages of an interpersonally open and self-reflective way of navigating the world and likely having decided (or taken for granted) that their advantages (e.g., viewing oneself and others in more complex and nuanced ways) outweigh the disadvantages (e.g., a tendency to overanalyze and/or pathologize self and others), clinicians might naturally wish their clients to move in this direction, including speaking more openly about their experiences, needs, wishes, feelings, and fears. But again, it is helpful to remember that this is not suitable for everyone—a Robert Mankoff cartoon from *The New Yorker* that I (BAF) often use in my presentations at professional meetings depicts a psychotherapy client saying to his therapist, "Look, call it denial if you like, but what goes on in my personal life is none of my own damn business."

Although most clinicians probably do not need research evidence to support the value of accepting a different perspective than their own, it is worth noting that recent studies have indicated that not all experience warrants extensive examination. Traumatic experience may be a good example. Our colleague at Teachers College, George Bonanno, has demonstrated convincingly that *expressive flexibility*, the ability to both suppress and express emotions and thoughts, is a highly adaptive regulatory strategy (e.g., Bonanno & Burton, 2013; Bonanno, Papa, Lalande, Westphal, & Coifman, 2004). Everything does not have to be talked out; in fact, as Bonanno has shown, it is a mistake to assume that all individuals who have experienced trauma need to engage in debriefing about these events. Some individuals will be retraumatized by this seemingly benign and well-intentioned strategy.

Consistent with this perspective, it is important for therapists to recognize the positive function of evasion and lying (at least for some clients some of the time). It does protect the self, it does allow clients to hide when they need to hide, and it can serve to enhance clients' sense of autonomy. As the Spanish novelist Javier Marias (2013) observed, "Lying . . . both benefits and prejudices all of us equally, and [serves as] our one remaining redoubt of freedom" (p. 246). The point is that some patients need these secrets, these private pieces of information, as a means of retaining their agency or pride or even as a way of maintaining a sense of superiority vis-à-vis their therapist, as in, "While you're in charge here and while I'm supposed to be telling you my most private information, I don't have to feel so one-down because I have information and experiences that you don't know that I have." In his (2010) book, *The Liar in Your Life: The Way to Truthful Relationships*, Feldman wrote that lying helps us navigate situations in which we feel we do not quite measure up. He further suggested that although "conversations involving lies are less warm, less intimate, less comfortable than those that are more honest . . . some deception can be extremely helpful in accomplishing goals that are an essential to an individual's or society's continued functioning" (pp. 24–26).

But what to do in the cases of those clients who do seem to be psychologically minded, who do value self-awareness, but who struggle nonetheless to reveal themselves? One could wait for the client to fill in the gaps or revise his or her story—"as it is a human thing to have a secret, it is also a human thing, sooner or later, to reveal it" (Roth, 2001, p. 338)—and this strategy, one that privileges therapist patience, can be productive. As in the earlier example of the client who waited a week before informing her therapist of her angry feelings, sometimes clients need time to process distressing feelings toward the therapist or provide the details of their drug abuse or sexual infidelities—and they need the therapist to wait a beat or two or a week or two to disclose this material. But this strategy may also have its limits—therapists can be too patient, in essence colluding with that part of their client's ambivalence that prefers staying unknown. Being endlessly patient may mean the client never gets to the truth that he or she (sort of) wants and/or produces therapies that last for years, or far longer than they need to.

Still, this waiting position has its adherents. For example, one prominent person-centered therapist, John Shlien, offered the following advice:

"Let the patient keep his secret until the pain of bearing it is greater than the shame of revealing it" (1984, p. 393). Although understanding the rationale of this advice from a person-centered perspective that eschews any indications of therapist directiveness, it strikes us that this position does not allow sufficient room for the therapist to help resolve the client's ambivalence about sharing secrets or clarifying misrepresentations. Moreover, as both past research (e.g., Farber, Berano, & Capobianco, 2004) and our current research have indicated, most clients when feeling uncertain about disclosure seem to prefer some form of engagement on the part of the therapist, including gentle questioning and inquisitiveness about omissions, inconsistencies, and puzzling details. The therapist can simply ask (as many do), "Can you say more about that"? Or he or she may wonder aloud about missing pieces in a client's narrative: "I'm wondering whether I'm missing something" or "I have a sense there's more here." Some therapists might also add a more relational piece: "Please help me understand what you're trying to tell me," "Is there something I can do to make this easier to talk about?" "Are you okay with sharing with me what you're experiencing?" Adding empathy to the mix may further help with this process: "I sense that this is really difficult to talk about, but I don't think I'm getting the whole picture yet" or "It feels to me like you're really struggling to let me know what happened to you." As Wiley (1998) observed, "Whatever their [lies'] purpose the psychotherapist must adopt a noncondemning, empathetic approach if therapy is to continue" (p. 890). It is critical for clinicians to be aware of the difference between clients being found and being found out.

In a similar vein, Wachtel (2008) suggested that therapists should attempt to expand or "amplify" the client's story rather than being suspicious of its truth value. The task, according to Wachtel, is to show the patient that he does not yet know the whole truth about himself or his experience, that there is "more to him than he has thought" (p. 193). We imagine that an intervention honoring this perspective might take the form "I'm wondering whether there are other parts of what you're talking about that are painful or hard to talk about." As Goldstein (2014) wisely observed, therapists must be prepared to engage clients not in the absence of their anxiety but in the full presence of it.

Although this book is intentionally focused on those aspects of client deceit that are conscious—secrets kept, lies told, thoughts and feelings withheld—here, per Wachtel and Goldstein and, of course, Freud and his followers as well, we may be in that wide but fuzzy realm of client unawareness of what they are leaving out of their narrative. That is, what clients do not tell us is not only a result of what they consciously omit or fabricate but also of those experiences to which they do not have conscious access. Whether we call it *repression* (as per Freud) or relatedly *motivated forgetting* (B. Weiner,

1968) or even the *unthought known* (Bollas, 1987), individuals sometimes do not remember events (e.g., trauma) that are too painful or cannot articulate events that have been experienced too early in childhood to be encoded verbally. Although these memories are difficult to retrieve, they tend to remain in storage. There is a large and controversial literature on the validity of the concept of repression, especially regarding child abuse cases (e.g., Memon & Young, 1997). Here, though, we simply note that the therapist who senses an absence of this sort—a seemingly nonconscious omission on the part of the client—can effectively acknowledge his or her confusion: "I'm sorry, but I'm confused. You've told me 'a' and 'b,' but then all of a sudden 'e' and 'f' happened. I'm not sure how you got from one place to the other." The therapist's confusion is a way of making clients feel they are not doing something wrong, all the while helping them fill in the gaps in their narrative of which they have been unaware.

Another means for therapists to facilitate disclosure and mitigate deceit is through their honest disclosures of what they are experiencing in the room. Therapist *authenticity*—self-disclosure in the here and now or what is sometimes referred to as *immediacy disclosures* (Hill & Knox, 2002)—can greatly facilitate openness on the part of clients. McWilliams (2004) suggested, "The more emotionally genuine the therapist is, the more the patient can open up without shame" (p. 53). Adrienne Rich (1979) also weighed in on the role of authenticity (and courage) in the pursuit of truth between any individuals, emphasizing the importance of both parties knowing that each is constantly trying to extend the possibilities of truth between them. The following is an example of this approach from a paper by Goldstein and Suzuki (2015), one marked with a degree of irreverence that the founder of dialectical behavior therapy, Marsha Linehan, would surely appreciate:

> I was once sitting with a remarkably obsessional and frozen man, and in spite of great efforts on my part to pay attention . . . my mind had wandered, and I was lost in my own thoughts. My patient, who generally noticed nothing about others, says to me, "Where are you? Are you paying attention?" . . . I heard myself say, "I think you're right; my mind was elsewhere." The patient, to his credit, asked, "Where were you?" Sensing a shift in him, I decided to dive in. "Do you actually want to know?" I asked. "Yes," he responded, so I told him, feeling quite embarrassed, "I was on the back nine of my favorite golf course." He asked, "Was I really that boring?" and I responded by asking him if he had been at all interested in what he had been talking about. "Actually, not really," he said. So I responded, "Since neither of us were interested in what you were talking about, why don't you tell me what is it that you do want to say, that you're not getting to? Let's see what we've got"—which we then proceeded to do. (p. 453)

The goal then of virtually all forms of intervention focused on concealment and deception in therapy is to help the client trust that he or she gets more from expressing the truth, with all its attendant positive consequences (e.g., greater therapist access to information that may facilitate treatment, deeper connection with the therapist, a sense of authenticity, a feeling of relief), than the negative reinforcement that occurs as a consequence of avoiding the anxiety of speaking honestly about a potentially shameful or otherwise fraught topic.

This general stance further assumes that the clinical work to be done around nonconcealment or distortion is not just about getting the client to reveal more extensively and honestly but that discussing why such expression has been difficult opens up significant areas of exploration into character, defenses, fears, relational patterns, self-esteem, trust, and a variety of other avenues that are likely to be equally valuable and clinically productive. For example, the therapist may begin to understand better the underlying message that a client is communicating, or perhaps acting out, with his or her dishonesty (e.g., "I don't trust you" or "I am worried about being rejected or ashamed"; Kottler & Carlson, 2011). Open-ended therapist questions—for example, "What do you think would happen if you shared this with me?" "What parts of yourself are you protecting by keeping this from me?" "In what other areas of your life does this happen?" "How would telling me change things between us?"—may illuminate significant and otherwise hard-to-reach aspects of the client's personality, especially characterological patterns of relating to others. In fact, it could be argued that understanding the etiology of and motives behind various forms of evasiveness has greater potential clinical pay-off than the truth about any specific issue.

One other, overarching ingredient must be brought into this discussion of what the therapist has to provide to further client honesty and uncover previously obscured aspects of resistance and character: He or she has to serve as a secure attachment figure, a safe base, such that patients feel sufficiently safe to explore and articulate their most shameful or feared parts of themselves (Bowlby, 1988; Farber, Lippert, & Nevas, 1995). That is, all these aspects of therapist engagement—empathy, curiosity, gentle questioning, and clarification—are greatly dependent for their effectiveness on the gradual establishment of the therapist as a safe base for exploration, one critical aspect of an effective therapeutic alliance. Mark Twain (1992) once suggested that we should never tell the truth to people who are not worthy of it, a maxim that may well have relevance to clients in psychotherapy.

The development of a safe base is especially important when therapists are working with clients who are in the borderline range of pathology and/or who have been abused or otherwise traumatized. Courtois's (1999) description of the phenomenology of traumatized patients serves as an excellent example of the fragile dynamics at play here:

> The patient may be beset by shame and anxiety and terrified of being judged and "seen" by the therapist. The therapist, in turn, may be perceived as a stand-in for other untrustworthy and abusive authority figures to be feared, mistrusted, challenged, tested, distanced from, raged against, sexualized, etc., or may be perceived as a stand-in for the longed-for good parent or rescuer to be clung to, deferred to, and nurtured by, or the two may alternate in unpredictable kaleidoscopic shifts (especially when the patient is highly dissociative and is easily triggered). (p. 190)

Given these dynamics, one can readily see how the establishment (and nearly constant reestablishment) of a safe environment is a prerequisite to honest client disclosure. The following is an example, drawn from my (BAF's) supervision of a doctoral student. Sometime in the first few weeks of her work with an angry woman in her 20s, someone diagnosable with borderline personality disorder, the student asked her to speak more about her feelings of hostility toward her mother. The problem, though, was that the student trainee also added the phrase, "Because I'm wondering whether there are other ways of seeing this." In response to this phrase, the patient became quite angry and frustrated, wondering whether the therapist believed her and was on her side or her mother's. It took quite a deal of clinical work to heal this rupture. Although this exchange may have occurred any time during treatment with a fragile client, the rupture here was especially likely early in treatment. Our point is that the therapist must be reasonably certain that he or she is providing a secure therapeutic base before pursuing greater client truth, especially when working with traumatized or otherwise fragile patients.

A MORE CONFRONTATIONAL PERSPECTIVE ON ENGAGING WITH CLIENTS' CONCEALMENT AND LIES

Despite our sense, and that of many others, that curiosity, engagement, empathy, and encouragement are the preferred components of an effective approach to client concealment or deception, there are those who endorse a somewhat more aggressive position. For example, Gediman and Lieberman (1996) promoted a more direct approach, recommending that lies be addressed as soon as they occur and that clients be implored to tell everything. They suggested checking in with one's therapeutic intuition as to whether something important has been concealed and, if that seems to be the case, pointing out inconsistencies in clients' stories or confronting them directly with a statement such as, "I have a feeling that something has been left out" (p. 53). Still, they recognized that "timing and dosage must be respected" (p. 54) in terms of how much and how far to challenge a client.

Kernberg (1975) also advocated for a more confrontational approach, though it is important to note that his stance was formulated specifically as a means to work with clients who are overtly deceitful. He contended that lies by patients reflect their pessimism regarding the possibility of honest, genuine relationships; his stance is that any indications of patient deceit have to be immediately confronted and challenged so that therapy can continue to be an authentic encounter.

For the most part, then, this more aggressive stance is recommended not as an across-the-board strategy but rather in several specific circumstances: when concealment has moved into outright deceit, when nontruth (broadly defined) is manifest in the here and now of the therapeutic relationship, and when the therapist is treating individuals with a history of or current potential for self-harm (e.g., suicidal clients, those with substance abuse problems or other addictions, those with eating disorders) or with personality disorders (e.g., antisocial personality disorder) in which lying and disregard for the rights of others are common features.

The following example of a more aggressive, confrontational stance, drawn from one of the informal interviews we conducted with colleagues of ours, should help illustrate this point. A client with a 1:00 appointment was not in the waiting room when his therapist returned from lunch at exactly 1:00. This was somewhat surprising because he was usually early and had never been more than 1 to 2 minutes late for this long-standing appointment time. His therapist waited and at 1:10 texted him to make sure he was okay. He answered the text almost immediately, avowing that he was in fact there at the scheduled appointment time, had waited 5 minutes, and then left. His therapist simply said, "Hmm, let's talk about this next time." At the next appointment, the therapist asked, "What happened last week"? The client clung to his initial story. The therapist considered letting it go, but decided, in fact, it was important not to. He told the client that he (the therapist) was there at 1:00—he was quite sure of it—and then stayed silent for a minute. The client wavered a bit, "Well, I thought, I'm pretty sure, it was already a few minutes after 1:00 when I left." "Okay," the therapist said, "but I'm wondering what else you think might have been going on." The client said, "What do you mean?" "Well," said the therapist, "I suspect that you might not have wanted to be there, or you might have felt relief when you left. I'm wondering whether there was something about our work in the last session or maybe the sessions before that felt frustrating to you."

With that hypothesis as a prompt, they began to discuss the client's feelings at the moment he (prematurely) left the office the week before, his sense that the therapist had not listened sensitively enough to some hard-to-discuss material some weeks before that, and arguably most important, his resistance to revealing these and other anxiety-laden feelings in therapy out of fear that the therapist would be angry, hurt, disappointed, or rejecting. The importance here lies not in the client's filling in the blanks of this particular story or in his acknowledgement that he was not revealing the truth of the situation but rather in an understanding of his resistance and character, a part of the work likely to lead not only to increased self-awareness but also to an improved alliance, greater depth in subsequent work, and greater access to material that may lead to more successful treatment. In a similar vein, Marcos (1972) noted that it is through engaging productively with the conflict and shame that are frequent concomitants of client deception that therapists may begin to understand better what clients are often communicating with their dishonesty.

With those at risk of harming themselves or others, including individuals who cut or otherwise self-abuse or abuse others (e.g., domestic partners or children) or who are substance abusers, eating disordered, or at risk of suicide, it becomes imperative to gain as soon as possible as good an understanding as possible of the truth of the situation. Wiley's (1998) comments regarding working with substance abusers resonate with clinical work with these other at-risk groups; he advocated for "a more confrontive and active approach on the part of the therapist" (p. 890), pointing to 12-step programs that combine confrontation with support. Accepting at face value the attestations of clients with a history of deception and dangerous behaviors can put multiple people at risk, including both members of the therapeutic dyad. In extreme, potentially life-threatening situations, clinicians, especially those who work in inpatient settings, may have to use drug testing, weigh-ins, signed reports from administrators at auxiliary programs (e.g., parent training programs), and/or mandatory phone check-ins to monitor the veracity of client reports of their behaviors.

To state what should be clinically obvious: Engagement cannot, or at least should not, include overreaction in the form of criticism, disappointment, admonishment, or moralizing. In this regard, it is helpful for clinicians to remember that people often keep secrets or lie because they believe that the recipient of this information will react poorly to the truth. Confronting clients with the "wrongness" of their actions invariably induces shame and subsequent defensiveness, a doubling down on half-truths or lies in the service of self-preservation. The following is an example, drawn from our interviews, of a client who refrained from talking about her current relationships because she believed her therapist would have a judgmental attitude about her sexual experiences:

> There's definitely the fear of judgment. . . . When I talk about my relationships, or even like the number of relationships I have had, that number makes me feel really guilty. I'm always scared I'm gonna come in and talk

> about somebody new, and she's never done this so I have no basis for this, but I feel like she's gonna be like, "Oh like, another person?" Like, "Oh my god, how many more people are we needing to talk about this week"?

Although it is fairly clear that this client's fears are at least somewhat based on projection—that is, she feels guilty about the nature of her sexual experiences—this narrative nevertheless serves to illustrate the potential consequences on subsequent disclosure of a client's fear of being judged.

We thus reiterate the importance of a clinical approach that blends the need for tactful awareness and questioning of what has been concealed or distorted with a good dose of acceptance, support, and acknowledgment that this may be an issue that at least in part resides in the relationship. The therapist who is invariably and exclusively accepting, nonquestioning, and nonskeptical is likely to provide a space in which the client can too easily hide. The therapist who is too eager to root out secrets or confront apparent deception is likely to induce therapeutic ruptures or actual termination from treatment.

Some readers may have observed that there are many parallels between the work on client deception and that on alliance rupture and repair. Indeed, some of the consequences of one type of alliance rupture—what Safran, Muran, and Eubanks-Carter (2011) termed a *withdrawal rupture*—include avoidant storytelling, appeasing, abstract communication, and minimal responsiveness, all forms of client concealment. This should be no surprise: As noted earlier in this book, an effective therapeutic alliance facilitates open, honest client disclosure; conversely, an alliance rupture interferes with this process. Moreover, there is a good degree of overlap between some of the approaches we have offered here regarding working with client secrets and lies and suggestions made in the literature regarding dealing with instances of alliance ruptures. Resolving alliance ruptures may involve validating the client's defensive position, acknowledging the therapist's contribution to the rupture, and eliciting the client's thoughts and feelings about what occurred (Eubanks-Carter, Muran, & Safran, 2015).

DEALING WITH SECRETS AND LIES: WHAT ABOUT "BEFORE" AND "AFTER"?

Clinicians, we believe, should develop an approach to clients' deceptive behavior that is consistent with the general stance of evidence-based psychological practice—that is, an approach that is based on the available research and clinical evidence but also reflects their personal and professional preferences as well as the immediate exigencies of the treatment at hand. Moreover, a comprehensive approach to client concealment and deception would include not only the specifics of a clinician's responses at the point of awareness that something is being hidden or distorted but also some sense of what might be said or what ground rules established at the beginning of treatment regarding disclosure, as well as some strategy or guidelines for following up on whatever interventions have been implemented when client lies or secrets have been felt to be in the treatment room.

What then might therapists do at the outset of treatment to maximize the possibility of client truthfulness? To begin with, we restate our belief that therapists have to recognize the inevitability of some client concealment and the possibility of some overt lying. Simply put, it is going to happen, and therapists should not be surprised when it does. Therapists should remember too how hard it was (or still is) for them to reveal sensitive information or difficult emotions (e.g., shame, anger, vulnerability) to their therapists or clinical supervisors. We also reiterate that therapists should keep in mind the positive psychological functions of deception (e.g., a need to feel autonomous, the human wish to feel valued and respected), as well as the fact that evasions from the truth provide important clinical data. The therapist who is unprepared for dishonesty or experiences it as an affront may experience strong negative reactions when deception occurs. Furthermore, we believe that the therapist should be aware as much as possible of his or her sensitivities and biases. The therapist who has let her patient know of her opposition to guns has made it unlikely that her client will let her know about his extensive gun collection; the therapist who has let slip that he is pro-life makes it far more difficult for his patient to let him know about her abortion. More generally, a therapist's values, vulnerabilities, and apprehensions are likely to be communicated, even unintentionally, to clients, affecting the extent to which they feel comfortable in honestly discussing certain topics. This, of course, is often among the main reasons cited as to why therapists themselves should be in therapy and avail themselves of supervision during their careers.

The following is an example, drawn from one of our interviews, of how a therapist's seeming discomfort in dealing with money and the cost of therapy affected a client's ability to discuss this issue:

> I was hesitant about entering therapy in the first place because of the cost of therapy and being a student I don't have a lot of finances, so I didn't want it to be an issue and I feel like my therapist, every time I say like, "Oh, when do I have to pay you or when's the bill due?" it seems like she doesn't want to make that the focus of the session, whereas for me I just want to get it off my mind, and so I will have a check for her and she'll say, "Oh, you can give that to me at the end," or I'll ask her if she has a bill for me and she'll say, "Yeah, I'll give that to you at the end," so it just makes me feel uncomfortable talking anything about that.

Apart from being attentive to their attitudes and blind spots, therapists should prepare clients for the work, including the hard work of disclosure, that lies before them. In this vein, Kahn, Achter, and Shambaugh (2001) described how it could be beneficial to normalize the disclosure process, explaining to clients the value of sharing distress with caring others both within and outside the therapy setting. Similarly, Vasquez (cited in De Angelis, 2008) recommended that early in the therapeutic process therapists tell their clients that "they'll get more out of therapy the more authentically genuine they can be about their life" (p. 33). Martin (cited in De Angelis, 2008) advised that therapists set a tone of consistent, unconditional acceptance for clients early on in therapy: "I want them to know I'll still accept and care about them no matter what they have to tell me" (p. 33). The task from this perspective is to become the therapist whose clients believe that he or she is entirely welcoming of the truth and can be trusted to regard it, with the exception of several notable (primarily life-threatening) situations, with complete confidentiality.

Informing or reminding clients about the bounds of confidentiality surrounding the therapeutic relationship typically provides a necessary degree of safety for honest disclosure. One of my (BAF's) patients, a therapist herself, asked for reassurance at our first therapy session that I would never use any aspects of our work together at professional meetings or in publications. We discussed the reasons for her anxiety about this, the rules about confidentiality, and her need for reassurance, but I did agree to her request. Only by doing so could the work begin. The consequences of not discussing confidentiality or, far worse, not abiding by these dictates is well illustrated in the following online comment: "I told my therapist my most deepest darkest secrets . . . and she took them and used me and them in a paper which she presented at a conference without my knowledge or permission . . . so much for confidentiality and ethics!" (Rosemary, 2016). One cannot imagine this therapy proceeding at this point.

Important, too, is what occurs following a courageous disclosure on the part of the patient. Turning to Nancy McWilliams (2004),

> One way to communicate acceptance and dissolve shame is by what I think of as the "Yeah . . . so?" response, either verbally or nonverbally. In other words, we take in whatever the patient has confessed with a tone or look of unsurprised matter-of-factness, implying that we are not quite sure why this is such a big deal. Sometimes we make a quick connection that allows us to make a casual comment to the effect that given what the person has said about his or her family of origin, the disclosure is hardly surprising. Or we mutter a comment such as, "Well, naturally," or adopt a puzzled tone and ask, "So what's so terrible about that?" when a patient seems to be drowning in shame. (p. 137)

Although McWilliams (2004) suggested several ways of expressing acceptance of clients' disclosures, others have touted the value of positive regard as an appropriate and effective follow-up to hard-fought truths. One of the interviewed participants in our study explained how her therapist's comments following some of her difficult disclosures served to reinforce her resolve to continue the hard work: "He said, 'You always work up to the edge of what is possible.'"

WHAT CAN I DO? TAKE-HOME POINTS FOR CLINICIANS

- Discuss the process of disclosure before eliciting disclosure. Explore with clients what they can expect when trying to discuss more difficult material. Explain why disclosure can be valuable for treatment and how it aligns with their specific presenting problems and goals for treatment. It can be helpful if clients know that they may experience the very emotions that motivate avoidance (e.g., shame) but that such feelings are generally endurable and often come with feelings of pride, relief, and authenticity after disclosing.
- Provide positive feedback when clients show the courage to be more open. This can help to defuse shame associated with disclosure while also promoting feelings of mastery and strengthening the therapeutic relationship.
- Ask directly. Clients tell us they are willing to discuss almost anything, but many balk at taking the first step. Taking the lead on shameful topics may be required. Therapists who do not introduce challenging topics can communicate to the client that these areas are off limits. Model for clients that all topics are discussable in therapy.
- Start with more general inquiries before easing into specifics. Although we should never shy away from specifics, a gradual approach into emotionally evocative material works better for most clients—for example, asking more broadly about relationships before moving to anything specifically sex related or starting with depression symptoms before moving to questions about suicidality.
- Use language that feels comfortable and authentic to the client. Sometimes this means adopting their specific terminology (i.e., a *hookup* is not always a *relationship*). At other times, clients may not bring topics up because they do not yet have the words to do so; you may have to help develop the right language to

address topics that clients have not found a way to speak of on their own.

- Be aware of your tone. Acting too eager, excessively empathic, or overemotional in response to a disclosure—or alternately, seeming unaffected, like you have "seen it all before"—are all good ways to have clients shut down. For the most part, therapists have to balance curiosity with acceptance and understanding of clients' limits for disclosure at any one time.
- For clients experiencing suicidality, make your explanation about the limits of confidentiality as open, thorough, and interactive as possible. Provide clarity about the triggers for hospitalization because the majority of clients who report dishonesty about this topic describe fears—often unrealistic fears—that they would be forcibly hospitalized for merely having suicidal thoughts. Invite questions and help clients distinguish what situations may or may not require a higher level of care to keep them safe so that they feel a measure of control over the process.
- Take a frank look at your own competence, comfort, and biases before addressing difficult disclosures with clients. Clients can be perceptive and are often on the lookout for signs that the therapist is hesitant or judgmental. We all have blind spots, but we can do our best to be thoughtful and seek out further training to fill any gaps and to know that a referral to a better-equipped colleague is sometimes the best course of action.
- Be aware of the role of diversity regarding client disclosures. Virtually all clients want to feel understood and accepted by their therapist before making emotionally risky disclosures; these perceptions may be influenced greatly by therapists' sensitivity to issues of gender, sexual orientation, age, race, ethnicity, language, immigration, or religious affiliation. Clients' perceptions of therapists' beliefs or attitudes—for example, toward substance use, divorce, or contemporary political issues—also impact their ability to disclose. When needed, judicious self-disclosure on the part of the therapist can clear up any confusion, facilitating client disclosure and reducing felt stigma.
- Revisit tough topics because the dynamics around disclosure can change over time. Some clients will wait until they feel more trust in the therapeutic relationship, and some will make "test" disclosures, letting out small secrets to see how the therapist reacts.
- Be prepared to not ever know. Even when it is clear something important is being hidden, clients may decide discussion is not

necessary or helpful to their therapy or that they cannot tolerate the perceived consequences of disclosure, some of which may be practical or emotional impacts of which we are not even aware.

- Metacommunicate about disclosure throughout the course of treatment. When talking seems to fail, there is a rich tradition of talking about talking in psychotherapy. Inviting clients to imagine what it would be like to make certain disclosures—without pressure to do so—can enhance feelings of agency and open up the world of feelings that is holding them back.
- Remember that dishonesty can serve important functions for clients, such as increasing feelings of autonomy, setting boundaries, or helping maintain self-esteem through impression management. Clients who are dishonest are generally not out to dupe the therapist; they are, for the most part, reacting to the human desire to feel safe and understood.

FINAL NOTES

That so many clients seem to struggle with being honest with their therapists is perhaps both inevitable and troubling. It is inevitable in the sense that people are rarely fully honest or fully disclosing in any interpersonal situation. We are constantly doing the work of impression management, of attempting to find a balance between wanting to be genuine in our expression of self and wanting to "sell" some not quite accurate sense of who we are in an effort to fit others' expectations and judgments and to lessen our feelings of fear, guilt, or shame. And so, clients dissemble—to protect themselves from their therapists' judgments and presumed subsequent reactions and to preserve their often unrealistic and fragile sense of who they should be and how they should act.

But this is a troubling state of affairs as well. Our data, and those of others, suggest that clinicians are often acting from a quite incomplete script, making decisions on the basis of incomplete or falsified information. There is some combination at play here of the natural tendency for people to dissemble and clinicians' inability to provide a sufficiently safe place for clients to disclose some quite significant clinical information. Although therapy is a somewhat safe place, a place where most clients do reveal a good deal of their innermost thoughts and feelings (Farber, 2006), it appears as if there are true limitations. This is not surprising for those who have studied personal relationships in general, but we sense that limitations in client honesty, along with its clinical implications, have not been sufficiently addressed in the professional literature or clinical training programs.

Although client honesty will never be totally unbounded, clinicians who address issues of emotional safety, trust, confidentiality, and disclosure in the earliest stages of therapy—and how these may be impacted by racial, ethnic, gender, or sexual orientation differences—and who revisit these issues periodically throughout treatment are likely to encounter more open and engaged clients. In a related vein, although most clinicians are aware of the importance of such relational elements as empathy and positive regard, some would undoubtedly profit from more focused attention on the dynamics of the relationship per se. We also argue for the need for increased therapist training in identifying and resolving therapeutic ruptures as a means to attenuate client inclinations toward dishonesty in the room. Last, we believe that renewed attention to the possibilities and benefits of pretherapy client "role induction" (e.g., C. L. Patterson, Anderson, & Wei, 2014) could sensitize clients to expectations regarding therapeutic tasks, including honest disclosure. Although we are far from advocating a return to Freud's dictum about the need for patients to say everything on their mind without censorship (the *fundamental rule* of psychoanalysis), we believe he was right in at least several respects: that it is important for clients to understand the need for honesty and why they struggle with this process, that clinicians do need to monitor what is and is not being honestly disclosed by clients, and that greater client honesty should be both a focus and goal of clinical work.

Future research on client dishonesty is surely needed, especially in the areas of client minimization of emotional distress and client avoidance of discussions of the current state of the therapeutic relationship. The groundbreaking work of Hill, Thompson, Cogar, and Denman (1993) on "things left unsaid" and by Safran and Muran (2000) on the identification and repair of therapeutic ruptures are excellent examples of research that has begun to move the field to a greater awareness of the clinical implications of client dishonesty or reluctance to disclose significant clinical material. Still, more is needed to identify further those specific therapeutic practices that increase or decrease the probability of client dishonesty. As we understand more about the processes that inhibit or facilitate client disclosure, we are likely to be in a better position to help our clients heal.

REFERENCES

Akhtar, S., & Parens, H. (Eds.). (2009). *Lying, cheating, and carrying on: Developmental, clinical, and sociocultural aspects of dishonesty and deceit*. Lanham, MD: Jason Aronson.

American Psychiatric Association. (2013). *Diagnostic and statistical manual of mental disorders* (5th ed.). Arlington, VA: Author.

Anonymous. (2016, October 27). Re: Why people lie to their therapists [Blog comment]. Retrieved from https://www.psychologytoday.com/us/blog/in-therapy/201610/why-people-lie-their-therapists

Ariely, D. (2013). *The honest truth about dishonesty: How we lie to everyone—especially ourselves*. New York, NY: HarperCollins.

Austen, J. (1816). *Emma*. London, England: John Murray. http://dx.doi.org/10.1093/oseo/instance.00080853

Bagarozzi, D. A., Sr. (2007). Understanding and treating marital infidelity: A multidimensional model. *The American Journal of Family Therapy, 36*, 1–17. http://dx.doi.org/10.1080/01926180601186900

Barbaro, M. (2015, November 8). Candidates stick to the script, if not the truth. *The New York Times*, p. A1.

Barclay, C. R. (1986). Schematization of autobiographical memory. In D. C. Rubin (Ed.), *Autobiographical memory* (pp. 82–99). Cambridge, MA: Cambridge University Press. http://dx.doi.org/10.1017/CBO9780511558313.010

Barnes, J. (2011). *The sense of an ending*. London, England: Jonathan Cape.

Baumann, E. C., & Hill, C. E. (2016). Client concealment and disclosure of secrets in outpatient psychotherapy. *Counselling Psychology Quarterly, 29*, 53–75. http://dx.doi.org/10.1080/09515070.2015.1023698

Bellow, S. (2006). *The adventures of Augie March*. London, England: Penguin Classics. (Original work published 1953)

Berano, K., & Farber, B. A. (2006, June). *Asian-American and Caucasian self-disclosure in psychotherapy: The Influence of Asian values and individualism-collectivism*. Paper presented at the meeting of the Society for Psychotherapy Research, Edinburgh, Scotland.

Berry, M. D., & Lezos, A. N. (2017). Inclusive sex therapy practices: A qualitative study of the techniques sex therapists use when working with diverse sexual populations. *Sexual and Relationship Therapy, 32*, 2–21. http://dx.doi.org/10.1080/14681994.2016.1193133

Beutler, L. E., Moleiro, C., & Talebi, H. (2002). Resistance in psychotherapy: What conclusions are supported by research. *Journal of Clinical Psychology, 58*, 207–217. http://dx.doi.org/10.1002/jclp.1144

Black, T., & Haines, R. (Producers), & Washington, D. (Producer & Director). (2002). *Antwone Fischer* [Motion picture]. United States: Fox Searchlight Pictures.

Blanchard, M., & Farber, B. A. (2016). Lying in psychotherapy: Why and what clients don't tell their therapist about therapy and their relationship. *Counselling Psychology Quarterly*, *29*, 90–112. http://dx.doi.org/10.1080/09515070.2015.1085365

Blanchard, M., & Farber, B. A. (2018). "It is never okay to talk about suicide": Patients' reasons for concealing ideation in psychotherapy. *Psychotherapy Research*. http://dx.doi.org/10.1080/10503307.2018.1543977

Blow, A. J., & Hartnett, K. (2005). Infidelity in committed relationships II: A substantive review. *Journal of Marital and Family Therapy*, *31*, 217–233. http://dx.doi.org/10.1111/j.1752-0606.2005.tb01556.x

Bok, S. (1999). *Lying: Moral choice in public and private life*. New York, NY: Vintage Books.

Bollas, C. (1987). *The shadow of the object: Psychoanalysis of unknown thought*. London, England: Free Association Books.

Bonanno, G. A., & Burton, C. L. (2013). Regulatory flexibility: An individual differences perspective on coping and emotion regulation. *Perspectives on Psychological Science*, *8*, 591–612. http://dx.doi.org/10.1177/1745691613504116

Bonanno, G. A., & Field, N. P. (2001). Examining the delayed grief hypothesis across 5 years of bereavement. *American Behavioral Scientist*, *44*, 798–816. http://dx.doi.org/10.1177/0002764201044005007

Bonanno, G. A., Keltner, D., Holen, A., & Horowitz, M. J. (1995). When avoiding unpleasant emotions might not be such a bad thing: Verbal-autonomic response dissociation and midlife conjugal bereavement. *Journal of Personality and Social Psychology*, *69*, 975–989. http://dx.doi.org/10.1037/0022-3514.69.5.975

Bonanno, G. A., Papa, A., Lalande, K., Westphal, M., & Coifman, K. (2004). The importance of being flexible: The ability to both enhance and suppress emotional expression predicts long-term adjustment. *Psychological Science*, *15*, 482–487. http://dx.doi.org/10.1111/j.0956-7976.2004.00705.x

Bond, C. F., Levine, T. R., & Hartwig, M. (2015). New findings in non-verbal lie detection. In P. A. Granhag, A. Vrij, & B. Vershuere (Eds.), *Detecting deception: Current challenges and cognitive approaches* (pp. 37–58). Hoboken, NJ: Wiley.

Bongar, B., & Sullivan, G. (2013). *The suicidal patient: Clinical and legal standards of care*. Washington, DC: American Psychological Association. http://dx.doi.org/10.1037/14184-000

Bowlby, J. (1969). *Attachment and loss: Attachment*. New York, NY: Basic Books.

Bowlby, J. (1973). *Attachment and loss: Vol. 2. Separation*. New York, NY: Basic Books.

Bowlby, J. (1988). *A secure base*. New York, NY: Basic Books.

Bresin, K., & Schoenleber, M. (2015). Gender differences in the prevalence of nonsuicidal self-injury: A meta-analysis. *Clinical Psychology Review*, *38*, 55–64. http://dx.doi.org/10.1016/j.cpr.2015.02.009

Brown, D., & Scheinman, A. (Producers), & Reiner, R. (Producer & Director). (1992). *A few good men* [Motion picture]. United States: Columbia Pictures Corporation.

Brown, G. K., Ten Have, T., Henriques, G. R., Xie, S. X., Hollander, J. E., & Beck, A. T. (2005). Cognitive therapy for the prevention of suicide attempts: A randomized controlled trial. *JAMA, 294*, 563–570. http://dx.doi.org/10.1001/jama.294.5.563

Bryan, C. J., & Rudd, M. D. (2006). Advances in the assessment of suicide risk. *Journal of Clinical Psychology, 62*, 185–200. http://dx.doi.org/10.1002/jclp.20222

Burckell, L. A., & Goldfried, M. R. (2006). Therapist qualities preferred by sexual-minority individuals. *Psychotherapy: Theory, Research, Practice, Training, 43*, 32–49. http://dx.doi.org/10.1037/0033-3204.43.1.32

Burgo, J. (2013, April 12). Lying to our clients [Blog post]. Retrieved from http://www.afterpsychotherapy.com/lying-to-our-clients

Byers, E. S. (2011). Beyond the birds and the bees and was it good for you?: Thirty years of research on sexual communication. *Canadian Psychology/Psychologie canadienne, 52*, 20–28. http://dx.doi.org/10.1037/a0022048

Campbell, R., & Raja, S. (2005). The sexual assault and secondary victimization of female veterans: Help-seeking experiences with military and civilian social systems. *Psychology of Women Quarterly, 29*, 97–106. http://dx.doi.org/10.1111/j.1471-6402.2005.00171.x

Campbell, R., Wasco, S. M., Ahrens, C. E., Sefl, T., & Barnes, H. E. (2001). Preventing the "second rape": Rape survivors' experiences with community service providers. *Journal of Interpersonal Violence, 16*, 1239–1259. http://dx.doi.org/10.1177/088626001016012002

Castonguay, L. G., & Hill, C. E. (Eds.). (2017). *How and why are some therapists better than others: Understanding therapist effects*. Washington, DC: American Psychological Association. http://dx.doi.org/10.1037/0000034-000

Center for Behavioral Health Statistics and Quality. (2015). *Behavioral health trends in the United States: Results from the 2014 National Survey on Drug Use and Health*. Retrieved from https://www.samhsa.gov/data/sites/default/files/NSDUH-FRR1-2014/NSDUH-FRR1-2014.pdf

Centers for Disease Control and Prevention. (2012, September 14). Surveillance for violent deaths—National Violent Death Reporting System, 16 states, 2009. *Morbidity and Mortality Weekly Report*. Retrieved from https://www.cdc.gov/mmwr/preview/mmwrhtml/ss6106a1.htm

Centers for Disease Control and Prevention. (2018). *Welcome to WISQARS*. Retrieved from https://www.cdc.gov/injury/wisqars/

Cevallos, D. (2016, October 23). Trump versus accusers: Who would win in court? *CNN*. Retrieved from http://www.cnn.com/2016/10/23/opinions/could-trump-sue-accusers-cevallos/

Chaffin, C., Donen, J., Milchan, A., & Witherspoon, R. (Producers), & Fincher, D. (Director). (2014). *Gone girl* [Motion picture]. United States: Twentieth Century Fox.

Christie, R., & Geis, F. (1970). *Studies in Machiavellianism*. New York, NY: Academic Press.

Coetzee, J. M. (1980). *Waiting for the barbarians*. London, England: Penguin.

Coetzee, J. M. (1999). *Disgrace*. London, England: Penguin.

Coetzee, J. M., & Kurtz, A. (2015). *The good story: Exchanges on truth, fiction and psychotherapy*. New York, NY: Viking.

Cornell Research Program for Self-Injury Recovery. (2018). *About self-injury: Detection, intervention, & treatment*. Retrieved from http://www.selfinjury.bctr.cornell.edu/about-self-injury.html#tab12

Courtois, C. A. (1999). *Recollections of sexual abuse: Treatment principles and guidelines*. New York, NY: Norton.

Cowles, G. (2015, October 23). 'The Art of Memoir' by Mary Karr [Review of the book]. *The New York Times*. Retrieved from https://www.nytimes.com/2015/10/25/books/review/the-art-of-memoir-by-mary-karr.html?rref=collection%2Fbyline%2Fgregory-cowles&action=click&contentCollection=undefined®ion=stream&module=stream_unit&version=latest&contentPlacement=112&pgtype=collection

Cramer, P. (2006). *Protecting the self: Defense mechanisms in action*. New York, NY: Guilford Press.

Curtis, D. A., & Hart, C. L. (2015). Pinocchio's nose in therapy: Therapists' beliefs and attitudes toward client deception. *International Journal for the Advancement of Counselling, 37*, 279–292. http://dx.doi.org/10.1007/s10447-015-9243-6

De Angelis, T. (2008, January). An elephant in the office: Experts discuss why clients withhold truth, and what practitioners can do about it. *Monitor on Psychology, 39*(1), 33.

DeLong, L. B., & Kahn, J. H. (2014). Shameful secrets and shame-prone dispositions: How outcome expectations mediate the relation between shame and disclosure. *Counselling Psychology Quarterly, 27*, 290–307. http://dx.doi.org/10.1080/09515070.2014.908272

DePaulo, B. M. (2004). The many faces of lies. In A. G. Miller (Ed.), *The social psychology of good and evil* (pp. 303–326). New York, NY: Guilford Press.

DePaulo, B. M., & Bell, K. L. (1996). Truth and investment: Lies are told to those who care. *Journal of Personality and Social Psychology, 71*, 703–716. http://dx.doi.org/10.1037/0022-3514.71.4.703

DePaulo, B. M., & Kashy, D. A. (1998). Everyday lies in close and casual relationships. *Journal of Personality and Social Psychology, 74*, 63–79. http://dx.doi.org/10.1037/0022-3514.74.1.63

DePaulo, B. M., Kashy, D. A., Kirkendol, S. E., Wyer, M. M., & Epstein, J. A. (1996). Lying in everyday life. *Journal of Personality and Social Psychology, 70*, 979–995. http://dx.doi.org/10.1037/0022-3514.70.5.979

Depue, B. E., Banich, M. T., & Curran, T. (2006). Suppression of emotional and nonemotional content in memory: Effects of repetition on cognitive control. *Psychological Science, 17*, 441–447. http://dx.doi.org/10.1111/j.1467-9280.2006.01725.x

DeScioli, P., Christner, J., & Kurzban, R. (2011). The omission strategy. *Psychological Science, 22*, 442–446. http://dx.doi.org/10.1177/0956797611400616

Deutsch, H. (1955). The impostor: Contribution to ego psychology of a type of psychopath. *The Psychoanalytic Quarterly, 24*, 483–505. http://dx.doi.org/10.1080/21674086.1955.11925999

de Waal, F. B. M. (1986). Deception in the natural communication of chimpanzees. In R. Mitchell & N. Thompson (Eds.), *Deception: Perspectives on human and nonhuman deceit* (pp. 221–244). New York, NY: SUNY Press.

Dillard, S. (2013, November 24). Re: Do psychologists lie to their patients? [Online forum comment]. Retrieved from https://www.quora.com/Do-psychologists-lie-to-their-patients

Downs, A. (2006). *The velvet rage: Overcoming the pain of growing up gay in a straight man's world.* Cambridge, MA: Da Capo Press.

Drake, A. (2017). *Carefrontation: Breaking free from childhood trauma.* New York, NY: Regan Arts.

Drum, D. J., Brownson, C., Burton Denmark, A., & Smith, S. E. (2009). New data on the nature of suicidal crises in college students: Shifting the paradigm. *Professional Psychology: Research and Practice, 40*, 213–222. http://dx.doi.org/10.1037/a0014465

Duba, J. D., Kindsvatter, A., & Lara, T. (2008). Treating infidelity: Considering narratives of attachment. *The Family Journal, 16*, 293–299. http://dx.doi.org/10.1177/1066480708323198

Dunn, M. (2014). *The unspeakable: And other subjects of discussion.* New York, NY: Farrar, Straus & Giroux.

Ebert, R. (2002, May 26). Great movie: *Rashomon.* [Review of the movie *Rashomon*]. Retrieved from http://www.rogerebert.com/reviews/great-movie-rashomon-1950

Ekman, P. (1992). *Telling lies: Clues to deceit in the marketplace, politics, and marriage* (2nd ed.). New York, NY: Norton.

Ekman, P. (2001). *Telling lies: Clues to deceit in the marketplace, politics, and marriage* (3rd ed.). New York, NY: Norton.

Ekman, P., & Friesen, W. V. (1969). Nonverbal leakage and clues to deception. *Psychiatry, 32*, 88–106. http://dx.doi.org/10.1080/00332747.1969.11023575

Eliot, T. S. (1920). Gerontion. In *Collected poems.* Boston, MA: Harcourt.

Erat, S., & Gneezy, U. (2012). White lies. *Management Science, 58*, 723–733. http://dx.doi.org/10.1287/mnsc.1110.1449

Eubanks-Carter, C., Burckell, L. A., & Goldfried, M. R. (2005). Enhancing therapeutic effectiveness with lesbian, gay, and bisexual clients. *Clinical Psychology: Science and Practice, 12*(1), 1–18. http://dx.doi.org/10.1093/clipsy.bpi001

Eubanks-Carter, C. F., Muran, J. C., & Safran, J. D. (2015). *Rupture Resolution Rating System (3RS): Manual.* Unpublished manuscript, Mount Sinai-Beth Israel Medical Center, New York, NY.

Evans, M., & Barker, M. (2010). How do you see me? Coming out in counselling. *British Journal of Guidance & Counselling, 38*, 375–391. http://dx.doi.org/10.1080/03069885.2010.503698

Exley, F. (1968). *A fan's notes*. New York, NY: Random House.

Farber, B. A. (1989). Psychological-mindedness: Can there be too much of a good thing? *Psychotherapy: Theory, Research, Practice, Training, 26*, 210–217. http://dx.doi.org/10.1037/h0085421

Farber, B. A. (2006). *Self-disclosure in psychotherapy*. New York, NY: Guilford Press.

Farber, B. A., Berano, K. C., & Capobianco, J. A. (2004). Clients' perceptions of the process and consequences of self-disclosure in psychotherapy. *Journal of Counseling Psychology, 51*, 340–346. http://dx.doi.org/10.1037/0022-0167.51.3.340

Farber, B. A., Berano, K., & Capobianco, J. (2006). A temporal model of patient disclosure in psychotherapy. *Psychotherapy Research, 16*, 463–469. http://dx.doi.org/10.1080/10503300600593250

Farber, B. A., Feldman, S., & Wright, A. J. (2014). Client disclosure and therapist response in psychotherapy with women with a history of childhood sexual abuse. *Psychotherapy Research, 24*, 316–326. http://dx.doi.org/10.1080/10503307.2013.817695

Farber, B. A., & Hall, D. (2002). Disclosure to therapists: What is and is not discussed in psychotherapy. *Journal of Clinical Psychology, 58*, 359–370. http://dx.doi.org/10.1002/jclp.1148

Farber, B. A., Khurgin-Bott, R., & Feldman, S. (2009). The benefits and risks of patient self-disclosure in the psychotherapy of women with a history of childhood sexual abuse. *Psychotherapy: Theory, Research, Practice, Training, 46*, 52–67. http://dx.doi.org/10.1037/a0015136

Farber, B. A., Lippert, R. A., & Nevas, D. B. (1995). The therapist as attachment figure. *Psychotherapy: Theory, Research, Practice, Training, 32*, 204–212. http://dx.doi.org/10.1037/0033-3204.32.2.204

Farber, B. A., & Sohn, A. E. (2007). Patterns of self-disclosure in psychotherapy and marriage. *Psychotherapy: Theory, Research, Practice, Training, 44*, 226–231. http://dx.doi.org/10.1037/0033-3204.44.2.226

Fedde, F. (2009). *Secret keeping and working alliance: The impact of concealment on the therapeutic process and the development of a solid client-therapist relationship* (Doctoral dissertation). Available from ProQuest Digital Dissertations. (AAT 3400158)

Feldman, R. (2009). *The liar in your life: The way to truthful relationships*. New York, NY: Twelve.

Feldman, R. S., Forrest, J. A., & Happ, B. R. (2002). Self-presentation and verbal deception: Do self-presenters lie more? *Basic and Applied Social Psychology, 24*, 163–170. http://dx.doi.org/10.1207/S15324834BASP2402_8

Ferrari, J. R., Groh, D. R., Rulka, G., Jason, L. A., & Davis, M. I. (2008). Coming to terms with reality: Predictors of self-deception within substance abuse recovery.

Addictive Disorders & Their Treatment, 7, 210–218. http://dx.doi.org/10.1097/ADT.0b013e31815c2ded

Findlay, R. (2012). Talking about sex: Narrative approaches to discussing sex life in therapy. *International Journal of Narrative Therapy & Community Work, 2*, 11–33.

Finkelstein, N. B. (2011). *Substance abuse treatment: Addressing the specific needs of women*. Collingdale, PA: Diane.

Fiona. (2013, April 13). Re: Lying to our clients [Blog comment]. Retrieved from http://www.afterpsychotherapy.com/lying-to-our-clients/

Fluckiger, C., Del Re, A. C., Wampold, B. E., & Horvath, A. O. (2019). Alliance in adult psychotherapy. In J. C. Norcross & M. J. Lambert (Eds.), *Psychotherapy relationships that work* (Vol. 1, pp. 37–69). New York, NY: Oxford University Press.

Foa, E. B., Hembree, E. A., & Rothbaum, B. O. (2007). *Prolonged exposure therapy for PTSD: Emotional processing of traumatic experiences (treatments that work)*. New York, NY: Oxford University Press.

Foa, E. B., Keane, T. M., Friedman, M. J., & Cohen, J. (Eds.). (2010). *Effective treatments for PTSD: Practice guidelines from the International Society for Traumatic Stress Studies* (2nd ed.). New York, NY: Guilford Press.

Ford, C. V. (1996). *Lies! Lies! Lies! The psychology of deceit*. Washington, DC: American Psychiatric Publishing.

Forrest, G. G. (2010). *Self-disclosure in psychotherapy and recovery*. New York, NY: Rowman & Littlefield.

Freimuth, M. (2005). *Hidden addictions: Assessment practices for psychotherapists, counselors, and health care providers*. Lanham, MD: Jason Aronson.

Freud, S. (1926). Inhibitions, symptoms and anxiety. In J. Strachey (Ed. & Trans.), *The standard edition of the complete psychological works of Sigmund Freud* (Vol. 20, pp. 75–176). London, England: Hogarth.

Freud, S. (1933). *New introductory lectures on psychoanalysis*. Oxford, England: Norton.

Freud, S. (1953). Fragment of an analysis of a case of hysteria. In J. Strachey (Ed. & Trans.), *The standard edition of the complete psychological works of Sigmund Freud* (Vol. 7, pp. 7–122). London, England: Hogarth Press. (Original work published 1905)

Freud, S. (1958). On beginning the treatment. In J. Strachey (Ed. & Trans.), *The standard edition of the complete psychological works of Sigmund Freud* (Vol. 12, pp. 121–144). London, England: Hogarth Press. (Original work published 1913)

Frey, J. (2003). *A million little pieces*. New York, NY: First Anchor Books.

Gabbard, G. O. (2014). *Psychodynamic psychiatry in clinical practice*. Washington, DC: American Psychiatric Publishing.

Gabbard, G. O., & Wilkinson, S. M. (2000). *Management of countertransference with borderline patients*. Northvale, NJ: Jason Aronson.

Gans, J. S., & Weber, R. L. (2000). The detection of shame in group psychotherapy: Uncovering the hidden emotion. *International Journal of Group Psychotherapy, 50*, 381–396. http://dx.doi.org/10.1080/00207284.2000.11491015

Ganzini, L., Denneson, L. M., Press, N., Bair, M. J., Helmer, D. A., Poat, J., & Dobscha, S. K. (2013). Trust is the basis for effective suicide risk screening and assessment in veterans. *Journal of General Internal Medicine, 28*, 1215–1221. http://dx.doi.org/10.1007/s11606-013-2412-6

Garrett, N., Lazzaro, S. C., Ariely, D., & Sharot, T. (2016). The brain adapts to dishonesty. *Nature Neuroscience, 19*, 1727–1732. http://dx.doi.org/10.1038/nn.4426

Gediman, J. S., & Lieberman, H. K. (1996). *The many faces of deceit: Omissions, lies, and disguise in psychotherapy*. Hillsdale, NJ: Jason Aronson.

Geller, J. D. (2014, April). *Courage and the effective practice of psychotherapy*. Paper presented at the meeting of the American Psychological Association, Division 39, New York, NY.

Gentilello, L. M., Samuels, P. N., Henningfield, J. E., & Santora, P. B. (2005). Alcohol screening and intervention in trauma centers: Confidentiality concerns and legal considerations. *The Journal of Trauma: Injury, Infection, and Critical Care, 59*, 1250–1255. http://dx.doi.org/10.1097/01.ta.0000188668.10758.40

George, J. F., & Robb, A. (2008). Deception and computer-mediated communication in daily life. *Communication Reports, 21*, 92–103. http://dx.doi.org/10.1080/08934210802298108

Gervais, R. (Producer & Director), Lin, D., Obst, L., & Obst, O. (Producers), & Robinson, M. (Director). (2009). *The invention of lying* [Motion picture]. United States: Warner Brothers.

Gilbert, D. (2006). *Stumbling on happiness*. New York, NY: Knopf.

Gochros, H. L. (1986). Overcoming client resistances to talking about sex. *Journal of Social Work & Human Sexuality, 4*, 7–15. http://dx.doi.org/10.1300/J291v04n01_05

Goffman, E. (1959). *The presentation of self in everyday life*. Garden City, NY: Doubleday.

Golaszewska, M. (2010). The problem of truth and falsehood in the anthroposphere. In P. Majkut & A. J. L. Carrillo Canán (Eds.), *Deception: Essays from the Outis Project on Deception, Society for Phenomenology and Media* (pp. 136–142). Bucharest, Romania: Zeta Books.

Goldstein, G. (2014, May). *The analyst's authenticity: "If you see something, say something."* Paper presented at the Westchester Center for the Study of Psychoanalysis and Psychotherapy, White Plains, NY.

Goldstein, G., & Suzuki, J. Y. (2015). The analyst's authenticity: "If you see something, say something." *Journal of Clinical Psychology, 71*, 451–456. http://dx.doi.org/10.1002/jclp.22181

Goligher, T. (Producer), & Haigh, A. (Director). (2015). *45 years* [Motion picture]. United Kingdom: BFI Film Fund.

Gordon. (2013, April 12). Re: Lying to our clients [Blog comment]. Retrieved from http://www.afterpsychotherapy.com/lying-to-our-clients/

Grant, B. F., Stinson, F. S., Dawson, D. A., Chou, S. P., Dufour, M. C., Compton, W., . . . Kaplan, K. (2004). Prevalence and co-occurrence of substance use disorders and independent mood and anxiety disorders: Results from the National Epidemiologic Survey on Alcohol and Related Conditions. *Archives of General Psychiatry*, *61*, 807–816. http://dx.doi.org/10.1001/archpsyc.61.8.807

Gray is the color of truth. (2017, June 11). *Quote Investigator*. Retrieved from https://quoteinvestigator.com/2017/06/11/gray-truth/

Green, J. D., Hatgis, C., Kearns, J. C., Nock, M. K., & Marx, B. P. (2017). The Direct and Indirect Self-Harm Inventory (DISH): A new measure for assessing high-risk and self-harm behaviors among military veterans. *Psychology of Men & Masculinity*, *18*, 208–214. http://dx.doi.org/10.1037/men0000116

Greenhut, R. (Producer), & Allen, W. (Director). (1983). *Zelig* [Motion picture]. United States: Jack Rollins & Charles H. Joffe Productions.

Guthrie, J., & Kunkel, A. (2013). Tell me sweet (and not-so-sweet) little lies: Deception in romantic relationships. *Communication Studies*, *64*, 141–157. http://dx.doi.org/10.1080/10510974.2012.755637

Hall, D. A., & Farber, B. A. (2001). Patterns of patient disclosure in psychotherapy. *Journal of the American Academy of Psychoanalysis*, *29*, 213–230. http://dx.doi.org/10.1521/jaap.29.2.213.17262

Hamilton, L., & Armstrong, E. A. (2009). Gendered sexuality in young adulthood: Double binds and flawed options. *Gender & Society*, *23*, 589–616. http://dx.doi.org/10.1177/0891243209345829

Hancock, J. T., Toma, C., & Ellison, N. (2007). The truth about lying in online dating profiles. *Proceedings of the SIGCHI Conference on Human Factors in Computing Systems*, 449–452. http://dx.doi.org/10.1145/1240624.1240697

Harris, S. K., Herr-Zaya, K., Weinstein, Z., Whelton, K., Perfas, F., Jr., Castro-Donlan, C., . . . Levy, S. (2012). Results of a statewide survey of adolescent substance use screening rates and practices in primary care. *Substance Abuse*, *33*, 321–326. http://dx.doi.org/10.1080/08897077.2011.645950

Hatcher, R. L., & Gillaspy, J. A. (2006). Development and validation of a revised short version of the Working Alliance Inventory. *Psychotherapy Research*, *16*, 12–25. http://dx.doi.org/10.1080/10503300500352500

Hawton, K., & Harriss, L. (2007). Deliberate self-harm in young people: Characteristics and subsequent mortality in a 20-year cohort of patients presenting to hospital. *The Journal of Clinical Psychiatry*, *68*, 1574–1583. http://dx.doi.org/10.4088/JCP.v68n1017

Heath, N. L., & Nixon, M. K. (2009). Assessment of nonsuicidal self-injury in youth. In M. K. Nixon & N. L. Heath (Eds.), *Self-injury in youth: The essential guide to assessment and intervention* (pp. 143–170). New York, NY: Routledge.

Henn, F., Sartorius, N., Helmchen, H., & Lauter, H. (Eds.). (2013). *Contemporary psychiatry*. New York, NY: Springer.

Henretty, J. R., & Levitt, H. M. (2010). The role of therapist self-disclosure in psychotherapy: A qualitative review. *Clinical Psychology Review*, *30*, 63–77. http://dx.doi.org/10.1016/j.cpr.2009.09.004

Herman, J. L. (1992). *Trauma and recovery: The aftermath of violence—from domestic abuse to political terror*. New York, NY: Basic Books.

Herman, J. L., & Harvey, M. R. (1997). Adult memories of childhood trauma: A naturalistic clinical study. *Journal of Traumatic Stress, 10*, 557–571. http://dx.doi.org/10.1002/jts.2490100404

Hill, C. E., Gelso, C. J., & Mohr, J. J. (2000). Client concealment and self-presentation in therapy: Comment on Kelly (2000). *Psychological Bulletin, 126*, 495–500. http://dx.doi.org/10.1037/0033-2909.126.4.495

Hill, C. E., & Knox, S. (2002). Self-disclosure. In J. Norcross (Ed.), *Psychotherapy relationships that work: Therapist contributions and responsiveness to patients* (pp. 255–265). New York, NY: Oxford University Press.

Hill, C. E., & Lambert, M. J. (2004). Methodological issues in studying psychotherapy processes and outcomes. In M. J. Lambert (Ed.), *Bergin and Garfield's handbook of psychotherapy and behavior change* (5th ed., pp. 84–135). New York, NY: Wiley.

Hill, C. E., Thompson, B. J., Cogar, M., & Denman, D. W. (1993). Beneath the surface of long-term therapy: Therapist and client reports of their own and each other's covert processes. *Journal of Counseling Psychology, 40*, 278–287. http://dx.doi.org/10.1037/0022-0167.40.3.278

Hill, C. E., Thompson, B. J., & Corbett, M. M. (1992). The impact of therapist ability to perceive displayed and hidden client reactions on immediate outcome in first sessions of brief therapy. *Psychotherapy Research, 2*, 143–155. http://dx.doi.org/10.1080/10503309212331332914

Hom, M. A., Stanley, I. H., Podlogar, M. C., & Joiner, T. E., Jr. (2017). "Are you having thoughts of suicide?" Examining experiences with disclosing and denying suicidal ideation. *Journal of Clinical Psychology, 73*, 1382–1392. http://dx.doi.org/10.1002/jclp.22440

Hook, A., & Andrews, B. (2005). The relationship of non-disclosure in therapy to shame and depression. *British Journal of Clinical Psychology, 44*, 425–438. http://dx.doi.org/10.1348/014466505X34165

Howard, J. C. (2017, April 29). Harper Lee's raw truth. *The New York Times*, pp. C1, C4.

Howard, V., & Holmshaw, J. (2010). Inpatient staff perceptions in providing care to individuals with co-occurring mental health problems and illicit substance use. *Journal of Psychiatric and Mental Health Nursing, 17*, 862–872. http://dx.doi.org/10.1111/j.1365-2850.2010.01620.x

Hyman, S. E., Malenka, R. C., & Nestler, E. J. (2006). Neural mechanisms of addiction: The role of reward-related learning and memory. *Annual Review of Neuroscience, 29*, 565–598. http://dx.doi.org/10.1146/annurev.neuro.29.051605.113009

Jackson, D., & Farber, B. A. (2018, June). *Therapist dishonesty*. Paper presented at the meeting of the Society for Psychotherapy Research, Amsterdam, Netherlands.

Jacobs, A. J. (2009). *The guinea pig diaries: My life as an experiment*. New York, NY: Simon & Schuster.

Jacobs, T. (2016, September). *Patients' secrets, analysts' secrets: Some reflections on their interaction.* Paper presented at Scientific Program Meeting, New York Psychoanalytic Society and Institute.

Jensen, L. A., Arnett, J. J., Feldman, S. S., & Cauffman, E. (2004). The right to do wrong: Lying to parents among adolescents and emerging adults. *Journal of Youth and Adolescence, 33,* 101–112. http://dx.doi.org/10.1023/B:JOYO.0000013422.48100.5a

Jessica. (2013, April 13). Re: Lying to our clients [Blog comment]. Retrieved from http://www.afterpsychotherapy.com/lying-to-our-clients/

Jingo, M. (Producer), & Kurosawa, A. (Director). (1950). *Rashomon* [Motion picture]. Japan: Daiei Motion Picture Company.

Jobes, D. A. (2006). *Managing suicidal risk: A collaborative approach.* New York, NY: Guilford Press.

Jobes, D. A., & Ballard, E. (2011). The therapist and the suicidal patient. In K. Michel & D. A. Jobes (Eds.), *Building a therapeutic alliance with the suicidal patient* (pp. 51–61). Washington, DC: American Psychological Association. http://dx.doi.org/10.1037/12303-003

John. (2013, April 12). Re: Lying to our clients [Blog comment]. Retrieved from http://www.afterpsychotherapy.com/lying-to-our-clients/

Johnson, G. (2013, July 29). Re: Lying to our clients [Blog comment]. Retrieved from http://www.afterpsychotherapy.com/lying-to-our-clients/

Jourard, S. M. (1971). *Self-disclosure: An experimental analysis of the transparent self.* Oxford, England: Wiley.

Kahn, J. H., Achter, J. A., & Shambaugh, E. J. (2001). Client distress disclosure, characteristics at intake, and outcome in brief counseling. *Journal of Counseling Psychology, 48,* 203–211. http://dx.doi.org/10.1037/0022-0167.48.2.203

Kahn, J. H., & Hessling, R. M. (2001). Measuring the tendency to conceal versus disclose psychological distress. *Journal of Social and Clinical Psychology, 20,* 41–65. http://dx.doi.org/10.1521/jscp.20.1.41.22254

Kalish, N. (2004, January). How honest are you? *Reader's Digest, 164,* 114–119.

Kashy, D. A., & DePaulo, B. M. (1996). Who lies? *Journal of Personality and Social Psychology, 70,* 1037–1051. http://dx.doi.org/10.1037/0022-3514.70.5.1037

Kelly, A. E. (1998). Clients' secret keeping in outpatient therapy. *Journal of Counseling Psychology, 45,* 50–57. http://dx.doi.org/10.1037/0022-0167.45.1.50

Kelly, A. E. (2000). Helping construct desirable identities: A self-presentational view of psychotherapy. *Psychological Bulletin, 126,* 475–494. http://dx.doi.org/10.1037/0033-2909.126.4.475

Kelly, A. E. (2002). *The psychology of secrets.* New York, NY: Plenum Press. http://dx.doi.org/10.1007/978-1-4615-0683-6

Kelly, A. E., & Yip, J. J. (2006). Is keeping a secret or being a secretive person linked to psychological symptoms? *Journal of Personality, 74,* 1349–1370. http://dx.doi.org/10.1111/j.1467-6494.2006.00413.x

Kelly, A. E., & Yuan, K. H. (2009). Clients' secret keeping and the working alliance in adult outpatient therapy. *Psychotherapy: Theory, Research, Practice, Training, 46*, 193–202. http://dx.doi.org/10.1037/a0016084

Kernberg, O. F. (1975). A systems approach to priority setting of interventions in groups. *International Journal of Group Psychotherapy, 25*, 251–275. http://dx.doi.org/10.1080/00207284.1975.11491899

Kettlewell, C. (1999). *Skin game: A memoir*. New York, NY: St Martin's Griffin.

Khantzian, E. J. (1985). The self-medication hypothesis of addictive disorders: Focus on heroin and cocaine dependence. *The American Journal of Psychiatry, 142*, 1259–1264. http://dx.doi.org/10.1176/ajp.142.11.1259

Khantzian, E. J. (1997). The self-medication hypothesis of substance use disorders: A reconsideration and recent applications. *Harvard Review of Psychiatry, 4*, 231–244. http://dx.doi.org/10.3109/10673229709030550

Klonsky, E. D. (2011). Non-suicidal self-injury in United States adults: Prevalence, sociodemographics, topography and functions. *Psychological Medicine, 41*, 1981–1986. http://dx.doi.org/10.1017/S0033291710002497

Klonsky, E. D., & Lewis, S. P. (2014). Assessment of nonsuicidal self-injury. In M. K. Nock (Ed.), *The Oxford handbook of suicide and self-injury* (pp. 337–355). New York, NY: Oxford University Press.

Knapp, M. L. (1984). The study of nonverbal behavior vis-à-vis human communication theory. In A. Wolfgang (Ed.), *Nonverbal behavior: Perspectives, applications, intercultural insights* (pp. 15–40). Lewiston, NY: Hogrefe.

Knight, R., Shoveller, J. A., Oliffe, J. L., Gilbert, M., Frank, B., & Ogilvie, G. (2012). Masculinities, 'guy talk' and 'manning up': A discourse analysis of how young men talk about sexual health. *Sociology of Health & Illness, 34*, 1246–1261. http://dx.doi.org/10.1111/j.1467-9566.2012.01471.x

Knox, D., Schacht, C., Holt, J., & Turner, J. (1993). Sexual lies among university students. *College Student Journal, 26*, 269–272.

Knox, S., & Hill, C. E. (2003). Therapist self-disclosure: Research-based suggestions for practitioners. *Journal of Clinical Psychology: In Session, 59*, 529–539. http://dx.doi.org/10.1002/jclp.10157

Kohut, H. (1966). Forms and transformations of narcissism. *Journal of the American Psychoanalytic Association, 14*, 243–272. http://dx.doi.org/10.1177/000306516601400201

Kolmes, K., Stock, W., & Moser, C. (2006). Investigating bias in psychotherapy with BDSM clients. *Journal of Homosexuality, 50*, 301–324. http://dx.doi.org/10.1300/J082v50n02_15

Kottler, J., & Carlson, J. (2011). *Duped: Lies and deception in psychotherapy*. New York, NY: Routledge.

Krebs, P. M., Norcross, J. C., Nicholson, J. M., & Prochaska, J. O. (in press). Stages of change and psychotherapy outcome. *Journal of Clinical Psychology: In Session, 74*(11).

Kronner, H. W. (2013). Use of self-disclosure for the gay male therapist: The impact on gay males in therapy. *Journal of Social Service Research, 39*, 78–94. http://dx.doi.org/10.1080/01488376.2012.686732

Kutappa, M. (2013, November 28). Re: Do psychologists lie to their patients? [Online forum comment]. Retrieved from https://www.quora.com/Do-psychologists-lie-to-their-patients

Ladany, N., Hill, C. E., Corbett, M. M., & Nutt, E. A. (1996). Nature, extent, and importance of what psychotherapy trainees do not disclose to their supervisors. *Journal of Counseling Psychology, 43*, 10–24. http://dx.doi.org/10.1037/0022-0167.43.1.10

Lane, J. D., & Wegner, D. M. (1995). The cognitive consequences of secrecy. *Journal of Personality and Social Psychology*, 69, 237–253. http://dx.doi.org/10.1037/0022-3514.69.2.237

Langer, R. (2010). When the patient does not tell the truth. *Psychoanalytic Social Work, 17*, 1–16. http://dx.doi.org/10.1080/15228871003676549

Larson, D. G., & Chastain, R. L. (1990). Self-concealment: Conceptualization, measurement, and health implications. *Journal of Social and Clinical Psychology*, 9, 439–455. http://dx.doi.org/10.1521/jscp.1990.9.4.439

Larson, D. G., Chastain, R. L., Hoyt, W. T., & Ayzenberg, R. (2015). Self-concealment: Integrative review and working model. *Journal of Social and Clinical Psychology, 34*, 705–729. http://dx.doi.org/10.1521/jscp.2015.34.8.705

Leaky, R. E., & Lewin, R. (1978). *People of the lake: Mankind and its beginnings*. New York, NY: Anchor Press.

Lemma, A. (2005). The many faces of lying. *The International Journal of Psychoanalysis*, 86, 737–753. http://dx.doi.org/10.1516/KN9J-2AU5-TB95-FRLH

Lenzenweger, M. F., Lane, M. C., Loranger, A. W., & Kessler, R. C. (2007). DSM–IV personality disorders in the National Comorbidity Survey Replication. *Biological Psychiatry, 15*, 62, 553–564.

Levine, T. R., Kim, R. K., & Hamel, L. M. (2010). People lie for a reason: Three experiments documenting the principle of veracity. *Communication Research Reports, 27*, 271–285. http://dx.doi.org/10.1080/08824096.2010.496334

Levine, T. R., McCornack, S. A., & Avery, P. B. (1992). Sex differences in emotional reactions to discovered deception. *Communication Quarterly*, 40, 289–296. http://dx.doi.org/10.1080/01463379209369843

Levine, T. R., Serota, K. B., Carey, F., & Messer, D. (2013). Teenagers lie a lot: A further investigation into the prevalence of lying. *Communication Research Reports, 30*, 211–220. http://dx.doi.org/10.1080/08824096.2013.806254

Levine, T. R., Serota, K. B., Shulman, H., Clare, D. D., Park, H. S., Shaw, A. S., . . . Lee, J. H. (2011). Sender demeanor: Individual differences in sender believability have a powerful impact on deception detection judgments. *Human Communication Research, 37*, 377–403. http://dx.doi.org/10.1111/j.1468-2958.2011.01407.x

Levinson, E. (1991). *The purloined self: Interpersonal perspective in psychoanalysis.* New York, NY: Contemporary.

Lewis, H. B. (1971). *Shame and guilt in neurosis.* New York, NY: International Universities Press.

Lewis, M. (1993). The development of deception. In M. Lewis & C. Saarni (Eds.), *Lying and deception in everyday life* (pp. 90–105). New York, NY: Guilford Press.

Linehan, M. (1993). *Cognitive-behavioral treatment of borderline personality disorder.* New York, NY: Guilford Press.

Linehan, M. M., Comtois, K. A., Brown, M. Z., Heard, H. L., & Wagner, A. (2006). Suicide Attempt Self-Injury Interview (SASII): Development, reliability, and validity of a scale to assess suicide attempts and intentional self-injury. *Psychological Assessment, 18,* 303–312. http://dx.doi.org/10.1037/1040-3590.18.3.303

Linquist, L., & Negy, C. (2005). Maximizing the experiences of an extrarelational affair: An unconventional approach to a common social convention. *Journal of Clinical Psychology, 61,* 1421–1428. http://dx.doi.org/10.1002/jclp.20191

Livingston, R., & Farber, B. A. (1996). Beginning therapists' responses to client shame. *Psychotherapy: Theory, Research, Practice, Training, 33,* 601–610. http://dx.doi.org/10.1037/0033-3204.33.4.601

Lizzie. (2013, April 12). Re: Lying to our clients [Blog comment]. Retrieved from http://www.afterpsychotherapy.com/lying-to-our-clients/

Loftus, E. F., & Palmer, J. C. (1974). Reconstruction of automobile destruction: An example of the interaction between language and memory. *Journal of Verbal Learning & Verbal Behavior, 13,* 585–589. http://dx.doi.org/10.1016/S0022-5371(74)80011-3

Love, M., Blanchard, M., & Farber, B. A. (2016, November). *Self-concealment, honesty, and the psychotherapeutic relationship.* Paper presented at the meeting of the North America Society for Psychotherapy Research, Berkeley, CA.

Lovejoy, M., Rosenblum, A., Magura, S., Foote, J., Handelsman, L., & Stimmel, B. (1995). Patients' perspective on the process of change in substance abuse treatment. *Journal of Substance Abuse Treatment, 12,* 269–282. http://dx.doi.org/10.1016/0740-5472(95)00027-3

Lupoli, M. J., Jampol, L., & Oveis, C. (2017). Lying because we care: Compassion increases prosocial lying. *Journal of Experimental Psychology: General, 146,* 1026–1042. http://dx.doi.org/10.1037/xge0000315

Macdonald, J., & Morley, I. (2001). Shame and non-disclosure: A study of the emotional isolation of people referred for psychotherapy. *British Journal of Medical Psychology, 74,* 1–21.

Mallinckrodt, B., Porter, M. J., & Kivlighan, D. M., Jr. (2005). Client attachment to therapist, depth of in-session exploration, and object relations in brief psychotherapy. *Psychotherapy: Theory, Research, Practice, Training, 42,* 85–100. http://dx.doi.org/10.1037/0033-3204.42.1.85

Maltsberger, J. T. (1986). *Suicide risk: The formulation of clinical judgment.* New York, NY: New York University Press.

Marcos, L. R. (1972). Lying: A particular defense met in psychoanalytic therapy. *The American Journal of Psychoanalysis, 32,* 195–202. http://dx.doi.org/10.1007/BF01872516

Marias, J. (2013). *The infatuations.* New York, NY: Alfred A. Knopf.

Markowitz, D. M., & Hancock, J. T. (2014). Linguistic traces of a scientific fraud: The case of Diederik Stapel. *PLoS One,* 9(8), e105937. http://dx.doi.org/10.1371/journal.pone.0105937

Martel, Y. (2001). *Life of Pi.* Toronto, Ontario, Canada: Knopf.

Martin, L. E. (2006). *Lying in psychotherapy: Results of an exploratory study* (Doctoral dissertation). Available from ProQuest dissertations and Theses database. (UMI No. 3253137)

McCornack, S. A., & Levine, T. R. (1990). When lies are uncovered: Emotional and relational outcomes of discovered deception. *Communication Monographs, 57,* 119–138. http://dx.doi.org/10.1080/03637759009376190

McCornack, S. A., Morrison, K., Paik, J. E., Wisner, A. M., & Zhu, X. (2014). Information manipulation theory 2: A propositional theory of deceptive discourse production. *Journal of Language and Social Psychology, 33,* 348–377. http://dx.doi.org/10.1177/0261927X14534656

McDonnell, M. (Producer), & Singer, B. (Producer & Director). (1995). *The usual suspects* [Motion picture]. United States: PolyGram Filmed Entertainment.

McWilliams, N. (1994). *Psychoanalytic diagnosis: Understanding personality structure in the clinical process.* New York, NY: Guilford Press.

McWilliams, N. (2004). *Psychoanalytic psychotherapy: A practitioner's guide.* New York, NY: Guilford Press.

Memon, A., & Young, M. (1997). Desperately seeking evidence: The recovered memory debate. *Legal and Criminological Psychology, 2,* 131–154. http://dx.doi.org/10.1111/j.2044-8333.1997.tb00339.x

Messer, S. B. (2002). A psychodynamic perspective on resistance in psychotherapy: Vive la résistance. *Journal of Clinical Psychology, 58,* 157–163. http://dx.doi.org/10.1002/jclp.1139

Meyer, I. H. (2003). Prejudice, social stress, and mental health in lesbian, gay, and bisexual populations: Conceptual issues and research evidence. *Psychological Bulletin, 129,* 674–697. http://dx.doi.org/10.1037/0033-2909.129.5.674

Meyer, P. (2010). *Liespotting: Proven techniques to detect deception.* New York, NY: St. Martin's Press.

Michel, K., & Jobes, D. A. (Eds.). (2011). *Building a therapeutic alliance with the suicidal patient.* Washington, DC: American Psychological Association. http://dx.doi.org/10.1037/12303-000

Mikulincer, M., & Nachshon, O. (1991). Attachment styles and patterns of self-disclosure. *Journal of Personality and Social Psychology, 61*, 321–331. http://dx.doi.org/10.1037/0022-3514.61.2.321

Miller, G. R., Mongeau, P. A., & Sleight, C. (1986). Fudging with friends and lying to lovers: Deceptive communication in personal relationships. *Journal of Social and Personal Relationships, 3*, 495–512. http://dx.doi.org/10.1177/0265407586034006

Miller, N. S., & Flaherty, J. A. (2000). Effectiveness of coerced addiction treatment (alternative consequences): A review of the clinical research. *Journal of Substance Abuse Treatment, 18*, 9–16. http://dx.doi.org/10.1016/S0740-5472(99)00073-2

Miller, W. R., & Rollnick, S. (2012). *Motivational interviewing: Helping people change* (3rd ed.). New York, NY: Guilford Press.

Mitchell, S. A., & Black, M. J. (1995). *Freud and beyond: A history of modern psychoanalytic thought.* New York, NY: Basic Books.

Miville, M. (2016, October 31). *The last word in Latina/o mental health: TC takes the lead in preparing bilingual counselors to serve the nation's fastest growing population.* Retrieved from http://www.tc.columbia.edu/articles/2016/november/the-last-word-in-latinao-mental-health/

Mohr, D. C. (1995). Negative outcome in psychotherapy: A critical review. *Clinical Psychology: Science and Practice, 2*, 1–27. http://dx.doi.org/10.1111/j.1468-2850.1995.tb00022.x

Molly. (2014, November 3). Re: Lying to our clients [Blog comment]. Retrieved from http://www.afterpsychotherapy.com/lying-to-our-clients/

Montemurro, B., Bartasavich, J., & Wintermute, L. (2015). Let's (not) talk about sex: The gender of sexual discourse. *Sexuality & Culture, 19*, 139–156. http://dx.doi.org/10.1007/s12119-014-9250-5

Morrison, L. L., & Downey, D. L. (2000). Racial differences in self-disclosure of suicidal ideation and reasons for living: Implications for training. *Cultural Diversity and Ethnic Minority Psychology*, 6, 374–386. http://dx.doi.org/10.1037/1099-9809.6.4.374

Muise, A. (2011). Women's sex blogs: Challenging dominant discourses of heterosexual desire. *Feminism & Psychology, 21*, 411–419. http://dx.doi.org/10.1177/0959353511411691

Neuendorf, K. A. (2002). *The content analysis guidebook.* Thousand Oaks, CA: Sage.

Newman, C. F. (1997). Establishing and maintaining a therapeutic alliance with substance abuse patients: A cognitive therapy approach. *NIDA Research Monograph, 165*, 181–206.

Newman, C. F., & Strauss, J. L. (2003). When clients are untruthful: Implications for the therapeutic alliance, case conceptualization, and intervention. *Journal of Cognitive Psychotherapy, 17*, 241–252. http://dx.doi.org/10.1891/jcop.17.3.241.52534

Nock, M. K., Holmberg, E. B., Photos, V. I., & Michel, B. D. (2007). Self-Injurious Thoughts and Behaviors Interview: Development, reliability, and validity in an adolescent sample. *Psychological Assessment, 19*, 309–317. http://dx.doi.org/10.1037/1040-3590.19.3.309

Norton, R., Feldman, C., & Tafoya, D. (1974). Risk parameters across types of secrets. *Journal of Counseling Psychology, 21*, 450–454. http://dx.doi.org/10.1037/h0037100

Palmieri, J. J., & Stern, T. A. (2009). Lies in the doctor–patient relationship. *Primary Care Companion to the Journal of Clinical Psychiatry, 11*, 163–168. http://dx.doi.org/10.4088/PCC.09r00780

Park, H. S., Levine, T. R., McCornack, S. A., Morrison, K., & Ferrara, M. (2002). How people really detect lies. *Communication Monographs, 69*, 144–157. http://dx.doi.org/10.1080/714041710

Parks, W. F. (Producer), & Spielberg, S. (Producer & Director). (2002). *Catch me if you can* [Motion picture]. United States: DreamWorks.

Pattee, D., & Farber, B. A. (2008). Patients' experiences of self-disclosure in psychotherapy: The effects of gender and gender role identification. *Psychotherapy Research, 18*, 306–315. http://dx.doi.org/10.1080/10503300701874534

Patterson, C. L., Anderson, T., & Wei, C. (2014). Clients' pretreatment role expectations, the therapeutic alliance, and clinical outcomes in outpatient therapy. *Journal of Clinical Psychology, 70*, 673–680. http://dx.doi.org/10.1002/jclp.22054

Patterson, J., & Kim, P. (1991). *The day America told the truth.* New York, NY: Prentice-Hall.

Paul, G. L. (1967). Strategy of outcome research in psychotherapy. *Journal of Consulting Psychology, 31*, 109–118. http://dx.doi.org/10.1037/h0024436

Paulhus, D. L., & Williams, K. M. (2002). The dark triad of personality: Narcissism, Machiavellianism, and psychopathy. *Journal of Research in Personality, 36*, 556–563. http://dx.doi.org/10.1016/S0092-6566(02)00505-6

Peckover, S., & Chidlaw, R. G. (2007). Too frightened to care? Accounts by district nurses working with clients who misuse substances. *Health & Social Care in the Community, 15*, 238–245. http://dx.doi.org/10.1111/j.1365-2524.2006.00683.x

Pennebaker, J. W. (1985). Traumatic experience and psychosomatic disease: Exploring the roles of behavioral inhibition, obsession, and confiding. *Canadian Psychology/Psychologie canadienne, 26*, 82–95. http://dx.doi.org/10.1037/h0080025

Pennebaker, J. W., Kiecolt-Glaser, J. K., & Glaser, R. (1988). Confronting traumatic experience and immunocompetence: A reply to Neale, Cox, Valdimarsdottir, and Stone. *Journal of Consulting and Clinical Psychology, 56*, 638–639. http://dx.doi.org/10.1037/0022-006X.56.4.638

Pope, K. S., & Tabachnick, B. G. (1994). Therapists as patients: A national survey of psychologists' experiences, problems, and beliefs. *Professional Psychology: Research and Practice, 25*, 247–258. http://dx.doi.org/10.1037/0735-7028.25.3.247

Porter, S., & ten Brinke, L. (2010). The truth about lies: What works in detecting high-stakes deception? *Legal and Criminological Psychology, 15*, 57–75. http://dx.doi.org/10.1348/135532509X433151

Pridham, S. (2013, April 12). Re: Lying to our clients [Blog comment]. Retrieved from http://www.afterpsychotherapy.com/lying-to-our-clients/

Prochaska, J. O., DiClemente, C. C., & Norcross, J. D. (1992). In search of how people change. Applications to addictive behaviors. *American Psychologist, 47*, 1102–1114. http://dx.doi.org/10.1037/0003-066X.47.9.1102

Radcliffe, P., & Stevens, A. (2008). Are drug treatment services only for 'thieving junkie scumbags'? Drug users and the management of stigmatised identities. *Social Science & Medicine, 67*, 1065–1073. http://dx.doi.org/10.1016/j.socscimed.2008.06.004

Regan, A. M., & Hill, C. E. (1992). Investigation of what clients and counselors do not say in brief therapy. *Journal of Counseling Psychology, 39*, 168–174. http://dx.doi.org/10.1037/0022-0167.39.2.168

Reissing, E. D., & Giulio, G. D. (2010). Practicing clinical psychologists' provision of sexual health care services. *Professional Psychology: Research and Practice, 41*, 57–63. http://dx.doi.org/10.1037/a0017023

Rennie, D. (1994). Clients' deference in psychotherapy. *Journal of Counseling Psychology, 41*, 427–437. http://dx.doi.org/10.1037/0022-0167.41.4.427

Resnick, P. J. (2002). Recognizing that the suicidal patient views you as an adversary. *Current Psychiatry, 1*, 8.

Reynolds, L., Smith, M. E., Birnholtz, J. P., & Hancock, J. T. (2013). Butler lies from both sides: Actions and perceptions of unavailability management in texting. *Proceedings of the 2013 Conference on Computer Supported Cooperative Work, 16*, 769–778. http://dx.doi.org/10.1145/2441776.2441862

Rhodes, R., Hill, C. E., Thompson, B. J., & Elliott, R. (1994). Client retrospective recall of resolved and unresolved misunderstanding events. *Journal of Counseling Psychology, 41*, 473–483. http://dx.doi.org/10.1037/0022-0167.41.4.473

Rich, A. (1979). *On lies, secrets, and silence: Selected prose, 1966–1978*. New York, NY: Norton.

Rieff, P. (1959). *Freud: The mind of the moralist*. New York, NY: Viking Press.

Ritov, I., & Baron, J. (1990). Reluctance to vaccinate: Omission bias and ambiguity. *Journal of Behavioral Decision Making, 3*, 263–277. http://dx.doi.org/10.1002/bdm.3960030404

Rogers, C. R. (1957). The necessary and sufficient conditions of therapeutic personality change. *Journal of Consulting Psychology, 21*, 95–103. http://dx.doi.org/10.1037/h0045357

Rogers, C. R. (1959). A theory of therapy, personality and interpersonal relationships, as developed in the client-centered framework. In S. Koch (Ed.), *Psychology: A study of science* (pp. 184–256). New York, NY: McGraw-Hill.

Rogers, C. R., Gendlin, E. T., Kiesler, D., & Truax, C. (Eds.). (1967). *The therapeutic relationship and its impact: A study of psychotherapy with schizophrenics*. Madison: University of Wisconsin Press.

Rosemary. (2016, November 5). Re: Why people lie to their therapist [Blog comment]. Retrieved from https://www.psychologytoday.com/us/blog/in-therapy/201610/why-people-lie-their-therapists

Roth, P. (2001). *The human stain*. United States: New York, NY: Vintage Books.

Rudd, M. D., Joiner, T., Brown, G. K., Cukrowicz, K., Jobes, D. A., Silverman, M., & Cordero, L. (2009). Informed consent with suicidal patients: Rethinking risks in (and out of) treatment. *Psychotherapy: Theory, Research, Practice, Training, 46*, 459–468. http://dx.doi.org/10.1037/a0017902

Saarni, C. (1982). Social and affective functions of nonverbal behavior: Developmental concerns. In R. S. Feldman (Ed.), *Development of nonverbal behavior in children* (pp. 123–147). New York, NY: Springer-Verlag. http://dx.doi.org/10.1007/978-1-4757-1761-7_5

Safran, J. D., & Muran, J. C. (2000). *Negotiating the therapeutic alliance: A relational treatment guide*. New York, NY: Guilford Press.

Safran, J. D., Muran, J. C., & Eubanks-Carter, C. (2011). Repairing alliance ruptures. *Psychotherapy, 48*, 80–87. http://dx.doi.org/10.1037/a0022140

Sakamoto, K., & Gupta, S. (2014). Lie acceptability. In T. R. Levine (Ed.), *Encyclopedia of deception* (pp. 596–598). Thousand Oaks, CA: Sage. http://dx.doi.org/10.4135/9781483306902.n224

Saltz, G. (2006). *Anatomy of a secret life: The psychology of living a lie*. New York, NY: Morgan Road Books.

Sarah. (2013, April 15). Re: Lying to our clients [Blog comment]. Retrieved from http://www.afterpsychotherapy.com/lying-to-our-clients/

Saypol, E., & Farber, B. A. (2010). Attachment style and patient disclosure in psychotherapy. *Psychotherapy Research, 20*, 462–471. http://dx.doi.org/10.1080/10503301003796821

Schalet, A. T. (2011). *Not under my roof: Parents, teens, and the culture of sex*. Chicago, IL: University of Chicago Press. http://dx.doi.org/10.7208/chicago/9780226736204.001.0001

Schiller, D., Monfils, M. H., Raio, C. M., Johnson, D. C., LeDoux, J. E., & Phelps, E. A. (2010). Preventing the return of fear in humans using reconsolidation update mechanisms. *Nature, 463*, 49–53. http://dx.doi.org/10.1038/nature08637

Schonbar, R. A. (1967). The fee as a focus for transference and countertransference. *American Journal of Psychotherapy, 21*, 275–285. http://dx.doi.org/10.1176/appi.psychotherapy.1967.21.2.275

Schottenfeld, R. S. (1994). Assessment of the patient. In M. Galanter & H. D. Kleber (Eds.), *Textbook of substance abuse treatment* (pp. 25–33). Washington, DC: American Psychiatric Press.

Seery, M. D., Silver, R. C., Holman, E. A., Ence, W. A., & Chu, T. Q. (2008). Expressing thoughts and feelings following a collective trauma: Immediate responses to 9/11 predict negative outcomes in a national sample. *Journal of Consulting and Clinical Psychology, 76*, 657–667. http://dx.doi.org/10.1037/0022-006X.76.4.657

Serota, K. B., Levine, T. R., & Boster, F. J. (2010). The prevalence of lying in America: Three studies of self-reported lies. *Human Communication Research, 36*, 2–25. http://dx.doi.org/10.1111/j.1468-2958.2009.01366.x

Serota, K. B., Levine, T. R., & Burns, A. (2012, November). *A few prolific liars: Variation in the prevalence of lying*. Paper presented at the meeting of the National Communication Association, Orlando, FL.

Shea, S. C. (1999). *The practical art of suicide assessment: A guide for mental health professionals and substance abuse counselors*. New York, NY: Wiley.

Sheila, A. (2013, April 12). Re: Lying to our clients [Blog comment]. Retrieved from http://www.afterpsychotherapy.com/lying-to-our-clients/

Shlien, J. M. (1984). Secrets and the psychology of secrecy. In R. F. Levant & J. M. Shlien (Eds.), *Client centered therapy and the person centered approach: New directions in theory, research and practice* (pp. 390–399). New York, NY: Praeger.

Showalter, E. (2017, May 28). Claims to fame: A new biography of Hemingway focuses on the man, not the legend. *The New York Times Book Review*, p. 16.

Simha-Alpern, A. (2007). "I finally have words!" Integrating a psychodynamic psychotherapeutic approach with principles of emotional intelligence training in treating trauma survivors. *Journal of Psychotherapy Integration, 17*, 293–313. http://dx.doi.org/10.1037/1053-0479.17.4.293

Slepian, M. L., Masicampo, E. J., & Galinsky, A. D. (2016). The hidden effects of recalling secrets: Assimilation, contrast, and the burdens of secrecy. *Journal of Experimental Psychology: General, 145*, e27–e48. http://dx.doi.org/10.1037/xge0000194

Slepian, M. L., Masicampo, E. J., Toosi, N. R., & Ambady, N. (2012). The physical burdens of secrecy. *Journal of Experimental Psychology: General, 141*, 619–624. http://dx.doi.org/10.1037/a0027598

Smith, M. K., Trivers, R., & von Hippel, W. (2017). Self-deception facilitates interpersonal persuasion. *Journal of Economic Psychology, 63*, 93–101. http://dx.doi.org/10.1016/j.joep.2017.02.012

Snyder, D. K., & Doss, B. D. (2005). Treating infidelity: Clinical and ethical directions. *Journal of Clinical Psychology, 61*, 1453–1465. http://dx.doi.org/10.1002/jclp.20194

Sonne, J. L., & Jochai, D. (2014). The "vicissitudes of love" between therapist and patient: A review of the research on romantic and sexual feelings, thoughts, and behaviors in psychotherapy. *Journal of Clinical Psychology, 70*, 182–195. http://dx.doi.org/10.1002/jclp.22069

Sorsoli, L., Kia-Keating, M., & Grossman, F. K. (2008). "I keep that hush-hush": Male survivors of sexual abuse and the challenges of disclosure. *Journal of Counseling Psychology, 55*, 333–345. http://dx.doi.org/10.1037/0022-0167.55.3.333

Spence, D. P. (1982). *Narrative truth and historical truth: Meaning and interpretation in psychoanalysis*. New York, NY: Norton.

Spranca, M., Minsk, E., & Baron, J. (1991). Omission and commission in judgment and choice. *Journal of Experimental Social Psychology, 27*, 76–105. http://dx.doi.org/10.1016/0022-1031(91)90011-T

Staebler, K., Helbing, E., Rosenbach, C., & Renneberg, B. (2011). Rejection sensitivity and borderline personality disorder. *Clinical Psychology & Psychotherapy, 18*, 275–283. http://dx.doi.org/10.1002/cpp.705

Stiles, W. B. (1987). "I have to talk to somebody": A fever model of disclosure. In V. J. Derlega & J. H. Berg (Eds.), *Self-disclosure: Theory, research, and therapy* (pp. 257–282). New York, NY: Plenum Press. http://dx.doi.org/10.1007/978-1-4899-3523-6_12

Stiles, W. B. (1995). Disclosure as a speech act: Is it psychotherapeutic to disclose? In J. W. Pennebaker (Ed.), *Emotion, disclosure, and health* (pp. 71–91). Washington, DC: American Psychological Association. http://dx.doi.org/10.1037/10182-004

Stouthamer-Loeber, M. (1986). Lying as a problem behavior in children: A review. *Clinical Psychology Review, 6*, 267–289. http://dx.doi.org/10.1016/0272-7358(86)90002-4

Substance Abuse and Mental Health Services Administration. (2011). *Results from the 2010 National Survey on Drug Use and Health: Summary of findings*. Retrieved from https://www.samhsa.gov/data/sites/default/files/NSDUHNationalFindingsResults2010-web/2k10ResultsRev/NSDUHresultsRev2010.pdf

Substance Abuse and Mental Health Services Administration. (2014). *Results from the 2013 National Survey on Drug Use and Health: Mental health findings*. Retrieved from: http://www.samhsa.gov/data/sites/default/files/NSDUHmhfr2013/NSDUHmhfr2013.pdf

Sue, D. W., & Sue, D. (1999). *Counseling the culturally different: Theory and practice* (3rd ed.). New York, NY: Wiley.

Suzuki, J. Y., & Farber, B. A. (2016). Towards greater specificity of the concept of positive regard. *Person-Centered and Experiential Psychotherapies, 15*, 263–284. http://dx.doi.org/10.1080/14779757.2016.1204941

Swannell, S. V., Martin, G. E., Page, A., Hasking, P., & St John, N. J. (2014). Prevalence of nonsuicidal self-injury in nonclinical samples: Systematic review, meta-analysis and meta-regression. *Suicide and Life-Threatening Behavior, 44*, 273–303. http://dx.doi.org/10.1111/sltb.12070

Talwar, V., & Crossman, A. (2011). From little white lies to filthy liars: The evolution of honesty and deception in young children. In J. Benson (Ed.), *Advances in child development and behavior* (Vol. 40, pp. 139–179). Burlington, VT: Academic Press. http://dx.doi.org/10.1016/B978-0-12-386491-8.00004-9

Talwar, V., & Lee, K. (2011). A punitive environment fosters children's dishonesty: A natural experiment. *Child Development, 82*, 1751–1758. http://dx.doi.org/10.1111/j.1467-8624.2011.01663.x

Talwar, V., Murphy, S. M., & Lee, K. (2007). White lie-telling in children for politeness purposes. *International Journal of Behavioral Development, 31*, 1–11. http://dx.doi.org/10.1177/0165025406073530

Tangney, J. P., Miller, R. S., Flicker, L., & Barlow, D. H. (1996). Are shame, guilt, and embarrassment distinct emotions? *Journal of Personality and Social Psychology, 70*, 1256–1269. http://dx.doi.org/10.1037/0022-3514.70.6.1256

Tavernise, S. (2016, December 7). As fake news spreads lies, more readers shrug at the truth. *The New York Times*, p. 1A.

Tenbrunsel, A. E., & Messick, D. M. (2004). Ethical fading: The role of self-deception in unethical behavior. *Social Justice Research, 17*, 223–236. http://dx.doi.org/10.1023/B:SORE.0000027411.35832.53

Thomas, P. M. (2005). Dissociation and internal models of protection: Psychotherapy with childhood abuse survivors. *Psychotherapy: Theory, Research, Practice, Training, 42*, 20–36. http://dx.doi.org/10.1037/0033-3204.42.1.20

Thompson, B., & Hill, C. E. (1991). Therapist perceptions of client reactions. *Journal of Counseling & Development, 69*, 261–265. http://dx.doi.org/10.1002/j.1556-6676.1991.tb01500.x

Thompson, M. G. (2001). *The ethic of honesty: The fundamental rule of psychoanalysis.* Amsterdam, Netherlands: Rodopi.

Tolman, D. L. (2002). Female adolescent sexuality: An argument for a developmental perspective on the new view of women's sexual problems. *Women & Therapy, 24*, 195–209. http://dx.doi.org/10.1300/J015v24n01_21

Touchstone Pictures (Producer), & Oz, F. (Director). (1991). *What about Bob?* [Motion picture]. United States: Bueno Vista Pictures.

Treeby, M., & Bruno, R. (2012). Shame and guilt-proneness: Divergent implications for problematic alcohol use and drinking to cope with anxiety and depression symptomatology. *Personality and Individual Differences, 53*, 613–617. http://dx.doi.org/10.1016/j.paid.2012.05.011

Trivers, R. (2011). *The folly of fools: The logic of deceit and self-deception in human life.* New York, NY: Basic Books.

Twain, M. (1992). *Collected tales, sketches, speeches and essays 1852–1890.* New York, NY: Library of America.

Twain, M. (2009). *On the decay of the art of lying.* Portland, OR: The Floating Press. (Original work published 1882)

Ullman, S. E. (1996). Correlates and consequences of adult sexual assault disclosure. *Journal of Interpersonal Violence, 11*, 554–571. http://dx.doi.org/10.1177/088626096011004007

Ullman, S. E., Filipas, H. H., Townsend, S. M., & Starzynski, L. L. (2007). Psychosocial correlates of PTSD symptom severity in sexual assault survivors. *Journal of Traumatic Stress, 20*, 821–831. http://dx.doi.org/10.1002/jts.20290

Ullman, S. E., Townsend, S. M., Filipas, H. H., & Starzynski, L. L. (2007). Structural models of the relations of assault severity, social support, avoidance coping, self-blame, and PTSD among sexual assault survivors. *Psychology of Women Quarterly, 31*(1), 23–37. http://dx.doi.org/10.1111/j.1471-6402.2007.00328.x

van Boekel, L. C., Brouwers, E. P., van Weeghel, J., & Garretsen, H. F. (2013). Stigma among health professionals towards patients with substance use disorders and its consequences for healthcare delivery: Systematic review. *Drug and Alcohol Dependence, 131*, 23–35. http://dx.doi.org/10.1016/j.drugalcdep.2013.02.018

Van Den Bergh, N., & Crisp, C. (2004). Defining culturally competent practice with sexual minorities: Implications for social work education and practice. *Journal of Social Work Education, 40*, 221–238. http://dx.doi.org/10.1080/10437797.2004.10778491

Van Swol, L. M., Braun, M. T., & Malhotra, D. (2012). Evidence for the Pinocchio Effect: Linguistic differences between lies, deception by omissions, and truth. *Discourse Processes, 49*, 79–106.

Vearnals, S., & Campbell, T. (2001). Male victims of male sexual assault: A review of psychological consequences and treatment. *Sexual and Relationship Therapy, 16*, 279–286. http://dx.doi.org/10.1080/14681990123228

von Hippel, W., & Trivers, R. (2011). The evolution and psychology of self-deception. *Behavioral and Brain Sciences, 34*, 1–16. http://dx.doi.org/10.1017/S0140525X10001354

Vrij, A., Nunkoosing, K., Paterson, B., Oosterwegel, A., & Soukara, S. (2002). Characteristics of secrets and the frequency, reasons and effects of secrets keeping and disclosure. *Journal of Community & Applied Social Psychology, 12*, 56–70. http://dx.doi.org/10.1002/casp.652

Wachtel, P. L. (2008). *Relational theory and the practice of psychotherapy*. New York, NY: Guilford Press.

Wallhed Finn, S., Bakshi, A. S., & Andréasson, S. (2014). Alcohol consumption, dependence, and treatment barriers: Perceptions among nontreatment seekers with alcohol dependence. *Substance Use & Misuse, 49*, 762–769. http://dx.doi.org/10.3109/10826084.2014.891616

Walsh, B. W. (2006). *Treating self-injury: A practical guide*. New York, NY: Guilford Press.

Walsh, B. W. (2014). *Treating self-injury: A practical guide* (2nd ed.). New York, NY: Guilford Press.

Warren, F. (2005). *PostSecret: Extraordinary confessions from ordinary lives*. New York, NY: William Morrow.

Weber, A. (2002). Survey results: Who are we? And other interesting impressions. *Loving More Magazine, 30*, 4–6.

Weiner, B. (1968). Motivated forgetting and the study of repression. *Journal of Personality, 36*, 213–234. http://dx.doi.org/10.1111/j.1467-6494.1968.tb01470.x

Weiner, M. F., & Schuman, D. W. (1984). What patients don't tell their therapists. *Integrative Psychiatry, 2*, 28–32.

Weinshel, E. M. (1979). Some observations on not telling the truth. *Journal of the American Psychoanalytic Association, 27*, 503–531. http://dx.doi.org/10.1177/000306517902700301

Weiss, R. D., Najavits, L. M., Greenfield, S. F., Soto, J. A., Shaw, S. R., & Wyner, D. (1998). Validity of substance use self-reports in dually diagnosed outpatients. *The American Journal of Psychiatry, 155*, 127–128. http://dx.doi.org/10.1176/ajp.155.1.127

Whiten, A., & Byrne, R. W. (1988). Tactical deception in primates. *Behavioral and Brain Sciences, 11*, 233–273. http://dx.doi.org/10.1017/S0140525X00049682

Whiten, A., & Byrne, R. W. (Eds.). (1997). *Machiavellian intelligence II: Extensions and evaluations*. New York, NY: Cambridge Univeristy Press. http://dx.doi.org/10.1017/CBO9780511525636

Whitlock, J., Muehlenkamp, J., Eckenrode, J., Purington, A., Baral Abrams, G., Barreira, P., & Kress, V. (2013). Nonsuicidal self-injury as a gateway to suicide in young adults. *Journal of Adolescent Health, 52*, 486–492. http://dx.doi.org/10.1016/j.jadohealth.2012.09.010

Widlitz, M., & Marin, D. B. (2002). Substance abuse in older adults. An overview. *Geriatrics, 57*, 29–34.

Wiley, S. D. (1998). Deception and detection in psychiatric diagnosis. *Psychiatric Clinics of North America, 21*, 869–893. http://dx.doi.org/10.1016/S0193-953X(05)70046-0

Winnicott, D. W. (1956). On transference. *The International Journal of Psychoanalysis, 37*, 386–388.

Winnicott, D. W. (1960). The theory of the parent–infant relationship. *The International Journal of Psychoanalysis, 41*, 585–595.

Winterson, J. (2016, October 23). Interiority complex. *The New York Times*, p. BR21.

Wise, T. (2012). *Waking up: Climbing through the darkness*. Charleston, SC: Missing Peace.

Witkiewitz, K., & Marlatt, G. A. (2004). Relapse prevention for alcohol and drug problems: That was Zen, this is Tao. *American Psychologist, 59*, 224–235. http://dx.doi.org/10.1037/0003-066X.59.4.224

Wurmser, L. (1981). *The mask of shame*. Baltimore, MD: Johns Hopkins University Press.

Yalom, I. D. (1970). *The theory and practice of group psychotherapy*. New York, NY: Basic Books.

Yalom, I. D. (1992). *When Nietzsche wept: A novel of obsession*. New York, NY: Basic Books.

Yalom, I. D. (1997). *Lying on the couch*. New York, NY: Harper.

Yalom, I. D. (2002). *The gift of therapy: An open letter to a new generation of therapists and their patients*. New York, NY: HarperCollins.

Yalom, I. D. (2015). *Creatures of the day: And other tales of psychotherapy*. New York, NY: Basic Books.

Zahl, D. L., & Hawton, K. (2004). Repetition of deliberate self-harm and subsequent suicide risk: Long-term follow-up study of 11,583 patients. *The British Journal of Psychiatry, 185*, 70–75. http://dx.doi.org/10.1192/bjp.185.1.70

INDEX

ABOUT THE AUTHORS

Barry A. Farber, PhD, received his doctorate from Yale University in 1978. The following year he became a member of the clinical psychology faculty at Teachers College, Columbia University, where he's been ever since. He was director of clinical training there for 24 years and also served two stints as department chair. He has varied interests within the area of psychotherapy research, including the nature and consequences of therapists' provision of positive regard, the role of informal supervision in psychotherapy training, and the extent to which patients, therapists, supervisors and supervisees do and don't honestly disclose to each other. He is the author of several previous books, including *Self-Disclosure in Psychotherapy* (2006), *The Psychotherapy of Carl Rogers: Cases and Commentary* (1998), and *Rock 'n Roll Wisdom: What Psychologically Astute Lyrics Can Teach About Life and Love* (2007). He served 6 years on the Executive Council of the American Psychological Association's Division 29 (Society for the Advancement of Psychotherapy), maintains a small private practice of psychotherapy, and currently serves as editor of the *Journal of Clinical Psychology: In Session.*

Matt Blanchard, PhD, is a Phi Beta Kappa graduate of the University of Pennsylvania and received his doctorate from Columbia University in 2017. Previously a reporter for the *Philadelphia Inquirer* and editor-in-chief of the *Graduate Student Journal of Psychology*, he is now in clinical practice as a staff psychologist at New York University's Gallatin School of Individualized Study.

Melanie Love, MA, graduated with honors from Johns Hopkins University and will receive her doctorate in clinical psychology from Columbia University in 2019. Her research focusing on factors affecting disclosure of sexual content in psychotherapy has been published in *Psychotherapy Research* and the *Journal of Clinical Psychology: In Session*, and her master's thesis was the recipient of APA Division 29's Donald K. Freedheim award in 2017. She was previously the editor-in-chief of the *Graduate Student Journal of Psychology*. Melanie is currently in clinical practice as a doctoral intern at Temple University's Counseling Center.